Who Gets What?
The New Politics of Insecurity

The authors of this timely book, *Who Gets What?*, harness the expertise from across the social sciences to show how skyrocketing inequality and social dislocation are fracturing the stable political identities and alliances of the postwar era across advanced democracies. Drawing on extensive evidence from the United States and Europe, with a focus especially on the United States, the authors examine how economics and politics are closely entwined. Chapters demonstrate how the new divisions that separate people and places, and fragment political parties, hinder a fairer distribution of resources and opportunities. They show how employment, education, sex and gender, and race and ethnicity affect the way people experience and interpret inequality and economic anxieties. Populist politics have addressed these emerging insecurities by deepening social and political divisions, rather than promoting broad and inclusive policies.

Frances McCall Rosenbluth is Damon Wells Professor in the Department of Political Science at Yale University. She writes widely about the politics and political economy of democratic accountability. Her books include *Women, Work, and Power* (with Torben Iversen, 2010), *Forged Through Fire* (with John Ferejohn, 2016), and *Responsible Parties* (with Ian Shapiro, 2018).

Margaret Weir is Wilson Professor of Public and International Affairs and Political Science at Brown University. She has written and edited several volumes on social policy, race, and employment in the United States. Professor Weir also served as director of the MacArthur Foundation Network on Building Resilient Regions and is currently working on a book entitled, *The New Metropolis: The Politics of Spatial Inequality in Twenty-First Century America*.

SSRC Anxieties of Democracy

Editors

John A. Ferejohn, *New York University*
Ira Katznelson, *Columbia University*
Deborah J. Yashar, *Princeton University*

With liberal democracies afflicted by doubt and disquiet, this series probes sources of current apprehensions and explores how such regimes might thrive. What array of pressures most stresses democratic ideas and institutions? Which responses might strengthen these regimes and help them flourish?

Embedded in the Social Science Research Council's program on "Anxieties of Democracy," the series focuses on how representative institutions – including elections, legislatures, political parties, the press and mass media, interest groups, social movements, and policy organizations – orient participation, learning, and accountability.

The volumes in the series further ask how particular policy challenges shape the character of democratic institutions and collective actors, and affect their capacity to address large problems in the public interest. These challenges include, but are not limited to: (1) designing democratic institutions to perform successfully under conditions of social and political polarization; (2) managing and orienting contemporary capitalism and alleviating hierarchies of inequality; (3) addressing questions of membership, including population movements and differentiated citizenship; (4) choosing policies to balance national security and civil liberty; (5) exploring the effects of global climate on citizens and the human impact on the environment; (6) managing the development of media and information technologies to ensure they enhance, rather than degrade, robust pluralism and civil political engagement.

Other Books in the Series

Can America Govern Itself? Frances E. Lee and Nolan McCarty

Social Media and Democracy: The State of the Field and Prospects for Reform Nathaniel Persily and Joshua A. Tucker

The Disinformation Age: Politics, Technology, and Disruptive Communication in the United States W. Lance Bennett and Steven Livingston

Who Gets What? The New Politics of Insecurity Frances McCall Rosenbluth and Margaret Weir

Sponsored by the Social Science Research Council

The Social Science Research Council (SSRC) is an independent, international, nonprofit organization driven by its mission to mobilize social science for the public good. Founded in 1923, the SSRC fosters innovative research, nurtures new generations of social scientists, deepens how inquiry is practiced within and across disciplines, and amplifies necessary knowledge on important public issues.

The SSRC is guided by the belief that justice, prosperity, and democracy all require better understanding of complex social, cultural, economic, and political processes. We work with practitioners, policymakers, and academic researchers in the social sciences, related professions, and the humanities and natural sciences. We build interdisciplinary and international networks, working with partners around the world to link research to practice and policy, strengthen individual and institutional capacities for learning, and enhance public access to information.

Who Gets What?

The New Politics of Insecurity

Edited by

FRANCES MCCALL ROSENBLUTH
Yale University

MARGARET WEIR
Brown University

CAMBRIDGE
UNIVERSITY PRESS

University Printing House, Cambridge CB2 8BS, United Kingdom

One Liberty Plaza, 20th Floor, New York, NY 10006, USA

477 Williamstown Road, Port Melbourne, VIC 3207, Australia

314–321, 3rd Floor, Plot 3, Splendor Forum, Jasola District Centre,
New Delhi – 110025, India

103 Penang Road, #05–06/07, Visioncrest Commercial, Singapore 238467

Cambridge University Press is part of the University of Cambridge.

It furthers the University's mission by disseminating knowledge in the pursuit of education, learning, and research at the highest international levels of excellence.

www.cambridge.org
Information on this title: www.cambridge.org/9781108840200
DOI: 10.1017/9781108879170

© Frances McCall Rosenbluth and Margaret Weir 2021

This publication is in copyright. Subject to statutory exception and to the provisions of relevant collective licensing agreements, no reproduction of any part may take place without the written permission of Cambridge University Press.

First published 2021

A catalogue record for this publication is available from the British Library.

ISBN 978-1-108-84020-0 Hardback
ISBN 978-1-108-79413-8 Paperback

Cambridge University Press has no responsibility for the persistence or accuracy of URLs for external or third-party internet websites referred to in this publication and does not guarantee that any content on such websites is, or will remain, accurate or appropriate

Contents

List of Figures   *page* ix
List of Tables   xi
Author Biographies   xiii
Acknowledgments   xviii

1 Introduction: The New Politics of Insecurity
   Frances McCall Rosenbluth and Margaret Weir   1

PART I PEOPLE

2 Race, Remembrance, and Precarity: Nostalgia and Vote Choice in the 2016 US Election
   Andra Gillespie   25

3 The End of Human Capital Solidarity?
   Ben Ansell and Jane Gingrich   52

4 Public Opinion and Reactions to Increasing Income Inequality
   Kris-Stella Trump   79

5 Engendering Democracy in an Age of Anxiety
   Alice Kessler-Harris   103

PART II PLACES

6 Keeping Your Enemies Close: Electoral Rules and Partisan Polarization
   Jonathan Rodden   129

7 America's Unequal Metropolitan Geography: Segregation and the Spatial Concentration of Affluence and Poverty
   Douglas S. Massey and Jacob S. Rugh   161

8 Redistribution and the Politics of Spatial Inequality in America
   Margaret Weir and Desmond King   188

                    PART III POLITICS

9 Electoral Realignments in the Atlantic World
   Carles Boix   213
10 Political Parties in the New Politics of Insecurity
   Christian Salas, Frances McCall Rosenbluth, and Ian Shapiro   237
11 The Peculiar Politics of American Insecurity
   Jacob S. Hacker and Paul Pierson   259
12 The Anxiety of Precarity: The United States in Comparative
   Perspective
   Kathleen Thelen and Andreas Wiedemann   281
13 Increasing Instability and Uncertainty among American
   Workers: Implications for Inequality and Potential Policy
   Solutions
   *Elizabeth O. Ananat, Anna Gassman-Pines, and Yulya
   Truskinovsky*   307

Index   329

Figures

1.1	Income Gini Ratio of Householder in the United States, 1947-2019	*page* 2
2.1	Respondent perceptions of American progress in 8 and 50 years	37
2.2	Top-line statistics for independent variable measures	38
3.1	Education and support for Remain in the UK referendum on leaving the European Union	59
3.2	Average satisfaction with democracy by education level across the ESS	60
3.3	Standard deviation of satisfaction with democracy by education level across the ESS	61
3.4	Average redistribution preferences by education level across the ESS	65
3.5	Standard deviation of redistribution preferences by education level across the ESS	68
3.6	Mismatched graduates and satisfaction – ESS	71
3.7	Mismatched graduates and political attitudes – ESS	72
3.8	Firm size and economic satisfaction	74
6.1	Three examples of party systems: Two potential dimensions of political conflict	138
6.2	Euclidian distance from non-proximate parties, three examples	139
6.3	Average absolute ideological distance between respondent and the most proximate party, ANES, 1972–2016	141
6.4	Average absolute ideological distance between respondent and the most distant party, ANES, 1972–2016	142

6.5	Share of the population with "quite cold or unfavorable feelings" about one or both parties, ANES, 1972–2016	143
6.6	Partisan ideological spread, Dalton Index applied to CMP data, 1959–2007	146
6.7	Voter assessments of party ideology, Sweden 2014 and the United States 2012	148
6.8	Voter assessments of party system polarization and the effective number of parties, CSES Modules 3 and 4	150
6.9	Voter assessments of party distances from themselves and the effective number of parties, CSES Modules 3 and 4	152
7.1	Class distributions by race 1970–2010	166
7.2	Segregation between income classes by race 1970–2000	167
7.3	Class isolation by race 1970–2010	170
7.4	Spatial concentration of affluence for whites and Asians in US Metropolitan Areas 2010	171
7.5	Spatial concentration of affluence for blacks and Hispanics in US metropolitan areas 2010	173
7.6	Spatial concentration of white and Asian poverty in US metropolitan areas 2010	174
7.7	The production of concentrated affluence and poverty	176
9.1	Evolution of labor productivity and median earnings in the United States, 1913–2016	215
9.2	Polarization in economic policy positions in Europe	220
9.3	Political polarization in advanced democracies, 1945–2010	221
9.4	Abstention, 1918–2016	223
9.5	European parties – as proportion of voters and electors, 1918–2016	225
11.1	Public and private social protection spending by country	261
12.1	Illustrative typology of risk amplification for labor market risk	286
12.2	Strictness of employment protection	288
12.3	Unemployment insurance replacement rate, weighted by share of unemployed receiving regular unemployment benefits, average in the 2000s	289
12.4	Out-of-pocket health spending, 2015	291
12.5	Poverty rates among individuals living in households with at least one worker, 2016	292
12.6	Share of youth not in employment, education or training	294
12.7	Consumer credit and housing loans as a share of disposable income	295
12.8	The comparative view of intensity of different types of risks over time	297

Tables

2.1	Descriptive statistics, JWJI 2016 Election National Survey	page 35
2.2	Crosstabulations of independent variables and nostalgia measures	40
2.3	Crosstabulations of racial resentment and nostalgia with Trump vote intention	41
2.4	Logistic regression of Trump vote on racial resentment, nostalgia, and economic precarity	42
2.5	Logistic regression of Trump vote on racial resentment, nostalgia, and economic precarity by race of respondent	44
3.1	European Social Survey – Mismatched degrees and satisfaction	70
3.2	Mismatched degrees and satisfaction: By age	73
7.1	Metropolitan-level variables used in analysis of the concentration of affluence and poverty in 2010	164
7.2	Equations predicting concentration of affluence for whites, Asians, blacks, and Hispanics in 2010	177
7.3	Equations predicting the concentration of poverty for whites, Asians, blacks, and Hispanics in 2010	181
8.1	Public policies and spatial inequalities	190
9.1	Change in employment share of each category in the United States	217
9.2	Rate of abstention in Finland, France, and the United Kingdom	224
9.3	Reported vote for "populist" parties in selected countries, mid-2000s	228

10.1	Industrial jobs and voter support	244
10.2	Industrial jobs and fragmentation on left parties	245
10.3	Industrial jobs and left party fragmentation	246
10.4	Fragmentation on left parties and policy choice and outcome	247

Author Biographies

Elizabeth Oltmans Ananat is the Mallya Chair in Women and Economics at Barnard College, Columbia University, and a faculty research affiliate of the National Bureau of Economic Research. She studies the causes and consequences of the intergenerational transmission of poverty and inequality and has authored many peer-reviewed publications on forces affecting US economic mobility, including racial segregation, access to family planning, and government programs. Her most recent work focuses on the destabilizing effects of employment restructuring on families, including "Linking Job Loss, Inequality, Mental Health, and Education" (with Anna Gassman-Pines, Dania Francis, and Christina Gibson-Davis), published in *Science* in 2017.

Ben Ansell is Professor of Comparative Democratic Institutions at Nuffield College and the University of Oxford. He is currently co-editor of *Comparative Political Studies* and Principal Investigator of the European Research Council project WEALTHPOL. His work spans a wide array of topics in political economy, from the politics of education, to inequality and democratization, to more recent work on housing, wealth, and populism. His book, coauthored with David Samuels, *Inequality and Democratization: An Elite-Competition Approach* (Cambridge University Press, 2014) won the Woodrow Wilson Award for the best book in political science in 2014. He was made Fellow of the British Academy in 2018.

Carles Boix is the Robert Garrett Professor of Politics and Public Affairs at Princeton University and Director of the Institutions and Political

Economy Research Group at the University of Barcelona. His most recent books include *Political Order and Inequality* (Cambridge University Press, 2015) and *Democratic Capitalism at the Crossroads: Information Technology and Its Impact on Employment, Wages and Politics* (Princeton University Press, 2019). He is a Guggenheim Fellow and a member of the American Academy of Arts and Sciences.

Anna Gassman-Pines is Bass Connections Associate Professor of Public Policy and Psychology & Neuroscience in the Sanford School of Public Policy at Duke University and a faculty affiliate of Duke's Center for Child and Family Policy. Her research focuses on the development of low-income children in the United States. She is the author of many peer-reviewed journal articles related to parental work, anti-poverty programs and child development, including "Food Instability and Academic Achievement: A Quasi-Experiment using SNAP Benefit Timing" (with Laura Bellows), which was published in the *American Education Research Journal* in 2018. She is currently studying the effects of schedule unpredictability among service workers on worker and family well-being.

Andra Gillespie is Associate Professor of Political Science and Director of the James Weldon Johnson Institute for the Study of Race and Difference at Emory University in Atlanta, Georgia. She earned her BA from the University of Virginia and her PhD in Political Science from Yale University. Gillespie teaches courses on American politics, race and politics, and qualitative methodology. She has written or edited three books, the most recent of which is *Race and the Obama Administration: Symbols, Substance and Hope* (Manchester University Press, 2019).

Jane Gingrich is Associate Professor of Comparative Political Economy at the University of Oxford and tutorial fellow at Magdalen College. Her first book, *Making Markets in the Welfare State* (Cambridge University Press, 2011), examined marketization in health and education. Her more recent work has looked at policy feedbacks in welfare and education reform and the structuring power of institutions on political behavior and voting. She is currently working on two large projects. The first examines the changing fates of social democratic political parties. The second is funded by a European Research Council starting grant and looks at the comparative development of education systems.

Jacob S. Hacker is the Stanley B. Resor Professor of Political Science, Director of the Institution for Social and Policy Studies at Yale University, and a member of the American Academy of Arts and

Sciences. His most recent book, written with Paul Pierson, is *Let Them Eat Tweets: How the Right Rules in an Age of Extreme Inequality* (Liveright Publishing Corporation, 2020).

Alice Kessler-Harris is the R. Gordon Hoxie Professor of American History, Emerita, at Columbia University where she was also Professor in the Institute for Research on Women and Gender and held a faculty affiliate appointment in the Columbia University School of Law. Kessler-Harris specializes in the history of women, American labor, and twentieth-century social policy. Her books include *In Pursuit of Equity: Women, Men and the Quest for Economic Citizenship in Twentieth-Century America* (Oxford University Press, 2001).

Desmond King is the Andrew W. Mellon Professor of American Government at the University of Oxford and Fellow of Nuffield College, Oxford. His publications include *Separate and Unequal: African Americans and the US Federal Government* (Oxford University Press, 2007), with Rogers M. Smith, *Still a House Divided: Race and Politics in Obama's America* (Princeton University Press, 2013), and with Stephen Skowronek & John Dearborn, *Phantoms of the Beleaguered Republic: The Deep State and the Unitary Executive* (Oxford University Press, 2021). He is a Fellow of the American Academy of Arts and Sciences, the British Academy and the Royal Irish Academy.

Douglas S. Massey is the Henry G. Bryant Professor of Sociology and Public Affairs at Princeton University. He is a past president of the Population Association of America, the American Sociological Association, and the American Academy of Political and Social Science and an elected member of the American Academy of Arts and Sciences, the National Academy of Sciences, the American Philosophical Association, and the Academia Europea. He is author of the award-winning books *American Apartheid: Segregation and the Making of the Underclass* (Harvard University Press, 1996) and *Beyond Smoke and Mirrors: Mexican Immigration in an Age of Economic Integration* (Russell Sage Foundation, 2002).

Paul Pierson is the John Gross Professor of Political Science at the University of California–Berkeley and Director of the Berkeley Center for the Study of American Democracy. He is a member of the American Academy of Arts and Sciences. His most recent book, written with Jacob Hacker, is *Let Them Eat Tweets: How the Right Rules in an Age of Extreme Inequality* (Liveright Publishing Corporation, 2020).

Jonathan Rodden is Professor of Political Science and Senior Fellow at the Hoover Institution and the Stanford Institute for Economic Policy Research. His research focuses on topics in political economy including federalism, decentralization, political geography, redistricting, redistribution, and political polarization. His most recent book is *Why Cities Lose: The Deep Roots of the Urban-Rural Political Divide* (Basic Books, 2019).

Frances McCall Rosenbluth writes widely about the politics and political economy of democratic accountability. Her books include *Women, Work, and Power* (with Torben Iversen, Yale University Press, 2010); *Forged Through Fire: Military Conflict and the Democratic Bargain* (with John Ferejohn, Norton 2016); and *Responsible Parties: Saving Democracy from Itself* (with Ian Shapiro, Yale University Press, 2018).

Jacob S. Rugh is Associate Professor of Sociology at Brigham Young University. His work has been featured in *The Atlantic*, *FiveThirtyEight*, *National Public Radio*, and the *New York Times*. He is the winner of the Law & Society Association John Hope Franklin Prize for the best article on racism and the law based on his analysis in the landmark case of *Baltimore v. Wells Fargo*. His most recent article, "Why Black and Latino Home Ownership Matter to the Color Line and Multiracial Democracy," was published in *Race and Social Problems*.

Christian Salas is an economist specializing in game theory and political economy. He completed his doctoral studies at the University of Chicago and postdoctoral studies at Yale University. He currently works at Bates White Economic Consulting. He has written "Persuading Policy-Makers," published in the *Journal of Theoretical Politics*.

Ian Shapiro is Sterling Professor of Political Science at Yale University. His most recent books are *Politics Against Domination* (Harvard University Press, 2016); *Responsible Parties: Saving Democracy from Itself*, with Frances McCall Rosenbluth (Yale University Press, 2018); and *The Wolf at the Door: The Menace of Economic Insecurity and How to Fight It*, with Michael Graetz (Harvard University Press 2020).

Kathleen Thelen is the Ford Professor of Political Science at MIT. Her work focuses on the origins, evolution, and contemporary impact of political-economic institutions in the rich democracies. She is the author, mostly recently, of *Varieties of Liberalization and the New Politics of Social Solidarity* (Cambridge University Press, 2014). She is currently studying the American political economy in comparative-historical perspective.

Kris-Stella Trump is Assistant Professor of Political Science at the University of Memphis. She specializes in political psychology, public opinion, attitudes toward income inequality, and the politics of distribution. She received her PhD from Harvard University, and her work has appeared in *The Journal of Politics* and *Perspectives on Politics* among other outlets. Prior to joining the University of Memphis, she was Program Director for the Social Science Research Council's "Anxieties of Democracy" and "Media & Democracy" programs. She is the author of "Income Inequality Influences Perceptions of Legitimate Income Differences" (*British Journal of Political Science*, 2018).

Yulya Truskinovsky is a health economist who studies long-term care and aging. She received her doctorate in public policy from Duke University in 2016 and was a Sloan Fellow in Aging and Work at the Harvard Center for Population and Development Studies from 2016 to 2018. She is now Assistant Professor of Economics at Wayne State University. Her current research focuses on the impacts of social insurance programs on how individuals and families make decisions about work and family caregiving.

Margaret Weir is the Wilson Professor of Public and International Affairs and Political Science at Brown University. She has written and edited several volumes on social policy, race, and employment. In her recent work, she has served as Director of the MacArthur Foundation Network on Building Resilient Regions and is currently working on a book entitled *The New Metropolis: The Politics of Spatial Inequality in Twenty-First Century America*. Parts of this research have appeared in the *Urban Affairs Review*, *Regional Studies*, and *Perspectives on Politics*. With Frances McCall Rosenbluth, she co-directed the Working Group on Distribution for the Social Science Research Council's program on the "Anxieties of Democracy."

Andreas Wiedemann is Assistant Professor of Politics and International Affairs at Princeton University. He studies the comparative political economy of advanced democracies, focusing on financial markets, wealth inequality, and social policies. He is the author of *Indebted Societies: Credit and Welfare in Rich Democracies* (Cambridge University Press, 2021).

Acknowledgments

Frances McCall Rosenbluth and Margaret Weir

In 2014, the Social Science Research Council (SSRC) launched the Anxieties of Democracy program, an interdisciplinary project probing the political strains coursing through the world's advanced democracies. Working groups of the Anxieties project examined the tensions facing democratic governments and societies from different perspectives, including institutions, political participation, climate change, media, and the social safety net. The chapters in this volume represent the activities of this latter working group on society-wide distribution and welfare, charged with examining the challenges posed by economies that no longer deliver the security they once did.

We owe a big debt of gratitude to the Social Science Research Council and its former president, Ira Katznelson, who created the Anxieties of Democracy program and helped guide the early deliberations of our working group. Throughout the process of building the working group and organizing its meetings, we relied on the expert assistance of the SSRC staff. Anoush Terjanian, the first director of the program, got us off to a productive start. Kris-Stella Trump, who subsequently took over the reins of the program, offered astute guidance for our group meetings as the volume took shape. We are grateful to James Kirwan for his help in organizing the meetings. The SSRC's Cole Edick provided invaluable staff support, and research assistant Julia Hossain combed through every chapter as we put the finishing touches on the manuscript.

We are also grateful to the Yale MacMillan Center for International and Area Studies under the direction of Ian Shapiro and the Institution of Research and Policy Studies (IRPS) led by Jacob Hacker for generous funding of two rounds of stimulating discussions among the authors.

Two anonymous reviewers carefully read the manuscript and provided detailed comments on all of the chapters. Their insights about differences between the United States and Europe and their advice about connections across the chapters have significantly strengthened the volume. We also thank Cambridge University Press's editor Sara Doskow, for consummate skill and tireless good humor throughout the writing, review, and editing processes.

I

Introduction

The New Politics of Insecurity

Frances McCall Rosenbluth and Margaret Weir

Income inequality in the United States, after declining in the postwar years, has climbed steadily in recent decades (Figure 1.1). The pain caused by the 2020 pandemic only intensified fissures already deeply etched into American life. Communities of color suffered the most devastating health consequences and bore the brunt of the economic pain. Women found themselves pushed out of the labor force as they sought to combine work and family amid shuttered schools and minimal child care. Communities across America, long blighted by a loss of manufacturing jobs and the attending "deaths of despair" from suicides and opioid overdoses (Case and Deaton 2020), watched death tolls rise. In prosperous cities, the poor and the newly unemployed were little better off, confronted with eviction notices and bleak job prospects. Yet, even as lower income Americans found their lives upended, the wealth of America's billionaire class soared.

When Donald Trump strode onto the political stage boasting that he alone could fix the economic and social troubles confronting America, he threw down a challenge to politics-as-usual. His promise to "Make America Great Again," fortified by his rebuke of an elite-dominated political system, fell on receptive ears. For decades, as the American economy delivered volatility, not security, politics seemed to offer little help. On the contrary, government action seemed to reward the very people and institutions that had caused the economic turmoil so harmful to ordinary Americans. Indeed, long after the Great Recession had officially ended, millions of Americans had not regained lost ground.

Such political disquiet has not been confined to the United States. The world's liberal democracies have all experienced economic change and

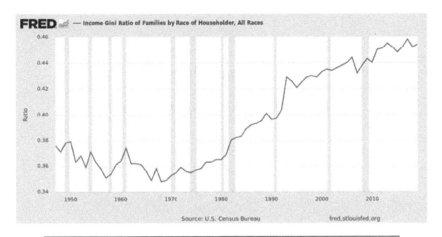

U.S. Census Bureau, Income Gini Ratio of Families by Race of Householder, All Races [GINIALLRF], retrieved from FRED, Federal Reserve Bank of St. Louis; https://fred.stlouisfed.org/series/GINIALLRF, October 6, 2020.

FIGURE 1.1 Income Gini Ratio of Householder in the United States, 1947-2019

significant challenges to long-entrenched political alliances and public norms. The shift away from manufacturing toward a service economy, the new rigors introduced by the open global economy, and the freer movement of people across national boundaries have stripped away the certainties of an earlier era. As confidence eroded in the capacity of representative government and political parties to alleviate the new insecurity, the field opened for a new kind of politics. Politicians who openly embraced racism, nationalism, and unilateral executive action now presented themselves as the alternative to the failures of liberal representative democracy and global connection.

Justifiably, much of the public attention has fixated on the bombast of racist and proto-authoritarian leaders. But the underlying fractures that gave rise to these troubling political developments run much deeper than a single leader: they have been decades in the making. The rifts that have pushed many liberal democracies onto perilous political terrain will not disappear quickly, even if future elections repudiate individual politicians or sideline some political parties.

This book harnesses the expertise of scholars from across the disciplines of history and the social sciences to probe how the economic and social transformations of the past forty years have introduced new risks and insecurities that fractured the solidarities of the postwar era. Focusing on the United States and European liberal democracies, the chapters show how the stable identities and alliances of the past have given way to a jumble of social cleavages and political rifts that now set the menu for politics. They reveal that the trend toward disaggregation in the late twentieth century, which historian Daniel Rogers (2011) called "the age of fracture," has continued apace. Instead of sweeping away class divides, however, political fragmentation has, if anything, deepened inequalities and rendered them more multifaceted. Fueled by fear and energized by the appeal of narrowly defined protections, the politics of fracture makes it difficult to address economic and social insecurity in broad and inclusive ways. Instead, a pervasive sense of insecurity has created fertile ground for populist politicians pushing politics toward ugly extremes once thought banished from public life.

Faced with these strains, can the democratic center hold? Can liberal democracies address insecurity in ways that maintain or rebuild broad solidarities? The chapters address these core questions from two perspectives. The first depicts how economic transformations and established institutions interacted over time to introduce new economic, social, and political cleavages. The chapters show that while these strains reverberated across Western democracies, they hit the United States with special ferocity. The second major question animating the volume considers how and in what ways the United States remains distinctive. The volume probes the role of America's deep racial divide and its meager forms of risk protection in aggravating fracture. They also show how new insecurities in Europe and America took different political expression in countries with proportional representation compared to those, like the United States, with majoritarian political institutions. In each, the end result weakened the hold of the political center on politics.

The social and political divisions that now slice through liberal democracies in Western Europe and the United States appear under many guises. To parse this complexity, we emphasize three core lines of fracture: people, places, and politics. These categories capture (1) the ideologies and attitudes linked to individual social position, (2) the spatial divisions that have become a hallmark of the new economy, and (3) the political institutions that segment the experience of insecurity and the political responses to it. In this Introduction, we first situate this volume with a review of research about the new economy and the divisions it has fostered. We then flesh out our analysis of people, places, and politics, showing how the chapters in each section build on and depart from existing research.

ECONOMIC TRANSFORMATIONS AND THE NEW POLITICS OF FRACTURE

Democracy and capitalism coexisted harmoniously when rapid industrialization after World War II brought untold prosperity to middle-class workers who formed the basis for stable social democratic politics in Europe and New Deal liberalism in the United States. Ambitious postwar plans for social insurance and full employment offered roadmaps for achieving these ideals. But by the 1970s, the postwar trajectory of economic growth stalled, as once reliable prescriptions failed to deliver prosperity (Stein 2010; Rogers 2011). Political leaders in the United States, and to a lesser degree those in Western Europe, exposed workers to alarming new insecurities as they sought to reboot economic growth under the banner of free markets and global trade. Unregulated technological change magnified insecurity by reducing the supply of good jobs. But decisions about how technology is used and the terms on which countries engage the global economy are deeply political. Governments can combat the dolorous effects of growing insecurities by offering compensation from losses with a menu of policies that includes education and training, increased social protection, public employment, and wage increases. But can governments chosen by increasingly divided electorates offer these policies?

The record to date is not encouraging and it is especially bleak in the United States. Across liberal democracies, many low-skilled but previously secure manufacturing jobs continue to disappear on account of capital-intensive production, in which technology increasingly substitutes for skilled labor, and because of greater dependence on trade and offshore outsourcing. These twin trends of technology and trade have swollen the ranks of citizens in the United States and Europe alike who get by on multiple part-time jobs, usually in the service economy and often without pension and health benefits (Neumark 2000; Standing 2011; Autor, Dorn, Hanson, Majlesi 2017). This includes the relatively high-skilled self-employed participants in the "gig economy" who work only as much and as often as they can line up customers on their own (Perez 2015; Sundararajan 2016).

Economic stress has not been shouldered equally. For those at the very top of the income spectrum in the United States – the top 1 percent – things have never been better. Over the forty years that incomes for most Americans have languished, the United States has become the most unequal among the advanced democracies. Between 1980 and 2018, the share of national income going to the top 1 percent rose from 11 percent to 20 percent, while the share of the bottom 50 percent dropped from 20 percent to 13 percent (Alvaredo et al. 2018, p. 81). In other liberal democracies, inequality grew but much less dramatically. In Western Europe, the share of national income going to the top 1 percent rose from 10 percent to 12 percent between 1980 and 2018, while the share going to the bottom 50 percent fell from 24 percent to 22 percent (Alvaredo et al. 2018, p. 70). Yet, the experience of insecurity has also grown in Western Europe as the share of workers on temporary contracts has risen and industrial jobs have declined markedly (Hall 2019).

Growing inequality poses a special problem in the United States. No longer can extreme levels of inequality in the United States be excused on the ground that high rates of social mobility compensate. As the cross-national comparison in economist Alan Krueger's "Great Gatsby Curve" shows, economic inequality is associated with declining intergenerational social mobility (Krueger 2015). Moreover, substantial evidence suggests that economic inequality restricts growth. In a sweeping analysis of growth and inequality in the United States since 1700, Lindert and Williamson (2016) show that the high rates of American inequality have not produced greater growth than in other liberal democracies. Heather Boushey (2019) goes further to argue that economic inequality restricts growth by distorting the flow of talent into the economy, limiting fair competition and reducing consumer demand.

The political stakes of insecurity and inequality are high: growing economic insecurity undermines democracy everywhere, as the electoral basis for moderation disappears. Why have the political systems across the liberal democracies found it so difficult to enact policy interventions that deliver prosperity and economic security for their citizens? Why instead have political strong men like Trump dominated politics and silver bullet solutions like Brexit won support? Why have political parties on the right and left grown at the expense of the center in Europe where the inequality has remained relatively low but insecurity has grown?

Existing research has sought to understand these fractures in different ways. Some analyses draw a direct line from economic dislocation to eroding solidarities. There is some evidence for this analysis. The decline of manufacturing across liberal democracies not only engendered discontent among former industrial workers; it also weakened unions, one of the central institutions anchoring postwar stability (Boix 2019). New forms of work in the gig economy have made it more difficult for workers to act on a shared interest (Thelen 2019). Likewise, industrial workers harmed by globalization and the decline of manufacturing jobs have provided important constituencies for the fringe parties that are hollowing out the center in European politics (Mair 2013). The splintering of the working class finds a counterpoint in the coalescence of wealth. As the fortunes of workers declined, the new concentrations of wealth vied to define the political agenda.

In addition to considering the economic causes of insecurity, the chapters in this book also probe the role of the social divisions, political institutions, and political actors in creating the specific fractures that now characterize politics in liberal democracies. These include the symbols, deeply embedded ideals, social identities, and political institutions that have long served as touchstones for interpreting and acting on economic and social challenges. But the unsettled nature of contemporary politics means that entrepreneurial politicians and parties have more freedom to wield these tools in new ways as they seek political advantage (Hall 2019; Iversen and Soskice 2019). Political and social fractures provide inroads for politicians and parties that cannot hope to win majorities or become part of governing majorities. Social divisions that blame the poor for their difficulties reduce pressure for raising taxes to fund more generous social programs. Spatial divisions drive new wedges between urban and rural areas and set up walls within metropolitan boundaries. Clearly, the new politics of insecurity is a multidimensional process that is played out in many different arenas.

BROKEN SOLIDARITIES AND THE NEW POLITICS OF INSECURITY

Analysts of advanced democracies note the exceptionally unsettled nature of contemporary politics as well as the complexity of interests and alliances vying for power (Beramendi et al. 2015; Hall 2019). We slice into this complexity by identifying three arenas of fracture: people: the social lenses through which people perceive and experience insecurity; place: which separates the winners and losers of globalization and, in the United States, divides the population by race and ethnicity., deepening social differences in the process; and policy and politics: which shape the social risks that different groups face and organize voters into bundles with distinctive appeals. The chapters explore the independent logics that create and sustain fractures in each arena. As we introduce the chapters, we consider the open questions in each of these domains, showing how the analyses in the chapters illuminate the divisions that contribute to unsettled politics and the implications for the politics of insecurity.

People

The social lenses through which people interpret rising inequality and insecurity produce distinct interpretations of what has been lost, if anything, why, and what should be done about it. Traditional class analysis drew a line from class position to support for redistribution: the economically less secure could be expected to form the core of support for redistribution. Instead, deepening divisions surrounding who or what is to blame for economic insecurity have boosted receptivity to new, more extreme political messages and limited the appeal of older more moderate politics. Research on political attitudes has highlighted intersecting lines of cleavage around social status, racial and ethnic divisions, and education. Each has been identified as a force in directing politics away from concerns about inequality and redistribution and bolstering support for right-wing populism.

In both Europe and the United States, research has documented the impact of declining social status as a crucial and powerful influence on attitudes supportive of populism. Examining twenty European democracies, Gidron and Hall (2017) argue that a sense of lost social status – measured by subjective feelings – is a powerful predictor of support for populism. Economic changes – especially the decline in occupations that require less education and the greater exposure to globalization – matter, but the sense of feeling shoved aside and disrespected by elites is on its own a powerful trigger for support for populism. Similarly, in the United States, Diana Mutz (2018) has traced support for Donald Trump to fears of lost status. She identifies the intertwined threats that underlie support for Trump as lost racial status and lost global status. Both particularly affect white Christian males, who long sat at the top of America's status hierarchy.

Andra Gillespie (Chapter 2, this volume) takes this analysis a step further by showing how nostalgia for a lost past drives support for Trump. Longing for a lost "golden age" has infused other historical periods when Americans confronted the anxieties associated with change and uncertainty (Cowie 2016, p. 227). Gillespie demonstrates that Trump took full advantage of this powerful social and political tool in his call to "make America great again." But nostalgia, she shows, reflects a tunnel vision of the past, incorporating only the perspective of those who believe their social dominance challenged. At the heart of that challenge lie perceived shifts in the racial hierarchy. Nostalgia is closely linked to racial resentment and to backlash against the election of America's first black president.

Of course, racist appeals, coded or not, are nothing new in American politics. The era that many remember with nostalgia featured bitter struggles over basic civil rights in the South and the openly racist candidacy of George Wallace, who won votes across the country with his vow to preserve segregation "forever." Gillespie's analysis shows the power of a savvy marketer to prime racist attitudes by combining open attacks on immigrants with gauzy references to a misremembered past.

Education level offers another source of anxiety related to social status and economic well-being. Because it bestows exceptional rewards on those with university degrees and imposes new deprivations on those with less education, the knowledge economy has amplified the significance of education. Analyses show the strong association between lower levels of education and support for Trump, Brexit, the Alternative für Deutschland (AfD) in Germany, and Marine Le Pen in France (Gidron and Hall 2017, p. S58). But the meaning of the educational divide is subject to debate. As Hall notes, education separates the winners and losers of the global economy, but it also marks off those with cosmopolitan values and those with more traditional values (Hall 2019). In her analysis of the 2016 election in the United States, Mutz (2018) shows that when perceived status threat is taken into account, education level has no impact on support for Trump.

Ben Ansell and Jane Gingrich (Chapter 3, this volume) bring a new lens to studying the impact of education on satisfaction with politics. Drawing on European data, they confirm the widely documented political dissatisfaction among those without a university education. But their work goes further to demonstrate distinctive attitudes among those with similar levels of education. They demonstrate divisions among graduates based on occupation, with public sector workers in health care and education more supportive of redistribution than those in the private finance, insurance, and real estate industries. Moreover, they show that a significant segment of college graduates holds jobs that are poorly matched with their qualifications. These mismatched workers are more likely to express dissatisfaction with the status quo than are people whose jobs better match their skills.

This analysis has stark implications. Economists studying skill-based technological change look to higher education as a solution to the problems confronting the less educated (Goldin and Katz 2010). But, as Ansell and Gingrich show, access to higher education has expanded greatly since the 1960s, but the economic benefits of a degree vary significantly. The mismatch in education and occupation that they identify suggests that the constituency for populist appeals extends more widely than most research would suggest.

As inequality has grown in many of the liberal democracies, a wealth of new research has sought to account for its impact on attitudes about policy and politics. Kris-Stella Trump (Chapter 4, this volume) provides a guide through this literature, focusing on attitudes toward rising top-level incomes. Research has shown that there is little relationship between the growth of inequality and support for redistribution: countries with more inequality do not exhibit greater support for redistribution, neither does support for redistribution rise when inequality grows worse (McCall and Kenworthy, 2009; McCall 2013). Seeking to understand why inequality has such limited effect on support for redistribution, studies have examined whether inadequate information – people underestimating the extent of inequality – is the problem. However, as Trump shows, experimental research reveals that the impact of more accurate information is mixed and depends greatly on the type of information and the conditions under which it is given.

Instead, Trump argues that attitudes about the deservingness of the poor are more important in shaping views about redistribution. In the United States, a large literature on the undeserving poor shows that racial stereotypes lie at the heart of harsh assessments of deservingness (Gilens 1999; Katz 2013). Yet, Trump shows that the United States is not alone in this regard: ethnic and racial divisions lower support for redistribution in Europe as well. Even so, in the United States, long-standing racial stereotypes and strong beliefs in meritocracy combine in unique ways to limit support for redistribution. If growing inequality challenges racial stereotypes or undermines faith in meritocracy, Trump concludes, American views may shift to support more redistribution.

Gender looms large in the experience and politics of inequality, for even though the gender wage gap has shrunk, opportunities and authority remain male-skewed even today. Alice Kessler-Harris (Chapter 5, this volume) situates the problem of gender solidarity in a trenchant analysis of the development of democracy and capitalism in the postwar America. She shows that even though the United States fell far short of the solidaristic policies of postwar European social democracies, New Deal social policies expanded in the decades after World War II. By the 1960s, federal action designed to temper capitalism and to lodge ideals of freedom within a system of social protection were gaining wide support. In this context, the emerging women's movement embraced broadly solidaristic goals, including a universal right to childcare.

Kessler-Harris documents the underlying tensions in the movement between those seeking freedom to function in a male-dominated society and those embracing social justice and wider social change. In the 1970s, she argues, gender solidarities evaporated in the context of newly dominant ideas about market freedom and individual responsibility. Similar to Kris-Stella Trump, Kessler-Harris finds that racialized ideas about individual responsibility and belief in meritocracy undermined support for broad redistributive policies. As unprecedented opportunities opened for privileged women at the top of the educational and income ladders, well-off women embraced individual rights in place of gender solidarity across economic lines. Broad class and gender alliances dissolved into fragmented identity politics and women became "just another interest group."

Together the chapters in this part document the challenges of preserving old solidarities and crafting new ones in the face of rising insecurity. The least controversial solution to insecurity – education – may not only be ineffective but may also actually expand the ranks of the discontented as cohorts of university graduates languish in jobs below their skill levels. Likewise, the social lenses through which people interpret insecurity fail to mobilize broadly based public responses to insecurity and lead away from robust public action. Political entrepreneurs such as Donald Trump in the United States and the Brexiteers in England direct public attention away from redistribution by promising a return to an idealized past where the sense of lost status can be restored. Despite concern about inequality, entrenched norms about deservingness, hard work, and meritocracy block support for redistribution. They also divide social groups, such as women, that might be expected to unite around a re-energized public role. These ideas are especially salient in the United States where racial stereotypes have long permeated debates about merit and redistribution. However, given the growing prominence of ethnic divisions linked to immigration in Europe, the United States may not be so different in this regard.

Place

Geographic diversity is an enduring fact of political life. Over the past two decades, however, economic and social divisions across place have attained an outsized significance. Rural voters backed the election of Donald Trump in large numbers, the majority of Brexit supporters reside in the economically stressed north of England, France's "yellow vest" protesters hail from the countryside, and support for the far right has grown sharply in economically distressed eastern Germany. The fracture of politics along rural-urban lines raises many questions. Why has the split become especially fierce in American politics? Are the central concerns of "left behind places" economic or status driven? In the United States, rural-urban divisions are accompanied by a second axis of spatial differentiation centered within metropolitan areas. The sharp division of US metropolitan areas into distinct enclaves defined by race, ethnicity, and income has existed for nearly a century. But new questions emerge about the impact of rising inequality on these divisions and about how the increasingly stark divisions across metros have affected the divisions within them.

The intensity of the rural-urban divide in the United States took many analysts by surprise after the 2016 election: rural and small-town America had played a central role in delivering the vote to Trump. Such regional divisions were a regular feature of nineteenth-century America when party politics pitted largely rural native Protestants against Catholic and Jewish immigrants concentrated in cities. The economic policies of the New Deal and the Great Society tempered these cultural divisions with broadly gauged economic benefits that assisted the poor and powerless everywhere. But demographic movements, along with political gerrymandering, accentuated regional differences well before Donald Trump entered the political arena. Voters in cities, beginning in the 1960s, had a greater affinity with "post-materialist" values: concerns with the environment, women's rights, gay rights, and immigration. Urban areas also benefitted disproportionately from the knowledge economy, leaving behind many "landscapes of despair" in rural areas (Moretti 2012; Monnat and Brown 2017). Katherine Cramer's (2016) study of Wisconsin depicts the development of "rural consciousness" infused with resentment of cities. Rural impoverishment generates a distinct "gradient of social conservatism" in blighted areas (Scala and Johnson 2017; Rodden 2019). Regional divisions, in turn, further weaken the capacity of political parties to offer national solutions to national problems.

Jonathan Rodden (Chapter 6, this volume) argues that, over time, two-party systems are increasingly impotent in the face of these regional differences. Already rooted in cities since the New Deal, Democrats readily responded to the new concerns of urban-based supporters of women's rights, environmentalism, civil rights, and immigration. Similarly, with the winners of the knowledge economy rooted in cities, the Democratic leadership embraced free trade. As a result, cities came to anchor a racially and ethnically diverse Democratic coalition that joined low-income service workers with high-income beneficiaries of the global economy. Republicans, by contrast, became entrenched in predominantly white rural areas left behind by the global economy and in exurban areas that rejected the cosmopolitan values embraced by Democrats. The two American parties, geographically rooted in rural and urban districts, respectively, have come to emphasize cultural differences at the expense of shared economic concerns.

The urban-rural division is one way that "place" influences the politics of insecurity. Given America's long history of legalized racial segregation, spatial divisions *within* metropolitan areas have also served as a powerful mechanism for creating and enforcing inequality across racial lines. A broad literature has documented that even after segregation became illegal, spatial separation across racial lines has persisted (Massey and Denton 1998; Rothstein 2017). These divisions have a profound impact on life opportunities, as Chetty and collaborators (Chetty, Hendren, Kline, Saez 2014) have shown in a series of important studies that tracks the impact of residence on long term-prospects for advancement. Research has also shown that economic segregation has risen as inequality has grown, and that the affluent increasingly cluster into their own neighborhoods (Reardon and Bischoff 2011; Jargowsky 2018).

Douglas Massey and Jacob Rugh (Chapter 7, this volume) add new dimensions to this work by examining the intertwined impact of growing inequality, the emergence of regional winners and losers in the knowledge economy, and the persistence racial segregation. Over the past forty years, they show, the United States has divided more sharply into pockets of wealth and concentrations of great need. The segregation of the affluent, they demonstrate, has become especially pronounced. These patterns are intensified by the persistence of racial segregation. The residential isolation of affluent whites and Asians and their spatial segregation from the poor are linked to racial segregation, which also exacerbates the concentration of poverty for African Americans and Hispanics. Massey and Rugh show that the geography of the global economy influences patterns of segregation. Metropolitan areas that are well connected to the global economy exhibit the greatest concentrations of affluence, while areas left behind by the global economy display the most extreme concentrations of poverty.

Margaret Weir and Desmond King (Chapter 8, this volume) show how citizens who have benefited from geographically specific wealth have used politics to lock in their advantages. Wealthier communities not only block entry to less affluent residents; they also attempt to secede from larger political jurisdictions if they feel their tax burdens are not commensurate with their services. Because budgets for schools and local public goods draw from local property taxes, the well off can save their tax dollars for their own children and withhold them from their needier neighbors. By contrast, a very different approach to redistribution is emerging in big diverse cities that benefit from agglomeration economies. These cities have spearheaded a host of new measures that expand the public sector and support low-wage workers, including minimum wage increases, work-family policies, and community benefit agreements, which require developers to provide employment, housing, or neighborhood amenities to benefit low-income residents. Although formidable political barriers limit the reach of these policies – and state governments have indeed blocked many – they offer a new vision for government's role in assisting workers and their families.

Economic and social divisions now appear across liberal democracies, but they are especially acute in American politics. The two-party system, entrenched patterns of racial segregation, and the rules for creating local political jurisdictions promote sharper divisions in political identities and access to public goods. These forces have produced dramatically different life chances depending on residential location. They also lead to very different assessments of appropriate political action, making it difficult to build broad solidarities across geographic lines. However, in cities benefitting from agglomeration economies, advocates have been able to use their power to implement a range of new policies designed to address insecurity. Whether and how these policy entrepreneurs can extend the geographical reach of these policies remains to be seen.

Politics and Policies

The economic transformations of the past four decades reverberated through the politics and policy landscapes of Western Europe and the United States. In the process, they created widespread new insecurities and robbed the political center of once reliable voters. In Western Europe, industrial workers cut loose from their earlier political moorings lent support to parties on the far right and far left. In the United States, the old New Deal coalition that brought white industrial workers into the same party as African Americans collapsed, as many white workers with less education deserted the Democratic Party. The blame for and proposed solutions to insecurity range widely, but calls for protection from global trade and pressures to block immigration signaled that a new politics was afoot. But disaffected industrial workers were not the only new force in politics. At the top of the economic spectrum, concentrations of great wealth – especially in the United States – have accelerated the flow of big money into political campaigns, amplifying the voice of those at the top. The chapters by Boix; Salas, Rosenbluth, and Shapiro; and Hacker and

Pierson examine the political processes that hollow out centrist politics in the face of rising economic and status insecurities.

Carles Boix (Chapter 9, this volume) examines how economic transformations linked to global trade and automation set the stage for political realignment in Europe and the United States. His chapter shows how the economic foundations of the old political order crumbled under the weight of trade and technical change. As well-paying manufacturing jobs disappeared, sharp income inequalities arose in the United States and employment levels stagnated in Western Europe. Although dissatisfaction mounted and trust in government fell as the economy failed to deliver the security it once had, the initial political response was muted. Instead, the disaffected simply dropped out of politics; the center held but lacked the firm foundation it once enjoyed. It was not until after the 2008 recession, Boix argues, that a new brand of political entrepreneur gained traction. In place of the broad social policies supplied by the welfare state, populist politicians promised to enhance security with protection from globalization and strong national borders to block immigration. Boix concludes his analysis with a grim prognosis. If policies such as expanded education and universal basic income fail to win support, some form of oligarchical capitalism that offers little to those affected by technical change may define the future.

Underscoring Boix's warning that a shrinking industrial workforce poses new challenges for democratic politics, Christian Salas, Frances McCall Rosenbluth, and Ian Shapiro (Chapter 10, this volume) provide evidence that fewer industrial jobs translate into party fragmentation in proportional electoral systems, thereby weakening the left even in the traditionally social democratic countries of Europe. Proportional representation has worked well in postwar Europe in providing broad coalitions of support for free trade with compensation and for growth with welfare. Businesses and labor were both well represented in parliaments, and sometimes, as in Germany's Grand Coalitions, within the ruling legislative coalition. However, fewer industrial jobs have weakened unions and the left political party representing them, leaving insecure citizens to vote for more radical parties including those on the far right. This finding puts the spotlight on institutional structures, including electoral rules, that shape the incentives of politicians and the choices offered to voters. It also cautions against a view, common among American academics, that proportional representation (PR) is necessarily a way to create political consensus. If PR's successes rested on a structure of organized labor that is on the wane, it may not offer the promise of welfare improvements for the United States that its proponents desire.

That is not to say, however, that single member district systems have insulated themselves against the dangers of populism either. In both the United States and Britain, voters unhappy with their economic lots have blamed political parties for their woes, demanding more decentralized control of party leadership and candidate selection. In Britain, London's prosperity has not been shared in the rest of the country, creating wide rifts within both parties. In the United States, meanwhile, a growing number of electoral districts are "safe" for one party or the other, because of demographic patterns and partisan gerrymandering as Rodden (Chapter 6, this volume) describes. In districts in which primary battles are the principal form of electoral competition and accountability, politicians who fail to cater to the more extreme interests within their districts can be challenged only by more extreme co-partisans. Moreover, political parties in America are susceptible to capture by extremists and can rely on a range of institutional tools to block majority-supported policy. Thus have money and cultural mobilization pushed aside debate over economic policy in American politics.

Jacob Hacker and Paul Pierson (Chapter 11, this volume) describe this process in the United States, showing how the Republican Party has been able to win power with an agenda supportive of highly inegalitarian policies and to use its power to block redistributive proposals. They document the rise of insecurity in the United States, asking why it has not produced stronger political support for a robust set of measures designed to buffer insecurity. The answer, they posit, lies in both the demand and the supply sides of policy. Republicans, Hacker and Pierson argue, have packaged together increasingly open racist appeals with inegalitarian economic policies, combining a coalition of lower-income whites and high-income elites. Emphasizing racialized group identities helps to dampen demand for new redistributive policies from voters while the capture of the party's economic agenda by extreme elites supplies the party with an agenda that actively fosters inequality. Hacker and Pierson show that the bar for challengers proposing more extensive redistribution remains high. Not only are Republicans assisted by a political geography and media world that isolate their supporters, they have also successfully weakened unions, the main organized force for solidarity on which the Democratic Party historically relied.

Kathleen Thelen and Andreas Wiedemann (Chapter 12, this volume) document a variety of policy responses to socioeconomic risk across the developed democracies, suggesting that a race to the bottom is not inevitable or uniform. To be sure, weaker workplace protections have amplified the risks borne by individuals across these countries. New sources of risk associated with credit markets augment these burdens further in the United States and Britain. But to different degrees, countries combine increased risks in labor markets with policies designed to buffer their impact. Neoliberal reforms in the labor market do not, they argue, necessarily translate into increased individual risk. Comparing liberal democracies across policy domains, they measure levels of risk exposure in the labor market as well as collective coverage of those risks in policy. They show that European social democracies, especially in Scandinavia, have survived relatively well and manage to protect their citizens from risks far better than countries like the United States. Thelen and Wiedemann acknowledge that workers everywhere are now more likely to face the loss or downgrading of their jobs, but they point out that countries with strong traditions of social democracy such as Denmark offer social insurance of various kinds including job retraining, unemployment insurance, single-payer health care, and universal retirement pensions.

Thelen and Wiedemann show that the United States is an outlier, with individuals exposed to very high levels of labor market risk and weak collective coverage. As a result, they argue, Americans face what they call "risk contagion," where risks in one domain spill over to create more risk in other areas. Because so few buffers are built into American social and economic policies, risks are likely to compound, leaving people with no footholds for climbing out of economic distress.

Nowhere are these dynamics more visible than in America's low-wage labor market. Elizabeth Ananat, Anna Gassman-Pines, and Yulya Truskinovsky (Chapter 13, this volume) zero in on the distinctive problems of low-skilled Americans. They show that the decline of manufacturing and the rise of service sector employment have increased income volatility for low-skilled workers over the past thirty years. Compounding this economic insecurity, employers in the low-wage sector have introduced new scheduling practices that made work hours unpredictable. As Alice Kessler-Harris (Chapter 5, this volume) documents, the divided women's movement meant the loss of a potentially powerful force supporting robust childcare policies. As a consequence, American public policy has historically offered only weak support for workers juggling care responsibilities. At a time when most caregivers are also workers and when the need for care associated with an aging population is increasing, Ananat, Gassman-Pines, and Truskinovsky show, the burden on low-wage workers has become untenable. They discuss a range of initiatives, including minimum wage increases, advance scheduling regulations, and paid family leave, that are forging new strategies to address the challenges these workers face. Policies designed to assist low-wage workers face less ideological resistance because the questions about deservingness discussed by Kris-Stella Trump (Chapter 4, this volume) are much less salient. Although these initiatives are mainly confined to politically sympathetic, relatively affluent localities, their focus on workers may help them gain broader support.

As exposure to risk has shifted, so too has politics. The anxieties engendered by social and economic strains have eroded centrist coalitions in Europe and have allowed more extreme voices new prominence in both Europe and the United States. But what drives these shifts? How do majoritarian vs. proportional representation systems affect the prospects of entrepreneurial politicians from the fringes to build political support?

The United States, as these chapters document, remains distinctive. Across the board, labor market, social, and financial policies expose Americans to considerably greater risk than is common in European countries. The New Deal and some past successes notwithstanding, America's two-party system has failed in the past few decades to produce a centrism capable of crafting stable support to those suffering from economic risks. The United States is unique in the ability of elites with an extreme economic agenda to capture the Republican Party, to perpetuate the racist nostalgia described by Gillespie (Chapter 2, this volume), and to use the levers of government to block or undermine broadly gauged policies directed at insecurity. But European countries are also not immune to extremism, as new parties eat away at the center. With protectionism from trade and immigrants at the core of their appeal, these parties have paid less attention to crafting new policies to address the economic strains that confront displaced industrial workers.

CONCLUSION

In the postwar decades, it was easy to think that democracy and capitalism were a natural pair, a golden formula. Constitutional democracies commanded world power, prosperity, and universal admiration. At the close of the war, the British sociologist T. H. Marshall divined a natural historical progression that led from civil rights, to political rights, to social rights. Citizens would now be able to use the power of democracy to break down entrenched class inequalities, and the world would be a better place. Although Marshall's hope for an end to inequality remained elusive, the agenda of expanding economic security drove postwar politics in liberal democracies.

The world today, however, appears radically different: growing wealth disparities have fueled political extremism, economic protectionism, and anti-immigrant xenophobia. Missing have been the heroic responses of the New Deal or the Marshall Plan.

The fragile economic foundations of representative democracy have long been understood: if tolerance, moderation, and generosity follow more easily from comfort and security, the reverse is also true. The wars that consumed the Western world in the first half of the twentieth century taught us those lessons, and the global economic institutions forged after the war were meant to guarantee against the repeat of bare-knuckle capitalism at home or beggar-thy-neighbor protectionism toward other nations (Polanyi 1944; Ruggie 1982). Have those lessons been forgotten? Is the genie out of the bottle, never to return?

Egalitarian politics, without a doubt, sit less steadily on an economy of capital-intensive production and global integration. It is in the perversity of things that the politics of redistribution is easiest for uniformly well-off voters, and hardest when the need is dire (Moene and Wallerstein 2001). The chapters of this book provide ample evidence of the challenges of creating political consensus when interests have become so disparate, and no political system is immune from the temptation of cheap, symbolic appeals. Both the American-style majoritarian systems and European proportional representation systems provide openings for politicians who thrive on division.

In the United States, the takeover of the Republican Party by extremist elements defied the long-standing nostrum that two-party systems converge in the center. Pulled to the right by business mobilization, a political geography that magnified divisions, and new media spouting extremist views, Republicans placed their political bets on alliances with well-organized groups including Christian conservatives and the National Rifle Association. With Trump at the helm and no credible plan to address insecurity, the party unapologetically embraced an ugly ethnonationalism designed to arouse and divide. Europe democracies have experienced no full-scale party takeovers; however, systems of proportional representation have allowed challenges from the fringes to eat away at the center. These include openly fascist parties peddling racist themes banished from European politics since the 1930s.

The hard-won lesson of the past decades underscores the fact that solidarity must be actively built, nurtured, and updated if it is to endure (Banting and Kymlicka 2017). Political actors hoping to fashion and sustain broader solidarities face a daunting task. The solutions they offer for alleviating insecurity will not yield quick results and their political appeals remain less emotionally arousing than the poisonous mix of scapegoating, nostalgia, and fear concocted by political extremists. But in neither European democracies nor United States does the strategy of fear and hate command majorities. The longer-term strategy for recovering a broad political center dedicated to finding solutions to insecurity will need to build civil society groups that can support solidarity, most importantly labor unions. This task is particularly urgent in the United States, where unions face direct attacks. In addition, features of the political system that amplify extremes need to be reformed where possible. The challenge for single member district systems such as the United States and Britain is to redraw district lines to force parties to compete on broadly appealing policies (Rosenbluth and Shapiro 2018). This is no easy task in a world with agglomeration economies that crowd some people into successful local economies and leave others behind. Even in a system of politically lopsided districts, however, political parties can begin to challenge partisan isolation by actively fielding candidates and competing in districts where they face significant disadvantages.

Efforts to reconstitute a stable political center must prevent the erosion of policies that yield widespread benefits, and they must introduce new security-enhancing initiatives that can command broad public support. Barak Obama's health care expansion and his Consumer Financial Protection Bureau both represented steps in this direction, even though both weakened under Trump. Initiatives in American states and in local governments demonstrate, albeit in small ways, that government can respond to growing economic insecurity. Western European democracies have the advantage of entrenched expectations of and widespread appreciation for redistributive policies. Those policies are needed now, to maintain democratic stability, as never before. Even as the left fragments with the decline of industrial jobs, and the far-right preys on the newly insecure, inclusive postwar policies have been weakened but not yet dismantled. The world holds its breath and hopes that the center holds.

REFERENCES

Alvaredo, Facundo, Lucan Chancel, Thomas Piketty, Emmanuel Saez, and Gabriel Zucman. 2018. World Inequality Report 2018. World Inequality Lab. https://wir2018.wid.world

Autor, David, David Dorn, Gordon Hanson, and Kaveh Majlesi, 2017, "Importing Political Polarization? The Electoral Consequences of Rising Trade Exposure," MIT Working Paper.

Banting, Keith and Will Kymlicka. 2017. *The Strains of Commitment: The Political Sources of Solidarity in Diverse Societies*. New York: Oxford University Press.

Beramendi, Pablo, Silja Häusermann, Herbert Kitschelt, and Hanspeter Kriesi, eds. 2015. *The Politics of Advanced Capitalism*. New York: Cambridge University Press.

Boix, Carles. 2019. *Democratic Capitalism at the Crossroads: Technological Change and the Future of Politics*. Princeton: Princeton University Press.

Boushey, Heather. 2019. *Unbound: How Inequality Constricts Our Economy and What We Can Do About It*. Cambridge, MA: Harvard University Press.

Chetty, Raj, Nathaniel Hendren, Patrick Kline, and Emmanuel Saez. 2014. "Where Is the Land of Opportunity? The Geography of Intergenerational Mobility in the United States. *The Quarterly Journal of Economics* 129(4): 1553–1623.

Cowie, Jefferson. 2016. *The Great Exception: The New Deal and the Limits of American Politics*. Princeton: Princeton University Press.

Cramer, Katherine J. 2016. *The Politics of Resentment: Rural Consciousness in Wisconsin and the Rise of Scott Walker*. Chicago: University of Chicago Press.

Gidron, Noam and Peter A. Hall. 2017. "The Politics of Social Status: Economic and Cultural Roots of the Populist Right." *British Journal of Sociology* 68 (S1): S57–S84.

Gilens, Martin. 1999. *Why Americans Hate Welfare: Race, Media, and the Politics of Antipoverty Policy*. Chicago: University of Chicago Press.

Goldin, Claudia and Lawrence F. Katz. 2010. *The Race between Education and Technology*. Cambridge, MA: Belknap Press.

Hall, Peter A. 2019. "The Electoral Politics of Growth Regimes." *Perspectives on Politics* 18(1): 1–26. DOI:10.1017/S1537592719001038

Hertel-Fernandez, Alexander. 2019. *State Capture: How Conservative Activists, Big Businesses, and Wealthy Donors Reshaped the American States – and the Nation*. Oxford: Oxford University Press.

Inglehart, Ronald. 1977. *The Silent Revolution: Changing Values and Political Styles Among Western Publics*. Princeton: Princeton University Press.

Iversen, Torben and David Soskice. 2019. *Democracy and Prosperity: Reinventing Capitalism through a Turbulent Century*. Princeton: Princeton University Press.

Jargowsky, Paul A. 2018. "The Persistence of Segregation in the 21st Century." *Law and Inequality: A Journal of Theory and Practice* 36:2.

Katz, Michael B. 2013. *America's Enduring Confrontation with Poverty: Fully Updated and Revised*. 2nd edn. Oxford: Oxford University Press.

Krueger, Alan B. 2015. "The Great Utility of the Great Gatsby Curve." Brookings Institution. www.brookings.edu/blog/social-mobility-memos/2015/05/19/the-great-utility-of-the-great-gatsby-curve/

Lindert, Peter H. and Jeffrey G. Williamson. 2016. *Unequal Gains: American Growth and Inequality since 1700*. Princeton: Princeton University Press.

Mair, Peter. 2013. *Ruling the Void: The Hollowing of Western Democracy*. London: Verso.
Massey, Douglas S. and Nancy A. Denton. 1998. *American Apartheid: Segregation and the Making of the Underclass*. Cambridge, MA: Harvard University Press.
McCall, Leslie. 2013. *The Undeserving Rich: American Beliefs about Inequality, Opportunity, and Redistribution*. Cambridge: Cambridge University Press.
McCall, Leslie and Lane Kenworthy. 2009. "Americans' Social Policy Preferences in the Era of Rising Inequality." *Perspectives on Politics* 7(3): 459–484.
Moene, Karl Ove and Michael Wallerstein. 2001. "Inequality, Social Insurance, and Redistribution." *The American Political Science Review* 95(4): 859–874.
Monnat, Shannon and David L. Brown. 2017. "More than a Rural Revolt: Landscapes of Despair and the 2016 Presidential Election." *Journal of Rural Studies* 55: 227–236.
Moretti, Enrico. 2012. *The New Geography of Jobs*. Boston, New York: Houghton Mifflin Harcourt.
Mutz, Diana C. 2018. "Status Threat, Not Economic Hardship, Explains the 2016 Presidential Vote." *Proceedings of the National Academy of Sciences* 115 (19): E4330–E4339.
Neumark, David, ed. 2000. *On the Job: Is Long Term Employment a Thing of the Past?* New York: Russell Sage.
Perez, Thomas. 2015. "Rising to the Challenge of a 21st Century Workforce." Monthly Labor Review, US Bureau of Labor Statistics.
Polanyi, Karl. 1944. *The Great Transformation*. Boston: Beacon Press.
Reardon, Sean F. and Kendra Bischoff. 2011. "Income Inequality and Income Segregation." *American Journal of Sociology* 116(4): 1092–1153.
Rodden, Jonathan. 2019. *Why Cities Lose: The Deep Roots of the Urban-Rural Political Divide*. New York: Basic Books.
Rogers, Daniel T. 2011. *Age of Fracture*. Cambridge MA, London: Harvard University Press.
Rosenbluth, Frances and Ian Shapiro. 2018. *Responsible Parties: Saving Democracy from Itself*. New Haven: Yale University Press.
Rothstein, Richard. 2017. *The Color of Law: A Forgotten History of How Our Government Segregated America*. New York: Liveright.
Ruggie, John Gerard. 1982. "International Regimes, Transactions, and Change: Embedded Liberalism in the Postwar Economic Order." *International Organization* 36(2): 379–415.
Scala, Dante J. and Kenneth M. Johnson. 2017. "Political Polarization along the Rural-Urban Continuum? The Geography of the Presidential Vote, 2000–2016." *The Annals of the American Academy of Political and Social Science* 672(1): 162–184.
Standing, Guy. 2011. *The Precariat: The New Dangerous Class*. London: Bloomsbury.
Stein, Judith. 2010. *Pivotal Decade: How the United States Traded Factories for Finance in the Seventies*. New Haven: Yale University Press.
Sundararajan, Arun. 2016. *The Sharing Economy: The End of Employment and the Rise of Crowd-Based Capitalism*. Cambridge, MA: MIT Press.

Thelen, Kathleen. 2019. "The American Precariat: U.S. Capitalism in Comparative Perspective." *Perspectives on Politics* 17(1): 5–27.

Williamson, Vanessa, Theda Skocpol, and John Coggin. 2011. "The Tea Party and the Remaking of Republican Conservatism," *Perspectives on Politics* 9 (1): 25–43.

Wilson, William Julius. 1996. *When Work Disappears: The New World of the Urban Poor*. New York: Knopf.

PART I

PEOPLE

2

Race, Remembrance, and Precarity

Nostalgia and Vote Choice in the 2016 US Election

Andra Gillespie

INTRODUCTION

In 2013, the A&E Network briefly suspended reality TV star Phil Robertson, of *Duck Dynasty*, because of controversial comments he made about homosexuality and race in an interview with *GQ* magazine (Magary 2013). At the time of the article's publication, most of the uproar in popular culture focused on the racist and anti-LGBTQ nature of Robertson's comments. However, a closer reading of the profile also revealed the general importance of nostalgia to Robertson's world view. Throughout Drew Magary's recounting of his day shadowing Phil Robertson, the discussion often veered to talk of reverting to a simpler time. For instance, Robertson's controversial comments about race centered on his recounting a sanitized version of the history of mid-twentieth-century race relations between poor blacks and whites in his Louisiana hometown – the kind of history where everyone got along. When they discussed the role of faith in public life, Robertson attributed American cultural decline to increasing secularization. For Robertson, returning to the "founding principles" of Christianity served as the template for restoring American greatness. "It's the direction he would like to point everyone," Magary writes, "Back to the woods. Back to the pioneer spirit. Back to God. 'Why don't we go back to the old days?' he asked me at one point" (Magary 2013).

Given the fact that Donald Trump won handily among white Evangelicals, it is not surprising that members of Robertson's family were ardent Trump supporters.[1] Phil Robertson actually started off as a Ted Cruz supporter,

---

[1] Robertson's son Willie was an ardent supporter of Trump and spoke at the 2016 Republican National Convention. Though Willie's wife Korie did vote for Trump because

"because I knew that he was a strict constitutionalist, and I know that he does vet his thinking through the Bible" (Guest 2016). When Donald Trump secured the nomination, though, Robertson enthusiastically endorsed him, explaining that partisan loyalty and retrospective voting motivated his choice. In his view, electing a Democratic president would usher in more of the same policies with which he had disagreed over the previous eight years. In his view, Trump would at least offer something different (Guest 2016).

This chapter considers whether Phil Robertson's point of view is generalizable to a larger population of Trump voters. Scholars and pundits have considered the role that perceived loss of social dominance, policy preferences, demographic factors, racial identity and resentment, and survey sampling techniques played in predicting (or incorrectly predicting) 2016 vote choice (see Mutz 2018; Tyson and Maniam 2016; Jardina 2019, 240–244; Gelman and Azari 2017). Rodden (Chapter 6, this volume) shows how rural residence and Republican Party identification have converged. Using Phil Robertson as my inspiration, I would like to consider the role that nostalgia – and the interaction between racial attitudes and nostalgia – played in understanding attitudes toward Donald Trump. After a brief literature review – where I draw upon literature in the humanities, history, sociology, political psychology, and political theory to explain the relevance of nostalgia to social and political phenomena–I present quantitative data from an original data set that asked questions about nostalgia and racial resentment to demonstrate the role that nostalgia played in predicting a person's likelihood of voting for Donald Trump.

DEFINING NOSTALGIA: WHEN AND WHY IS IT IMPORTANT?

Nostalgia literally means "a painful (i.e. physical) longing *(algos)* for home *(nostos)*" (Farrar 2011, 727, original emphasis). In their analysis of how museum curators reckon with the past, Amy Levin and Joshua Adair define nostalgia as "a unique way of knowing that valorizes certain positive aspects of the past, endowing them with importance as truths" (Levin and Adair 2017, 85). The implication of this definition is that nostalgia involves creating an idealized version of the past, one that emphasizes the positive things that people or communities want to remember, while deemphasizing or omitting memories of things that are negative or troubling.

---

of his pro-life views, she has been more critical of Trump, both before and after his election (Gangel et al. 2017).

Discussions of nostalgia are often ancillary to but not absent in the academic work of social scientists. Political theorists discuss nostalgia most explicitly. For instance, Jeanne Morefield (2014) engages the concept of "nostalgia" in her comparative study of the perceived decline of British and American global supremacy. Morefield's overall argument is that American and British politicians and political theorists are so committed to the idea that their respective countries are liberal (in the classical sense) that when confronted with episodes of illiberal behavior (e.g., racism or human rights abuses), they tend to view them as aberrations of their nations' founding principles instead of intrinsic features of Anglo-American empire. Furthermore, Morefield contends that defenders of Anglo-American liberalism engage in this defense in part because they fear that their nation is in decline. By shoring up Anglo-American classical liberalism, she argues, these theorists invoke the past as a means of system maintenance – that is, as an attempt to promote a path to maintain an Anglo or American hegemony justified by the perception that liberal values are superior (Morefield 2014, 2–17).

Nostalgia is perceived as a largely conservative project. George Hawley, for instance, renders paleoconservatives, who can be described as conservatives who resist aspects of modernity (Hawley pejoratively describes them as those who "simply refuse to get with the times") as the keepers of nostalgia (Hawley 2016, 180). However, Morefield argues that even ideological progressives uncritically accept the notion of a glorious, unproblematic American or British political heritage when they embrace the narrative that America or Britain has long embraced democracy and equality without acknowledging how many people had to be marginalized to provide freedom and equality for the privileged within these societies (Morefield 2014, 19).

Other work corroborates the idea that in policy debates, it is easy to romanticize the past in an effort to create a template for current deliberations. For Americans, the middle part of the twentieth century stands out as the aspirational standard. Yuval Levin notes that both liberals and conservatives venerate the 1950s and 1960s and long to return America to that past, but for different reasons. Liberals might romanticize the protest movements of the 1960s (the civil rights movement at the beginning of the decade and the antiwar and women's movements at the end of the decade), for instance; conservatives long for the stability and cultural coherence of the time period of the 1950s until the Kennedy assassination in 1963 (Levin 2016, 18–23).

That thinkers across the ideological spectrum point to the mid-twentieth century as the object of their nostalgic desire is telling. Though they long for different aspects of mid-century life and culture, Levin argues that that time period is significant in part because the prosperity of the era was real. Moreover, he contends that the era was so culturally relevant that even people born in subsequent generations harbor nostalgia for that time. For instance, he notes that the millennial-led Occupy Wall Street protests of the early 2010s tried to recapture the spirit of 1960s protests as though that would legitimate their cause (Levin 2016, 23–24).

To be sure, an accurate rendering of the history of the mid-twentieth-century United States would not omit the fact that the prosperity masked serious inequalities that systematically disadvantaged marginalized groups economically, socially, and politically. For some, the notion of mid-century prosperity could extend beyond material well-being to ideas about the social dominance of traditionally privileged groups – whites in general and white men in particular. As sociologist and antiracist educator Robin DiAngelo contends:

Romanticized recollections of the past and calls for a return to former ways are a function of white privilege . . . . Claiming that the past was socially better than the present is also a hallmark of white supremacy . . . it calls out to a deeply internalized sense of superiority and entitlement and the sense that any advancement for people of color is an encroachment on this entitlement.

The past was great for white people (and white men in particular) because their positions went largely unchallenged. (DiAngelo 2018, 59)

Other social scientists have also discovered a nexus between nostalgia for white racial advantage and policy preferences. For instance, those who study gun control argue that those who support gun rights (who are often but not exclusively white) often do so out of a sense of trying to maintain or reclaim racial or gender advantages. Angela Stroud observes that the white male "concealed carry" permittees she interviewed often invoked their role as family protectors or the perceived pervasiveness of crime (presumed to be committed by black or Latino perpetrators) as a justification for their gun ownership. Stroud (2016) views these justifications as the manifestation of a desire to preserve their masculinity. Likewise, Jennifer Carlson interviewed black and white gun owners who used the language of reclamation to justify their gun ownership. Her respondents explicitly discussed their intention to take their communities back from criminals (also presumed to be black or brown) (Carlson 2015).

For Carlson, the language of "taking back" one's community implies a desire for a nostalgic return to an imagined past. One of her interviewees (a black man) actually invoked the fictional town of Mayberry (from the 1960s sitcom *The Andy Griffith Show*) to explain his motivation for having a gun. For Carlson, this invocation is loaded with multiple meanings. She writes, "Mayberry expresses a nostalgic longing for a 'state of mind' ... about a particular version of America" (Carlson 2015, 11). That version of America was patriarchal but stable: men could earn enough to support their families on income from one stable job. As she interprets it, the practice of carrying a gun was a manifestation of the loss of that mid-twentieth-century stability. As such, when men carried guns, they did so in part to "mourn Mayberry," or to lament the loss of the stability that had characterized the 1950s and 1960s (Carlson 2015, 13).

Jonathan Metzl more explicitly ties gun culture to race and nostalgia. He argues that white men in particular suffer from a "crisis of authority" (Metzl 2019, 53), in which they have had trouble adjusting to a perceived loss of power. Ironically, subordinate groups cannot suffer from this crisis because their subordination should have inured them to any new loss of status. Metzl argues that guns are one way for white men to restore the sense of authority that they may have lost to the civil rights movement, feminism, and economic dislocation (Metzl 2019).

Metzl goes beyond gun rights debates to find relationships between feelings of nostalgia and opposition to other social policies, namely health care reform and education funding. In his interviews with working-class white men in Tennessee about Medicaid expansion, he found that many of these respondents opposed the expansion – despite their own need for health care – because they viewed Medicaid expansion as tantamount to welfare, an unfair entitlement for undeserving minorities. In contrast, Metzl's black respondents tended to support expanded Medicaid options as a community good that benefited all (Metzl 2019, 121–169).

Metzl sees the resistance to health care among his white respondents as an extension of their investment in their white identity. As counterintuitive as it may seem to some people, Metzl argues that his white respondents invested in a whiteness that was in tension with modernity. Metzl invokes historian C. Vann Woodward's notion of the "'divided mind' ... in which Southerners, and Southern white men in particular, seek the material gains of modern America while still holding fast to mores, prejudices, or historical traumas of their regional pasts" (Metzl 2019, 144). He later connects this nostalgic reading of Southern history, where the federal government was the bad guy that damaged the South, to a general suspicion of government programs that would expand federal authority (Metzl 2019, 148). Thus, health care becomes infused with historic, racially tinged baggage that upends a social order that previously placed white men on top.

Metzl's third case study examines cuts to educational spending in Kansas under Governor Sam Brownback. Metzl starts by describing Kansas as "a state awash in nostalgia. Locals often talk about the *old* Kansas, the Kansas *we grew up with*, the land of yesteryear in which forward looking citizens got along and got things done" (Metzl 2019, 193, original emphasis). Despite the state's reputation for outstanding schools, in the early 2010s Kansas voters elected politicians who pledged to cut budgets, including expenditures for education. Metzl found that these austerity politicians justified their actions on the ground of cutting waste, particularly in urban (code: minority) school districts that allegedly overspent without contributing their fair share of taxes (Metzl 2019, 196). However, the consequences of the austerity program were that all school districts lost money and student performance faltered statewide (Metzl 2019, 226). Thus, according to Metzl's interpretation, Kansas voters initially saw budget cuts as a way to recalibrate a perceived imbalance of minority-serving school districts getting too much money. Voters rethought this position when the austerity proved untenable, but the implied connection between race, nostalgia, and initial policy preferences was unmistakable here, too.

Other scholars have shown the ways that nostalgic memories can be selective, especially when it comes to race. Sociologist Kristen Lavelle interviewed white senior citizens who had lived through the civil rights movement in Greensboro, North Carolina to gauge their memories of the era and the period immediately before and after. She found consistent evidence that her respondents' memories did not match the historical record. Her respondents portrayed their individual interactions with African Americans (usually workers in their families' employ) during segregation as friendly, often familial, and they tended to portray themselves as not racist (Lavelle 2015, chap. 2).

Lavelle reports additional evidence to corroborate the fact that respondents had a unique way of remembering the civil rights era. Their memories of key occurrences were hazy compared to other contemporaneous events. For instance, while respondents could remember exactly where they were and what they were doing when John F. Kennedy was assassinated, they could not remember when the Woolworth sit-ins took place. While they reported strong feelings about Robert Kennedy's assassination, they tended to not talk about the murder of Martin Luther King Jr. in the same robust terms. They emphasized the tragedy of King's loss to his immediate family, not his significance as a civil rights leader. Some downplayed his importance by focusing on his alleged marital infidelity. One woman even swore that she did not know who King was until he was assassinated. (Lavelle 2015, chap. 4).

Lavelle also notes that her respondents tended to focus on their own inconveniences when recounting how the civil rights movement affected their lives. Respondents talked about how afraid they were of civil rights protesters, even during nonviolent protests. (Lavelle speculates that they may have conflated nonviolent protests of the early 1960s with uprisings that took place later in the decade.) One of the respondents suggested that the manager at Woolworth's instructed servers to wait on the sit-in participants but that the servers were too afraid to do so. This type of amnesia continued with their recollections of school desegregation. Most of Lavelle's respondents, who were parents of school-age children at the time of desegregation, lamented the loss of their neighborhood schools, complained about how bussing inconvenienced their children, and sometimes claimed that their children developed negative views of blacks because black students bullied them (Lavelle 2015, chaps. 4–5).

Lavelle's (2015) overall assessment is that her respondents lacked empathy, historical context, and an appreciation of the structural inequalities that consistently disadvantaged their black neighbors. However, she contends that her respondents' selective memory is actually a normal part of maintaining white privilege. She argues, "denial is integral to how dominant groups are accustomed to managing both their past *and* their present" (Lavelle 2015, 189, original emphasis).

The social science findings complement other, humanities-oriented work that finds that race and racial hierarchies are intimately connected to notions of nostalgia. As Kloeckner (2015) notes, one of the themes of the Great Recession novels he studies are the ways that white men have to reconsider their masculinity in light of their new precarity. Dudden (1961) notes the ways that racial conservatism, or the desire to maintain the traditional racial hierarchy of slavery, compelled the US South to violently defend its old way of life. In her analysis of historic preservation districts, Farrar (2011) acknowledges that the nostalgia that compels developers to try to recreate or preserve the essence of a place's particular historic aesthetic often causes them to overlook the histories of poor, immigrant, and/or minority communities that often lived in those same places at different times.

Hawley (2016) also sees the connections to race in his discussion of nostalgic paleoconservatism. While he hesitates to tie paleoconservatism to white nationalism, he recognizes the connections between this form of conservative ideology and racist ideas. He notes, for instance, that prominent paleoconservative Sam Francis was a member of the Council of Conservative Citizens (196) and that Thomas Fleming, editor of the paleoconservative journal *Chronicles,* argued that Southern conservatives wanted to go back to

a way of life, of a social order and a moral order for which the people of the 1860s went to war ... he is not so delighted with the mobility and tawdriness of modern life, with the fast food and fast buck artist who seem intent on turning the New South into a suburb of Chicago. He does not like to see family farms swallowed up by Agribusiness .... Above all, he knows the value of stability and the price of progress. (Fleming, quoted in Hawley 2016, 191)

Hawley's discussion of paleoconservatives has clear links to the current political moment. Fleming's nostalgia for the 1860s presages 2017 Alabama Senate candidate Roy Moore's pronouncement to an African American questioner that America was last great when "families were united – even though we had slavery – they cared for one another.... Our families were strong, our country had a direction" (Mascaro 2017).

Nostalgia and the Rise of Donald Trump

Moore enjoyed the support of President Trump in his unsuccessful bid against Doug Jones. Like Moore, Donald Trump's political messaging was nostalgic, racially loaded, and potent. Sociologist and theologian Nichole Phillips argues that Trump's most visible campaign slogan, *Make America Great Again*, was especially effective because of its invocation of a prior era of greatness that coincided with racial hierarchy. She argues that Trump's

most eloquent tool is *nostalgia*, a "memory of place" that ... grants permission for white middle America to recapture times when public and private spaces were circumscribed by social controls to manage a growing population. Furthermore, his use of *nostalgia* recalls a former time when efforts to "sanitize" and "sterilize" unwanted, polluted and *politicized* social bodies from the American body politic were legally allowed. By hearkening back to a "romanticized" past, Trump seems to suggest and "unofficially" sanction the formation of a racially differentiated society. (Phillips 2018, 48, original emphasis)

In addition, there is evidence that Trump appealed strongly to whites who were invested in their racial identity, even after controlling for racial resentment and stereotyping. Ashley Jardina examined a number of possible predictors of positive feelings for Donald Trump, as measured by feeling thermometer rates. Regardless of her model specifications, white consciousness was a statistically significant predictor of warm (or positive) feelings for Trump. In other words, whites who more strongly identified with their whiteness reported warmer feelings for Donald Trump, as did those who reported higher levels of racial resentment and those who reported more stereotypical attitudes toward minorities (Jardina 2019, 239–242).

Though she uses the term "nostalgia" only once in her examination of the relationship between perceptions of declining social dominance and support for Donald Trump in the 2016 election, Diana Mutz's (2018) foregrounding of social dominance in this discussion has obvious connections to discussions of nostalgia. If one can lose status, it is not surprising that they would long for it and seek to gain it back. Race was clearly implicated in this discussion of status loss. Mutz writes, "Those who felt that the hierarchy was being upended – with whites discriminated against more than blacks, Christians discriminated against more than Muslims, and men discriminated against more than women – were more likely to support Trump" (Mutz 2018, 9).

Survey data also corroborates the link between nostalgia and 2016 vote choice. In their 2016 American Values Survey, the Public Religion Research Institute (PRRI) asked respondents if they thought that American culture and way of life had improved since the 1950s. Over 60 percent of respondents who thought that America had improved since the 1950s indicated support for Hillary Clinton, while more than half of respondents who thought that America was worse in 2016 compared to the 1950s said that they supported Donald Trump (Public Religion Research Institute 2016).

The extant literature suggests that nostalgia is a powerful political and social tool. Nostalgia is often used in attempts to restore or maintain status quo privileges. Citizens who believe they are being displaced by change can invoke it to reestablish their legitimate role as active participants in or leaders of changing communities. Individuals may use nostalgia to overlook uncomfortable truths about their historical privileges. Politicians invoke nostalgia to rally citizens concerned about a loss of status.

Given the problematic and complicated history of US racial discrimination, it is not surprising that nostalgia often has racial undercurrents in the American context. One person's reminiscences of the "good old days" may invoke for others a time and place where they could not exercise full citizenship rights. Thus, it is important to consider whether or not political calls designed to invoke a storied past are nothing more than coded language that signals a willingness to accept old, discriminatory social hierarchies (see Kinder and Sanders 1996, 223–226, chap. 9).

HYPOTHESES AND DATA

With this in mind, this chapter seeks to explore the ways that nostalgia could be used to predict voting behavior in the 2016 election and whether nostalgia interacts with racial resentment. I hypothesize that (1) nostalgia will predict support for Donald Trump in 2016 and (2) voters who are nostalgic and racially resentful will also be more inclined to support Trump.

I do not expect that this relationship will be the same across different racial and ethnic groups. Racial minorities are not immune from harboring feelings of nostalgia, as evidenced by the African American research subject in Jennifer Carlson's study who said he carried a gun because he did not live in Mayberry (Carlson 2015, 11). However, minority respondents may not associate their "good old days" with a loss of racial dominance because of their groups' subordinate social position. Furthermore, because minorities are predicted to engage the past differently, I do not expect nostalgia to correlate with 2016 support for Donald Trump among nonwhite voters.

To explore these questions, I use data from the James Weldon Johnson Institute (JWJI) 2016 Election National Survey, an internet survey commissioned by Emory University and fielded by Qualtrics on November 7 and 8 (until 7 p.m. EST), 2016 (Gillespie 2016). Table 2.1 lists the unweighted descriptive statistics of the sample. The sample size includes 3,065 respondents, with oversamples of millennials, evangelical Christians, Asian Americans and minority Republicans. The sample also skews well-educated and affluent. While this does limit generalizability, it does create opportunities to explore nonwhite and Republican attitudes in greater depth.

The JWJI 2016 Election National Survey is advantageous because it includes two retrospective questions, which I use as proxies for nostalgia. Respondents were asked to assess whether America was better off than it had been eight years and fifty years before. The eight-year impression question was meant to prime respondent attitudes about the Obama administration. Realistically, one could argue that comparisons of America in 2016 versus 2008 are more retrospective than nostalgic (see Fiorina 1981). However, retrospection is an important component of nostalgia, and given the fact that respondents were asked to compare the present with eight and fifty years prior, the contrast between the two earlier eras is helpful.

The question about whether America was better off fifty years before was intended to prime attitudes about the era of the civil rights movement, which coincides with the tail end of the era identified with America's cultural apex. Though fifty years before 2016 is 1966 – just after the passage of the Voting Rights and Civil Rights Acts – evidence suggests that respondents' historical recollections of the era are not always precise (Lavelle 2015, chap. 4). Moreover, as Levin (2016) notes, the 1960s are more of an idea than an exact time period. What is more important is that Americans romanticize the mid-twentieth century (from the end of World

TABLE 2.1 *Descriptive statistics, JWJI 2016 Election National Survey*

Variable	Percentage
Gender	
Male	43.0%
Female	57.0%
Age	
18–34	28.5%
35–49	26.6%
50–64	28.8%
65 and older	16.1%
Race/Ethnicity (Select all that apply)	
White	60.1%
Black	12.0%
Latino/a	18.3%
Asian American	15.1%
Party ID	
Republican	31.0%
Democratic	51.1%
Independent/Other	17.9%
Ideology	
Liberal	34.8%
Moderate	26.0%
Conservative	39.2%
Income	
Under $30K	15.4%
$30–$49K	15.9%
$50–$79K	26.1%
$80K or more	42.5%
Education	
No College (includes associates degree)	37.0%
College Degree (includes grad/prof. degrees)	63.0%
Religion	
Evangelical Christian	32.5%

Source: JWJI 2016 Election National Survey. Figures are based on the unweighted sample and reflect valid percentages, which exclude missing responses.

War II to the middle part of the 1960s) as being the period of peak American ascendance. Scholars disagree on the exact periodization, but the consensus is that this rough time frame is often the object of nostalgia (see also Caputi 2005, chap. 1; Dwyer 2015, 3, 5).

I use logistic regression analysis to test the relationship between nostalgia, racial resentment, and vote choice. The dependent variable is 2016 vote choice for Donald Trump, coded as a binary variable. The primary independent variables include the aforementioned nostalgia questions and racial resentment (I use Sears' (1988) standard racial resentment scale). To test an alternate hypothesis – that perceptions of personal economic precarity will predict support for Trump – I include three questions in which respondents could indicate vulnerability or concern with precarity: whether they, when asked to rate their most important election issue, cited trade or unemployment as their top issue; whether the respondent is a union member; or whether the respondent reported having lost a manufacturing job. For the models that include the eight-year nostalgia measure, I also include favorability ratings of Barack Obama as a covariate.

FINDINGS

Figure 2.1 includes the top-line responses for the nostalgia questions. About 44 percent of respondents thought America was worse off than it had been eight years prior, compared to about 40 percent who thought it was better and 17 percent who thought it was the same. When the question instructs respondents to compare America to fifty years before, the same proportion said America was better, while 47 percent said that it was worse, and about 14 percent said that it was the same.

Figure 2.2 shows the top-line data for the other independent variables of interest: perceptions of economic precarity (a), Obama favorability (b), and racial resentment (c). As Figure 2a shows, few respondents reported the type of economic positioning that one would have expected to correlate with support for Trump. About 9 percent of respondents ranked trade or unemployment as their top issue in 2016. Nine percent of respondents were union members, and 5 percent of respondents had lost a manufacturing job.

Respondents in this sample had a generally favorable impression of Barack Obama (b). Nearly 60 percent of respondents reported having a favorable impression of him. About 37 percent of respondents had an unfavorable impression of him. An additional 3 percent of respondents reported neutral feelings.

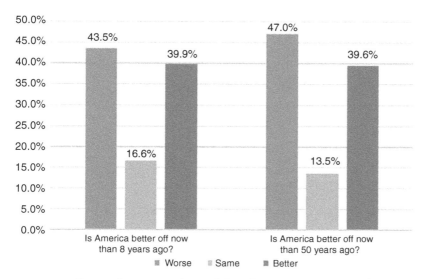

FIGURE 2.1 Respondent perceptions of American progress in 8 and 50 years
Source: JWJI 2016 Election National Survey. Figures are based on the unweighted sample, reflect valid percentages, and may include rounding error.

To measure racial resentment (c), I use Sears' (1988) four-question racial resentment battery. This battery asks respondents to agree or disagree (strongly or somewhat, with a neutral response category) with four questions about how to interpret black/white inequality (i.e., if white ethnics could succeed in the face of discrimination, then so can blacks; slavery and discrimination explain black/white inequality; if blacks tried hard, they would succeed like others; and blacks have gotten more than they deserve). If respondents affirm (strongly or somewhat) with the racially conservative part of the question (e.g., they disagree that slavery explained black/white inequality or agree that blacks got more than they deserved), their response is coded as 1. These responses are then added together. An additive score of 0 would indicate that the respondent gave no racially conservative responses, while a score of 4 would reveal that all of a respondent's answers were racially conservative. As Figure 2.2c indicates, nearly 36 percent of respondents gave no racially resentful responses. About 38 percent gave one or two racially conservative responses. About 26 percent gave three or four racially conservative responses.

Table 2.2 includes crosstabulations of the independent variables. The top rows look at the relationship between racial resentment and

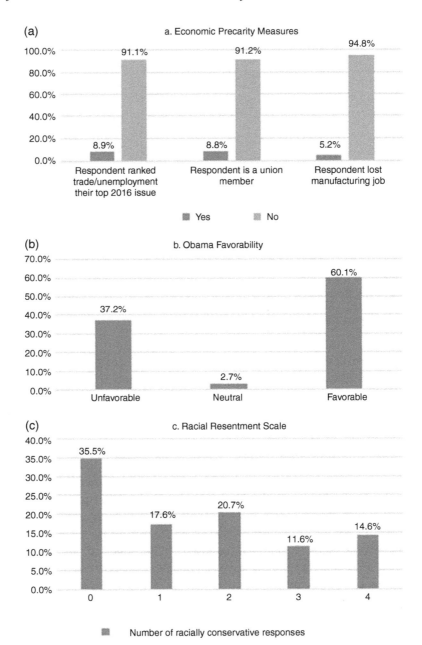

FIGURE 2.2 Top-line statistics for independent variable measures
Source: JWJI 2016 Election National Survey. Figures are based on the unweighted sample, reflect valid percentages, and may include rounding error.

perceptions of nostalgia. The data seems to indicate a relationship between racial resentment and perceptions of nostalgia. Respondents who reported no racial resentment were more likely to say that America had improved in eight and fifty years. As respondents reported higher levels of racial resentment, they were more likely to think that America had been better eight or fifty years before. Similarly, respondents who had negative perceptions of President Obama were far more likely to report that America was worse off in 2016 than it was eight and fifty years prior, while those with favorable impressions of him were more likely to report that America was better off in the present than it had been previously.

The relationship between the designated precarity measures and nostalgia are less clear. Those who listed trade and unemployment as their most important issue were about 14 percentage points more likely to say that America was worse in 2016 than it had been eight years before, but they were only about 4 percentage points more likely to believe that America was worse than it had been fifty years before. Nearly half of union members believed that America was better in 2016 than it had been eight or fifty years before. Respondents who had lost a manufacturing job were about 5 percentage points more likely to think that America had improved in eight years but were 2 percentage points more likely to believe that America was worse in 2016 than it had been fifty years earlier.

Table 2.3 presents crosstabulations of the key dependent variable (2016 vote choice, coded here as a binary measure of whether respondents planned to vote for Trump (For this variable, I use the vote question that all respondents answered–there was a vote question asked of early voters that does elicit slightly different responses for some respondents)) and the primary independent variables. There does appear to be a bivariate relationship between racial resentment and support for Trump. As a respondent's score on the racial resentment scale increases, their likelihood of voting for Trump increases. Conversely, respondents with the lowest racial resentment scores were the least likely to report voting for Trump.

Trump voters are also more likely to believe that America was better off in the past than in the present. Nearly all the respondents (93 percent) who thought that America was better off in 2016 than in 2008 said that they were not voting for Trump, as did 88 percent of voters who thought America was better off in 2016 compared fifty years before. To be sure, respondents who thought that America was better in the past were more split in their vote preferences. Only 57 percent of voters who thought that America was better off in 2008 compared to 2016 voted for Trump. And voters who responded

TABLE 2.2 Crosstabulations of independent variables and nostalgia measures

Obama favorability	Is America better off now than 8 years ago?			Is America better off now than 50 years ago?		
	Worse	Same	Better	Worse	Same	Better
Unfavorable	963 (82.0%)	137 (11.7%)	75 (6.4%)	897 (76.5%)	105 (9.0%)	171 (14.6%)
Neutral	39 (45.9%)	30 (35.3%)	16 (18.8%)	39 (45.9%)	30 (35.3%)	16 (18.8%)
Favorable	372 (19.6%)	354 (18.7%)	1168 (61.7%)	545 (28.8%)	288 (15.2%)	1058 (55.9%)
Racial Resentment						
0	274 (24.8%)	228 (20.7%)	602 (54.5%)	350 (31.8%)	204 (18.5%)	547 (49.7%)
1	198 (36.1%)	100 (18.2%)	251 (45.7%)	226 (41.2%)	67 (12.2%)	256 (46.6%)
2	280 (43.5%)	91 (14.2%)	272 (42.3%)	295 (46.0%)	77 (12.0%)	270 (42.1%)
3	244 (67.8%)	52 (14.4%)	64 (17.8%)	240 (66.7%)	39 (10.8%)	81 (22.5%)
4	361 (79.5%)	47 (10.4%)	46 (10.1%)	352 (77.7%)	33 (7.3%)	68 (15.0%)
Trade/Unemployment most important 2016 issue	126 (44.8%)	67 (23.8%)	88 (31.3%)	117 (41.9%)	55 (19.7%)	107 (38.4%)
Respondent is a union member	98 (35.1%)	42 (15.1%)	139 (49.8%)	110 (39.4%)	33 (11.8%)	136 (48.7%)
Respondent had lost manufacturing job	64 (38.6%)	28 (16.9%)	74 (44.6%)	77 (46.4%)	16 (9.6%)	73 (44.0%)

Source: JWJI 2016 Election National Survey. Figures are based on the unweighted sample.

TABLE 2.3 *Crosstabulations of racial resentment and nostalgia with Trump vote intention*

	Trump voters	Non-Trump voters
Racial resentment		
0	121 (11.0%)	984 (89.0%)
1	107 (19.5%)	442 (80.5%)
2	219 (34.1%)	424 (65.9%)
3	200 (55.6%)	160 (44.4%)
4	310 (68.3%)	144 (31.7%)
8-Year Nostalgia		
America is worse now	787 (57.2%)	589 (42.8%)
America is the same	96 (18.3%)	429 (81.7%)
America is better now	85 (6.7%)	1176 (93.3%)
50-Year Nostalgia		
America is worse now	732 (49.4%)	751 (50.6%)
America is the same	90 (21.2%)	335 (78.8%)
America is better now	146 (11.7%)	1103 (88.3%)

Source: JWJI 2016 Election National Survey. Figures are based on the unweighted sample.

that America was better fifty years ago were nearly evenly split in their vote preferences for Trump versus the other candidates.

To test these relationships further, I constructed logistic regression models, which I present in Table 2.4. The models here include all respondents. I regress 2016 support for Donald Trump on perceptions of whether America was better off eight or fifty years before and respondents' level of racial resentment. (Unless otherwise specified in Table 2.3, all variables are coded as dummy variables. For the racial resentment variable, respondents who answered three or four of the questions in the racially conservative direction were coded as 1.) In addition, I include precarity measures (union membership, manufacturing job loss, and perception of trade or jobs as the most important issue) and Obama favorability as covariates. I also include standard control variables, including gender, age, race, party, ideology, income, education, and evangelical religious identification.

In the first model, nostalgia is measured as a comparison to 2008 – a classic "are you better off now than when the incumbent took office" framing. Respondents who thought America was better off in 2008 were more than twice as likely to report voting for Donald Trump than those who thought America had improved in eight years. Moreover, respondents who answered

TABLE 2.4 *Logistic regression of Trump vote on racial resentment, nostalgia, and economic precarity*

	IV=2008 Nostalgia		IV=1966 Nostalgia	
	B (S.E.)	Odds Ratio	B (S.E.)	Odds Ratio
Constant	−2.635 (0.277)**	0.072	−2.597 (0.278)**	0.075
Racially resentful (binary)	0.617 (0.130)**	1.854	0.652 (0.129)**	1.919
US better off in the past	0.793 (0.138)**	2.210	0.476 (0.131)**	1.610
Negative Obama favorability (binary)	1.668 (0.139)**	5.301	1.823 (0.136)**	6.188
Trade or unemployment as most important issue	−0.241 (0.199)	0.786	−0.192 (0.198)	0.825
Experienced manufacturing job loss	0.656 (0.260)**	1.928	0.600 (0.261)**	1.822
Union member	−0.075 (0.219)	0.928	−0.082 (0.219)	0.922
Male	0.242 (0.123)**	1.274	0.220 (0.123)*	1.246
Age (4 category interval)	0.001 (0.061)	1.001	0.016 (0.061)	1.017
Black	−0.821 (0.251)**	0.440	−0.786 (0.250)**	0.456
Latino/a	−0.445 (0.162)**	0.641	−0.444 (0.163)**	0.641
Asian American	−0.409 (0.168)**	0.664	−0.387 (0.168)**	0.679
Republican	1.081 (0.149)**	2.949	1.075 (0.148)**	2.929
Democrat	−0.862 (0.174)**	0.422	−0.925 (0.173)**	0.396
Liberal	−0.684 (0.198)**	0.504	−0.687 (0.198)**	0.503
Conservative	0.552 (0.141)**	1.736	0.635 (0.140)**	1.888
Income ($10K intervals to $100K; $50K intervals to $150K+)	−0.003 (0.020)	0.997	−0.002 (0.020)	0.998
Less than a BA	0.446 (0.134)**	1.562	0.427 (0.134)**	1.533
Evangelical Christian	0.062 (0.131)	1.064	0.034 (0.130)	1.035
N	3050		3045	
Cox and Snell R-sq	0.458		0.456	

Source: IWJI 2016 Election Survey. Figures are based on the unweighted sample.

three or more racial resentment questions in the more conservative way were about 85 percent more likely to vote for Trump. Respondents who disliked Barack Obama were more than five times as likely to report voting for Trump. In addition, respondents who reported having lost a manufacturing job were nearly twice as likely to say that they were voting for Trump.

It is important to note that a number of control variables predicted vote choice as well. Not surprisingly, men and Republicans were significantly more likely to vote for Trump, and Democrats were significantly less likely to vote for Trump. Likewise, liberals were more likely to oppose Trump, while conservatives were more likely to vote for Trump. (In the case of party and ideology, pure Independents and moderates were the comparison categories.) In addition, respondents with less than a bachelor's degree were about 56 percent more likely to vote for Trump, while members of the three main racial and ethnic minority groups were between 33 percent and 56 percent less likely to vote for Trump.

The second model replicates the first equation, except for the fact that it changes the eight-year nostalgia question to the fifty-year framing. As Table 2.4 shows, voters who thought America was better off in the 1960s than in 2016 were 61 percent more likely to support Trump. Similarly, respondents with high levels of racial resentment were about twice as likely likely to support Trump. Those who had lost manufacturing jobs were also about 82 percent more likely to vote for Trump, and those who disliked Obama increased their likelihood of supporting Trump sixfold. As in the first model, men (at $p<.1$), Republicans, conservatives, and those without four-year college degrees were more likely to support Trump, while liberals, Democrats, and racial/ethnic minorities were significantly more likely to vote against Trump.

I did attempt to interact racial resentment with perceptions that America was better off eight or fifty years before. In both models, the interaction terms were not statistically significant. As such I do not include them in the models shown here.

Racial Resentment, Nostalgia, and Support for Trump

To confirm the seemingly recursive relationship between racial resentment and nostalgia and support for Trump, it is helpful to run the models among whites and nonwhites separately. Table 2.5 presents the logistic regression models for the white and nonwhite subsamples. The first two models look at white respondents. Here, the models look similar to those in Table 2.4. Thinking America was better off in 2008 strongly predicts support for

TABLE 2.5 *Logistic regression of Trump vote on racial resentment, nostalgia and economic precarity by race of respondent*

	Whites				Nonwhites			
	IV=2008 Nostalgia		IV=1966 Nostalgia		IV=2008 Nostalgia		IV=1966 Nostalgia	
	B (S.E.)	Odds ratio	B (S.E.)	Odds ratio	B (S.E.)	Odds ratio	B (S.E.)	Odds ratio
Constant	−2.779 (0.344)**	0.062	−2.764 (0.347)**	0.063	−3.133 (0.446)**	0.044	−3.153 (0.445)**	0.043
Racially resentful (binary)	0.703 (0.160)**	2.020	0.689 (0.160)**	1.992	0.167 (0.506)	1.181	0.768 (0.448)*	2.154
US better off 8/50 years ago	0.928 (0.177)**	2.529	0.627 (0.167)**	1.871	0.431 (0.256)*	1.539	0.320 (0.255)	1.377
racially resentful*US better off 8/50 years ago					0.893 (0.513)*	2.441	−0.047 (0.452)	0.954
Negative Obama favorability (binary)	1.666 (0.180)**	5.289	1.832 (0.174)**	6.246	1.851 (0.259)**	6.364	1.911 (0.260)**	6.762
racially resentful*negative Obama favorability					−0.417 (0.496)	0.659	−0.170 (0.483)	0.844
Trade or unemployment as most important issue	−0.366 (0.282)	0.693	−0.328 (0.280)	0.720	−0.081 (0.278)	0.922	−0.025 (0.278)	0.976
Experienced manufacturing job loss	0.650 (0.332)**	1.916	0.633 (0.330)*	1.882	0.735 (0.428)*	2.085	0.534 (0.433)	1.706
Union member	−0.210 (0.274)	0.811	−0.228 (0.273)	0.796	0.146 (0.375)	1.157	0.217 (0.376)	1.242
Male	0.160 (0.159)	1.174	0.118 (0.157)	1.125	0.456 (0.199)**	1.577	0.434 (0.198)**	1.544
Age (4 category interval)	0.009 (0.075)	1.009	0.031 (0.075)	1.031	0.044 (0.106)	1.045	0.048 (0.105)	1.050

(*continued*)

	Model 1			Model 2			Model 3			Model 4		
Republican	1.109	(0.184)**	3.031	1.115	(0.183)**	3.051	0.963	(0.255)**	2.620	0.941	(0.255)**	2.564
Democrat	-0.792	(0.216)**	0.453	-0.865	(0.214)**	0.421	-0.988	(0.296)**	0.372	-1.054	(0.294)**	0.348
Liberal	-0.811	(0.247)**	0.445	-0.827	(0.246)**	0.437	-0.537	(0.337)	0.585	-0.490	(0.338)	0.613
Conservative	0.360	(0.178)*	1.434	0.459	(0.176)**	1.583	0.827	(0.236)**	2.287	0.936	(0.236)**	2.549
Income ($10K intervals to $100K; $50K intervals to $150K+)	0.004	(0.025)	1.004	0.009	(0.025)	1.009	-0.008	(0.033)	0.992	-0.009	(0.033)	0.992
Less than a BA	0.433	(0.165)**	1.543	0.391	(0.164)**	1.478	0.399	(0.230)*	1.490	0.433	(0.230)*	1.542
Evangelical Christian	0.251	(0.166)	1.286	0.212	(0.165)	1.236	-0.330	(0.211)	0.719	-0.335	(0.211)	0.715
N	1833			1831			1217			1214		
Cox and Snell R-sq	0.487			0.483			0.379			0.378		

Source: JWJI 2016 Election Survey. Figures are based on the unweighted sample.

*p<.1; **p≤.05

Trump in 2016, as does being racially resentful and having experienced a manufacturing job loss. In all three cases, white respondents reporting these attitudes were about 2 to 2.5 times as likely to report voting for Trump. Control variables are also strong predictors of vote choice. Republicans, conservatives, and those without bachelor's degrees are more likely to support Trump, while liberals and Democrats were less likely to report voting for Trump. Unlike the previous models, though, white men are not more likely to vote for Trump than white women.

Of the variables already discussed, Republican Party identification is the strongest predictor of support for Trump. That factor is eclipsed, however, by harboring negative attitudes toward Barack Obama. Respondents who gave Obama negative favorability ratings were more than five times as likely to report voting for Trump. There would be good reason to consider the interaction between racial resentment and negative feelings for Obama. However, when I added interaction terms to the model to test that relationship (and the interaction between racial resentment and thinking America was better off in the past), those interactions were not statistically significant.

Changing the nostalgia variable to one that compares America in 2016 to America in 1966 does little to change these relationships. White respondents who were nostalgic for the America of the 1960s were about 87 percent more likely to indicate that they were supporting Trump in the election. And as in the previous model, antipathy towards Barack Obama is an extremely strong predictor of voting for Donald Trump. White respondents who harbored negative views of Obama were more than six times as likely to express support for Trump. Racially resentful voters were also more likely to report voting for Trump. As in the previous model, respondents who reported a manufacturing job loss were nearly twice as likely to support Trump. Similarly, Republicans, conservatives and respondents without bachelor's degrees were also more likely to vote for Trump. Conversely, Democrats and Liberal voters were significantly less likely to support Trump, and gender was not significant.

The right-hand side of Table 2.5 replicates these same models among nonwhites. Unlike the models for white respondents, interaction terms are worth discussing in the context of nonwhite voting behavior. As such, I include them in the models and report them here. The relationship between nostalgia, racial resentment, and support for Donald Trump is different for nonwhites. While nostalgia for 2008 does predict nonwhite support for Donald Trump (at the $p<.1$ level), longing for the 1960s has no relationship with 2016 vote preference. In the eight year nostalgia model, racial resentment is insignificant. However, resentment does predict nonwhite vote choice in the fifty year nostalgia model (again, at the p<.1 significance level)..

The control variables behave in the expected directions. Whether the nostalgia reference point is 2008 or 1966, nonwhite Republicans, conservatives, and respondents without bachelor's degrees are more likely to vote for Trump (the significance of education is p<.1). Democrats are significantly less likely to vote for Trump. Unlike in the white subsample, though, gender does predict vote choice among nonwhites, with men of color being significantly more likely to report voting for Trump.

The most interesting relationships in these models among nonwhites are the relationships between racial resentment, Obama favorability, and vote choice. I have already noted the relationship between racial resentment and nonwhite support for Trump when nostalgia is framed as a fifty year measure. In addition to that, nonwhites who dislike Obama were overwhelmingly more likely to support Trump in 2016. By itself, racial resentment is not significant in the eight year nostalgia model, but when resentment interacts with nostalgia for 2008, it too, positively predicts Trump support among nonwhites (though at the p<.1 significance level).

ANALYSIS

The analysis presented confirms the idea that nostalgia predicted support for Donald Trump in 2016. Whether nostalgia was operationalized in a more retrospective sense (Did the respondents believe that America was better off after Obama than before Obama?) or in a classic sense (Is America better off in the present than two generations ago?), respondents who thought that America had been better in the past were more likely to vote for Trump. This feeling of nostalgia did not preclude other factors predicting support for Trump. Racial resentment independently predicts support for Trump, as does having lost a manufacturing job (particularly in the context of nostalgia for 2008). Generally speaking, partisanship and ideology predict support for Trump, with Republicans and conservatives being more likely to support Trump, in contrast with Democrats and liberals, who voted against Trump.

These relationships are mediated by race/ethnicity. Consistent with what we know about minority voting behavior (see Segura and Bowler 2011), nonwhites reported a lower propensity for voting for Trump. When I disaggregate the sample to model voting behavior among whites and nonwhites, I find that nostalgia operates distinctly among different populations, even in a sample like this with an oversample of conservative minorities. While nostalgia is a strong predictor of support for Trump among whites, it barely registers as a significant predictor of Trump support among nonwhites; and even then, it is only in the context of nostalgia for 2008. While racial resentment alone does not predict nonwhite support for Trump in the context of 2008 nostalgia (It is signficant at the p<.1 level in the context of 1966 nostalgia), the interaction of racial resentment (or conservatism) and nostalgia for 2008 is correlated with 2016 vote choice (though at the p <.1 level, too). Gender also seems to matter more for nonwhites than whites. Men of color seem to be driving the gender gap in these models. This, too is not surprising, especially when we consider the fact that majorities of white men and women (overall) voted for Trump in 2016 and that gender gaps in voting exist in communities of color, too (Junn 2017; Gillespie and Brown 2019). The place where there are consistent similarities is on the one significant economic precarity measure. Whites and nonwhites who lost manufacturing jobs expressed similar levels of support for Trump in the models that framed nostalgia as a longing for the recent past.

Collectively, these findings point to a few important insights about the factors that influence vote choice. Nostalgia for 2008 is arguably a proxy for retrospective voting. As such, it is not surprising that white and nonwhite voters who thought that America was better off before Barack Obama became president would vote for the nominee of the opposing party in 2016. However, it is less likely that perceptions of America's well-being relative to 1966 are functions of retrospective voting. That respondents who thought that America was better off in the mid-1960s were more likely to support Trump suggests that researchers should not discount the importance of nostalgia in their explanations of vote choice.

The data also shows that racial resentment operates differently among whites and nonwhites. While resentment significantly predicts the voting behavior of whites, it is barely significant in predicting the behavior of nonwhites, and that is only in the context of fifty year nostalgia. Future studies should probe deeper to understand what racial resentment means in nonwhite populations and how it influences voting behavior in the context of other factors like nostalgia.

Future studies should also continue to question the recursivity of the relationships between these variables.

The general lack of interaction effects in this study suggests that these relationships are independent, but this question warrants future examination and testing with non-recursive modeling.

CONCLUSION

Overall, this analysis points to the idea that we should not rule out nostalgia as a factor in predicting vote choice. The survey used here did not include questions about social dominance orientation, so it may be the case that nostalgia is a proxy for a loss of social status. And to be sure, while this chapter shows that racial resentment and nostalgia independently predict vote choice (particularly among whites), it does not capture the determinants of nostalgia. If the lack of interaction effects between racial resentment and nostalgia holds up in non-recursive modeling, it still does not preclude the possibility of relationships between other types of bias. For instance, the racial resentment battery clearly measures anti-black resentment, but it does not speak to other types of racial or ethnic prejudices (Kinder and Sanders 1996, 106). In particular, resentments targeting women and immigrants, particularly Hispanic or Asian Americans, may not be captured fully in the Sears (1988) battery.[2] Future models should consider how new types of resentments inform vote choice and should also probe the relationship between those biases and feelings of nostalgia.

REFERENCES

Abramowitz, Alan. 2016. "Will Time for Change Mean Time for Trump?" *PS: Political Science and Politics.* 49(4): 659–660.

Caputi, Mary. 2005. *A Kinder, Gentler America: Melancholia and the Mythical 1950s.* Minneapolis: University of Minnesota Press.

Carlson, Jennifer. 2015. *Citizen-Protectors: The Everyday Politics of Guns in an Age of Decline.* New York: Oxford University Press.

DiAngelo, Robin. 2018. *White Fragility: Why It's So Hard for White People to Talk About Racism.* Boston: Beacon Press.

Dudden, Arthur. 1961. "Nostalgia and the American." *Journal of the History of Ideas.* 22(4): 515–530.

Dwyer, Michael D. 2015. *Back to the Fifties: Nostalgia, Hollywood Film and Popular Music of the Seventies and Eighties.* New York: Oxford University Press.

Farrar, Margaret. 2011. "Amnesia, Nostalgia and the Politics of Place Memory." *Political Research Quarterly.* 64(4): 723–735.

Fiorina, Morris. 1981. *Retrospective Voting in American National Elections.* New Haven: Yale University Press.

Gangel, Jamie, Sophie Tatum, and Javier De Diego. 2017. "Duck Dynasty's Korie Robertson to Trump: 'Say You Were Wrong' on Charlottesville." *CNN.com.*

---

[2] The author would like to thank Sergio García-Rios for influencing her thoughts on this matter.

August 25. Retrieved from www.cnn.com/2017/08/24/politics/korie-robertson-duck-dynasty/index.html, May 13, 2019.

Gelman, Andrew and Julia Azari. 2017. "19 Things We Learned from the 2016 Election." *Statistics and Public Policy.* 4(1): 1–10, DOI:10.1080/2330443X.2017.1356775

Gillespie, Andra. 2016. JWJI Election 2016 National Survey. [Statistical dataset]. Atlanta: Emory University.

Gillespie, Andra and Nadia E. Brown. 2019. "#BlackGirlMagic Demystified: Black Women as Voters, Partisans and Political Actors." *Phylon.* 56(2): 37-58.

Guest, Steve. 2016. "'Duck Dynasty' Patriarch Phil Robertson Supports Trump Now." *The Daily Caller.* May 10. Retrieved from https://dailycaller.com/2016/05/10/duck-dynasty-patriarch-phil-robertson-supports-trump-now/, May 14, 2019.

Hawley, George. 2016. *Right Wing Critics of American Conservatism.* Lawrence: University Press of Kansas.

Jardina, Ashley. 2019. *White Identity Politics.* New York: Cambridge University Press.

Junn, Jane. 2017. "The Trump Majority: White Womanhood and the Making of Female Voters in the US." *Politics, Groups and Identities.* 5(2): 343–352.

Kloeckner, Christian. 2015. "Risk and Nostalgia: Fictions of the Financial Crisis." *Amerikastudien/American Studies.* 60(4): 463–478.

Kinder, Donald and Lynn Sanders. 1996. *Divided by Color.* Chicago: University of Chicago Press.

Lavelle, Kristin. 2015. *Whitewashing the South: White Memories of Segregation and Civil Rights.* New York: Rowman and Littlefield.

Levin, Amy and Joshua G. Adair. 2017. "Nostalgia as Epistemology." In *Defining Memory: Local Museums and the Construction of History in America's Changing Communities.* Amy Levin and Joshua G. Adair (eds.). New York: Rowman and Littlefield. 85–88.

Levin, Yuval. 2016. *The Fractured Republic: Renewing America's Social Contract in the Age of Individualism.* New York: Basic Books.

Magary, Drew. 2013. "What the Duck?" *GQ* magazine. December 18. Retrieved from www.gq.com/story/duck-dynasty-phil-robertson, May 13, 2019.

Mascaro, Lisa. 2017. "In Alabama, the Heart of Trump Country, Many Think He's Backing the Wrong Candidate in Senate Race." *Los Angeles Times.* September 21. Retrieved from www.latimes.com/politics/la-na-pol-alabama-senate-runoff-20170921-story.html, May 13, 2019.

Metzl, Jonathan. 2019. *Dying of Whiteness: How the Politics of Racial Resentment Is Killing America's Heartland.* New York: Basic Books.

Morefield, Jeanne. 2014. *Empire Without Imperialism: Anglo-American Decline and the Politics of Deflection.* New York: Oxford University Press.

Mutz, Diana. 2018. "Status Threat, Not Economic Hardship, Explains the 2016 Presidential Vote." *Proceedings of the National Academy of Science.* 115(19): E4330–E4339. Retrieved from https://doi.org/10.1073/pnas.1718155115, May 16, 2019.

Phillips, Nichole. 2018. *Patriotism Black and White: The Color of American Exceptionalism.* Waco, TX: Baylor University Press.

Public Religion Research Institute. 2016. PRRI 2016 American Values Survey [Statistical Dataset]. Washington, DC: Public Religion Research Institute.

Sears, David. 1988. "Symbolic Racism." In *Eliminating Racism: Perspectives in Social Psychology*. Phyllis Katz and Dalmas Taylor (eds.). New York: Springer US. 53–84.

Segura, Gary and Shaun Bowler. 2011. *The Future Is Ours: Minority Politics, Political Behavior, and the Multiracial Era of American Politics*. Washington, DC: CQ Press.

Stroud, Angela. 2016. *Good Guys with Guns: The Appeal and Consequences of Concealed Carry*. Chapel Hill: University of North Carolina Press.

Tyson, Alec and Shiva Maniam. 2016. "Behind Trump's Victory: Divisions by Race, Gender and Education." Pew Research Center. November 9. Retrieved from www.pewresearch.org/fact-tank/2016/11/09/behind-trumps-victory-divisions-by-race-gender-education/, May 13, 2019.

3

The End of Human Capital Solidarity?

Ben Ansell and Jane Gingrich

INTRODUCTION

The electoral victories of Brexit and Donald Trump in 2016 have spurred a wave of increasingly fraught analyses by political scientists of the rise of populism and of dissatisfaction with democracy reaching to countries thought of as 'core' Western liberal democracies (Foa and Mounk 2016; Levitsky and Ziblatt 2018; Rosenbluth and Weir, Chapter 1, this volume). Along with divisions defined by race and gender (see Gillespie (Chapter 2, this volume) and Kessler-Harris (Chapter 5, this volume), many commentators have noted that underlying these political cleavages has been a growing gap in the political preferences between those with and without university educations. Degree holders have become increasingly cosmopolitan and liberal on social issues, whereas those without degrees have become less comfortable with these changes and their implications for their understanding of local communities.

What scholars have paid rather less attention to is differences *within* these groups. The education cleavage has emerged following several decades of unprecedented expansion in the provision of higher education. It would, we argue, be rather surprising if this mass expansion in higher education had left the composition of graduates the same. Instead, as higher education has expanded, university graduates have become more heterogeneous economically – no longer is higher education the preserve of a small cadre of managers and professionals. The so-called sociocultural professions have expanded particularly dramatically, but graduates have also entered the broader service sector in large numbers. Given these changes, does it really make sense to think of university graduates as an undifferentiated 'elite' cosmopolitan class? And if not, how should we think of them?

A second question emerges. Are university graduates really that satisfied with the status quo, as recent accounts of populism have suggested? Democracy and capitalism often coexist in a somewhat uneasy bargain between a small group of economic winners and the wider voting public. Not all graduates can win equally in this system, at least not to the same extent as their predecessors in the 1960s and 1970s. While on average graduates may be more supportive of the bargain underpinning democratic capitalism, they too may not find it meeting all of their expectations. In particular, we argue that the political views of graduates are shaped by the degree to which their occupation matches their graduate status – how well does the labour market reward their investment in education? Put simply, graduates' expectations may be unfulfilled compared to historical expectations.

We start by considering existing literature explaining the growing gap in socio-economic outcomes (a) between the 'skilled' and 'unskilled' and (b) among the skilled. The former story is well known, the latter somewhat less so. Most economists agree that growing gaps in wages between skilled and unskilled workers reflect the role of 'skill-biased technical change' – that is, recently adopted technologies depend on highly skilled workers to operate effectively, meaning that this group of workers benefits disproportionately from the expansion of usage of these technologies. But there are also reasons to believe that among skilled workers, wage inequality is growing substantially. This reflects two mechanisms. Some skilled workers are making substantially less than they might expect since they are 'mismatched' in the labour market, taking on roles that do not typically require high levels of skill. This is an important, but understudied, group, whose employment is more precarious than perhaps they had expected (see Thelen and Wiedemann, Chapter 12, this volume). However, there is also a group of skilled workers who are benefiting disproportionately, in this case because of differences *among firms*, due in part to 'winner take all' markets and uncompetitive sectors.

We begin our empirical analysis by examining where graduates *do* differ from non-graduates. We argue that for three reasons, we might expect university graduates to be more satisfied than non-graduates with the democratic status quo: their position in the economic structure, their cultural norms associated with support for democracy, and their greater representation by political elites. We show that consistent with these claims and with recent election results, graduates are quite distinct from non-graduates in their satisfaction with the democratic system and that their preferences as a group are more homogeneous than those of non-graduates.

We then turn to examine differences *among* graduates, emphasizing a growing internal divergence on questions of economic policy and attitudes towards redistribution. We also note that even in terms of satisfaction with democracy, graduates may not be as coherent as they appear. Using data on skill mismatch with jobs, we show that mismatched graduates, whose labour market status belies their education, appear increasingly dissatisfied with their lot in life and with democracy itself, less trustful of politicians, and more attracted to populist right parties. We also show that, by contrast, those graduates in large firms – the key beneficiaries of recent growth – are most satisfied with the economy.

The title of this chapter refers to 'the end of human capital solidarity'. We think about this in two ways. First, it may not make sense to think of university graduates – those with high human capital – as a uniform, homogeneous, solidaristic group today. It is not obvious that graduates share similar political preferences or view one another's welfare solidaristically. Indeed, in the United States, graduates are arguably the most politically polarized group, perhaps helping to explain America's particularly venomous debates among elites (Hacker and Pierson, Chapter 11, this volume). Second, we think of the solidarity of graduates with non-graduates. While graduates may be a more diverse group than sometimes portrayed, on average they have clearly benefitted more than non-graduates from economic change over the past few decades. But are they willing to keep up their end of the bargain underpinning democratic capitalism – paying higher rates of taxation to those less fortunate to maintain political and social peace? How will graduates respond to the populist upsurge in terms of their sympathies for non-graduates if the price to be paid is restrictions on the liberal global markets which have so benefitted the university educated? These cleavages around the democratic bargain may be especially threatening to the stability of contemporary democracy.

THE EDUCATION DEBATE

Two key facts shape how we should understand the returns to education over the past few decades and their likely political consequences. The first is well known: on average the returns to education have risen substantially since the 1970s, even as the supply of education has increased. This in turn has heightened differences in the labour market experiences of those with high skills – usually proxied for by a university degree – and those without.

The second is more recent and less well known: there are growing gaps in the economic outcomes associated with holding a university degree. That is, socio-economic variation is increasing *among* the 'high skilled'. This latter development reflects a widening at both the top and bottom of income distribution among graduates. As university enrollment has expanded, some graduates have found themselves in 'non-graduate' jobs, which pay commensurately lower salaries – we term this 'mismatch' and its economic (and perhaps political) consequences resemble those from earlier eras of 'over education'. At the top of the wage distribution scale, superstar firms in uncompetitive product markets have been able to capture and distribute rents among their high-skilled staff – hence graduates working for top financial, tech, legal, and other firms have reaped returns substantially beyond what might be predicted from their skills alone. We refer to this dynamic as 'winner-take-all', a phrase that of course has both economic (Frank and Cook 2010) and political (Hacker and Pierson 2011) variants.

In this section, we discuss existing literature from economics and political science that sets out the causes and consequences of these twin shifts – between the high and low skilled and among the high skilled. Let us begin with the now well-established story about the growing returns to skill since the 1970s. That higher-skilled workers receive higher wages than lower-skilled workers is of course not surprising – basic human capital theory, as inspired by Becker (2009), views skills as important and accordingly remunerated parts of the production process. What is less obvious is why a particular bundle of skills might become more valuable over time – particularly if the supply of skills in the economy is actually growing, which all else equal ought to lower returns to skill. To address this apparent contradiction, economists have explored the role of technology in increasing the demand for skills to a level that exceeded the negative supply effect. In particular, they have emphasized *skill-biased technical change* – technological developments that are complementary with skilled labour, thereby raising demand for skills and the associated wages (Goldin and Katz 1996). Goldin and Katz (2009) refer to the pattern of returns to skill as a 'race' between education and technology – the former increasing skills supply and thereby reducing returns, the latter increasing skills demand and raising returns.

Not only has skill-biased technical change pulled apart the high skilled from the unskilled; it has also been accompanied by a 'hollowing out' of the middle of the skill distribution as many routinizable tasks have been replaced by machinery, robots, or software (Autor, Levy, and Murnane 2003). Goos and Manning (2007) and Goos, Manning, and Salomons (2009) show that this has led to a long-run decline in employment in middle-paid, middle-skilled jobs since the early 1990s – with the labour market increasingly divided into 'lovely jobs' for the high skilled and 'lousy jobs' for the low skilled.[1] The combination, then, of skill-biased technical change with hollowing out implies an ever greater economic polarization based on skills, particularly noticeable when comparing university graduates to non-graduates. It has also accompanied a more general decline in the labour share of national income, heightening this growing inequality (Karabarbounis and Neiman 2013; Schwellnus, Kappeler, and Pionnier 2017).

What are the political implications of this kind of economic polarization? We will explore this question empirically in the next section; however, before doing so, it is worth laying out some basic expectations. Our focus in this chapter is on satisfaction, both economic and political. Clearly in the former case, we would expect low-skilled workers to be less satisfied with the state of the economy and with their life more broadly, and for the reverse to be true among high-skilled workers. The political implications follow this pattern: if low-skilled workers are falling behind economically, their dissatisfaction with their economic circumstances is likely to spill over into negative assessments of the government, of politicians in general, and of how democracy is functioning – those assessments in turn may lead them to support anti-systemic or populist parties. By contrast, one would expect high-skilled voters to be more supportive of the political status quo and incumbent mainstream politicians and parties.

As already noted, this bifurcation of the labour market into high and low skilled has happened even as policymakers have expanded the supply of higher education. Ansell (2008) shows that since the 1960s in many OECD countries, enrollment rates in higher education have increased from less than 5 per cent to more than 50 per cent. While this expansion has not led to a collapse in the wage premium received by graduates – because of the compensating demand effect – it has almost necessarily produced a more heterogeneous group of university graduates. Even

---

[1] It is worth noting that there is not complete consensus on the skill-biased technical change polarization argument. Mishel, Shierholz, and Schmitt (2013) argue that these trends have been exaggerated, particularly the rise of low-wage service employment.

though on average this group has continued to diverge from non-graduates, there is growing variation in economic outcomes among the high skilled. Broadly this comes from two forces: first mismatched graduates in lower-paying/traditionally non-graduate jobs and second high-skilled workers in 'market-dominant' firms who, because of the winner-take-all characteristic of a number of important sectors, are receiving wage returns well beyond what one might expect from skills alone.

We begin with the mismatched group. The expansion of higher education by governments does not deterministically produce an expansion in private and public sector jobs that can use these skills effectively. Product and labour markets may not be immediately able to adjust to skill-biased production. Or there may be political and institutional blockages – many skilled professions are able to assemble high and often rather arbitrary barriers to entry – think, for example, of the profession of public notaries in Italy or in France, which require a national exam and have regional quotas. In either case, many graduates end up in jobs that traditionally did not require graduates and that fail to employ their skills. This phenomenon of over qualification or mismatch has been identified in many environments, including in liberal labour markets such as the United Kingdom (Green and Zhu 2010) – it does appear, however, to be especially prevalent in rigid labour markets such as those in Southern Europe (Mavromaras and McGuinness 2012; McGowan and Andrews 2015; Oliveira, Santos, and Kiker 2000).

What are the implications for the economic and political satisfaction of mismatched university graduates? Ansell and Gingrich (2017, 2018) argue that patterns of mismatch vary systematically across European labour markets, with countries with protected labour markets more exposed, and that mismatched individuals are less likely to vote, have less trust in politicians, and are more opposed to immigration than other graduates. We can extend the claims in those articles to broader questions about economic and political satisfaction.

Mismatch matters because it violates the expectations that students undertaking higher education have about their likely life courses. Where jobs fail to live up to expectations, the loss is doubled: first of the investment in time, and increasingly financial resources, from going to university, and second because of the increased emphasis – both rhetorically and in wage premia – of education as the sole path to economic success. If attaining education proves inadequate, despite its costs and apparent importance, it should not surprise us that the mismatched feel deeply frustrated both with their own experience in the economy and with the political system in general that has produced it. This should drive generalized dissatisfaction and more specifically greater support for anti-system political parties. In a sense, this is just a return to a long historical experience with the frustration of over education, important in cases from colonial indigenous elites in Ghana to the 1968 movement in France. But when over education becomes a mass phenomenon, as opposed to the preserve of a disgruntled would-be elite, its implications may be even more profound.

The growing divergence among the high skilled is not only a story about disappointed, mismatched graduates. There is also an increasing skew at the upper end of the wage distribution scale among the high skilled. Part of this may reflect highly productive individuals who can take advantage of ever growing international markets for their highly valued and scarce skills. For certain individuals in the entertainment, sports, artificial intelligence, and other creative or scientific industries, this may truly reflect their global marginal productivity. For others, though, this likely reflects their holding jobs in particularly high-paying firms. In other words, some firms may be able to capture rents or market position in ways that supersede the contribution of skills and capital alone to firm output (Andrews et al. 2016; Autor et al. 2017; Barth et al. 2014).

Where rents permit super-profits, employees of these firms, typically degree holders, benefit disproportionately compared with employees of smaller or less well-positioned firms. This further widens returns among the high skilled and is likely to mean that high-skilled individuals working in larger, particularly multinational firms in particular industries will be particularly well paid and especially satisfied with the economic and political status quo. But these winner-take-all markets also create substantial resentment among those who have not benefitted. As wages detach from skills, citizens become suspicious that claims about meritocracy are not fully justified. At the same time the beneficiaries of these dynamics are likely to justify their wage premia with reference to their own merit. Where economic advantage can spill over into political power, the winners of winner-take-all have the incentive and ability to institutionalize their status (Hacker and Pierson 2011).

HUMAN CAPITAL SOLIDARITY? EDUCATION STILL MATTERS

Scholars and pundits alike have pointed to a new 'educational rift' in advanced democracies (Goodwin and Heath 2016; Inglehart and

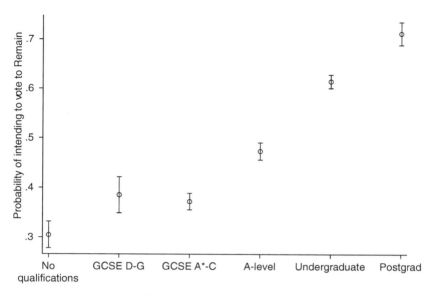

FIGURE 3.1 Education and support for Remain in the UK referendum on leaving the European Union (BES 2016)

Norris 2016). At the aggregate level, places with higher levels of education were less likely to vote in favor of Brexit, for Marine le Pen in France, for the Alternative for Germany (AfD) party, or for Donald Trump. At the individual level, the educated are also less likely to cast a ballot for a populist candidates or causes. Figure 3.1 provides a striking example. Using data from the British Election Survey, undertaken just before the Brexit referendum, it shows the estimated probability of intending to vote Remain by educational groups in Britain, using a simple logit specification controlling for age, income, and gender, and with dummies for each of the 378 local authorities. The predicted relationship between education and satisfaction with the status quo in Britain (i.e., Remain) is very strong – whereas individuals with no qualifications were estimated to have around a 30 per cent chance of supporting Remain; this rises to more than 70 per cent for those with a postgraduate degree.

This rejection of populism rests upon a more general satisfaction with democracy. Figures 3.2 and 3.3 show the mean levels of satisfaction with democracy and the standard deviation of satisfaction with democracy between 2002 and 2016 in a number of European countries, broken

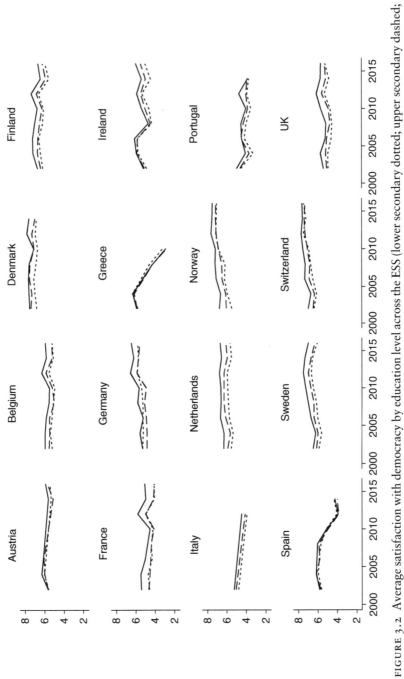

FIGURE 3.2 Average satisfaction with democracy by education level across the ESS (lower secondary dotted; upper secondary dashed; graduates unbroken)

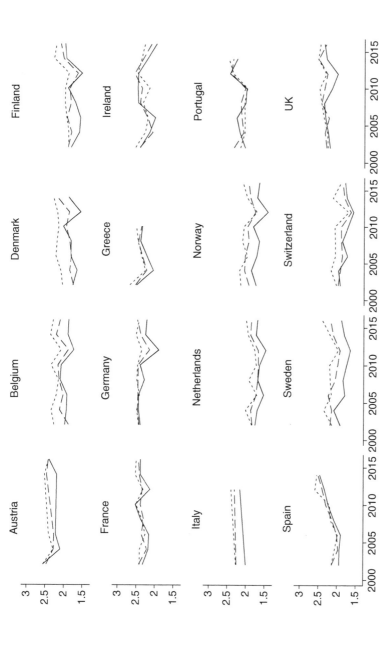

FIGURE 3.3 Standard deviation of satisfaction with democracy by education level across the ESS (lower secondary dotted; upper secondary dashed; graduates unbroken)

down by education group.² Figure 3.2 shows that in nearly every context, those with university degrees are more satisfied with democracy than other educational groups.³ Moreover, Figure 3.3 demonstrates that, in general, those with degrees are more homogenous in their levels of satisfaction. It is worth noting that these are average associations of satisfaction with education – we are not netting out the role of income, gender, or race, all of which are strongly correlated with educational achievement in Europe and beyond. We will return in the following sections to models that take such covarying factors into account. Still, the overall distinction between educated groups is striking.

Why are the educated more satisfied with democracy? Much of the debate about recent populist surges has focused on the relative explanatory power of economic versus cultural versus political factors. Those emphasizing economic roots to populism point to growing divergences at the individual and geographic levels related to structural economic changes (Autor et al. 2016). By contrast, others have pointed to the superior explanatory power of non-economic variables, such as cultural values and racial animosity (Inglehart and Norris 2016). Finally, a third group points to the interaction between the political system and populist movements, arguing that mobilization occurs when the representative process appears to swerve away from the interests of voters – something associated with both political gridlock and polarization in the United States (Oliver and Rahn 2016) but also its opposites, de-polarization and cartelization, in Europe (Katz and Mair 2009).

While these explanations are at times cast as competing hypotheses, they are not mutually exclusive and, indeed, may be reinforcing. In each, however, education is a key part of the mechanism linking economic, cultural, and political variables to democratic satisfaction. We briefly take each of these logics in turn.

First, those with college degrees are often economic 'winners' – particularly in the current moment. One of the defining features of post-industrial economies is the complementarity between high levels of general skills and technology (Goldin and Katz 2009). Scholars debate the

---

² These figures are drawn from the European Social Survey waves 1–7. Respondents are asked to rate their satisfaction with democracy on an eleven-point scale, range from completely dissatisfied (0) to completely satisfied (10).

³ The average within-country standard deviation in support for democracy is around two points. In a number of cases in Figure 3.2, the gap between satisfaction of those with lower secondary and those with university education is more than one full point – thus accounting for half of a standard deviation.

extent to which skill-biased technological change explains growing inequality in advanced democracies; however, the skill premium has grown nearly everywhere, even in countries with historically low gaps due to collective wage bargaining (for an overview, see Autor, 2014). Moreover, geographic regions with greater concentrations of human capital are increasingly successful relative to other regions (Moretti 2012). Economic satisfaction is highly correlated with satisfaction with democracy and with the government – across the European Social Survey sample, the correlations across these three measures range between 0.55 and 0.65.

Second, education itself may impart values that are congruent with both the principles of liberal democracy and greater satisfaction with the status quo. Inglehart and Norris (2016) have long pointed to cultural divides among individuals in advanced democracies. These divides are highly associated with education. The causal effect of education itself is debated, but there is some evidence that education can impart more culturally liberal values – a core predictor of populist support and, in some cases, democratic satisfaction.[4] In addition to imparting particular values, more education may simply teach more acceptance of the status quo.

Finally, those with more education are everywhere more likely to see themselves represented in politics. Carnes (2013), in his work on working-class representation, shows the dominance of high-education groups in electoral politics, something demonstrated as well in the United Kingdom and elsewhere (Alexiadou 2015, 2016; Carnes and Lupu 2016). In left-wing parties, the shift towards more professional politicians and the decline of trade unions as major recruiters have meant that almost all politicians now are university educated.

In short, the role of education in inoculating voters against anti-system parties and in creating satisfaction with the principles of democracy is overdetermined; educated voters are more likely to have economic success (and live in prosperous areas), more likely to have culturally liberal values, and more likely to be represented by the

---

[4] Scholars disagree about the extent to which schools and colleges have an independent causal effect on attitudes and behaviours, and where long-run effects do exist, what about the schooling experience actually matters? (See, for example, Berinsky and Lenz 2011; Hillygus 2005; Kam and Palmer 2008; Marshall 2016; Mendelberg, McCabe, and Thal 2016; Neundorf, Niemi, and Smets 2016; Niemi and Junn 2005; Persson 2015; Surridge 2016.)

political mainstream. Given the fairly homogenous support of the highly educated for democracy, they might appear to be a democratic bulwark.

Of course, this cleavage raises the concern that as the highly educated and less educated drift apart in views about the merits of the status quo, there is ever less political solidarity between the satisfied high skilled and the dissatisfied low skilled. The next section, indeed, suggests that education is not as stabilizing for democracy as the previous analysis suggests, nor are the preferences of the educated as homogenous as they might appear.

HUMAN CAPITAL SOLIDARITY? DIVERSE GRADUATES

The broader electoral picture shows the highly educated moving further away politically from the less educated. But we should not let this mislead us into thinking that the educated are a coherent, homogenous, and solidaristic group. As we now show, there are strong reasons to believe that new cleavages are emerging *among* the educated in terms of their attitudes towards both the place of government in the economy and the desirability of democracy as a whole. We take each of these concerns in turn.

Economic Divides

Earlier we noted how trends in structural economic and cultural change, along with patterns of political representation, have pulled apart the highly educated from the less educated in terms of their satisfaction with how democracy operates in their countries. But what of the other half of the bargain of democratic capitalism? When it comes to attitudes towards capitalism – or more precisely, whether people think the government should play a role in directly redistributing the spoils from capitalism – graduates are far less solidaristic, in terms of their attitudes towards the less well off and among themselves as a group.

The former claim – that the highly educated are less supportive of government redistribution than the less well educated – should not surprise us. Since education has become so closely correlated with economic outcomes, on average the educated will indeed be the net losers of any such transfer. Figure 3.4 shows that in the case of every country in the European Social Survey for which we have data, graduates are less

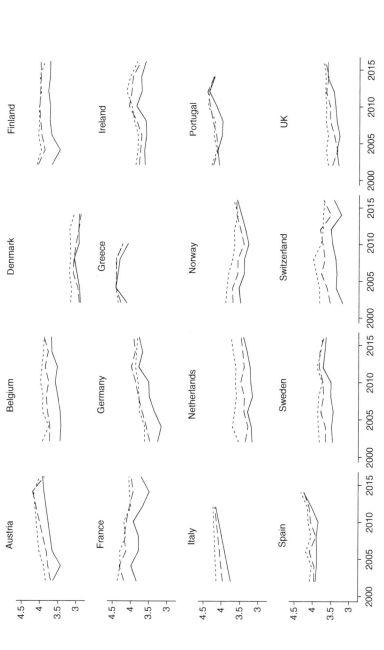

FIGURE 3.4 Average redistribution preferences by education level across the ESS (lower secondary dotted; upper secondary dashed; graduates unbroken)

supportive of increased redistribution than are those with only lower or upper secondary education.[5]

And yet this kind of finding does occasionally surprise commentators who have, in part because of populist victories at elections, often associated less-educated people with voting for right-wing parties that are typically anti-redistribution. How can this be the case then? The answer lies in part in the splits among the highly educated – with a vocal and politically active group of graduates increasingly supportive of left-wing government and redistribution. Who are these graduates and why have their economic preferences diverged from the typically more anti-redistributive views of the highly educated?

Earlier we alluded to the effects of the mass expansion of higher education that occurred from the 1960s onwards across the advanced industrial world (Ansell 2008). It would be surprising if such a surge in the supply of graduates had been absorbed uniformly by the labour market into the types of jobs that graduates had held in the 1950s. Indeed, part of the background to massified higher education was a growing demand among new so-called sociocultural professions for university-educated workers (Oesch 2013). Mass higher education hence implied a more economically diverse pool of graduates. Two sectors were particularly important in absorbing these new graduates – the public sector, particularly in sociocultural professions such as teaching and healthcare – and the 'high-productivity' private service sector – the so-called FIRE industries (finance, insurance, and real estate). Thus mass higher education produced a surge in employment in two rather distinct directions (Ansell and Gingrich 2013) – each of which had counterposed implications for redistributive attitudes. Sociocultural workers in the public sector tended to favor higher redistribution for a number of reasons. First, higher taxation supported a growing public sector. Second, public sector workers were typically not among the best paid (and hence most taxed) citizens. And third, more contentiously, individuals with more 'altruistic' attitudes were attracted towards such professions. Meanwhile workers in the FIRE industries were well paid, concerned about the size of government, and more potentially acculturated to the benefits of market forces. Mass

---

[5] That being the case, there has been some convergence of attitudes in a few cases over the long period of post-crisis austerity, notably in Germany, Norway, Portugal, Spain, and the United Kingdom. The typical gap between redistributive preferences of graduates and those with lower secondary education appears to be around 0.5 points – this is half of the overall within-country typical standard deviation.

higher education then has produced a split among graduates in views about redistribution, driven by the diversity in occupations they have taken on (Häusermann and Kriesi 2011; Kitschelt and Rehm 2014).

Figure 3.5 follows on from Figure 3.4 but shows the standard deviation of redistributive preferences by education level, as opposed to the mean. The figure shows a rather stark contrast with the equivalent figure for satisfaction with democracy – indeed, the opposite pattern. In terms of redistributive attitudes, graduates are *more* diverse than non-graduates, whereas with regards to satisfaction with democracy, they were less diverse.

These figures have some intriguing implications for the contemporary shape of party competition. Parties on both the left and right can potentially find allies among groups of graduates – neither is likely to be able to capture graduates as a group any more. For right-wing parties, this means that university graduates are no longer their base, and they have often had to combine socially conservative and populist themes as a counterweight to anti-redistribution policies as they seek to attract working-class support. For left-wing parties, the tension has emerged between their traditional base of the working-class and their new base of sociocultural professionals – both of whom support higher redistribution but often have very different reactions towards sociocultural attitudes and immigration (Gingrich and Häusermann 2015). Moreover, sociocultural professionals may still balk at very high levels of redistribution. One consequence of this jumbling of party bases is that the capitalism component of the democratic capitalism bargain may produce less electoral tension across parties, forcing the debate to occur within parties.

Dashed Expectations about Democracy

We know that graduates have become increasingly diverse politically and are arguably responsible for the high levels of political polarization seen over the past few decades. But to what extent has polarization turned into dissatisfaction with the other side of the bargain of democratic capitalism: democracy itself? After all, despite their diversity, most graduates still fare better economically (and in terms of social and cultural capital) than non-graduates. We now turn to examining which graduates are less satisfied with their own fortunes and with democracy itself. While this group may be relatively small in number, as we shall see, its position lies between that of non-graduates and more-satisfied graduates, making them potentially

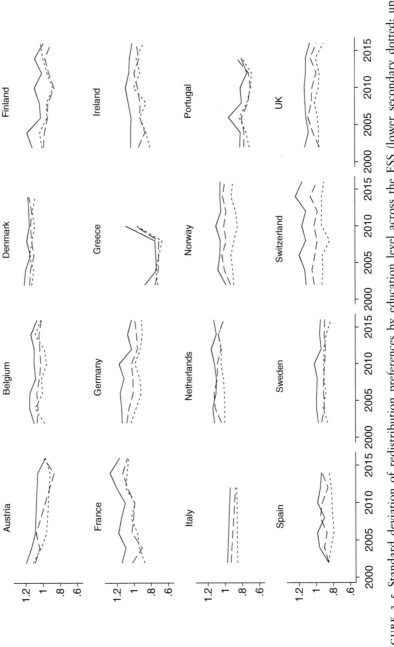

FIGURE 3.5 Standard deviation of redistribution preferences by education level across the ESS (lower secondary dotted; upper secondary dashed; graduates unbroken)

important swing voters and hence major players in the close recent victories for populist campaigns.

What makes graduates less satisfied? We argue that core to understanding their attitudes and behaviour is thinking about graduates' expectations associated with having completed a university degree. In the 1960s and 1970s, fewer than 20 per cent (and often far less) of the population completed a degree and having done so was generally considered a ticket to a secure, decently remunerated 'graduate-level' job. With the mass expansion of higher education, a degree may no longer meet these expectations. Still, most people enter higher education with the expectation that the job they end up with will be one that uses their degree. For those who nonetheless find themselves working in jobs that are not traditionally graduate level, these dashed expectations are likely to produce dissatisfaction with their lot, and potentially with the political and economic system in which they live.

Building on earlier work examining mismatch between jobs and graduates (Ansell and Gingrich 2017), we now turn to examining whether graduates who end up in non-graduate jobs are indeed less satisfied, at least in terms of what we can elicit from survey responses. Using data on occupations drawn from previous analyses of the European Community Household Panel (ECHP) and the European Union Statistics on Income and Living Conditions (EU-SILC), we are able to code every industry-occupation combination with more than forty respondents per country in these surveys – we refer to these as distinct 'jobs'. For each such job, we then examine how many respondents in these surveys have university degree–level qualifications.

We can then use this job data to match respondents in the European Social Survey – a separate survey that focuses on asking social and political questions – to their industry and occupation combination and characteristics of that job. In particular, we are interested in whether individuals have education levels matching those typical in the particular kind of job they have. Where individuals have a university degree and are in a job where the majority of holders of that job in that country have degrees, we refer to them as 'matched'. Where, on the other hand, degree holders are in a job where fewer than a majority of people in that job have a degree, we refer to them as 'mismatched'. Clearly, these are blunt categories – many high-paying jobs such as stockbroking used to have very few graduates and are now dominated by, presumably happy, university graduates. Still, the measure does capture the degree to which graduates' labour market expectations have been satisfied by a 'typical' graduate job.

With this concept in hand we can examine how heterogeneity among university graduates might affect their satisfaction with the bargain of democratic capitalism. Is it the case that mismatched graduates feel let down? Do they act on those feelings?

Table 3.1 uses six dependent variables that capture attitudes related to satisfaction. For each, we use dummies for being a 'mismatched graduate' or having no university-level education, with the omitted category being 'matched graduates'. Our data covers sixteen European countries over seven waves of surveys between 2000 and 2014. Our analyses are limited to individuals currently employed to more cleanly analyze the effect of job matching. We add controls for age, gender, (logged) income relative to the country-year mean, union membership, and year and country dummies and cluster standard errors by country-year. Models 1 through 5 use satisfaction measures which are responses on a zero to ten scale – accordingly we model this using linear regression. Model 6 by contrast is a binary dependent variable and we use a logit specification.

We begin with Models 1 through 4 which are various satisfaction measures. Model 1 examines satisfaction with 'how democracy works in

TABLE 3.1 *European Social Survey – Mismatched degrees and satisfaction*

	(1) Satis. Demo	(2) Satis. Econ.	(3) Satis. Gov.	(4) Satis. Life	(5) Trust Pol.	(6) Rad. Right
No Degree	-0.56***	-0.38***	-0.30***	-0.13***	-0.58***	1.62***
	(0.03)	(0.04)	(0.05)	(0.03)	(0.03)	(0.16)
Degree Mismatched	-0.10***	-0.09***	-0.04	-0.10***	-0.16***	0.60***
	(0.04)	(0.04)	(0.04)	(0.02)	(0.03)	(0.15)
Relative Income	0.27***	0.28***	0.16***	0.50***	0.18***	-0.21***
	(0.03)	(0.03)	(0.03)	(0.03)	(0.02)	(0.04)
Age	0.00	-0.00	0.00	-0.00	0.00	-0.01
	(0.00)	(0.00)	(0.00)	(0.00)	(0.00)	(0.00)
Gender	-0.22***	-0.33***	-0.13***	0.06***	-0.05**	-0.44***
	(0.02)	(0.03)	(0.03)	(0.02)	(0.02)	(0.06)
Union Member	0.08***	0.07***	0.16***	0.02	0.01	0.16**
	(0.03)	(0.03)	(0.04)	(0.02)	(0.02)	(0.07)
N	76740	77300	76640	77751	77262	47929

Note: Standard errors, clustered by country-year, in parentheses. * $p<0.10$, ** $p<0.05$, *** $p<0.01$. All models contain country and year dummies.

The End of Human Capital Solidarity?

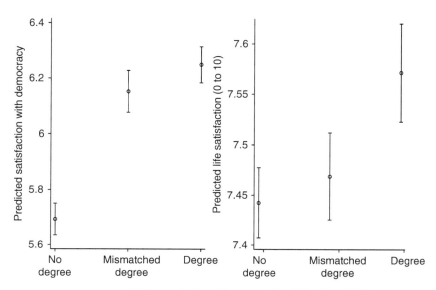

FIGURE 3.6 Mismatched graduates and satisfaction – ESS

[the respondent's] country'. Model 2 examines satisfaction with the 'present state of the economy in [the respondent's] country'. Model 3 examines satisfaction with the national government, and Model 4 examines how satisfied the respondent is 'with life as a whole'.

Except for Model 3 – satisfaction with the national government – there appear to be quite distinct differences between graduates in mismatched versus matched jobs, with the former less satisfied with their life, with the state of the economy, and with how democracy itself works. The substantive magnitude for mismatched graduates vis-à-vis matched graduates is moderate – about a third to a half the size of gender or a doubling of income. It is also notable, however, that save for the case of satisfaction with life, mismatched graduates still look much more similar to matched graduates than they do to non-graduates. Finally, non-graduates are especially unsatisfied – clearly the split between the skilled and unskilled is still larger than that among the skilled. These patterns can be seen in Figure 3.6.

In terms of attitudes towards politicians, though not satisfaction with the government itself, differences also appear between matched and mismatched graduates. The latter are less likely to trust politicians and more likely to vote for radical or populist right parties than are matched graduates. However, again we see that the biggest difference is

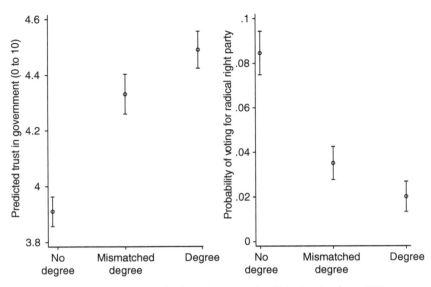

FIGURE 3.7 Mismatched graduates and political attitudes – ESS

between those without degrees and those with degrees. Figure 3.7 demonstrates these patterns. As we noted in the previous section, education clearly matters substantially as a core cleavage in terms of satisfaction with the political system. However, what these results show is that there are still noticeable differences between graduates who have had their labour market expectations met and those who have not. Moreover, these effects are similar in magnitude to, or larger than, the effects of gender or income.

Who is most impacted by having mismatched skills? Table 3.2 splits the sample into respondents below and above age forty, respectively. We see that it is younger citizens for whom lower or mismatched education has especially negative implications for satisfaction with economic and political life. In all cases, save support for the radical right, the effect of being mismatched is much more pronounced among the younger cohort. While these analyses have similar measures of mismatch, it is also the case that in the younger cohort's case the supply of higher education is much greater – hence the labour market for mismatched younger graduates is challenging in that many other mismatched graduates of a similar age are competing for jobs. By contrast, older mismatched workers are more likely to have acquired job security by virtue of seniority or work in jobs that did not previously require

TABLE 3.2 *Mismatched degrees and satisfaction: By age*

Under Forties	(1) Satis. Demo	(2) Satis. Econ.	(3) Satis. Gov.	(4) Satis. Life	(5) Trust Pol.	(6) Rad. Right
No Degree	−0.64***	−0.44***	−0.40***	−0.25***	−0.62***	1.86***
	(0.04)	(0.04)	(0.05)	(0.03)	(0.04)	(0.12)
Degree Mismatched	−0.14***	−0.10*	−0.08	−0.20***	−0.15***	0.59***
	(0.04)	(0.05)	(0.05)	(0.03)	(0.05)	(0.13)
Relative Income	0.24***	0.27***	0.12***	0.48***	0.14***	−0.16***
	(0.03)	(0.03)	(0.03)	(0.03)	(0.03)	(0.05)
Age	−0.00	−0.01*	−0.01**	−0.01***	−0.00*	−0.01
	(0.00)	(0.00)	(0.00)	(0.00)	(0.00)	(0.01)
Gender	−0.14***	−0.26***	−0.06*	0.03	−0.02	−0.55***
	(0.03)	(0.03)	(0.03)	(0.02)	(0.03)	(0.06)
Union Member	0.16***	0.13***	0.20***	−0.01	0.10***	−0.20***
	(0.03)	(0.04)	(0.04)	(0.02)	(0.04)	(0.08)
N	37845	38213	37793	38511	38142	19782

Over Forties	(1) Satis. Demo	(2) Satis. Econ	(3) Satis. Gov.	(4) Satis. Life	(5) Trust Pol.	(6) Rad. Right
No Degree	−0.49***	−0.28***	−0.21***	−0.03	−0.55***	1.60***
	(0.03)	(0.04)	(0.05)	(0.03)	(0.04)	(0.15)
Degree Mismatched	−0.05	−0.02	0.05	−0.02	−0.14***	0.70***
	(0.04)	(0.04)	(0.05)	(0.03)	(0.04)	(0.15)
Relative Income	0.32***	0.33***	0.22***	0.56***	0.23***	−0.24***
	(0.03)	(0.03)	(0.03)	(0.03)	(0.02)	(0.05)
Age	0.00	0.00	0.00**	0.01***	0.00***	−0.02***
	(0.00)	(0.00)	(0.00)	(0.00)	(0.00)	(0.00)
Gender	−0.26***	−0.36***	−0.16***	0.06***	−0.06**	−0.37***
	(0.02)	(0.03)	(0.03)	(0.02)	(0.03)	(0.06)
Union Member	0.04	0.06*	0.14***	0.02	−0.05*	0.21***
	(0.03)	(0.03)	(0.04)	(0.02)	(0.03)	(0.07)
N	54222	54520	54171	54798	54531	35564

a degree as a certification for entry but now do so for new entrants. Finally, since tuition fees are a relatively recent phenomenon in some of the countries in our sample, younger mismatched graduates should also face higher debt burdens related to their education. Hence, it is little surprise we find strong evidence that mismatch produces greater dissatisfaction among the young. The political implications of this are perhaps surprising – it could well be the 'never made it' young who are most driven towards populist causes in coming years, not older 'left-behind' citizens.

Finally, we briefly examine preferences among the top end of the graduate income distribution. Earlier we noted the importance of firms in determining the returns to skill of their high-skilled employees – with larger, multinational firms leading to higher returns to skill, beyond what would be predicted from information about education, age, and experience. Figure 3.8 shows the predicted impact of firm size for individuals with and without university degrees on satisfaction with the economy. Immediately apparent is that firm size *only* appears to matter for graduates – with individuals in larger firms happier with the state of the economy than those in smaller firms. But for non-graduates, there is no effect of firm size at all. While this is just suggestive evidence, we do see signs that one set of individuals – graduates in large firms – are pulling away from the rest.

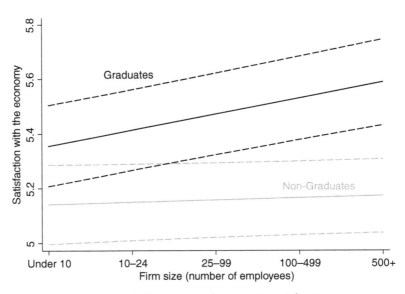

FIGURE 3.8 Firm size and economic satisfaction

CONCLUSION

Is education a salve for democracy in an era of populism and creeping authoritarianism? Our answer is unequivocally equivocal. On the whole, the highly educated are happy with how democracy works – at least more so than are those with less education. And since the former are economic, cultural, and political winners of the status quo, this should be no surprise. It is indeed conceivable that a continued expansion of educational opportunities to the less skilled might spread democratic norms to groups more sceptical of its current merits.

Yet, we should be cautious. As we have shown, graduates themselves are increasingly split. Even as they may agree on the merits of democracy, they diverge on the merits of capitalism. Moreover, even democracy itself is not universally approved by graduates – those degree holders who find themselves in decidedly non-graduate occupations are understandably frustrated and may take their dashed expectations out on the political system. Expanding education thus may just create more dissatisfaction if its recipients cannot find work that matches their expectations.

The past decade of politics in the advanced industrial world may have witnessed the first stirrings of this fracturing of the educated classes. In a world where ever fewer firms seek ever more hyper-skilled workers to reap enormous profits – the world of 'superstar firms' and their employees identified in David Autor et al. (2017) – only a small group of the skilled can identify as the real winners of economic and political life. Among the remainder of the university-educated, grievances about elites may become ever more salient, with growing resentments about access to prestigious universities and internships along with a suspicion that this access depends on financial favours, as in the recent US college admissions scandal.

The partisan consequences of these developments are likely to be profound. Graduates already inhabit spatially different parts of America from non-graduates – and elite graduates are concentrating in particularly benighted areas. Educational and regional divides could co-evolve, heightening the kinds of geographic polarization identified by Massey and Rugh (Chapter 7, this volume), Weir and King (Chapter 8, this volume), and Rodden (Chapter 6, this volume). Both unskilled workers *and* the dissatisfied, mismatched graduate class appear to be driven towards populist causes and parties that might heighten culture war battles but are unlikely to institute major redistributive economic reforms. Political battles and culture wars among graduates may become just as fierce as those between the high and low skilled. If there was ever an era of human capital solidarity, it seems unlikely to survive unscathed.

REFERENCES

Alexiadou, Despina. 2015. 'Ideologues, Partisans, and Loyalists: Cabinet Ministers and Social Welfare Reform in Parliamentary Democracies'. *Comparative Political Studies* 48 (8): 1051–86.
   2016. *Ideologues, Partisans, and Loyalists: Ministers and Policymaking in Parliamentary Cabinets*. Oxford University Press.
Andrews, Dan, Chiara Criscuolo, Peter N. Gal, and others. 2016. 'The Best Versus the Rest: The Global Productivity Slowdown, Divergence Across Firms and the Role of Public Policy'. OECD Background Paper.
Ansell, Ben W. 2008. 'University Challenges: Explaining Institutional Change in Higher Education'. *World Politics* 60 (2): 189–230.
Ansell, Ben, and Jane Gingrich. 2013. 'A Tale of Two Trilemmas: Varieties of Higher Education and the Service Economy'. In *Users Without a Subscription Are Not Able to See the Full Content. The Political Economy of the Service Transition*, ed. Anne Wren, 195. Oxford University Press.
   2017. 'Mismatch: University Education and Labor Market Institutions'. *PS: Political Science and Politics* 50 (2): 423–5.
   2018. 'Skills in Demand'. In *Worlds of Welfare Capitalism and Electoral Politics*, ed. Hanna Schwander, Philip Manow, and Bruno Palier. Oxford University Press.
Autor, David H. 2014. 'Skills, Education, and the Rise of Earnings Inequality Among the 'Other 99 Percent'. *Science* 344: 843–51.
Autor, David, David Dorn, Gordon Hanson, Kaveh Majlesi, and others. 2016. 'Importing Political Polarization? The Electoral Consequences of Rising Trade Exposure.' *NBER Working Paper* 22637.
Autor, David, David Dorn, Lawrence F. Katz, Christina Patterson, John Van Reenen, and others. 2017. *The Fall of the Labor Share and the Rise of Superstar Firms*. National Bureau of Economic Research.
Autor, David H., Frank Levy, and Richard J. Murnane. 2003. 'The Skill Content of Recent Technological Change: An Empirical Exploration'. *The Quarterly Journal of Economics*. JSTOR, 1279–333.
Barth, Erling, Alex Bryson, James C. Davis, and Richard Freeman. 2014. 'It's Where You Work: Increases in Earnings Dispersion Across Establishments and Individuals in the US'. National Bureau of Economic Research.
Becker, Gary S. 2009. *Human Capital: A Theoretical and Empirical Analysis, with Special Reference to Education*. University of Chicago Press.
Berinsky, Adam J., and Gabriel S. Lenz. 2011. 'Education and Political Participation: Exploring the Causal Link'. *Political Behavior* 33 (3): 357–73.
Carnes, Nicholas. 2013. *White-Collar Government: The Hidden Role of Class in Economic Policy Making*. University of Chicago Press.

Carnes, Nicholas, and Noam Lupu. 2016. 'Do Voters Dislike Working-Class Candidates? Voter Biases and the Descriptive Underrepresentation of the Working Class'. *American Political Science Review* 110 (4): 832–44.

Foa, Roberto Stefan, and Yascha Mounk. 2016. 'The Democratic Disconnect'. *Journal of Democracy* 27 (3): 5–17.

Frank, Robert H., and Philip J. Cook. 2010. *The Winner-Take-All Society: Why the Few at the Top Get so Much More Than the Rest of Us*. Random House.

Gingrich, Jane, and Silja Häusermann. 2015. 'The Decline of the Working-Class Vote, the Reconfiguration of the Welfare Support Coalition and Consequences for the Welfare State'. *Journal of European Social Policy* 25(1): 50–75.

Goldin, Claudia, and Lawrence F. Katz. 1996. 'The Origins of Technology-Skill Complementarity'. National Bureau of Economic Research.

2009. *The Race Between Education and Technology*. Harvard University Press.

Goodwin, Matthew J., and Oliver Heath. 2016. 'The 2016 Referendum, Brexit and the Left Behind: An Aggregate-Level Analysis of the Result'. *The Political Quarterly* 87(3): 323–32.

Goos, Maarten, and Alan Manning. 2007. 'Lousy and Lovely Jobs: The Rising Polarization of Work in Britain'. *The Review of Economics and Statistics* 89 (1): 118–33.

Goos, Maarten, Alan Manning, and Anna Salomons. 2009. 'Job Polarization in Europe'. *The American Economic Review* JSTOR 99 (2): 58–63.

Green, Francis, and Yu Zhu. 2010. 'Overqualification, Job Dissatisfaction, and Increasing Dispersion in the Returns to Graduate Education'. *Oxford Economic Papers* 62 (4): 740–63.

Hacker, Jacob S., and Paul Pierson. 2011. *Winner-Take-All Politics: How Washington Made the Rich Richer–and Turned Its Back on the Middle Class*. Simon & Schuster.

Häusermann, Silja, and Hanspeter Kriesi. 2011. 'What Do Voters Want? Dimensions and Configurations in Individual-Level Preferences and Party Choice'. In *Conference on the Future of Democratic Capitalism*, Zurich.

Hillygus, Sunshine D. 2005. 'The Missing Link: Exploring the Relationship Between Higher Education and Political Engagement'. *Political Behavior* 27 (1): 25–47.

Inglehart, Ronald, and Pippa Norris. 2016. 'Trump, Brexit, and the Rise of Populism: Economic Have-Nots and Cultural Backlash', *HKS Working Paper* No. RWP16-026.

Kam, Cindy D., and Carl L. Palmer. 2008. 'Reconsidering the Effects of Education on Political Participation'. *The Journal of Politics* 70 (3): 612–31.

Karabarbounis, Loukas, and Brent Neiman. 2013. 'The Global Decline of the Labor Share'. *The Quarterly Journal of Economics* 129 (1): 61–103.

Katz, Richard S., and Peter Mair. 2009. 'The Cartel Party Thesis: A Restatement'. *Perspectives on Politics* 7 (4): 753–66.

Kitschelt, Herbert, and Philipp Rehm. 2014. 'Occupations as a Site of Political Preference Formation'. *Comparative Political Studies* 47 (12): 1670–706.

Levitsky, Steven, and Daniel Ziblatt. 2018. *How Democracies Die*. Crown.

Marshall, John. 2016. 'Education and Voting Conservative: Evidence from a Major Schooling Reform in Great Britain'. *The Journal of Politics* 78 (2): 382–95.
Mavromaras, Kostas, and Seamus McGuinness. 2012. 'Overskilling Dynamics and Education Pathways'. *Economics of Education Review* 31 (5): 619–28.
McGowan, Muge Adalet, and Dan Andrews. 2015. 'Labour Market Mismatch and Labour Productivity'. OECD iLibrary.
Mendelberg, Tali, Katherine T McCabe, and Adam Thal. 2016. 'College Socialization and the Economic Views of Affluent Americans'. *American Journal of Political Science* 61 (3): 606–23.
Mishel, Lawrence, Heidi Shierholz, and John Schmitt. 2013. 'Don't Blame the Robots: Assessing the Job Polarization Explanation of Growing Wage Inequality'. *Economic Policy Institute Working Paper*.
Moretti, Enrico. 2012. *The New Geography of Jobs*. Houghton Mifflin Harcourt.
Neundorf, Anja, Richard G. Niemi, and Kaat Smets. 2016. 'The Compensation Effect of Civic Education on Political Engagement: How Civics Classes Make up for Missing Parental Socialization.' *Political Behavior* 38 (4): 921–49.
Niemi, Richard G., and Jane Junn. 2005. *Civic Education: What Makes Students Learn*. Yale University Press.
Oesch, Daniel. 2013. *Occupational Change in Europe: How Technology and Education Transform the Job Structure*. Oxford University Press.
Oliveira, M. Mendes de, Maria C. Santos, and Bill F. Kiker. 2000. 'The Role of Human Capital and Technological Change in Overeducation'. *Economics of Education Review* 19 (2): 199–206.
Oliver, J. Eric, and Wendy M. Rahn. 2016. 'Rise of the Trumpenvolk: Populism in the 2016 Election'. *The ANNALS of the American Academy of Political and Social Science* 667 (1): 189–206.
Persson, Mikael. 2015. 'Education and Political Participation'. *British Journal of Political Science* 45 (3): 689–703.
Schwellnus, Cyrille, Andreas Kappeler, and Pierre-Alain Pionnier. 2017. 'Decoupling of Wages from Productivity', no. 1373. https://doi.org/https://doi.org/10.1787/d4764493-en.
Surridge, Paula. 2016. 'Education and Liberalism: Pursuing the Link'. *Oxford Review of Education* 42 (2): 146–64.

4

Public Opinion and Reactions to Increasing Income Inequality

Kris-Stella Trump

In 2008, the Great Recession temporarily interrupted a decades-long rise in income inequality in the United States. The recession catalyzed the Occupy movement, which in turn pushed the phrase "the one percent" into the popular lexicon (typically referring to the top one percent of income earners, and occasionally wealth owners). However, despite this apparent surge in public interest in economic inequality, income inequality continued to grow after the recession, as "the one percent" of income earners disproportionately captured the gains from income growth. In total, over the past five decades, this group has nearly doubled their share of national income; income inequality in the United States now rivals that of the famously unequal 1920s.

This chapter asks how the public has (or has not) reacted to these economic trends. In a time of increasing income differences, with income accumulating at the very top of the income distribution, what has been the American public's reaction? Has public pressure to address economic inequality through public policy intensified – and if not, why not? In this chapter, I will review the recent literature on these questions. In doing so, I will draw on empirical evidence from within as well as beyond the United States, placing American public opinion toward income differences in comparative perspective.

Thank you to Josh Carpenter, William Franko, Frances McCall Rosenbluth, Margaret Weir, Julie Wronski, the contributors to this book volume, two anonymous reviewers, panel participants at the American Political Science Association's 2018 Annual Meeting, and participants at a Democratic Anxieties conference at the University of Bamberg in March 2019 for valuable feedback on earlier drafts of this chapter.

As the chapter will make clear, there is a significant and relatively recent literature to draw on; the economic changes of recent decades have led to a burst of activity from social scientists looking to understand the consequences of income inequality. This fortunate circumstance, however, necessitates placing some boundary conditions on the type of studies and research questions covered here. For the bulk of the chapter, I focus narrowly on the role that factual information about income differences plays in affecting attitudes toward inequality. At the end of the chapter, I will zoom out and place the takeaway points from this particular literature in a broader context of research on how social and political institutions (including the media, labor unions, and public policy) affect the public's reactions to facts about inequality.

A traditional way to pose the key question motivating this chapter is "why don't the poor soak the rich?" (Shapiro 2002). A more formal way to describe this puzzle is through rational choice: in a society with unequal incomes skewed toward the top, the median income earner's economic self-interest should cause them to demand income redistribution (Meltzer and Richard 1981). The chapter will start by observing that contrary to this prediction, increasing economic inequality is not consistently or strongly linked to support for redistribution. In other words, economic inequality can increase significantly without a corresponding growth in public support for "soaking the rich." I will then explore potential explanations for this phenomenon.

First, I will ask whether a lack of public awareness regarding increasing inequality is to blame. On the one hand, evidence clearly indicates that citizens commonly underestimate both wealth and income inequality. On the other hand, the existence of underestimation does not prove that a fully informed public would react any differently. Even if the public is unaware of the extent of inequality, the question remains of how they *would* react if they were aware.

This question is addressed in numerous recent experiments that inform people about inequality or expose them to income differences in various ways. Summarizing recent studies in this vein, I show that the impact of such information on attitudes is inconsistent and includes numerous null findings. The mixed results suggest that if information effects exist, they are likely to be contingent; that is, accurate information about inequality affects people's attitudes toward inequality only under specific circumstances. I tentatively suggest three conditions that may condition public responses to information about inequality: (a) whether information about one's own position in the income distribution is included, (b) whether economic mobility is implicated, and (c) whether inequality is seen as changeable.

With this summary of recent findings in hand, I turn to broader questions. First, I ask which variables *other* than accurate information impact support for redistribution. While the effects from information experiments are inconsistent and likely conditional, other research has demonstrated that cues about the deservingness of the beneficiaries of redistribution powerfully and consistently affect attitudes toward redistribution. In light of these effects, it seems likely that ideas surrounding the fairness of inequality and the deservingness of social groups (at both the winning and losing ends of inequality) are more important for support for redistribution than (in)accurate information about the extent of income inequality. In other words, knowing correct *facts* about inequality does not easily change people's *attitudes* toward inequality (with potential exceptions for the conditional effects mentioned earlier). Social perceptions regarding the fairness of inequality-producing mechanisms, as well as stereotypes regarding the deservingness of social groups, are powerfully shaped by sociopolitical institutions like political parties, the media, unions, and others. This insight, then, points us toward scholarship, both classic and recent, on the roles these institutions play in shaping normative interpretations of inequality.

Finally, I ask whether the United States is exceptional when it comes to public attitudes toward redistribution. Without disputing that there are some ways in which Americans' beliefs stand out in a comparative perspective (e.g., a higher than average belief in the role of hard work as opposed to luck determining one's lot in life), I argue that the dynamics through which we should understand support for redistribution are the same in the United States as they are in other industrialized countries. Americans, like others, evaluate inequality through a prism of deservingness, in which group stereotypes regarding deservingness feature heavily. And, like others, Americans are prone to underestimating inequality in their country (though it is unclear how consequential such underestimation is). Finally, Americans are more supportive of redistribution and more disapproving of inequality than the American exceptionalism narrative can make them seem. I conclude by arguing that to understand American exceptionalism in inequality-producing public policy, we need to look beyond public opinion and turn toward issues of representation and policy-making processes.

Before moving to the main content of this chapter, an important caveat is in order. This chapter focuses primarily on public reactions to increasing top-end incomes. This focus, combined with the short format of a book chapter, necessitates giving only brief descriptions of some broader contextual variables. In particular, questions of race and gender inequality undeniably structure conversations around the acceptability of income inequality, in the United States as well as elsewhere. While I cover these key variables relatively briefly in the main body of the chapter, this is not to imply they are unimportant. Toward the end of the chapter, I briefly discuss the importance of variables such as whether specific socioeconomic groups are perceived as deserving their lot in life. However, for a more detailed discussion of these factors, see the chapters by Andra Gillespie (Chapter 2, this volume) and Alice Kessler-Harris (Chapter 5, this volume). Additionally, Douglas Massey and Jacob Rugh (Chapter 7, this volume) address questions of geographic segregation (including income-based segregation), while Jacob Hacker and Paul Pierson (Chapter 11, this volume) discuss unequal political responsiveness. The current chapter, in other words, is intended to be read within the broader context of this edited volume.

MATERIAL SELF-INTEREST AND REACTIONS TO INCOME INEQUALITY

The material self-interest assumption is probably the most common theoretical foundation for studies of public reactions to income inequality. From this perspective, individuals who earn below-mean incomes should support redistribution, because they can expect to benefit from it (Meltzer and Richard, 1981). This basic expectation can be extended to argue that *increasing* inequality should lead to *increasing* demands for redistribution – this because the distance between median and mean incomes increases as incomes become more concentrated at the top of the income distribution (Kelly and Enns 2010).

This stylized material self-interest expectation has a mixed track record empirically. On the one hand, it is generally true that people with lower socioeconomic status support redistribution and taxation more than well-off people do (Amable 2009; Andersen and Curtis 2015). On the other hand, evidence generally does not support the hypothesis that high income inequality is associated with more intense public demand for redistribution.[1] In comparative perspective, for example, the public in

---

[1] In the bulk of this chapter, I follow a common convention in the literature, which is to think of public support for redistribution as agreement with relatively generic statements

more unequal countries does *not* tend to be more concerned about inequality than the public in more equal countries (Kenworthy and McCall 2008; Breznau and Hommerich 2019, though see Finseraas 2009; Andersen and Curtis 2015). In the United States, McCall (2013) shows that dissatisfaction with inequality has remained relatively steady (at consistently high levels) from the late 1980s onward, even though inequality has risen sharply during this time period. These findings are replicated, with additional subgroup analysis, in Ashok et al. (2015). Kelly and Enns (2010), Luttig (2013), and Wright (2017) all argue that increasing inequality in the United States may even have led to more conservative public opinion on issues of redistribution. Moving from national-level to local-level inequality in the United States, Johnston and Newman (2016) find no relationship between local income inequality and preferences for redistribution. Finally, both McCall (2013) and Franko (2016) find that increasing inequality may lead to more progressive opinions on some, though not all, aspects of redistributive public policy. In sum, the expected relationship between increasing inequality and increasing demand for redistribution is only found inconsistently in empirical analyses of this type.

Turning from cross-sectional survey data to evidence from field and/or experimental studies, results are also mixed. Sands (2017), in a field experiment, finds that seeing a poor person in a wealthy neighborhood (which serves as a reminder of inequality) leads to *lower* support for a "millionaire's tax." In a similar vein, Roth and Wohlfart (2016) use observational data and find that people who experienced more inequality growing up become less supportive of redistribution as adults. McCall et al. (2017), in a survey experiment, find that reading information about increasing income inequality *increases* support for redistribution, while experiments by Kuziemko et al. (2015) and Trump (2018) find that information about inequality does not change support for redistribution.

In sum, research findings are mixed on the question of whether high or increasing inequality leads to high or increasing support for redistribution. This conclusion applies both in comparative perspective and in the United States in particular. The conflicting evidence suggests that *if* inequality has an impact on public opinion toward redistribution, it is

---

such as "the government should do more to reduce income differences between the rich and the poor." Support for redistribution can also be measured through public support for specific policies that have various redistributive impacts; I return to the distinctions that these policies bring into the conversation later in this chapter.

likely to be conditional on other factors; such conditionality may explain otherwise conflicting findings. Having said this, it is important to point out that these findings do not mean that the public in general is *not concerned* with income inequality. On the contrary: the public in the United States generally agrees that inequality is "too high" (Page and Jacobs 2009; McCall 2013) and expresses sympathy with the poor (Piston 2018). It is *the extent* to which the public disapproves of inequality that is not consistently related to either levels or changes in inequality.

Why is demand for redistribution not responsive to increasing inequality? I first ask whether the public is simply too uninformed about growing inequality, followed by an examination of whether providing accurate information about inequality might affect public support for redistribution.

HOW ACCURATE ARE PERCEPTIONS OF INEQUALITY?

One plausible explanation for the lack of a relationship between inequality and support for redistribution is that the public is simply not aware of the extent of income inequality. The population in the United States tends to have relatively low levels of political information in general (Delli Carpini and Keeter 1997); they also do not perform very well when asked to give numeric estimates of politically relevant quantities (Kuklinksi et al. 2000). It would therefore not be surprising if citizens also struggled to accurately estimate income inequality. Indeed, the public in the United States as well as in other countries systematically underestimates income inequality (Osberg and Smeeding 2006; Kiatpongsan and Norton 2014) as well as wealth inequality (Norton and Ariely 2010). Since it is difficult (albeit not impossible, in the presence of elite cues) to react to phenomena that one is not aware of, this could explain why increasing inequality has not led to increasing public support for redistribution.

This argument becomes even more appealing if we consider that, if inequality levels are difficult for an average citizen to observe, then changes in inequality may be even harder to see. Studies show that citizens perceive substantial and relatively quick changes in inequality, such as those that occurred in post-Communist countries after the collapse of the Soviet Union (Gijsberts 2002; Kolczynska and Merry 2016). Smaller changes, however, such as the gradual growth in top-end inequality in the United States over a longer period of time, are probably not accurately perceived by the population (Gimpelson and Treisman 2018).[2]

Before describing these results in more detail, it is worth pausing here to emphasize the importance of operationalization choices. In studies that seek to measure public knowledge, operationalization is key – and this may be even truer in studies of economic inequality than in other studies of citizen knowledge. Developing survey items about inequality requires special care, because income inequality is a particularly abstract concept, and it can be numerically summarized in many ways. This makes intuitive survey questions about inequality a challenge to construct. The choice of survey questions also matters because it may not only affect the conclusions of one's study; it can also influence the design of follow-up studies in which participants are informed about real levels of inequality. For these reasons, in what follows I will consider operationalization choices in somewhat more detail than is usual in overview chapters of this type.

Good survey items about inequality should allow us to separate normative assessments of inequality from factual knowledge. This separation is crucial to the research agenda at hand, which seeks to understand how (a lack of) factual knowledge may affect normative attitudes. Because survey questions about knowledge need to stop short of encouraging normative assessments, we need to rule out using some common survey items, such as those that ask whether inequality is "too low," "just right," or "too high."

Additionally, the choice of survey question can significantly influence the results of a study. For example, in the case of wealth inequality, Norton and Ariely (2010) ask US respondents to estimate the *share of wealth* that belongs to different income quintiles. They find significant and widespread underestimation of inequality, as well as widely shared popular support for very low levels of inequality. Eriksson and Simpson (2012), however, demonstrate that asking a similar question but focusing on the *average wealth* of people in different quintiles yields different results. Perhaps most significantly, they find that this alternative phrasing shows the public endorsing higher wealth inequality than in the Norton and Ariely (2010) study.

Similar concerns apply when measuring perceptions of income differences. Using a similar approach as Norton and Ariely (2010), adapted to

---

[2] Note, however, that within the United States, changes in state- and local-level inequality may be more visible than national levels of inequality (Xu and Garand 2010; Franko and Witko 2017).

income rather than wealth, Boudreau and MacKenzie (2018a) find that Californians underestimate state-level income inequality.

However, using a set of visualizations (society depicted as pyramids/ladders), Niehues (2014) shows that overestimation of inequality is common, and that the extent of overestimation varies by country. A third way to measure perceived income differences is asking respondents to estimate how much money people in different vocations make in a year (e.g., factory worker, CEO of large national company). This approach finds significant underestimation of income inequality both cross-nationally (Kiatpongsan and Norton 2014) and in the United States (Osberg and Smeeding 2006). In an operationalization where respondents fill in their own histogram of household incomes in the United States, Page and Goldstein (2016) find that respondents underestimate income inequality and overestimate median incomes. Finally, Minkoff and Lyons (2017) find that simply asking whether inequality is "small" or "large" in one's local neighborhood is related to the actual income diversity in the local area. Their results indicate at least a somewhat accurate perception of inequality on the local level, though this approach does not allow a quantification of potential overestimation/underestimation.

While the results vary somewhat from study to study, the overall picture that emerges is that inequality, especially at the national level, is difficult for most citizens to perceive and that underestimation of income differences is very common, in the United States as well as cross-nationally.

While underestimation of inequality may be widespread, the studies cited earlier do not demonstrate that *if the public were more informed*, they would be more supportive of redistribution. To find out whether a more informed public would react to inequality differently, we need to look at studies that directly explore the link between factual knowledge of inequality and support for redistribution.

HOW WOULD OPINIONS ABOUT INEQUALITY CHANGE IF PEOPLE WERE BETTER INFORMED?

Public ignorance of inequality could explain why increasing inequality has not been met with increasing support for redistribution. For this to be the case, however, a well-informed citizen would need to react to inequality by demanding more redistribution, if it was in their economic self-interest to do so. In recent years, a literature that tests this link between information and attitudes has emerged. The results from this literature are quite mixed; as a whole, the results (1) suggest that information alone probably does not suffice to change concern about inequality or support for redistribution and (2) highlight the moderating role of fairness perceptions and, by extension, of social and political institutions in shaping reactions to income inequality.

First, looking at cross-sectional evidence, the most informative available studies regarding the impact of knowledge of increasing inequality come from Eastern Europe in the period immediately following the fall of the Soviet Union. As mentioned earlier, surveys suggest that in countries where inequality sharply increased after the fall of Communist regimes, the population started perceiving larger income differences (these perceptions were measured with the "occupational earnings" questions described earlier). However, these perceptions did not go hand in hand with changes in normative reactions, such as beliefs that inequality was too high or that more redistribution was needed (Gijsberts 2002; Kolczynska and Merry 2016). Instead, citizens started reporting higher occupational income differences as desirable, indicating that the population had come to see larger income differences as legitimate (Kelley and Zagorski 2004; for similar evidence from Chile, see Castillo 2012). Of course, observational studies like these suffer from a range of weaknesses, perhaps most prominently that the new democratic and capitalist regimes were seen as more legitimate than the previous Communist regimes. Increased regime legitimacy probably helped legitimate the growing income differences that accompanied the transitions, which leaves us with the question of how the public reacts to increasing inequality within democratic systems.

To establish whether inequality per se, net of confounding factors such as regime change, can cause increased support for redistribution, we need to turn to experimental research. Two recent studies, carried out in the United States and Sweden, use information treatments that mirror the occupational earnings questions used in the studies from Eastern Europe. In these experiments, respondents are told how much different occupational categories, including CEOs of large national companies, make per year. These studies show that informing people about the true extent of occupational income inequality does not change normative assessments of whether inequality is "too high;" neither does this information impact support for redistribution (Pedersen and Mutz 2018; Trump 2018). Further, and consistent with the correlational evidence discussed earlier, respondents who are exposed to such information start recommending higher income differences as ideal. These patterns probably occur in part because of anchoring processes (Pedersen and Mutz 2018) and partly because of motivated reasoning processes such as system justification, whereby people are motivated to interpret their social environment as fair (Garcia-Sanchez et al. 2018; Trump 2018).

Additional experiments have used different operationalizations than the occupational earnings questions. For example, Kuziemko et al. (2015) show their respondents a range of information that focuses primarily on growing inequality but also discusses taxation and economic growth. Despite the substantial information treatment, this study finds only a small effect of information on concerns about inequality, and no impact on support for redistribution. On the other hand, Boudreau and MacKenzie (2018b) inform Californians about the extent of inequality in their state (through pie charts displaying the share of income going to different income quintiles) and find that this information increases support for raising the marginal income tax rate among some subgroups of respondents.

Departing from numeric information about inequality, McCall et al. (2017) use a vignette that discusses rising inequality; they find that this treatment causes respondents to perceive less meritocracy in the United States, and to increase their support for redistribution. Conversely, in a field experiment in which people in a wealthy neighborhood are unobtrusively exposed to a poor individual (thus highlighting inequality), Sands (2017) finds that experiencing inequality makes people *less* supportive of redistributive public policy.

These mixed results jointly suggest that reactions to information about inequality are probably conditional, depending on variables such as the context in which information is received, respondent characteristics, and how information is presented. For example, based on the studies cited, support for redistribution is not affected by information about the high incomes of CEOs. On the other hand, when information about inequality is presented in a way that raises concerns about the existence of equal opportunity in society, support for redistribution increases. The key question becomes: under what conditions do citizens link information about income inequality to support for redistribution?

WHEN DOES INCOME INEQUALITY LEAD TO DEMAND FOR REDISTRIBUTION?

Without yet broadening our remit to the wider world of socioeconomic institutions, social stereotypes, and other such variables, this section will retain a narrow focus on the consequences of giving citizens accurate information about inequality, exploring its potentially conditional impact on opinions toward redistribution. Focusing on this narrower question and recent experimental evidence, three moderators emerge as potentially relevant. First, the respondents' ability to connect information about inequality to their economic self-interest may be important. Making this connection is not as straightforward for many citizens as simply reading income statistics; therefore, the way in which information is presented can be consequential. A second potentially relevant variable is how strongly citizens believe in meritocracy and upward mobility. And finally, the effect of information may depend on the citizens' perceptions of whether inequality is changeable (as opposed to an inevitable fact of life).

Awareness of One's Own Economic Position

For information about income inequality to change people's support for redistribution according to their economic self-interest, respondents need to connect inequality information with the consequences that increased redistribution would have on their own income. This may be a challenge for many citizens, not least because it is common for people to not be aware of their specific position in the income distribution (Boudreau and MacKenzie 2018a). Giving people information about the economy and inequality in a format that helps them connect the dots between inequality, redistribution, and their own economic outcomes may have a different effect from decontextualized information about inequality.[3]

Consistent with this line of reasoning, research suggests that learning one's specific position in the income distribution can affect attitudes toward redistribution. For example, Cruces et al. (2013) show that Argentinian respondents who overestimated their own position in the income distribution started supporting more redistribution after they were informed of their true ranking. Similarly, Karadja et al. (2017) show that Swedes who initially underestimated their own position became less supportive of redistribution after receiving correct information; individuals who also held right-wing political beliefs drove this effect. In a study carried out in California, Boudreau and MacKenzie (2018a) find that information about one's own position in the income distribution, as

---

[3] For similar arguments, see Bullock (2011) and Boudreau and MacKenzie (2014); both articles argue that citizens connect their values and interests to policy positions – when the circumstances are right.

well as information about growing income inequality, strengthens the relationship between personal economic circumstances and support for redistributive policies. Engelhardt and Wagener (2016) find that while information about one's own position does not change Germans' attitudes toward redistribution, additional information about whether one is a net contributor to or beneficiary of redistribution does affect support for redistribution in expected directions. Finally, however, Hoy and Mager (2019) carry out a standardized information experiment in ten countries, finding mixed results, and no impact of information on support for redistribution in the United States among a few other countries.

While information about one's position in the income distribution does not directly provide information about the *extent* of inequality, these results are nonetheless relevant to understanding the relationship between income inequality and economic attitudes. Jointly, the studies provide evidence that when individuals have the requisite information, they can *sometimes* connect their own position in society to their policy preferences. This evidence is also consistent with the broader observation that a person's socioeconomic position predicts their support for redistribution (Amable 2009). In conclusion, information about one's relative position may be a key piece of information for people to have, whenever they reason about inequality and redistribution. In fact, this information may be more important than information about the absolute distance between the top and the bottom of the income distribution.

Meritocracy and Upward Mobility

All else being equal, citizens tend to interpret the possibility of upward mobility as a sign of meritocracy, which in turn legitimizes the existence of inequalities of outcome (Shariff et al. 2016). The related hypothesis that the prospect of upward mobility reduces support for redistribution (Benabou and Ok 2001) is well known and empirical evidence supports it (Engelhardt and Wagener 2014; Day and Fiske 2017). Recent research, building on this insight, has asked whether the reverse relationship also exists: whether income inequality itself affects perceptions of meritocracy and equal opportunity. Unfortunately, studies so far disagree on the direction of this relationship, alternately suggesting either that inequality leads to increased perceptions of meritocracy (in turn justifying inequality) or that inequality leads to reduced perceptions of meritocracy (in turn delegitimizing inequality).

In a cross-sectional analysis, Mijs (2019) finds that citizens of relatively unequal countries are more likely to explain success in meritocratic terms. Similarly, local inequality in the United States is associated with an increased willingness to believe that people can get ahead if they are willing to work hard (Solt et al. 2016). Theoretically, such a relationship may occur because of motivated reasoning: people are motivated to believe that it is possible to improve one's lot in life, even in unequal circumstances (Kraus and Tan 2015).

However, experimental evidence suggests that the opposite relationship may hold: that information about high inequality may lead to doubts about how widespread equal opportunity is. McCall et al. (2017) find that a vignette about economic inequality decreases belief in meritocracy. Similarly, Davidai (2018) finds that information about unequal wealth distribution (between quintiles) reduces perceptions of upward mobility. Becker (2019) finds that information about income inequality between groups increases respondents' belief that the differences were due to circumstances (as opposed to individual effort). The experimental evidence thus contradicts the correlations found in observational data; reconciling these findings is an important task for future research.

Belief That Inequality Can Be Changed

Some evidence suggests that perceiving inequality as *changeable* may affect how people react to it. Johnson and Fujita (2012) show that perceptions of changeability affect how we engage with information about the status quo in general. The inequality-related implication of this finding is that perceiving inequality as inevitable may suppress support for redistribution. Consistent with this prediction, Pellicer et al. (2019) show that perceiving inequality as inevitable affects whether information about inequality leads South African respondents to support more redistribution. Only when inequality appears changeable does demand for redistribution increase in response to information about inequality.

Inevitability perceptions may also explain at least one set of conflicting findings in the literature. As mentioned earlier, McCall et al. (2017) find that exposing survey respondents to information about increasing income inequality increases beliefs that wealth and family background matter for getting ahead. In other words, inequality decreases belief that success is determined meritocratically. However, in analyses of cross-sectional, international surveys that use the same survey questions as those used by McCall et al. (2017), Mijs (2019) finds that income inequality is positively related to belief in meritocracy. It may be possible to reconcile these conflicting findings by observing that McCall et al.'s informational treatment included an implied message of changeability: the focus of the information treatment was on how inequality has changed over time, which necessarily implies that inequality *can* change. As per the Pellicer et al. (2019) argument, this perception of changeability may trigger demands that the government address inequality. Further research could shed useful light on how these findings complement each other.

BROADER CONTEXT: FAIRNESS AND DESERVINGNESS CONSIDERATIONS

Each of the variables discussed in the previous section – awareness of one's own position, perceptions of upward mobility, and perceptions of whether inequality can be changed – plays out in a broader context of culture and politics. Attitudes toward government policy are not only shaped by economic self-interest; they are also powerfully affected by perceptions of who deserves government help, and to what extent inequality can be considered fair (Hochschild 1981; Starmans et al. 2017). In this section, I will place the frequently conditional or contradictory effects of information that I have summarized earlier into a broader context, in which considerations of (frequently group-based) fairness and deservingness play a major role.

Addressing this broader context requires first pointing out that generic support for redistribution (frequently measured as agreement with statements such as "the government should do more to reduce income differences between the rich and the poor") can differ from attitudes toward particular policies that benefit specific social groups. So far, I have discussed support for redistribution as a unidimensional attitude, whose primary referent is the respondent's own expected loss or gain from redistribution. However, attitudes toward redistribution are also informed by what we think of *other* beneficiaries of government policy (Petersen 2012), and these additional considerations mean that attitudes toward redistribution can vary depending on whom we know or imagine the beneficiaries to be. For example, Cavaille and Trump (2015) show that attitudes regarding redistribution *to the poor* are not necessarily correlated with support for redistribution *from the rich* (see also Kluegel and Smith 1986 and Attewell 2019). Stereotypes regarding the poor and the rich influence attitudes toward policies that help these groups, and it is clear that these stereotypes matter in addition to economically self-interested attitudes.

The importance of stereotypes about social groups for attitudes toward public policy is made clear in a broad literature that emphasizes the concept of the "deserving poor" (Katz 1989). When the poor are seen as undeserving of government help, support for redistribution is lower. This dynamic can be particularly acute in racially or ethnically heterogeneous societies, where minority groups are frequently stereotyped as both poor and undeserving (Gilens 1999; Alesina and Glaeser 2004). In a related argument, Scheve and Stasavage (2016) emphasize the centrality of deservingness attitudes for redistributive tax policy, arguing that top marginal income tax rates have historically only been raised during or immediately after wars that involve mass mobilization. In other words, taxes on the rich are significantly increased only in situations where the sacrifices of the poor for the common good are abundantly clear (thus speaking to their deservingness), and there is societal agreement that the rich need to "pay their share."

So far, the experimental literature on reactions to information about inequality has not directly engaged with the question of how perceptions of group-based deservingness interact with increasing income inequality to shape support for redistribution. However, we know from experiments that explicitly include cues regarding the deservingness of welfare recipients that such cues can affect opinion so strongly as to remove partisan differences in support for redistribution (Petersen 2012; Petersen et al. 2012). The strength of findings in the literature on deservingness perceptions contrasts strongly with the weak and mixed findings in the literature on well-informed, economically self-interested reactions to inequality. Taking these sets of findings together, it seems probable that when it comes to changing public support for redistribution, opinions about the recipients of government help are more important than the public's knowledge about growing inequality. If this is true, then we should not expect increasing income inequality to affect public support for redistribution – unless growing inequality affects perceptions of how deserving either the rich or the poor are.

The proposition that public notions regarding fairness and deservingness are a key driver of support for redistribution highlights the importance of sociopolitical institutions that shape such notions. While information about high CEO salaries, on its own, may be inconsequential for attitudes toward redistribution, the activities of labor unions do affect such attitudes (Ahlquist and Levi 2013; Rueda and Pontusson 2000).

While simply informing people of the income distribution through the media may not be effective, the media also describes the universe of available policy options (Guardino 2019) and illustrates who the beneficiaries of such policies would be (Gilens 1999). Policies that reduce inequality create their own constituencies and feedback effects, affecting public opinion about inequality (Skocpol 1992; Pierson 1993; Campbell 2003; Mettler 2005; Michener 2018). In other words, the finding that information is not enough, on its own, to change support for redistribution directs our attention toward the broader societal institutions that structure public interpretations of what constitutes fairness.

IS THE UNITED STATES EXCEPTIONAL?

The United States is more unequal than most other industrialized countries; having experienced sustained growth in income inequality since the 1970s, it now has the highest levels of inequality since the famously unequal 1920s (Saez 2017). During this same period, however, American public opinion regarding inequality did not substantially change: from the late 1980s to the 2010s, agreement with statements like "inequality is too high" remained steady, with a majority of respondents either agreeing or strongly agreeing (McCall 2013). This pattern of increasing inequality, contrasted against stable (but generally disapproving) public opinion, raises the question of whether the United States is exceptional in that its population is particularly unlikely to object to growing income differences.

Arguments in favor of American exceptionalism point out that Americans overestimate upward mobility (Davidai and Gilovich 2015; Kraus and Tan 2015) and perceive more upward mobility than citizens of other wealthy industrialized countries (Alesina and Glaeser 2004). As described earlier, such beliefs make inequality more acceptable to the public (Engelhardt and Wagener 2014; Shariff et al. 2016). Another strand of the exceptionalism argument points out that the United States is a particularly racially and ethnically heterogeneous country, and that such heterogeneity is associated with lower support for redistribution (Alesina and Glaeser 2004). In fact, Alesina and Glaeser (2004) further argue that Americans' relatively strong belief in meritocracy is in fact endogenous to the relatively high racial and ethnic heterogeneity in the United States. Complementing this line of reasoning, Gilens (1999) shows that US minority groups – especially, but not only, African Americans – are stereotyped as undeserving in American culture, and that this reduces popular support for redistributive policies that are perceived to disproportionately benefit the minorities in question.

Whether these variables make the United States exceptional is a matter of perspective. There are no strong reasons to believe that the underlying mechanisms that explain popular support for redistribution – ethnic heterogeneity and perceptions of meritocracy – work differently in the United States than they do anywhere else. While the United States scores unusually high on these explanatory variables, all this means is that even if redistributive politics in the United States *looks* somewhat different to other countries, it nonetheless follows a similar logic (Alesina and Giuliano 2011).

Additionally, when it comes to the other relevant variables I have discussed in this chapter, the United States does not stand out as unusual. Overall, Americans are not significantly worse than citizens of other nations at estimating levels of income inequality (Osberg and Smeeding 2006), though they may be somewhat more likely to underestimate incomes at the very top (Kiatpongsan and Norton 2014). Both Osberg and Smeeding (2006) and Kiatpongsan and Norton (2014) further find that Americans report ideal levels of income inequality, in particular preferences for "leveling down" top incomes, that are comparable to the preferences expressed by citizens in other countries. Finally, while support for redistribution in the United States is lower than in other countries, it is more widely shared than the narrative of American exceptionalism might make it seem. Concern about the poor, belief that inequality is too high, and even direct support for government redistribution are shared by most Americans (Kluegel and Smith 1986; Page and Jacobs 2009; McCall 2013; Piston 2018).

If the United States is an outlier primarily due to racial/ethnic heterogeneity and (the resulting) higher rates of belief in meritocracy, and if it is subject to the same logics of redistributive politics that we observe in other countries, then what does this tell us about American public opinion in an age of increasing inequality? First, that while Americans – like other nationalities – underestimate the true extent of income inequality, informing them about it is unlikely to change how they feel about redistribution, except under particular circumstances. Second, perceptions of the possibility of upward mobility are important here, as they are everywhere, and may be affected by income inequality. In a country long known for an unusually strong belief that hard work gets you ahead, the hypothesis that income inequality may undermine perceptions of meritocracy is a particularly intriguing one. As mentioned earlier, however, at the moment evidence on this hypothesis is contradictory, which makes this an issue worthy of further study.

Finally, Americans have consistently been concerned about high inequality in recent decades (even though this concern has not intensified as inequality has increased). This points to a question outside the realm of public opinion studies: why has the political system not been responsive to this stable and broadly shared concern among its citizens? Even though the public does not react thermostatically to increasing income inequality, there is arguably sufficient concern about inequality among the American public to justify interventions that would at least reduce its rate of growth. The lack of such public policies in the United States raises questions about the political system in general, and differential responsiveness in particular. In other words, it would be too simple to attribute the lack of policy responses to growing inequality in the United States solely to lackluster demand for them among the public.

CONCLUSION

Even though income inequality in the United States has increased substantially since the 1970s, reaching historically high levels by the late 2010s, the public's concern about inequality and their support for redistribution plateaued during the same time period. Why did the increase in income inequality, driven by the top 1 percent of income earners capturing the lion's share of income growth over several decades, not lead to a stronger public backlash?

This chapter started by asking whether a lack of public awareness about the true extent of income differences is to blame, especially in the broader context of low levels of knowledge about political facts among most citizens. While it is true that Americans generally underestimate the prevalence of income inequality (and perceive themselves to be more middle class than they actually are), the evidence suggests that a lack of information is not the whole story. Informing citizens about inequality does not consistently change their normative attitudes toward inequality and redistribution, and economically self-interested reactions only seem to occur in particular circumstances.

When citizens can draw clear connections between their own economic position and proposed redistributive policies, they can and do react in accordance with their self-interest and/or their political values. However, the information that enables them to do this needs to be rich, for example, letting people know where they fall in the income distribution. More abstract representations of inequality either result in no changes in public support for redistribution or have indirect effects, such as by affecting perceptions of meritocracy.

These subtle and contingent findings contrast with the strong evidence that social stereotypes about the rich and the poor are powerful predictors of support for redistribution. People evaluate economic differences based on their perceptions of whether the rich and the poor seem to deserve their lot in life. These perceptions of fairness, in turn, are affected by racial and ethnic heterogeneity, with minority groups frequently stereotyped as undeserving. These findings redirect our attention to the sociopolitical institutions (such as labor unions, the media, and public policy) that shape public notions regarding the deservingness of socioeconomic groups and the fairness of inequality-producing mechanisms.

The United States does not have a unique political dynamic when it comes to public support for redistribution, despite standing apart in comparative contexts on some key variables, notably when it comes to believing that poverty is due to personal characteristics rather than bad luck. Even though the United States is an outlier when it comes to perceptions of the deservingness of the poor, it does not follow that the underlying political logics of economic inequality and redistribution are different here. If increasing inequality, for example, slowly changes public perceptions regarding the deservingness of the rich, then we may ultimately see increased support for redistribution in the Unites States, too. But even if this does not happen, it does not follow that public policies allowing disproportionate growth in top-end incomes in the United States have been fully sanctioned by the population. Disapproval of inequality has not risen in tandem with inequality, but it has been high and stable, with most Americans continuously concerned that inequality in the United States is too high. To give a full account of the political dynamics of inequality-ameliorating public policy in the United States, we need to look beyond public opinion, considering how the political system more broadly shapes public opinion and then translates public preferences into public policy.

REFERENCES

Ahlquist, John S., & Margaret Levi. (2013). *In the Interest of Others*. Princeton: Princeton University Press.

Alesina, A., & Giuliano, P. (2011). *Preferences for Redistribution. Handbook of Social Economics* (Vol. 1). Amsterdam: Elsevier B.V. https://doi.org/10.1016/B978-0-444-53187-2.00001-2

Alesina, A. F., & Glaeser, E. (2004). *Fighting Poverty in the U.S. and Europe: A World of Difference.* Oxford: Oxford University Press. http://nrs.harvard.edu/urn-3:hul.ebookbatch.OXSCH_batch:osouko199267669

Amable, B. (2009). The Differentiation of Social Demands in Europe. The Social Basis of the European Models of Capitalism. *Social Indicators Research, 91*(3), 391–426. https://doi.org/10.1007/s11205-008-9340-6

Andersen, Robert, & Curtis, J. (2015). Social Class, Economic Inequality, and the Convergence of Policy Preferences: Evidence from 24 Modern Democracies. *Canadian Review of Sociology/Revue Canadienne de Sociologie 52*(3): 266–288. https://doi.org/10.1111/cars.12077

Ashok, V., Kuziemko, I., & Washington, E. (2015). Support for Redistribution in an Age of Rising Inequality: New Stylized Facts and Some Tentative Explanations. *NBER Working Paper Series,* 59. https://doi.org/10.3386/w21529

Attewell, D. (2019). Education and the Multi-Dimensional Politics of Redistribution in Western Europe. Paper presented at the 2019 Annual Convention of the Midwest Political Science Association. Chicago.

Becker, Bastian. (2019). Mind the Income Gaps? Experimental Evidence of Information's Lasting Effect on Redistributive Preferences. *Social Justice Research.* https://doi.org/10.1007/s11211-019-00343-7

Benabou, R., & Ok, E. A. (2001). Social Mobility and the Demand for Redistribution: The POUM Hypothesis. *Quarterly Journal of Economics, 116*(2), 447–487.

Boudreau, C., & Mackenzie, S. A. (2014). Informing the Electorate? How Party Cues and Policy Information Affect Public Opinion about Initiatives. *American Journal of Political Science, 58*(1), 48–62. https://doi.org/10.1111/ajps.12054

(2018a). Misinformed in an Unequal World: How Accurate Information about Inequality and Income Affects Public Support for Redistributive Policies. Paper presented at the 2018 American Political Science Association Conference, Boston.

(2018b). Wanting What Is Fair: How Party Cues and Information About Income Inequality Affect Public Support for Taxes. *The Journal of Politics, 80*(2), 367–381. https://doi.org/10.2139/ssrn.2405294

Breznau, N., & Hommerich, C. (2019). No Generalizable Effect of Income Inequality on Public Support for Governmental Redistribution among Rich Democracies 1987–2010. *Social Science Research, 81,* 170–191. https://doi.org/10.1016/j.ssresearch.2019.03.013

Bullock, J. G. (2011). Elite Influence on Public Opinion in an Informed Electorate. *American Political Science Review, 105*(03), 496–515. https://doi.org/10.1017/S0003055411000165

Campbell, A. L. (2003). *How Policies Make Citizens: Senior Political Activism and the American Welfare State.* Princeton: Princeton University Press.

Castillo, J. C. (2012). Is Inequality Becoming Just? Changes in Public Opinion about Economic Distribution in Chile. *Bulletin of Latin American Research, 31*(1), 1–18.

Cavaille, C., & Trump, K.-S. (2015). The Two Facets of Social Policy Preferences. *The Journal of Politics*, 77(1), 146–160.

Cruces, G., Truglia, R. P., & Tetaz, M. (2013). Biased Perceptions of Income Distribution and Preferences for Redistribution: Evidence from a Survey Experiment. *Journal of Public Economics*, 98, 100–112. https://doi.org/10.1016/j.jpubeco.2012.10.009

Davidai, S. (2018). Why Do Americans Believe in Economic Mobility? Economic Inequality, External Attributions of Wealth and Poverty, and the Belief in Economic Mobility. *Journal of Experimental Social Psychology*, 79 (February), 138–148. https://doi.org/10.1016/j.jesp.2018.07.012

Davidai, S., & Gilovich, T. (2015). Building a More Mobile America – One Income Quintile at a Time. *Perspectives on Psychological Science*, 10(1), 60–71. https://doi.org/10.1177/1745691614562005

Day, M. V, & Fiske, S. T. (2017). Movin' on Up? How Perceptions of Social Mobility Affect Our Willingness to Defend the System. *Social Psychological and Personality Science*, 8(3), 267–274. https://doi.org/10.1177/1948550616678454

Delli Carpini, M. X., & Keeter, S. (1997). *What Americans Know About Politics and Why It Matters*. New Haven: Yale University Press.

Engelhardt, C., & Wagener, A. (2014). Biased Perception of Income Inequality and Redistribution. Hanover Economic Papers, dp-526.

(2016). What Do Germans Think and Know about Income Inequality? A Survey Experiment. ECINEQ Working Paper (No. 2016–389).

Eriksson, K., & Simpson, B. (2012). What Do Americans Know about Inequality? It Depends on How You Ask Them. *Judgment and Decision Making*, 7(6), 741–745.

Finseraas, H. (2009). Income Inequality and Demand for Redistribution: A Multilevel Analysis of European Public Opinion. *Scandinavian Political Studies*, 32(1), 94–119. https://doi.org/10.1111/j.1467-9477.2008.00211.x

Franko, W. (2016). Political Context, Government Redistribution, and the Public's Response to Growing Economic Inequality. *The Journal of Politics*, 78(4), 957–973.

Franko, W., & Christopher Witko. (2017). *The New Economic Populism: How States Respond To Economic Inequality*. New York: Oxford University Press.

García-Sánchez, E., Van der Toorn, J., Rodríguez-Bailón, R., & Willis, G. B. (2018). The Vicious Cycle of Economic Inequality: The Role of Ideology in Shaping the Relationship Between "What Is" and "What Ought to Be" in 41 Countries. *Social Psychological and Personality Science*, 10(8), 991–1001. https://doi.org/10.1177/1948550618811500

Gijsberts, M. (2002). The Legitimation of Income Inequality in State-socialist and Market Societies. *Acta Sociologica*, 45(4), 269–285. https://doi.org/10.1080/000169902762022860

Gilens, M. (1999). *Why Americans Hate Welfare: Race, Media, and the Politics of Antipoverty Policy*. Chicago: University of Chicago Press.

Gimpelson, V., & Treisman, D. (2018). Misperceiving Inequality. *Economics and Politics*, 30(1), 27–54. https://doi.org/10.1111/ecpo.12103

Guardino, M. (2019). *Framing Inequality: News Media, Public Opinion, and the Neoliberal Turn in U.S. Public Policy*. Oxford, New York: Oxford University Press.

Hochschild, J. (1981). *What's Fair? American Beliefs about Distributive Justice*. Cambridge, MA: Harvard University Press.

Hoy, C., and Mager, F. (2019). Why Are Relatively Poor People Not More Supportive of Redistribution? Evidence from a Randomized Survey Experiment across 10 Countries. *ECINEQ Working Paper 2019-489*.

Johnson, I. R., & Fujita, K. (2012). Change We Can Believe In: Using Perceptions of Changeability to Promote System-Change Motives over System-Justification Motives in Information Search. *Psychological Science*, 23(2), 133–140. https://doi.org/10.1177/0956797611423670

Johnston, C. D., & Newman, B. J. (2016). Economic Inequality and U.S. Public Policy Mood Across Space and Time. *American Politics Research*, 44(1), 164–191. https://doi.org/10.1177/1532673X15588361

Karadja, M., Möllerström, J., & Seim, D. (2017). Richer (and Holier) Than Thou? The Effect of Relative Income Improvements on Demand for Redistribution. *The Review of Economics and Statistics*, 99(2), 201–212.

Katz, M. (1989). *The Undeserving Poor: From the War on Poverty to the War on Welfare*. New York: Pantheon Books.

Kelley, J., & Zagorski, K. (2004). Economic Change and the Legitimation of Inequality: The Transition from Socialism to the Free Market in Central-East Europe. *Research in Social Stratification and Mobility*, 22, 319–364. https://doi.org/10.1016/S0276-5624(04)22011-X

Kelly, N. J., & Enns, P. K. (2010). Inequality and the Dynamics of Public Opinion: The Self-Reinforcing Link Between Economic Inequality and Mass Preferences. *American Journal of Political Science*, 54(4), 855–870. https://doi.org/10.1111/j.1540-5907.2010.00472.x

Kenworthy, L., & McCall, L. (2008). Inequality, Public Opinion and Redistribution. *Socio-Economic Review*, 6(1), 35–68. https://doi.org/10.1093/ser/mwm006

Kiatpongsan, S., & Norton, M. I. (2014). How Much (More) Should CEOs Make? A Universal Desire for More Equal Pay. *Perspectives on Psychological Science*, 9(6), 587–593. https://doi.org/10.1177/1745691614549773

Kluegel, J. R., & Smith, E. R. (1986). *Beliefs about Inequality: Americans' Views of What Is and What Ought to Be*. New York: Aldine De Gruyter.

Kolczynska, M., & Merry, J. J. (2016). Preferred Levels of Income Inequality in a Period of Systemic Change: Analysis of Data from the Polish Panel Survey, POLPAN 1988–2003. *Polish Sociological Review*, 2(194), 171–189.

Kraus, M. W., & Tan, J. J. X. (2015). Americans Overestimate Social Class Mobility. *Journal of Experimental Social Psychology*, 58, 101–111. https://doi.org/10.1016/j.jesp.2015.01.005

Kuklinski J. H., Quirk P. J., Jerit J., et al. (2000). Misinformation and the Currency of Citizenship. *Journal of Politics*, 62, 791–816.

Kuziemko, I., Norton, M. I., Saez, E., & Stantcheva, S. (2015). How Elastic Are Preferences for Redistribution? Evidence from Randomized Survey Experiments. *American Economic Review*, 105(4), 1478–1508. https://doi.org/10.1257/aer.20130360

Luttig, M. (2013). The Structure of Inequality and Americans' Attitudes Toward Redistribution. *Public Opinion Quarterly*, 77(3), 811–821. https://doi.org/10.1093/poq/nft025

McCall, L. (2013). *The Undeserving Rich: Beliefs about Inequality, Opportunity, and Redistribution in American Society*. Cambridge: Cambridge University Press.

McCall, L., Burk, D., Laperrière, M., & Richeson, J. A. (2017). Exposure to Rising Inequality Shapes Americans' Opportunity Beliefs and Policy Support. *Proceedings of the National Academy of Sciences*, 114(36), 9593–9598. https://doi.org/10.1073/pnas.1706253114

Meltzer, A. H., & Richard, S. F. (1981). A Rational Theory of the Size of Government. *Journal of Political Economy*, 89(5), 914–927.

Mettler, S. (2005). *Soldiers to Citizens: The G.I. Bill and the Making of the Greatest Generation*. New York: Oxford University Press.

Michener, J. (2018). *Fragmented Democracy: Medicaid, Federalism, and Unequal Politics*. Cambridge: Cambridge University Press.

Mijs, J. J. B. (2019). The Paradox of Inequality: Income Inequality and Belief in Meritocracy Go Hand in Hand. Forthcoming in *Socio-Economic Review*, 1–28. https://doi.org/10.1093/ser/mwy051

Minkoff, S. L., & Lyons, J. (2017). Living with Inequality: Neighborhood Income Diversity and Perceptions of the Income Gap. *American Politics Research*. https://doi.org/10.1177/1532673X17733799

Niehues, J. (2014). Subjective Perceptions of Inequality and Redistributive Preferences: An International Comparison. Cologne Institute for Economic Research: unpublished.

Norton, M. I., & Ariely, D. (2010). Building a Better America – One Wealth Quintile at a Time. *Perspectives on Psychological Science*, 6(1), 9–12.

Osberg, L., & Smeeding, T. (2006). "Fair" Inequality? Attitudes toward Pay Differentials: The United States in Comparative Perspective. *American Sociological Review*, 71(3), 450–473. https://doi.org/10.1177/000312240607100305

Page, B. I., & Jacobs, L. R. (2009). *Class War: What Americans Really Think About Economic Inequality*. Chicago: University of Chicago Press.

Page, L., & Goldstein, D. G. (2016). Subjective Beliefs about the Income Distribution and Preferences for Redistribution. *Social Choice and Welfare*, 47(1), 25–61. https://doi.org/10.1007/s00355-015-0945-9

Pedersen, R. T., & Mutz, D. C. (2018). Attitudes Toward Economic Inequality: The Illusory Agreement. *Political Science Research and Methods*, 1–17. https://doi.org/10.1017/psrm.2018.18

Pellicer, M., Piraino, P., & Wegner, E. (2019). Perceptions of Inevitability and Demand for Redistribution: Evidence from a Survey Experiment. *Journal of Economic Behavior and Organization*, 59, 274–288. https://doi.org/10.1016/j.jebo.2017.12.013

Petersen, M. B. (2012). Social Welfare as Small-Scale Help: Evolutionary Psychology and the Deservingness Heuristic. *American Journal of Political Science*, 56(1), 1–16. https://doi.org/10.1111/j.1540-5907.2011.00545.x

Petersen, M. B., Sznycer, D., Cosmides, L., & Tooby, J. (2012). Who Deserves Help? Evolutionary Psychology, Social Emotions, and Public Opinion about Welfare. *Political Psychology*, 33(3), 395–418. https://doi.org/10.1111/j.1467-9221.2012.00883.x

Pierson, P. (1993). When Effect Becomes Cause: Policy Feedback and Political Change. *World Politics*, 45(4): 595–628. https://doi.org/10.2307/2950710

Piston, S. (2018). *Class Attitudes in America: Sympathy for the Poor, Resentment of the Rich, and Political Implications*. New York: Cambridge University Press.

Roth, C., & Wohlfart, J. (2016). Experienced Inequality and Preferences for Redistribution. *SSRN Electronic Journal*. https://doi.org/10.2139/ssrn.2809655

Rueda, D., and Pontusson, J. (2000).Wage Inequality and Varieties of Capitalism. *World Politics* 52(3): 350–383.

Saez, E. (2017). Income and Wealth Inequality: Evidence and Policy Implications. *Contemporary Economic Policy*, 35(1), 7–25. https://doi.org/10.1111/coep.12210

Sands, M. L. (2017). Exposure to Inequality Affects Support for Redistribution. *Proceedings of the National Academy of Sciences*, 114(4), 663–668. https://doi.org/10.1073/pnas.1615010113

Scheve, K., & Stasavage, D. (2016). *Taxing the Rich: A History of Fiscal Fairness in the United States and Europe*. Princeton: Princeton University Press.

Shapiro, I. (2002). Why the Poor Don't Soak the Rich. *Daedalus*, 131(1), 118–128.

Shariff, A. F., Wiwad, D., & Aknin, L. B. (2016). Income Mobility Breeds Tolerance for Income Inequality: Cross-National and Experimental Evidence. *Perspectives on Psychological Science: A Journal of the Association for Psychological Science*, 11(3), 373–380. https://doi.org/10.1177/1745691616635596

Skocpol, Theda. (1992). *Protecting Soldiers and Mothers: The Political Origins of Social Policy in the United States*. Cambridge, MA: Belknap Press of Harvard University Press.

Solt, F., Hu, Y., Hudson, K., & Song, J. (2016). Economic inequality and belief in meritocracy in the United States. *Research & Politics*. https://doi.org/10.1177/2053168016672101

Starmans, C., Sheskin, M., & Bloom, P. (2017). Why People Prefer Unequal Societies. *Nature Publishing Group*, 1, 1–7. https://doi.org/10.1038/s41562-017-0082

Trump, K.-S. (2018). Income Inequality Influences Perceptions of Legitimate Income Differences. *British Journal of Political Science*, 48(4), 929–952. https://doi.org/10.1017/S0007123416000326

Wright, G. (2017). The Political Implications of American Concerns About Economic Inequality. *Political Behavior*, 1–23. https://doi.org/10.1007/s11109-017-9399-3

Xu, P., & Garand, J. C. (2010). Economic Context and Americans' Perceptions of Income Inequality. *Social Science Quarterly*, 91(5), 1220–1241.

5

Engendering Democracy in an Age of Anxiety

Alice Kessler-Harris

Why are established democracies facing dilemmas of legitimacy and capacity? I want to try to answer this question by exploring one of the central tensions in our society – between capitalism and democracy – and asking how the strain has played itself out in the late twentieth century. I argue that we understand that tension more fully if we explore the long history of women's quest for full economic and political participation – their search for inclusion in the democratic polity. I suggest that women's commitment to the social good helped tame late nineteenth- and twentieth-century capitalism, and that in the late twentieth century new economic circumstances and divisions among women may have helped sustain the triumph of capitalism over democracy.

Historians of the United States have long recognized the potential for conflict between capitalism and democracy without especially noting the roles that women have played (Appleby 2010, 433–435; Green 1980; Kessler-Harris 2012, 725–740). They have noted the use of ideas of freedom and liberty to provide a mantra that at once sustained popular belief in the right of individuals to accumulate wealth and justified the untrammeled use of capital. In the aftermath of nineteenth-century industrialization, they have documented the efforts of capitalists to maximize profits, enhance individual wealth, and shape the political process in their own interests. Interpretations of liberty as an individual right, historians have concluded, have left community well-being unprotected and suppressed most opportunities to foster the social good (Paulson 1997, 118–128). Historians have also followed efforts of racial/ethnic peoples and diverse groups of wage workers to expand their political roles by restraining the power of money, exercising a voice in the public sphere (often through trade unions), and redirecting expenditures in the public interest. But labor, to put it broadly, has not generally succeeded in taming capital with the result that capital has been able to limit the access of ordinary folk to democracy. Supreme Court Justice Louis Brandeis articulated the tension in the early twentieth century: "We may have democracy or we may have wealth concentrated in the hands of a few," he wrote, "but we can't have both" (qtd. in Dilliard, 1941, 42).

Women as a group have tended to enter the fray on the side of democracy. Valued historically for their roles in biological and social reproduction, they have fought to free themselves from stereotypes about their lack of reason and reliance on emotion to justify claims to full participation in political and economic life. Their political rights derived from their family positions, nineteenth-century women found themselves sharply divided by class and race. But women of every race were marginalized in the polity of most states. After they formally acquired the vote, custom, culture, race, and law continued to inhibit the full participation of all females in democratic practice. Their roles in capitalist accumulation generally subsumed in those of their male partners, and often invisible, women have also been denied even the limited rewards of male wage earners (Kessler-Harris, 1982). For most of the past, occupational segregation restricted female job choice, wages, and social mobility. Excluded as major players in the acquisition of wealth and in the play of politics, women have learned to live with very different definitions of freedom and liberty than their menfolk. For many twentieth-century women (and for most people of color), liberty would rest not on the freedom of individuals to achieve wealth and success but on the willingness of the society to provide the kinds of resources that would assure all of its members the capacity to contribute fully. A democracy that included women could, in the view of many, be achieved only if states ensured the fair distribution of resources such as education and family support. These positive liberties, to paraphrase the philosopher Isaiah Berlin, would underline individual opportunity for all and thus promote more inclusive political participation (Marshall 1991, 1–26; Villa 2008, 1–26).

In the United States, in contrast to much of Europe, the many efforts of women, working people, and reformers to provide a path to democracy through a commitment to the collective or social good generally fell afoul of the cry for liberty (Lichtenstein 2006). Allowing the mantras of freedom and liberty rather than calls to equality and democracy to govern their political choices and their legal and judicial arguments, Americans hesitated to constrain capital and the political power of wealth. To do so, most

Americans believed, would be ideologically abhorrent – labeled or mislabeled as socialist and un-American. Under those circumstances, labor struggles, public protests, and the efforts of marginalized people to make their voices heard in the political process had limited success. This changed during the Great Depression of the 1930s, when the economic crisis compelled attention to social concerns even at the price of liberty. Then, and for several decades afterward, greater attention to the well-being of citizens briefly encouraged restraints on capital and heightened the voices of the disadvantaged, including women. Under such banners as fairness, or social responsibility, and sometimes in the name of "the good society," government placed the liberty of capital second to that of the general welfare. Congress legislated financial support for the poor and aged; it encouraged skilled and unskilled workers to organized into unions strong enough to provide a countervailing force to capitalism. As Brandeis and others might have agreed, broadening concern from individual liberty to social well-being enhanced opportunities for citizens to participate in the polity. Briefly, movements for democracy flourished – among them a feminism that promised to challenge the preeminence of the individual. But a changing climate in the seventies brought with it questions about the legitimacy of democracy and anxiety about democracy itself.

In the pages that follow, I explore how the late twentieth-century women's movement, which embodied at least a modicum of hope for expanding the democratic vision, fell afoul of a push for increased corporate market share and profitability, disguised as freedom (Brown 2015, 17–46; Rottenberg 2018). The movement's initial concern with social transformation and caring gave way to a search for liberty and equality of opportunity for individuals and groups and divided the movement along paths that echoed racial and class tensions. As ideologies of free market individualism achieved new prominence, they tempted well-prepared women to advocate for equality with men and to support free market competition that promised to pave the way to opportunity for women. Aspirations to collective well-being, to social justice, or to fairness fell by the wayside. As they did so, the success of so-called mainstream feminists undermined visions of collective good that had brought women as a whole to the edge of greater democratic rewards. Economic opportunity for liberal, or mainstream, feminists came at the expense of social democratic visions.

In this respect, the US experience differs from that of Western Europe. Crucially, in the aftermath of World War II, the separate nations of Western Europe accepted greater or lesser forms of social democracy.

Ideologies of nation building there encouraged continuing strong state support for mothers, children, and community life as well as corporate regulation to encourage respect for working people. At the same time, the United States insisted on measuring well-being through higher living standards and greater consumption. The gendered implications of these differing belief systems have yet to be fully explored; in the framework that follows, we begin to see how understanding the differences might illuminate the struggles of all sorts of politically marginalized peoples (including African Americans, new immigrants, and the rural poor) and shape national social policies. In the United States, in the case of women (and perhaps elsewhere and for many others), the turn away from a belief in shared responsibility toward consumption accompanied and rationalized an alliance with identity politics, a renewed fragmentation of collective sensibilities, and a diminution of the democratic spirit. Tracing these changes among women illuminates the power of belief systems and helps us understand the mechanisms that fostered the powerful ideological commitments of the late twentieth century.

Historians generally agree that the 1960s revealed an ongoing search for inclusion, respect, and participation on the part of ordinary folk (Bloom and Breines 2000; Boskin and Rosenstone 1972; Isserman and Kazin, 2004). They disagree about the origins of women's quest for these signs of full citizenship. Some point to the discussions and recommendations of the President's Commission on the Status of Women (PCSW), created in 1961 by the newly elected president John Fitzgerald Kennedy (Harrison 1988). Others attribute the spark to the civil rights movement that caught fire in the 1950s, and led women of every race and socioeconomic level to search for a democratic voice and equal treatment under the law (Evans 1979). Both events played significant roles, but these origin stories set the stage for divisions that would emerge in later years that drew women in different directions. Both, crucially, drew on democratic aspirations.

We begin with the commission: President Kennedy had relied on the labor movement and working people to support his election. Barely defeating Richard Nixon for the presidency in 1960, Kennedy offered a high-level position in the Department of Labor to Esther Peterson, one of his key supporters. Peterson, conscious that women had been excluded from most of the democratic gains of the postwar period or included in them mostly as family members, promptly asked him to initiate a presidential commission to investigate the status of women. Its purpose, in the words of Kennedy's charge, would be the full realization of women's rights "which should be respected and fostered as part of our nation's commitment to human dignity, freedom, and democracy." He expected the commission's final report to include recommendations for federal and state services to increase women's economic and political potential and thus enhance their roles in democratic life (Mead and Kaplan 1965, 207).

In modest, and yet influential, ways, the PCSW, as it came to be known, did just that. While remaining respectful of women's family roles as well as their roles in caring labor, the commission's major recommendations involved new paths to employment for women. These included federal and state government support for enhanced education, counseling, and job training for women; greater work opportunities for married women; and new definitions of full employment and unemployment insurance that would include them. Members of the commission proposed an Equal Pay Law that the president signed in 1963; they also defended the addition of "sex" to the categories among which employers could not discriminate in the 1964 Civil Rights Act (Kessler-Harris 2001). The language of freedom and democracy infused its recommendations. As Margaret Mead put it in her transmittal of the commission's report to the president, members believed "an important part of democracy to be the freedom of women to contribute to our society" (Mead and Kaplan 1965, 4). But freedom, as the commission's recommendations made clear, involved the opportunity for women to participate in the world's work: the provision of positive freedoms, as Isaiah Berlin would have called them. Concerned that the shift of women out of the home not undermine the family, the PCSW report called for government investments in childcare, family services, and community planning. Unusually, it proposed government regulations that would encourage labor organization among those who earned wages and suggested that federal employment might provide a model for equality in the workforce.

The PCSW's recommendations appeared in the same year that Betty Friedan published her devastating analysis of women's social roles (Friedan 1963). Together, the heightened conversations around *The Feminine Mystique* and the PCSW's state-based follow-ups propelled the emergence of the National Organization for Women (NOW) in 1966. NOW's founding members included Black, white, and Hispanic women; former members of President Kennedy's Commission on the Status of Women; and college professors, trade unionists, and political activists. Initially, NOW, as an organization, sought two kinds of freedom. Intent on achieving greater inclusion for women in politics, it sought economic equality by removing legal and cultural constraints to women's advancement and political representation. At the same time, informed by the rising tide of women, especially married women with children, entering the labor force, as well as by women's earlier shared participation in antiwar, civil rights, and anti-poverty activities, NOW's leadership advocated for social support systems that would enable women to take advantage of a new freedom.

In the first instance, NOW led a political movement for equal treatment under the law, reframing calls for fairness as demands for equality of opportunity and treatment consistent with that accorded to white males. Given equal pay and a fair shot at jobs, given a dropping of the barriers to promotion and advancement in the workforce, liberal feminists believed that they would soon achieve their goals. To do so, they relied on legislative and administrative change: government intervention rooted in a still far from universal belief that women deserved social and economic equality.

It took a while, but after Congress, in 1964, enjoined employers not to discriminate on the basis of sex, some economic barriers did indeed fall. The Equal Employment Opportunity Commission (EEOC) slowly came around to recognizing that denying women access to jobs constituted discrimination, eliminating, for example, the common practice of designating 'help wanted' advertisements under male and female labels. In the early 1970s, the EEOC added women to affirmative action programs. Around the same time, and under the intellectual leadership of Ruth Bader Ginsburg among others, courts began to redefine sexual discrimination to incorporate hostile work environments, sexual harassment, and differential treatment of women with children. These changes, occurring as they did just as the call for faith in markets and individual liberty expanded, seemed to threaten workingmen and their masculinity.

The mostly young women who had been influenced by the cultural revolution of the sixties and shaped by participation in civil rights and New Left protests situated their personal oppression at the heart of social change. Rather than demanding "equal rights" for women, they turned their attention to achieving an equality of power (Echols 1989; Evans 1979, 214–215). Relying on "consciousness raising" as their major strategy, they demanded the kinds of fundamental changes in sex roles and social relations conducive to female autonomy. Radical women believed that sexual freedom, reproductive control, and a newly egalitarian family would underline the quest for full economic and political participation.

Only systemic change, they believed, would create the more just society in which women could expect to assume positions of power.

Because women differed around how disadvantage had emerged, they disagreed as to solutions. Some placed the blame on what they called the patriarchal family and demanded freedom from it. They advocated as well reproductive choice within and outside the nuclear family. Their solutions involved dismantling the traditional family and the social institutions that supported it, including churches and schools and the books that children read. In the late 1960s, women from these groups sought cultural changes to effect a shift in consciousness. They protested the Miss America pageant's emphasis on stylized beauty, advocated for control of women's bodies, rejected traditional marriage and heterosexual normativity, and disputed the language and "symbol systems" that had long kept women in their places. Crucially, women confronted male and professional control of women's health, turning to self-help books and clinics to invest themselves with the knowledge they needed to make their own decisions. Those who held capitalism responsible insisted that limits on women's wage-earning roles and the sometimes artificial demands for unnecessary housework constrained women's hopes and their political voices. Academic women investigated socialism and Marxism hoping to find remedies to hierarchical governance and methods of resisting the power of wealth. More influential than their limited numbers might indicate, these more radical feminists kept alive the importance of creating a world view and an environment that would help promote a more just economic world. For them, freedom extended beyond individual liberty (DuPlessis and Snitow 1988; Wandersee 1998).

Feminists of all kinds sought access to power through increased participation and representation. They could, and did at first, share common concerns, agreeing, for example, on the negative effects of corporate power; on the disadvantages of a consumer society; on the idea, though not the method, of compensating household labor; and on color-blind, if not antiracist, policies. Crucially, they also agreed on many cultural issues most especially sharing a desire for more inclusive creation and wider distribution of knowledge. But increasingly the idea that freedom lay in dropping the barriers to women's advancement absorbed one group, while the second sought to change the rules of the game to encompass a new world view in which women's emotions and voices would play a central role.

We can see the battle play itself out in several late 1960s debates and most especially in the battle for universal childcare in the late 1960s and early 1970s. Conceived in the 1960s as a service to needy families, publicly subsidized childcare emerged then to provide poor mothers with coverage while they worked. Toward the end of the decade, feminists began to argue for childcare as a universal right that would give all mothers the capacity to decide whether or not to work. In 1966, NOW argued that European-style provisions for motherhood, including paid maternity leaves, nurseries, and day care centers would provide "true equality of opportunity and responsibility in society without conflict with their responsibilities as mothers and homemakers" (Danziger-Halperin, 2020, 1012; see also Kornbluh 2007, 95–100; Michel 1999; Swinth 2018, 156–179). By 1967, NOW was advocating for freely available public childcare centers accessible on the same basis as "parks, libraries and public schools" (Swinth 2018, 160, 166–167). But its energetic campaign for federal legislation that would fund childcare centers foundered on the meaning of "freedom," as it differed for different women. If universal childcare could provide freedom for educated mothers of the very young to engage in wage labor, it could also provide a mechanism for coercing poor and single mothers into earning wages. And, some feared, available childcare could tempt more comfortable mothers to abandon their children for the sake of wage labor.

For a few years, NOW and other advocacy groups wholeheartedly supported childcare as a universal right. In 1971, a coalition of feminist groups succeeded in getting Congress to pass an act to fund "Comprehensive Child Development." But those who feared that it might foster racial mixing at childcare centers as well as some who sanctioned the idea that women belonged at home opposed the bill. Providing government funding for childcare would, in the view of President Nixon, who vetoed the bill, "commit the vast moral authority of the National Government to the side of communal approaches to child-rearing over against the family centered approach." The government, he insisted, must "cement the family in its rightful position as the keystone of our civilization" (Swinth 2018, 168). His veto message articulated a growing fear of radical transformation in family life – a transformation already visible in growing female economic independence. In the aftermath of the rejection of universal childcare, NOW and many feminists pulled back, turning from a program that would have provided a broad benefit to all families to a legislative agenda that would focus on the rights of women in the workplace and beyond.

The National Welfare Rights Organization (NWRO), whose constituents were among the poorest women, continued the fight. It had a different vision of childcare. The NWRO pressed for resources that would allow these women to mother their children more effectively – a goal originally inscribed into the New Deal family aid programs in the 1930s and then accepted as in the national interest. Fearful that the push by middle-income women (who could afford to pay for their own childcare) would undercut the opportunity for poor women to care for their young, the NWRO argued, unsuccessfully it turned out, that mothering was a job in which the whole society had a stake.

In making these arguments, NWRO members drew on the long history of social welfare as it had developed in the United States when the depression of the 1930s shifted the ideological debate to include concern for social solidarity. During the depression years, policy makers had (unevenly to be sure) recognized the rights of children to maternal care through policies such as Aid to Dependent Children and by extending Social Security to the surviving children of workers and to their mothers. Even the need for labor during World War II had not turned the tide; wartime policies generally did not promote the entry of mothers into the workforce. Policies that placed the freedom of individual women in the context of what historian Bruce Shulman has called an "ideal of social solidarity… [a] conception of a national community with duties and obligations to one's fellow citizens" continued after the war (Schulman 2002, 15). In the thirty years that followed, widely shared beliefs in the state's capacity to safeguard the common welfare sustained the promise of democracy and encouraged individuals and groups to expand their demands on government and the state. The common wisdom in those days held that freedom could best be protected by enhancing the economic well-being of the population at large. Spending on the social good would, in the minds of liberals and those to the left, enhance the lives and experience of the majority, creating a more inclusive society and broadening the democratic base (Galbraith 1963).

The resulting systems had different names and different emphases in Europe and the United States. British economist William Beveridge's 1942 report sketched out the benefits and rights that would be necessary to establish a reunified citizenry in the wake of World War II (Beveridge, 2015). His 1944 follow-up made the case for full employment. These widely influential reports heralded the dawn of a general consensus that would emerge after the war that a stable prosperity required secure, more equal, and fairer economic arrangements. Attaining this standard required a cooperative relationship between democracy and capital, a commitment to regulation and planning that could effectively organize the economy without excess restraint. It would require sustained increases in efficiency, agreements to share the gains of productivity more equally between capital and labor by taxation and transfer payments, and full employment policies. To achieve these, European governments would be called on to promote the general welfare, corporations would be asked to pay their fair share of the costs, and labor would become a countervailing force to the market's profit-maximizing goals. Questions of gender, including who would earn wages, who would sustain and support families, and how social benefits would be distributed, became central to the economic calculus.

The United States hewed to something often called "liberal democracy." Unusually, it linked many protections and benefits to wage work rather than to citizenship or residence. In the common conception, men would remain the major breadwinners; their employers (pressed by trade unions) would provide social benefits including health care, old age pensions, and free time; women and their children would remain dependent on their menfolk, with government acting as backup (or husband) when male support failed. This version of the welfare state therefore never exacted the deep concessions from the corporate sector demanded by most Western European industrial countries. And it retained a gendered underpinning that relegated the benefits of women subsidiary to those of male workers.

Still, and despite ongoing resistance within wealthy and corporate elites, a generalized consensus around the wisdom of government intervention sustained constraints on capital that lasted through the Eisenhower years and into the 1960s. Large majorities in the postwar years agreed on such policies as adequate minimum wages, reasonable welfare payments, and basic old age pensions. Seizing the democratic impetus, an emboldened labor movement encouraged the spread of Social Security to domestic workers and farm workers as well as the disabled and the blind. It supported as well, better coverage for the surviving widows and underage children of male participants. Trade unions also pushed for expanded unemployment insurance to cover a greater share of the population. They championed health insurance for the poor and the aged. These initiatives fostered the appearance of a more human face for capitalism. The GI Bill offered the promise of social mobility; progressive taxation reduced economic inequality; federal subsidies for public transportation, schools, hospitals, and infrastructure enhanced the lives of the poorest (Galbraith 1956; Piketty 2017). Union negotiated health care benefits and rising standards of living inducted many working-class families into the more affluent society.

But there were those, left behind, who still sought the benefits of a consumer society and access to the democratic institutions that would provide it. When a rising civil rights movement protested exclusion of African Americans from good jobs, the threat of protest marches and wartime disruptions motivated legislators to pass a Fair Employment Practices Act. Full employment and universal health care emerged onto the political agenda at the end of the war. In 1954, a path-breaking Supreme Court decision (*Brown* v. *Board of Education*) ordered school desegregation and drew national attention to historically discriminatory education systems. Efforts to desegregate public accommodations followed soon after with women like Ella Baker, Fannie Lou Hamer, and Rosa Parks leading the grassroots organizing efforts of the civil rights movement. The fight for democracy served as a banner for the struggle of African Americans to join in the electoral process. As the crucial participation of leadership of women illustrates, it also encouraged women to measure their own progress by their capacity to participate in the polity (Lee 2005; Meyerowitz 1994; Ransby 2005).

Trade unions, which represented about a third of American workers in the 1950s, and constituted the core of resistance to untrammeled capitalism, opened their doors to the rising numbers of women giving them a chance at leadership positions. Lillian Roberts got her start as a health care worker before she rose to become executive secretary of the most powerful public sector union. Addie Wyatt joined the Packinghouse Workers Union and then became perhaps the most influential female trade unionist in the newly unified AFL-CIO. Everywhere women challenged seniority rules in efforts to create more inclusive workplaces. Dolores Huerta, who would spend her life organizing farm workers, began her activism in the mid-fifties as a community organizer advocating for housing, sanitary working conditions, and reduced hours of labor, as well as fairer wages.

By the sixties, a galvanized population, motivated by slogans of fairness, justice, and equal opportunity, sought inclusion in the democratic practice of political parties and the economic system. Huerta and Cesar Chavez founded the National Farm Workers' Union in 1962. That year, socialist Michael Harrington published *The Other America*, which exposed the plight of the poor and drew attention to the exclusion of most of the poorest members of society from the democratic process. Among the poor, women and their children constituted a large majority. The resulting surge of attention produced a poor people's movement (led by Martin Luther King Jr.) with an eclectic set of supporters and resulted, finally, in a "War on Poverty." Undoubtedly designed to distract attention from an escalating war in Vietnam, new government initiatives nevertheless produced housing subsidies, childcare services, and Head Start programs for small children from underprivileged families. Mid-decade, government-subsidized health insurance provided medical care for the aged (majority female) and for the poor – most of them single mothers and their children. With all of their defects, these additions and changes reveal just how firmly notions of social spending and social justice had become embedded in the nation's value system. Perhaps more important, they suggest the close relationship between a world view shaped by a concern for social well-being and the democratic impetus.

The women who participated in these activities, inspired by a vision of social justice, quickly learned the limits of their own power (Rosen, 2000). When the Democratic Party nominated presidential candidates without primary input from constituents, and thus violated the expectations of thousands of newly enrolled African American voters in Mississippi, droves of young people took to the streets in protest. The Democratic Party later changed its policies and yet made little room for women. Simultaneously Students for a Democratic Society (SDS), whose demand for "participatory democracy" drew young people into movements for social justice, continued to assign women to lesser tasks.

Women resisted, without significant effect. Presidential executive orders that mandated fair employment practices for federal workers and stricter occupational health and safety laws often excluded women. Administrators of the Equal Employment Opportunity Commission, created by Title VII of the Civil Rights Act of 1964, remained unable or unwilling to administer the act with respect to women. They simply did not see discrimination against women (Kessler-Harris 2001). In this context, women turned increasingly to the fight for inclusion: members of NOW pressured the EEOC to respond to the interests of women; the Women's Equity Action League (WEAL) filed lawsuits seeking to redress discrimination against professional women; unionized women took the lead in insisting that job-training programs include women; and affirmative action programs came slowly to include goals for females well as for African Americans.

However, the struggles and successes of some groups, as NOW and the NWRO discovered, increased fragmentation among women as well as between women and men. As the decade progressed, male and female African Americans and Black and white women increasingly confronted skilled white male workers who feared incursion on their jobs. A more or less peaceful civil rights movement morphed into urban disorder when it proved unable to satisfy the needs of the urban poor or the demands for Black Power (Rodgers 2011, 77–144). By the early 1970s, the emerging women's movement faced the tensions of an austerity politics that promoted racial antagonism, class division, and normative heterosexuality. In this context, a robust commitment to collective solutions through government action tottered. A fragile belief in social responsibility and an expanded democracy diminished. Individuals and their representatives claimed special treatment in recognition of their identification as members of particular groups. The emergence of what came to be called "identity politics" pitted groups against one another, producing a decline in public commitment to social justice, shared responsibility, and equality that had inspired pledges to restrain capitalism. To some, the value of an expanded democracy no longer seemed self-evident. Had democracy gone too far?

Women were not exempt from these tensions; by the mid-seventies, those who sought freedom to function in a male-dominated society found their interests diverging from those who continued to focus on social justice and wider social change. Their differences might well have been left to play themselves out, had it not been for an economic crisis that weighted the scales with a rising chant to cast off the fetters of government in favor of market freedom. The crisis came in many shapes, but at its core was a decline in economic productivity that shrank the capacity of government and corporations to distribute an ever-enlarging pie of profits (Thurow 1970). Seeking greater profits, corporations walked away from the social compromise of the postwar years, abandoning their commitments to labor- and factory-based communities. They could do this because new technologies released them from the fixed machine costs they had earlier required and reliance on a stable cohort of experienced workers. We have seen the results in globalization, unregulated capital flows, and labor migration. At home, corporations sought cheaper labor wherever they could find it; experimented with temporary, contingent, and part-time labor to reduce the costs of benefits; undermined trade unions wherever they could; and fought against the labor regulations and capital constraints they had earlier accepted. The crisis signaled the turn of the economy to "post industrialism" (Borstelmann 2012; Schulman 2002; Stein 2011). It created a labor market more amenable to women at the top, but it also produced huge numbers of poorly remunerated jobs into which women were disproportionately channeled. As Ansell and Gingrich (Chapter 3, this volume) demonstrate, disgruntled workers turned to political solutions.

The economic demands of the 1970s joined a revived call for individual freedom that replaced the postwar mantra of social justice. Rooted in nineteenth-century notions of the sanctity of property, the new mantra focused on protecting the liberty of individuals from the predations of government through the mechanism of the free market. Antagonism to big government had been around since at least the 1940s, put forward by the Austrian economists Friedrich Hayek and Ludwig Von Mises and debated by a slowly growing cohort of economists connected with the Mont Pelerin Society. These voices grew louder as discontent with the perceived economic failures of the seventies rose. Apostles, who included political scientist James Buchanan and economist Milton Friedman, drew on the economic uncertainties to enhance fears of big government and to denigrate governmental intervention or regulation of any kind (Burgin 2015; Jones 2014). Social services and social spending, they argued, undermined the free market. To preserve that market, they would need to defuse public faith in such government-provided services as schools, the military, and welfare for the poor. They would, in short, need to delegitimize democratic voice.

Nancy McLean and others have documented the skepticism of members of this group toward democratic practice and their fears that too much democracy would undermine the free flow of money. Economist Milton Friedman and political scientist James Buchanan argued that democracy was, after all, the enemy of the market, and that restricting democratic access would pave the way to market freedom. In the sixties and seventies, their ideas spread through an expanding network of "public choice" theorists supported by the wealth of committed individuals (MacLean 2017; Mayer 2016). In the seventies, along with the transforming economy, wealth inequality dramatically expanded, and a small but influential number of conservative thinkers found their opportunity to restore the full play of capital in an unregulated marketplace. Newly active conservative social scientists insisted that less reliance on "big government" and greater faith in the market would ultimately increase the freedom of all. Liberty justified the growing influence of money in the political process (Hacker and Pierson 2011; Rodrik 2012). The accompanying ideological changes (generally identified as neoliberalism) increased skepticism among those unable to keep up with the changes and exacerbated competition among working people, further fragmenting and reducing their political influence.

As they emerged in the 1970s and took practical form in the 1980s, market-driven ideas of individual freedom proved to be insidious.

Neoliberalism promoted a particularly aggressive or raw form of capitalism rooted in the assumption that the market was the best (perhaps the only) determinant of freedom. Insisting that markets provided the most accurate form of information and therefore the most efficient path to profits, neoliberals attempted to destroy the welfare state whose minimum wages, unemployment benefits, and tax subsidies for the poor interfered with market operations. Faith in market solutions and mistrust of big government discouraged planning and encouraged a reduction in public services; a shedding of publicly owned assets; and a deregulation of major industries, including airlines, banking, and financial services. It blocked investment in such public goods as schools, hospitals, and housing; discouraged spending for legal services for the poor; and reduced spending for public transportation. More circuitously, but no less decisively, it blocked the achievement of a universal health insurance program. Precipitous declines in public investment in such amenities as parks, beaches, and museums communicated the message that only private accumulation of wealth could offer a good life. Disdaining public responsibility for such social ills as poverty, unemployment, underpaid jobs, and lack of housing and health care, neoliberals argued that every individual needed to exercise personal responsibility. Under these circumstances, appeals to social investment and the social good fell under the churning wheels of privatization.

The new world view touched everyone, but its particular effect on women provides a bellwether for the resulting dissolution of social solidarity that had fueled the expansion of democracy in earlier years. Grasping the mantra of personal responsibility as an invitation to enter the meritocracy, a large and growing segment of the women's movement advocated strategies that would bring women's opportunities in line with those of men. Freedom replaced community as a primary value; equality replaced fairness as a basic goal. Growing divisions among women appeared in at least four ways.

First, mainstream feminists, organized in a range of advocacy groups took advantage of the moment to demand that women, in the words of the Fourteenth Amendment, be accorded "equal treatment under the law." The group of women who separated from NOW in 1969 to form the Women's Equity Action League (WEAL) turned into effective champions for advancing women's careers. WEAL lobbied for Title IX of the Higher Education Act of 1972, which banned sex discrimination in schools and colleges. It then went on to press elite educational and professional training institutions to open their doors to women – a move that generally benefited the privileged. And WEAL soon turned its attention to legal action, becoming a major advocate of the 1972 Equal Employment Opportunity Act, which granted enforcement power to the EEOC. Effective affirmative action for women followed, along with new jobs in technology, finance, and the service industries (Kessler-Harris 2003, 325–336; Turk 2016, 72–101; Wandersee 1988, 118–120). Together, advocates for wage-earning women and for political rights for women campaigned for an Equal Rights Amendment that passed Congress in 1973. Fiercely opposed by women who feared losing the benefits of their dependent positions within families, that amendment failed ratification before the extended 1982 deadline.

A shift in occupational structures and in educational opportunities created new paths to economic success for more privileged women and constituted a second source of division. The economic crisis of the 1970s paved the way. Rising unemployment and high rates of inflation encouraged women in formerly male-breadwinning families to earn wages outside the home. Declines in traditional, mostly male manufacturing jobs accompanied openings in new fields. Mid-level managerial jobs and professional opportunities opened to women just as women took advantage of newly available opportunities in professional and graduate schools. The two-income family slowly became the norm, creating tensions in the meaning of masculinity and the ideal of feminine subordination. Together these encouraged the creation of diverse family forms that included same-sex partnerships. As increasing numbers of women, including the mothers of small children, entered wage work, the idea that women might be economically independent altered expectations of families as economic units and promoted notions of partnerships within marriage.

WEAL, NOW, and other feminist organizations also campaigned for changes in divorce laws that would give women a greater share of accumulated marital property in most states. They insisted on access to credit for women as individuals, rather than as family members and promoted legislation that would give women access to mortgages based on their own earnings and financial records. As well, feminists fostered a reassessment of insurance strategies that disadvantaged women considered greater economic risks than men (Horan 2018; Kahn 2015; Schwartz 2018).

Third, a world view rooted in personal responsibility captured the public agenda in ways that divided women along class lines, fostering savage attacks on the well-being of ordinary folk, and particularly on African Americans. As doors began to open for more educated women in the 1970s, Americans lost interest in supporting the poor. The historian

Edward Berkowitz dates 1973 as the moment when New Deal welfare priorities gave way. Attention to the common good – the source of democratic impetus in the 1960s – fell by the wayside after that (Berkowitz 1973, 227). The change demeaned and then destroyed welfare programs for the poor and created new work requirements in return for subsidies of all kinds, including food and, most recently, medical care for children. While middle-income, generally white women benefited from the decade's greater access to opportunity, poor, often Black women found themselves desperately trying to fit wage work into family responsibilities. Pushed by congressional legislation into required wage work, the majority found themselves in low-paid, contingent, and temporary jobs that carried no pensions and no paid personal or vacation days and yet placed them beyond the reach of subsidized health services. Inadequate and means-tested childcare awaited children whose parents qualified. Shifting ideas about what was "fair" fueled the push for lesser provision for the poor.

The shift from an ideology of social justice cut the ground from under those who still valued the common welfare and the institutions that protected it. Growing mistrust of government replaced the old conviction that government might intervene to ameliorate the damage of capitalism. As Kris-Stella Trump (Chapter 4, this volume) notes, changing ideas about fairness could and did justify new government policies. An increasingly hostile public opinion blamed government-supported welfare programs for encouraging "laziness" among poor women. In its wake, families measured satisfaction by increased consumption rather than by kin and community relationships; workers buried the desire for job satisfaction in the search for higher wages. The Personal Responsibility Act of 1996 captured the consequences. It removed the federal government from efforts to ameliorate the lot of the poor through public welfare by distributing limited funds to state bodies that could use them for public purposes, or not.

These changes exacerbated the gap in differential services to rich and poor, producing a climate of resentment and fear among those "left behind." Ever-present fury and rage against the ethnic, racial, gender, and religious groups held responsible for one's own declining circumstances encouraged deep divisions that sometimes translated into a politics of incarceration that simply removed those who chose not to play the game from public view, and others elevated to power those who fed into the discomfort. Women, earlier among the chief architects of the American welfare state, drifted into the new pattern. In a world of personal responsibility, individuals, women among them, measured their interests against those of others, their alliances rotating around ethnic, religious, and racial identity rather than around class interest. As Black women separated from white, as women in the LGBTQ movement fought for access, as the wealthy employed the poor to care for children, as mothers asked for paid leaves from work that non-mothers would have to do, women no longer identified as a powerful collective. They became another assortment of special interests in a world where every identity group struggled to make its case.

Fourth and finally, a beleaguered labor movement faced rising demands of women for access to leadership, disrupting strategies that might have unified men and women across gender lines. In the neoliberal view, the most efficient and profitable production would come in a world where capital could search unhindered for the lowest wages. Achieving this end would require dismantling obstacles to the free movement of labor – chief among them organized labor. Yet neoliberal theories about the need for a more mobile, and more global, workforce happily coincided with corporate efforts to reduce the influence of labor unions (historically the loudest voice for regulation), or even to eliminate them. Unsurprisingly, the 1970s witnessed a variety of constraints on unions including government intervention in long strikes deemed against the national interest, restrictions on political spending, denial of collective bargaining rights to public unions, and the creation of a hostile National Labor Relations Board (Turk 2018, 93; Windham 2017).

As the countervailing power of labor diminished, corporations increasingly resisted sharing profits with labor, leaving unions with internal struggles around whether to protect the victories and save the jobs of the already unionized or to serve the unorganized. These struggles further undermined notions of social solidarity. Corporations dramatically exacerbated divisions as they turned increasingly to contingent, temporary, and precarious workforces or converted employees to "independent contractors." All these workers lacked such previously negotiated union benefits as paid vacations, sick days, adequate unemployment insurance, and old age pensions. In practice neoliberalism exacerbated the difficulties faced by workers, exacerbating wage volatility for both men and women, and destabilizing income for Black and white workers (Thelen and Widemann, Chapter 13, this volume). Workers, who had previously shared in capital's profits, found themselves entirely self-dependent. They faced barriers to new organizing efforts, destructive legislative changes to workplace safety laws, and corporate abandonment of whole communities without retraining, recompense, or responsibility.

Hostile strategies against labor unions, as historian Lane Windham tells us, occurred at a moment when women were actively pushing for union leadership and when female union membership climbed to new heights as a result of the efforts of workers in the public sector to organize (Windham, 2017). Unions themselves faced a divided membership. Upward of two-thirds of the new jobs went to women who, though they constituted the vanguard of workers in poorly paid and economically insecure jobs, seemed to be benefiting from male job loss. Traditional trade unions that had eagerly organized low-paid public sector employees seemed at a loss when faced with the new workforce. After all, they were already under pressure to meet training and hiring targets and to follow new rules about affirmative action. Some of the largest unions resisted demands to modify their timeworn practices of giving seniority and the best jobs to the longest-serving members. Women who demanded democratic inclusion often frightened traditional trade unionists who resisted representing marginal workers like those in domestic service.

In the mid- and late seventies, the idea that women shared common interests across class and racial lines all but vanished. Class and race divisions undermined solidaristic goals and diverted the women's movement from reliable support for social justice, and for campaigns for the common good, into a fragmented set of groups, each intent on achieving its own ends. Division took many forms. Advocates of reproductive freedom such as New York's RedStockings promoted reproductive choice among women and won abortion rights in New York and other states. At the same time, African American women believed abortion to be less an issue in their communities than the persistent use of sterilization to prevent Black women from bearing children. Women-identified-women challenged notions of common interest in sexuality, reproduction, and mothering. Some trade union women created a coalition to train female union leaders who might challenge sex-based apprenticeship, promotion, and discharge policies; other women shared negative views of trade unions as unredeemable bastions of white male privilege. Some feminists climbed academic and corporate ladders; others accused them of taking advantage of "global nannies" who abandoned their own children to care for those of others. Evangelical Christian women protested what they saw as hostility to men and accused feminists of destroying family life and family values. By the middle of the seventies, references to a "woman's" movement had given way to "women's movements." The change reflected the numbers of women who had taken advantage of marketplace freedom to enhance their own economic and social positions, even as they abandoned the spirit of collective social responsibility that had nurtured the women's movement in the sixties.

Perhaps the Equal Rights Amendment that went to the states for ratification in 1973 most effectively signaled a turn toward individual rights. The amendment, resisted by many women's groups for half a century, proposed that "Equality of rights under the law shall not be denied or abridged by the United States or by any State on account of sex." The idea of such an amendment, first introduced in 1923, had long been opposed by a majority of wage-earning women, trade union members, and female policy makers on the ground that it would deprive the neediest women of the special protections offered to them by law. The amendment said nothing about the social support systems necessary to ensure that women, and especially mothers, could take advantage of the opportunities offered to them as discriminatory barriers fell. But after 1970, powerful advocates of New Deal–type social legislation (including influential female labor leaders, NOW officers, and the Women's Bureau of the Department of Labor) changed their minds.

Getting the ERA through Congress was a singular achievement, suggesting that by the early 1970s, large numbers of feminists had, to paraphrase Judith Stein, "found common ground with corporations in opposing government intervention" (Stein 2011, 8). Though the amendment fell short of ratification, the struggle around it revealed the degree to which marketplace assumptions about politics had taken hold. Opposition came primarily from women who continued to value primary roles in male-headed families that sought market-driven success; support came from women poised to enter the marketplace and eager to earn the meritocratic awards that they were sure would await them. Divisions rotated around just how far the family could accommodate women's changing roles. In this environment, advocates of social well-being, of racial and economic justice, of efforts to eliminate poverty became marginal (Levenstein 2009; Orleck 2005; Schlafly et al. 2016).

Faced with a steep rise in inequality that has left many families in poverty while others benefited from enormous wealth, individual rights have lost some of their appeal. We see signs of a returning commitment to something that might be called social democracy in demands to tax unearned wealth and a growing movement for free public university education. At the other end of the scale, new organizations draw attention to the plight of caring workers whose low pay and unregulated working conditions subsidize the lifestyles of the affluent. New analyses point to family tensions produced by women's workforce aspirations, and to changes in definitions of masculinity that most men can no longer measure in the dollars they produce for their families. Political tensions thrive as family tensions increase.

Women's increasingly significant roles in the wage-earning economy raise crucial questions. As every adult becomes a wage earner, families increasingly agree on socializing the costs of child and elder care. Pressure to provide paid maternity and parental leaves rises. For the first time in a century, the idea of universal health care has achieved substantial political support. In the 1970s, only female activists called for supportive family policies. In 2019, political candidates of many stripes called for higher minimum wages, advance schedules for on-call workers, benefits for part-time workers, and paid family leaves. The search for answers has led to the social democratic regimes of Scandinavia that provide evidence of greater well-being. The robust social insurance programs in these countries offer answers that some in the United States label "socialist." The idea of the collective good now challenges the individualist ethos of a free market economy.

The economic crisis of 2008 revealed that the free market left on its own produced instability both in the financial sphere and in the social order. Declining economic security for many and the loss of homes produced a rising skepticism about the capacity of the free market to meet popular needs. The "Occupy" movement, the "Fight for Fifteen," "Black Lives Matter," "Justice for Janitors," demonstrations for environmental justice and climate change all indicate renewed interest in collective action to challenge corporate values and produce social change. The emergence of alternatives to traditional labor unions (known as "alt-labor") to better protect workers' rights as the workforce changes its shape suggests enthusiasm for collective action at family, community, and workplace levels. Such slogans as "Medicare for all" and campaigns for free education through college have caught the public imagination. After years of accepting a culture of sexism in the workplace, women have turned sexual harassment into a public matter. A #MeToo movement registered the dimensions of an endemic problem that crossed lines of class and race as well as gender.

The women's march that followed Donald Trump's inauguration and the several that succeeded it have demonstrated a rarely seen solidarity, pulling together issues of racism, inequality, sexual preference, unjust incarceration, reproduction, and migration under the leadership of a diverse group of women. Espousing issues of solidarity, speakers called on those assembled to advocate together for government funding and support for housing, income, education, social services, and environmental protection against corporate abuse and climate change. At least partly inspired by social protests, the largest proportion of women ever to run for public office found seats in Congress and in governorships and local arenas in 2018. Markedly, spokespeople articulated an explicitly oppositional ideology – one that decried excessive corporate profits and market-driven values in favor of compassion and caring. Women have demanded, and achieved, a larger political voice – one that once again speaks the values of a democratic socialism. Following their ascent, watching how they come together around issues of social caring might well provide clues to the emergence of a more egalitarian and more democratic society.

WORKS CITED

Appleby, Joyce. 2010. *Relentless Revolution: A History of Capitalism*. W.W. Norton.

Berkowitz, Edward D. 1973. *Something Happened: A Political and Cultural Overview of the Seventies*. Columbia University Press.

Beveridge, William Henry. 2015. *Full Employment in a Free Society (Works of William H Beveridge: A Report)*. Routledge.

Bloom, Alexander and Wini Breines, eds. 2000. *"Takin' It to the Streets:" A Sixties Reader*. Oxford University Press.

Borstelmann, Thomas. 2012. *The 1970s: A New Global History from Civil Rights to Economic Inequality*. Princeton University Press, 2012.

Boskin, Joseph and Robert A. Rosenstone. 1972. *Seasons of Rebellion: Protest and Radicalism in Recent America*. Holt, Rinehart and Winston.

Brown, Wendy. 2015. *Undoing the Demos: Neoliberalism's Stealth Revolution*. Zone Books.

Burgin, Angus. 2015. *The Great Persuasion: Reinventing Free Markets Since the Depression*. Harvard University Press.

Danziger-Halperin, Anna. 2020. "An Unrequited Labor of Love: Child Care and Feminism." *SIGNS: Journal of Women in Culture and Society*, 45 (4) 1011–1034.

de Schweinitz, Karl. 1972. *England's Road to Social Security: From the Statute of Laborers in 1349 to the Beveridge Report of 1949*. Barnes and Co.

Dilliard, Irving, ed. 1941. *Mr. Justice Brandeis, Great American*. Modern View Press.

DuPlessis, Rachel Blau and Ann Snitow, eds. 1998. *The Feminist Memoir Project: Voices of Women's Liberation*. Three Rivers Press.

Echols, Alice. 1989. *Daring to Be Bad: Radical Feminism in America, 1967–75*. University of Minnesota Press.

Evans, Sara. 1979. *Personal Politics; The Roots of Women's Liberation in the Civil Rights Movement and the New Left*. Knopf.
Friedan, Betty. 1963. *The Feminine Mystique*. W. W. Norton.
Friedman, Milton and Rose Friedman. 1980. *Free to Choose: A Personal Statement*. Houghton Mifflin.
Galbraith, John Kenneth. 1956. *American Capitalism: The Concept of Countervailing Power*. Houghton Mifflin.
  1963. *The Affluent Society*. Signet.
Green, James. 1980. *The World of the Worker: Labor in Twentieth Century America*. Hill and Wang.
Hacker, Jacob S. and Paul Pierson. 2011. *Winner-Take-All Politics: How Washington Made the Rich Richer – And Turned Its Back on the Middle Class*. Simon and Schuster.
Harrison, Cynthia. 1988. *On Account of Sex: The Politics of Women's Issues, 1945–1968*. University of California Press.
Horan, Caley. 2018. "Reopening a Closed Case: The Insurance Industry and the ERA," unpublished paper delivered at the American Society for Legal History, Houston, TX, November.
Isserman, Maurice and Michael Kazin. 2004. *America Divided: The Civil War of the 1960s*. Oxford.
Jones, Daniel Stedman. 2014. *Masters of the Universe, Hayek, Friedman and the Birth of Neo-Liberal Politics*. Princeton University Press.
Kahn, Suzanne. 2015. "Divorce and the Politics of the American Social Welfare Regime, 1969–2000," Unpublished dissertation, Columbia University.
Kessler-Harris, Alice. 2001. *In Pursuit of Equity: Women, Men and the Quest for Economic Citizenship in Twentieth Century America*. Bloomsbury.
  2003 [1982]. *Out to Work: A History of Wage Earning Women in the United States*. Oxford University Press.
  2012. "Capitalism, Democracy, and the Emancipation of Belief," *Journal of American History*, 99 (Winter), 725–740.
Kornbluh, Felicia. 2007. *The Battle for Welfare Rights: Politics and Poverty in Modern America*. University of Pennsylvania Press.
Lee, Chang Kai. 2005. *For Freedom's Sake: A Life of Fannie Lou Hamer*. University of Illinois Press.
Levenstein, Lisa. 2009. *A Movement without Marches: African American Women and the Politics of Poverty*. University of North Carolina Press.
Lichtenstein, Nelson. 2006. *American Capitalism: Social Thought and Political Economy in the Twentieth Century*. University of Pennsylvania Press.
MacLean, Nancy. 2017. *Democracy in Chains: The Deep History of the Radical Right's Stealth Plan for America*. Viking.
Marshall, T. H. 1991. *Citizenship and Social Class*. Pluto Press.
Mayer, Jane. 2016. *Dark Money: The Hidden History of the Billionaires Behind the Rise of the Radical Right*. Random House.
Mead, Margaret and Frances Bagley Kaplan, eds. 1965. *American Women: The Report of the President's Commission on the Status of Women and Other Publications of the Commission*. Charles Scribner's Sons.

Meyerowitz, Joanne. 1994. *Not June Cleaver: Women and Gender in Post-war America*. Temple University Press.

Michel, Sonya. 1999. *Children's Interests, Mother's Rights*. Yale University Press.

Orleck, Annelise. 2005. *Storming Caesar's Palace: How Black Mothers Fought Their Own War on Poverty*. Beacon Press.

Paulson, Ross Evans. 1997. *Liberty, Equality, and Justice: Civil Rights, Women's Rights and the Regulation of Business, 1865–1932*. Duke University Press.

Piketty, Thomas. 2017. *Capital in the Twenty-First Century*. Harvard.

Ransby, Barbara. 2005. *Ella Baker and the Black Civil Rights Movement: A Radical Democratic Vision*. University of North Carolina Press.

Rodgers, Daniel T. 2011. *Age of Fracture*. Belknap Press of Harvard University Press, 77–144.

Rodrik, Dani. 2012. *The Globalization Paradox: Democracy and the Future of the World Economy*. W. W. Norton.

Rosen, Ruth. 2000. *The World Split Open: How the Modern Women's Movement Changed America*. Viking.

Rottenberg, Catherine. 2018. *The Rise of NeoLiberal Feminism*. Oxford University Press.

Schlafly, Phyllis, Ed Martin and Brett M. Decker. 2016. *The Conservative Case for Trump*. Regnery.

Schulman, Bruce J. 2002. *The Seventies: The Great Shift in American Culture, Society and Politics*. DaCapo Press.

Schwartz, Allison. 2018. "The Persistent Gap Between Law's Promise and Performance: Fair Housing Laws and Women's Enduring Income Inequality." Unpublished paper delivered at the American Society for Legal History, Houston, TX, November.

Stein, Judith. 2011. *Pivotal Decade: How the U.S. Traded Factories for finance in the Seventies*. Yale University Press.

Swinth, Kirsten. 2018. *Feminism's Forgotten Fight: The Unfinished Struggle for Work and Family*. Harvard University Press.

Thurow, Lester C. 1970. *The Zero-Sum Society: Distribution and the Possibilities for Economic Change*. Basic Books.

Turk, Katherine. 2016. *Equality on Trial: Gender and Rights in the Modern American Workplace*. University of Pennsylvania Press.

  2018. "Labor Feminism Meets Institutional Sexism," *Labor: Studies in Working Class History* 15 (September), 72–101.

Villa, Dana. 2008. "Public Freedom Today" in *Public Freedom*. Princeton University Press, 1–26.

Wandersee, Winifred. 1988. *On the Move: American Women in the 1970s*. Twayne Publishers.

Windham, Lane. 2017. *Knocking on Labor's Door: Union Organizing in the 1970s and the Roots of a New Economic Divide*. University of North Carolina Press.

PART II

PLACES

6

Keeping Your Enemies Close

Electoral Rules and Partisan Polarization

Jonathan Rodden

The contemporary United States is often described as a society divided along a single, overarching left-right political dimension, with Democrats on one side and Republicans on the other. The parties are described as two hostile tribes (Chua 2018), where group membership now goes well beyond shared party loyalty and political preferences and has become a form of social identity (Mason 2014), in which members of the outgroup are viewed with disdain and enmity (Iyengar et al. 2019).

Yet the emerging narrative about American partisan tribalism is riddled with puzzles. First, Americans don't seem to have become more attached to their "in-groups," but rather, only more hostile toward their partisan out-groups (Abramowitz and Webster 2018). Moreover, an increasing share of Americans do not identify with either party (Pew Research Center 2016). And there is little evidence that Americans' attitudes or policy preferences on specific issues have actually diverged over time (Fiorina 2017). Rather, it appears that individuals who describe themselves as conservatives have sorted themselves into the Republican Party, and those who describe themselves as liberals have found their way to the Democrats – a phenomenon known as partisan sorting (Levendusky 2009). It is not clear why this type of sorting should lead people to view members of the out-party as those who would make a bad neighbor or unsuitable spouse for their child.

Furthermore, while voting behavior in Congress, as measured by roll-call voting scores, has become increasingly polarized (McCarty, Poole, and Rosenthal 2008), we do not see a similar bimodal distribution, either in presidential voting or in estimates of ideology, across congressional districts (Rodden 2015). Moreover, one cannot claim that the parties have become ideologically more cohesive or homogeneous over time. On the contrary, at the same moment that tribal hostilities across parties appear to be growing, the tribes seem to be in a competition with one another to see which can be the first to collapse from internal division. Tea Partiers and now Trumpist populists have gone into battle with establishment Republicans, and Democratic Socialists now hope to upend mainstream Democrats.

American tribalism becomes even more puzzling when we place it in comparative perspective and consider time-honored theories of party competition. The United States has the purest two-party system of any industrialized country. Classic theories suggest that two-party systems encourage the parties to adopt converging platforms. According to Anthony Downs:

> [T]he number of parties in existence molds the political views of rising generations, thereby influencing their positions on the [left-right] scale. In a [majoritarian system], since a two-party system is encouraged and the two parties usually converge, voters' tastes may become relatively homogenous in the long run; whereas the opposite effect may occur in a proportional representation structure. (1957, 124–125)

Indeed, building on variants of this logic, a large empirical literature purports to show that the American political parties are ideologically more similar to one another than are parties in most other countries, and that in majoritarian democracies with winner-take-all districts and relatively few parties, the parties are closer together, on average, than in countries with multiparty systems.

Yet this observation, and the conceptualization of "polarization" on which it is based, seems far removed from the kind of social and affective polarization now being described in the United States, the United Kingdom, and Canada. And it is difficult to find media or academic portrayals of Germany, with its multiparty system, as riven with ideological hatred between tribal adherents of the CDU and SPD, or in Sweden between the Conservative Alliance parties and the red-green coalition. In Germany and Austria, the mainstream parties of left and right enter into grand coalitions that would be unthinkable in the United Kingdom or the United States. In the Netherlands, rather than being consumed with mutual hostility, most of the parties are quite open to the prospect of forming coalitions, and governing coalitions often contain odd ideological bedfellows.

In this chapter, I explore the idea that these puzzles can be solved by letting go of the understanding of polarization as the movement of parties and their voters away from one another on a single, coherent all-encompassing left-right ideological dimension. We must understand that in advanced industrial democracies of the twenty-first century, the idea of unidimensional political competition is a fiction that is sometimes analytically useful, and sometimes not. In the study of ideological, social, and affective polarization, it may have led us astray. It seems axiomatic that polarization involves a single, over-arching dimension of conflict, and that multiple cross-cutting dimensions should help reduce polarization. This chapter argues the opposite. It explores the notion that the ideological distance between the parties' platforms, and between their voters, is better understood as the distance between the parties in a multidimensional Cartesian coordinate system.

To fix ideas, I focus on two dimensions: economic and social. However, the basic logic applies if we add additional dimensions, for example, related to environmental protection, immigration, or free trade. Over the course of the past century, with the rise of demands for racial equality, the women's movement, concerns about environmental degradation, and more recently fears about immigration and globalization, activists with strong preferences for changes from the status quo have pressured parties to adopt new positions, and the platforms of existing parties have diverged in areas where they were previously indistinguishable. This chapter explores what happens when voters' preferences are multidimensional – that is, when preferences on the dominant dimension of conflict – say economic redistribution – are not highly correlated with those on the newly politicized dimension – say social issues.

I argue that if preferences are sufficiently multidimensional in a two-party system, when the parties take divergent positions on a new issue dimension, even if voters' preferences don't change at all, the average voter can end up a bit further from the most proximate of the two parties, and substantially further from their non-proximate party in the two-dimensional space. Thus, as parties take divergent platforms on new issues, but the number of parties is constrained to two, voters perceive both parties as moving further away in the two-dimensional space.

However, this phenomenon is far more muted in a multiparty system, where parties are likely to spread themselves out in the multidimensional issues space. Instead of viewing a party system like that of Sweden or the Netherlands as a set of points on a single line from communist to far right, I view the parties as taking different mixtures of positions in the multidimensional space. If we imagine two societies with identical multidimensional preferences – one with a two-party system and the other with a multiparty system, voters in the multiparty democracy will be closer to their most proximate party, but also to the mean of the non-proximate parties. In other words, they perceive the partisan "out-groups" to be closer than voters in two-party democracies.

This perspective helps shed light on several of the puzzles of polarization described earlier. It helps explain why American voters have come to view partisan out-groups as extremely distant over the course of recent decades, while growing no closer to their in-group, even though on many individual political issues, Americans have not grown further apart. It may also explain why an increasing number of voters feel close to neither party. Instead of interpreting the catchall left-right scale used in survey research as a voter's placement of themselves and the parties on a single dimension of conflict, we can fruitfully understand it as an attempt by the survey respondent at a dimension-reduction exercise – an effort to convert locations in a multidimensional Cartesian coordinate system into a single vector. Consistent with this perspective, as the parties' platforms and reputations have diverged on new issues, the average American voter has come to see their most proximate party as moving slightly further away, while seeing the least proximate party as having moved much further away. This phenomenon may be at the heart of the rise of American-style affective and social polarization.

Next, I examine cross-national data. In contrast with the traditional unidimensional notion that two-party democracies tend to converge to the center and multiparty democracies tend toward ideological extremes, I show that in contrast with other countries, Americans perceive their parties as extremely far apart. Furthermore, it appears that more generally, countries with highly proportional electoral systems and multiparty systems perceive their parties to be closer together than do voters in majoritarian democracies with fewer parties.

This first step in this argument is to explore the changing issue politics of industrialized countries since World War II, and the extent to which the evolution of party platforms is shaped by political geography and electoral institutions. Next, I take a closer look at what this means for voters' perceptions of the parties' platforms, first in two-party systems and then in multiparty systems. Finally, I examine the evolution of those perceptions in the United States, and then in a larger sample of industrialized countries.

GEOGRAPHY, ISSUE EVOLUTION, AND ELECTORAL RULES

This chapter argues that most of what Americans refer to as partisan polarization is the result of two parties adopting divergent platforms on new dimensions of political conflict. This argument has much in common with Layman and Carsey's (2002) notion of "conflict extension," the portrayal of multidimensional politics in the United States by Miller and Schofield (2003, 2008), and the multidimensional approach to issue politics taken by Ahler and Broockman (2018). These scholars recognize that many voters maintain heterogeneous mixtures of preferences that do not fit neatly into the bundles offered by the two parties. Influential elites and activists, however, push the parties to adopt divergent positions on new issues. Opponents of abortion, for example, push the Republicans to take antiabortion positions, and supporters of abortion rights push the Democrats to adopt pro-choice positions. Immigration opponents enlist the Republicans to their cause, and advocates enlist the Democrats.

But why do the parties in majoritarian democracies end up with the specific bundles of positions that have emerged in the early twenty-first century? The bundles of platforms offered by the mainstream parties of left and right in the United Kingdom, Canada, Australia, and the United States are quite similar. This is remarkable, since there is no good philosophical or intellectual reason why gay rights and high taxes, for instance, "go together." Indeed, they are not bundled together in most European multiparty systems, each of which features one or more parties, often with roots in classical liberalism, that promote freedom in both the economic and social realms. And as demonstrated by the welfare chauvinism of European radical right parties, there is no particular reason to bundle anti–welfare state and anti-immigration positions. And it is even less clear why defense of the welfare state and global free trade should be bundled together by parties of the left.

Why exactly have elites pushed parties of the left in majoritarian democracies to advocate for redistribution and the welfare state, cosmopolitan social values, racial diversity, freer immigration, environmental protection, support for the knowledge economy, and global free trade? And why has the right come to support lower taxes, traditional social values, nativism, the natural resource industry, traditional manufacturing, and most recently protectionism? It is difficult to understand the evolution of these bundles in the twentieth century without understanding the political geography of industrialized societies (Rodden 2019).

The story starts with the mobilization of the urban industrial working class in the era of heavy industrialization in the late nineteenth and early twentieth centuries. Labor parties in Europe, the United Kingdom, and Australasia became advocates of urban workers around the turn of the twentieth century. The Democrats transformed themselves into such a party a few decades later under Franklin Roosevelt, as did the Cooperative Commonwealth Federation (CCF) and then the New Democratic Party (NDP) in Canada. By the 1950s, these parties of the left were predominantly urban parties.

Later in the twentieth century, as described by Dalton (1996) and Inglehart (1990), a host of new issues emerged. Above all, activists in the environmental and women's movements demanded changes to the status quo, and traditionalists pushed back. In the proportional democracies of Europe, new parties like the Greens emerged, and existing parties repositioned themselves in the multidimensional issue space. Preferences on these new issues were correlated with population density, with urban activists and voters taking more progressive positions, while exurban and rural activists and voters took more traditionalist positions. In majoritarian democracies, the parties of the left had already become dominant in urban districts during the era of heavy industry, and exurban and rural districts had become the core support bastions of the right. Thus, it was Labor and Democratic incumbents who were pressured by activists to promote progressive social and environmental positions, and incumbent legislators of the right who felt pressure to adopt traditionalist views.

The correlation between population density and "cosmopolitan" social views is quite pronounced in many societies. While the social upheavals that started in the 1960s led parties of the left and right to become diverse urban versus non-urban coalitions in majoritarian democracies, those same upheavals led to greater differentiation of the parties in the multidimensional issue space in the proportional electoral systems of Europe in the subsequent decades. For instance, Socialists and Social Democrats often maintained their emphasis on workers, while Greens and other parties courted urban youth and educated cosmopolitans. But in the majoritarian democracies, existing parties of the left took on both roles, slowly becoming parties not just of urban workers but also parties of urban cosmopolitans and environmentalists.

Race and the struggle for civil rights played an especially important role in this type of multidimensional politics in the United States. Initially, as the Democrats came to embrace an agenda that elevated the interests of urban workers during the New Deal, they also supported an agenda of racial oppression in the South. This slowly changed, however, via the geographic mechanism I have described. African American industrial workers became an important part of the Democrats' constituency in the urban congressional districts of the North, and they pressed Democratic congressional incumbents and challengers to adopt key early elements of the civil rights agenda, thus setting the seeds for a very slow transformation of the Democratic Party from a position of racial oppression – favored by its rural Southern base – to a racially progressive agenda favored by a segment of its burgeoning new Northern urban base (Schickler 2016).

In addition to race and the rise of social and environmental issues that Ronald Inglehart (1990) has referred to as "post-material," issue politics have also been affected by an important economic transformation documented in Boix (Chapter 9, this volume), among others: the rise of the globalized knowledge economy. While many urban centers have entered into a long decline during the era of globalization and deindustrialization, others have emerged as wealthy centers of knowledge-based industries. In addition to socially progressive attitudes, knowledge economy workers have developed sector-based interests in global free trade and relatively easy movement of people across borders. In Europe's multiparty systems, various parties of the left, right, and center have taken up the interests of highly educated urban knowledge economy employees. But in majoritarian democracies, as with cosmopolitan social issues, activists looking for political allies have turned to the parties that had already gained dominance in cities. Thus, parties of the left have become rather incongruous advocates for poor service workers, as well as for investments in universities and scientific research, immigration, and free trade.

Meanwhile, parties of the right – having built up a dominant position in exurbs and rural areas – have been mobilized as advocates for economic activities that take place outside city centers. These include not only agriculture and natural resource extraction but in recent decades, manufacturing. In several majoritarian countries, globalization skeptics in areas that are struggling to maintain a manufacturing base have turned to mainstream parties of the right. In the United States, the mainstream party of the right has turned to protectionism, and the Tories in the United Kingdom have embraced Brexit. In the United Kingdom and Australia, the urban Labor party advocates for the rights of immigrants, and the rural party feels pressure to adopt nativist positions due to electoral competition from smaller nativist parties, UKIP and One Nation. Due to a combination of (1) efforts to stave off losses to upstart far-right parties and (2) hostile take-overs due to primaries and other such mechanisms described by Salas, Rosenbluth, and Shapiro (Chapter 10, this volume), parties of the right in majoritarian democracies have begun to embrace much of the agenda of European far-right parties.

As a result of all this, the activation of new issue dimensions has had a pronounced geographic expression. In industrialized majoritarian democracies, including the United States, Britain, France, Australia, and Canada, there is a strong – and in some cases rapidly growing – correlation between population density and the vote shares of left parties (Rodden 2019). The key claim of this chapter is that these changes in issue politics are responsible for the rise of social polarization in the United States and other majoritarian countries, but even though many of the same issues have been politicized in proportional European democracies, the implications for social polarization are more subdued.

POLARIZATION AND MULTIDIMENSIONAL POLITICS

We are accustomed to thinking of social polarization as a unidimensional concept. Indeed, in much of the literature, and many of the chapters in this volume, the focus is on economic policy. It seems intuitive that a polarized society is one where preferences on a wide variety of issues are highly correlated, such that, for instance, those with socially liberal preferences also have economically liberal preferences. And we might suspect that, to the extent that these preferences overlap with party membership, race, and geography, this single overarching ideological dimension starts to become a salient social identity that evokes basic in-group/out-group dynamics that facilitate hostility. It is difficult, at first, to grasp the notion that social polarization might emerge not only in spite of but *because of* the fact that individuals' preferences in different issue areas are not highly correlated.

To see how this might be the case, let us examine Americans' attitudes on two dimensions of conflict: economic and moral. In joint work with Aina Gallego, using the American National Election Study, we have generated scales of economic and moral issue preferences. The items tap into the core substantive content of the economic and moral dimensions as defined in previous studies (Baldassarri and Goldberg 2014; Feldman and Johnston 2014; Treier and Hillygus 2009). The scales are normalized to have mean zero and a standard deviation of 1. Each panel in Figure 6.1 displays the moral scale on the horizontal axis and the economic scale on the vertical axis. As in the studies just cited, the scales are only weakly correlated (around .20). Around 58 percent of the population is not "cross-pressured": that is, they have preferences to the right or left of the median on both dimensions. The remaining 42 percent of the population has preferences either to the left of the economic median and to the right of the moral median, or to the right of the economic median but to the left of the moral median. In other words, public opinion can be characterized as multidimensional.

The idea behind Figure 6.1 is that each voter has a location in the two-dimensional Cartesian coordinate system created by these issue scales. The parties then offer platforms at specific locations. By all accounts, in the 1970s, the Democrats and Republicans had distinctive economic platforms, but their platforms on moral issues like abortion and gay rights were indistinguishable. In the 1976 presidential election between Gerald Ford and Jimmy Carter, for instance, it was unclear whether an antiabortion moral conservative should vote for the Republican or the Democratic candidate. This situation is captured by the hypothetical platforms displayed in the top panel of Figure 6.1 in red, where the parties' platforms are symmetrically arranged, one standard deviation away from the median voter on the economic dimension, but each party offers an identical platform at the position of the median voter on the moral dimension. We can then measure the distance between the parties – 2 units in the first example – as well as the distance between each individual and each of the two parties. The shading of the dots in the top panel of Figure 6.1 corresponds to the distance from each individual to the *least proximate* of the two parties.

Next, let us consider a situation in which the parties also develop divergent platforms on the moral values issue dimension. In the United States, for example, while maintaining divergent economic platforms, the parties began to also take clearly opposed positions in the 1980s on issues like gender, abortion, and the role of religion. To capture this type of platform shift, in the second panel of Figure 6.1, the parties' platforms are symmetrically arranged, one standard deviation from the position of the median voter, on *both* dimensions. With this change in platforms, the distance between the parties in the Cartesian plane increases from 2 to 2.8, even though the parties' platforms are unchanged on the economic dimension. Moreover, as indicated by the shading of the dots, the average voter is now further away from their least proximate party. In other words, the party system has become, in an important sense, more polarized.

Figure 6.2 provides kernel densities showing the distribution of individual distances from the non-proximate political party for each example. The solid line corresponds to the first example, where parties take

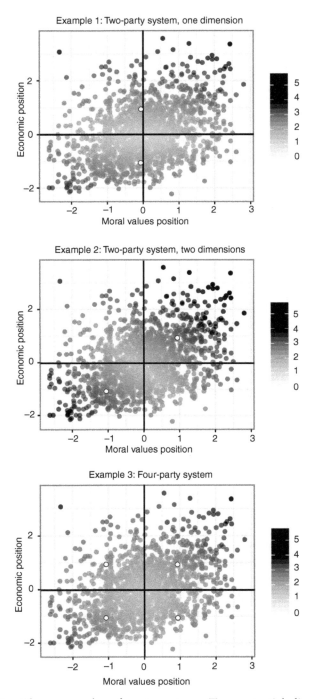

FIGURE 6.1 Three examples of party systems: Two potential dimensions of political conflict

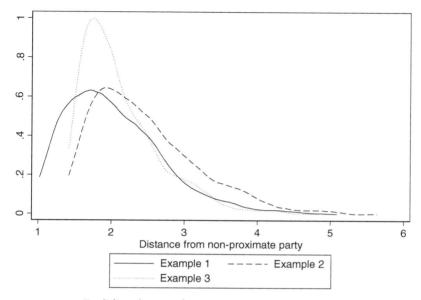

FIGURE 6.2 Euclidian distance from non-proximate parties, three examples

diverging platforms on only a single dimension of conflict, while the dashed line Four-corresponds to the second example, with platform divergence on both dimensions. After the platform shift, the vast majority of individuals are now further from the non-proximate party, and the average voter experiences an increase in ideological distance from the non-proximate party of around 0.41 units.

This is a very simple representation of the impact of multidimensional politics on political polarization in a two-party system. The story is quite different, however, if multiple political parties in a European-style system of proportional representation are able to occupy a wider diversity of coordinates in the two-dimensional space (see Laver and Schofield 1990). To capture this, the third example in Figure 6.1 is a four-party system, where parties are located symmetrically around the median in both directions. The first thing to notice about this arrangement is that voters are much closer to their most proximate party. The average distance to the most proximate party is 1.04 in the first example, and 1.08 in the second example, but 0.82 in the third example. This is a simple way to comprehend what is perhaps the most intuitive advantage of a multiparty system: voters can find a party that comes closer to their ideal point (see, for example, Lijphart 2012).

There is an additional advantage. In example 3, in terms of Euclidean proximity, the average voter is also closer to their second-ranked party than in either example 1 or example 2. Even the third-ranked party is closer to the average voter than the less proximate of the two parties in example 2. Clearly, averaging over the three non-proximate parties, voters are substantially closer to their partisan "enemies" in the four-party case. This is captured by the dotted kernel density in Figure 6.2, which displays the distribution of the average distance from the three non-proximate parties across individuals. By this measure, the multiparty system is less polarized than the two-party examples – even less so than the two-party case with only one dimension of political conflict (example 1).

These stylized examples provide a logic whereby voters in majoritarian systems with relatively few political parties might come to see the parties as increasingly polarized over time as parties take divergent platforms on new issues, even if the parties' platforms on the initial dimension of conflict and the voters' political views on both dimensions remain the same. And this logic also sheds light on the possible role of proportional representation as an antidote to polarization.

MULTIDIMENSIONAL POLITICS AND THE GROWTH OF POLARIZATION IN THE UNITED STATES

In empirical research on American and comparative polarization, survey researchers rely heavily on questions that ask respondents to place themselves, and the parties, on an ideological scale from far left to far right. Researchers typically interpret this scale as a straightforward assessment of positions on a single, all-encompassing left-right dimension of conflict. But in all likelihood, respondents are assessing the parties' platform and thinking of their own ideological placement as composed of a combination of issues like taxation, redistribution, race, cultural and social issues, environmental protection, and immigration policy. As a result, it might be more fruitful to interpret these scales as efforts by the survey respondent to collapse these multiple issue dimensions into a single vector. The perceived distance between party A and party B, or between one of the parties and the survey respondent, then, can be understood as the respondent's assessment of the Euclidean distance between the two parties in n-dimensional space.

With this understanding, as the parties' policy platforms, and perhaps more slowly their policy reputations, have grown apart since the 1970s on issues like race and religion, and as social polarization has risen, we should expect to see that the average voter perceives the ideologically *most proximate* party not as moving closer as ideological sorting and tribalism set in, but if anything, moving further away. Moreover, we should expect that respondents see the *least proximate* party as moving substantially further away.

Since 1972, the American National Election Study (ANES) has asked respondents to place both of the major parties and themselves on a 7-point scale. I calculate the absolute difference between each individual's self-placement and their assessment of the more proximate party, as well as the absolute difference between the self-placement and the assessment of the more distant party. I then take averages over all respondents for each presidential election year. In Figures 6.3 and 6.4, I plot both of these quantities over time.

It is clear that substantial partisan sorting took place over the period from 1972 to the 2016, whereby those who call themselves conservatives have become more likely to also call themselves Republicans and report voting for Republican candidates, while those who call themselves liberals

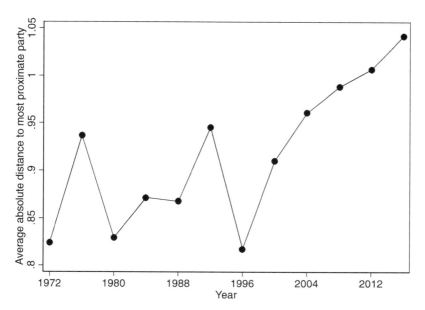

FIGURE 6.3 Average absolute ideological distance between respondent and the most proximate party, ANES, 1972–2016

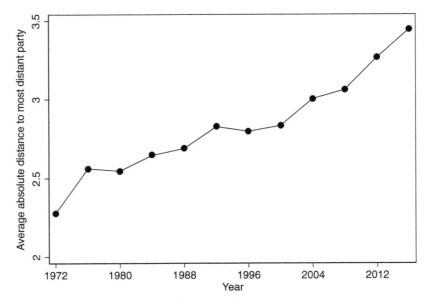

FIGURE 6.4 Average absolute ideological distance between respondent and the most distant party, ANES, 1972–2016

have become more likely to identify with and vote for Democrats (Fiorina 2017; Levendusky 2009). But Figure 6.3 reveals that during this period, voters have not come to see their most proximate party as ideologically closer today than they did in the 1970s. In fact, this distance has grown, especially since 1996, and is higher today (1.04) than in 1972 (0.82).

But as demonstrated in Figure 6.4, the most striking change has been in the perceived distance between American survey respondents and their non-proximate party. This distance has grown substantially over time. On the 7-point scale, the average ANES respondent saw their most distant party as 2.28 units away in 1972, while today, the distance has grown to 3.45.

In short, as parties have taken divergent platforms on a larger number of noneconomic issues, Americans have come to view their partisan out-group as ideologically very distant. When asked to place a party on a left-right scale, voters are likely thinking not only of the party's elites and its written platform but also its voters. It is not surprising that this growing perception of ideological distance might spill over into a broader social animosity. If one sees the other side as an advocate of baby killing or

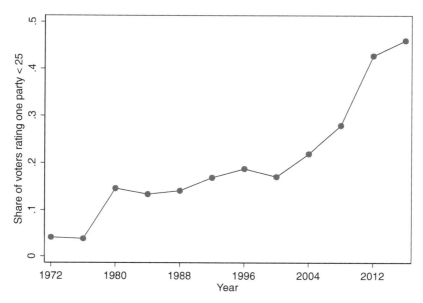

FIGURE 6.5 Share of the population with "quite cold or unfavorable feelings" about one or both parties, ANES, 1972–2016

placing children in cages, it is a short step to see them as potentially bad neighbors or unsuitable spouses for one's children.C While some of the more interesting constructs for measuring social polarization in recent work are not available over time, Figure 6.5 is based on so-called feeling thermometers in the ANES, where 100 is a "very warm or favorable feeling" toward the group, and 0 is "a very cold or unfavorable feeling." I simply generate a dummy that takes on the value 1 for all respondents who rate at least one of the parties less than 25 and calculate means for each year.

Figure 6.5 looks quite similar to Figure 6.4. Only around 5 percent of Americans had very cold feelings toward members of one of the parties in the 1970s. By 1996, it was around 19 percent, and today, 46 percent of the population feels this way.

Note that as Hacker and Pierson (Chapter 11, this volume) point out, there is a broad consensus among political scientists that American polarization since the early 1990s is asymmetric in the sense that Republican elites and elected officials have moved further to the right than Democrats have moved to the left. However, in terms of perceived ideological distance from and affective hostility toward the out-party, polarization appears to be somewhat more symmetric. Democrats and Republicans are rather similar in their growing sense of alienation from the out-party.

COMPARATIVE ANALYSIS

In short, Americans have come to see the parties as increasingly ideologically distant in recent decades, and this has been closely linked with an increasing hostility toward partisan out-groups. But this creates quite a puzzle for the dominant unidimensional model used by political scientists. Two-party systems, we are told, should always be more centrist than multiparty systems. The key insight of this chapter, however, is that a multidimensional starting point for thinking about party systems and ideological distance yields precisely the opposite intuition. As new dimensions of conflict are added over time in a system where the number of parties remains fixed at two, the Euclidean distance between the parties often increases, and for most voters, the Euclidean distance between themselves and the two parties also increases.

In a multiparty system, in contrast, parties should be able to occupy a larger part of the multidimensional issue space. As a result, the average Euclidian distance between the parties should be smaller, and voters should be closer to both their most proximate party and the average of the non-proximate parties. A party system like that in Sweden is best understood not as a series of points on a line offering a range of tax rates from 100 percent to zero but, rather, as a set of coordinates in multidimensional space. For instance, several parties on the Swedish right push for lower taxation and espouse free market principles, but the Center Party focuses on the needs of agricultural producers and has an environmentalist agenda. The Moderate Party favors gay marriage, European Union membership, and the maintenance of the welfare state. The Liberals have at times espoused more liberal immigration policies than the Social Democrats The Sweden Democrats, on the other hand, support greater investment in the welfare state, especially for the elderly, but restrictions on immigration.

Let us first proceed by quickly reviewing the expectations of the classic unidimensional perspective, and the empirical literature it has spawned, and then examine an empirical approach based on the notion that catchall party and self-placements in comparative surveys should be thought of not as generating a single policy line, but a vector created by coordinates in n-dimensional space.

Following from the insights of Anthony Downs (1957), the starting point for the political economy literature on electoral rules and polarization is summarized in Gary Cox's seminal paper: "The standard spatial model begins by assuming that electoral competition can fruitfully be modeled as taking place along a single left-right ideological dimension" (Cox 1990: 908). Cox treats parties as office-maximizers and demonstrates that equilibria in ordinary plurality systems tend toward a clustering of the parties in the middle of the ideological spectrum, in the same spirit as Hotelling (1929). The equilibria in proportional systems are such that "(1) each party has a fairly well-defined and narrow ideological appeal and (2) parties are dispersed fairly widely over the ideological spectrum" (p. 922). This leads to the hypothesis that declining district magnitude is associated with convergence of party platforms to the center. A series of formal models based on different assumptions and modelling strategies – all in the context of a unidimensional understanding of politics – yields broadly similar insights (Adams, Merrill, and Grofman 2005; Calvo and Hellwig 2011; Iaryczower and Mattozzi 2013; Matakos, Troumpounis, and Xefteris 2016). In these papers, smaller district magnitude and hence higher levels of electoral disproportionality place centripetal pressure on the largest parties. Proportional representation and larger numbers of parties create centrifugal incentives and result in non-centrist parties.

To assess the ideological spread of parties, scholars have used an index devised by Dalton (2008) that sums over deviations of each party j's ideological position, p_j from the party system average, $\bar{p}$, weighted by the party's vote share, V_j, as follows:

$$DI = \sqrt{\sum_j V_j \left(\frac{p_j - \bar{p}}{.5}\right)^2}$$

In order to estimate p_j, Dalton (2008) recommends using the average assessment of survey respondents in the Comparative Study of Electoral Systems, each of whom is asked to place each party in their country on an 11-point scale from left to right (0 to 10). Matakos et al. (2016) use data from the Comparative Manifesto Project (CMP), which relies on text analysis of party manifestos to make assessments about how the parties line up on a single, all-encompassing dimension of conflict.

The advantage of using the CMP data is that one can examine a panel of OECD countries covering a long period starting in 1959. Based on the data assembled by Matakos et al. (2016), Figure 6.6 provides a box plot

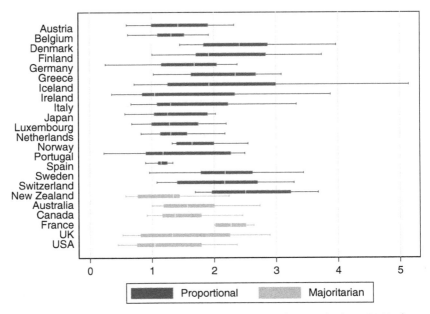

FIGURE 6.6 Partisan ideological spread, Dalton Index applied to CMP data, 1959–2007

by country of the Dalton Index using CMP data from 1959 to 2007, employing a blunt differentiation between majoritarian and proportional democracies.[1] On average, this measure of partisan spread is lower in majoritarian democracies. France, with its multi-round elections, and Australia, with its system of ranked-choice voting, look more similar to proportional democracies, but according to this approach, the United States, Canada, and the United Kingdom have been consistently among the least polarized democracies in the world, and they remain so today.

Note the separate observations in Figure 6.6 for New Zealand, which distinguish between the period before and after the transition to proportional representation in 1996. With this measurement approach, New Zealand's parties became much more spread out after adopting proportional representation. Matakos et al. (2016) focus on the relationship between electoral disproportionality and partisan spread (which they refer to as "polarization"), and it is robust whether one examines cross-section or

---

[1] Japan and Ireland are controversial cases, coded here as proportional.

time-series variation. There is also a relatively strong relationship between a larger number of effective political parties and this same measure of partisan spread. These same relationships can be discerned if one uses the Comparative Study of Electoral Systems to take a survey-based approach to measuring partisan spread rather than data on party manifestos. The lowest levels of estimated partisan spread appear to be in the majoritarian countries: the United States, Canada, Australia, and the United Kingdom are among the least centrifugal industrialized democracies by this measure, along with Ireland and Japan.[2]

Remarkably, whether one uses the manifesto- or survey-based approach with a unidimensional mind-set, one draws the conclusion that Sweden, with its multiparty system, has one of the most centrifugal party systems, and the United States, in spite all of the talk about polarization, has the most centripetal party system in the industrialized world.

On its own terms, this basic finding is quite intuitive if we imagine there is a single dimension of electoral conflict. Relative to majoritarian democracies with two or three internally heterogeneous parties, proportional representation can be understood as allowing extremists on the left and right to run under separate party labels. Thus, the extremes of the policy platforms offered by the parties are pulled outward. For instance, let us examine CSES data for Sweden and the United States. The first panel of Figure 6.7 provides kernel densities of voters' ideological assessments of the main Swedish parties in 2014, and the second panel does the same for the United States in 2012. The vertical lines correspond to the means from which the Dalton Index are calculated.

According to the Dalton Index, Sweden can be thought of as more widely spread, or "polarized" according to the contributors to this literature, than the United States because the means for the two American parties are relatively close to the center, while those for the Swedish parties are spread much more widely across the ideological spectrum. The United States simply does not have a separate party that voters, on average, view as having an ideological position that is far from the center, like the Vänsterpartiet (Left Party) or the Sweden Democrats.

Figure 6.7 makes it clear, however, that the party means in the United States mask striking heterogeneity in the assessments of American voters about the ideological locations of their political parties. In fact, a rather large density of Americans perceives the Democratic Party to be extremely

---

[2] Note that the correlation between ENP and the Dalton survey-based polarization measure does not hold up in the larger sample of non-OECD countries in the CSES.

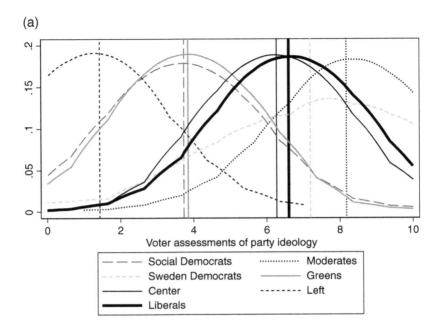
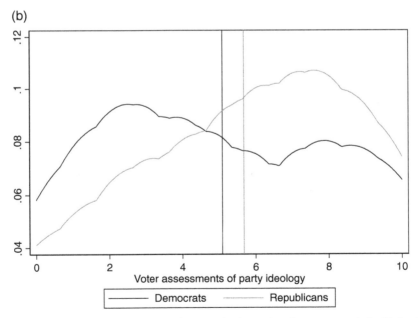

FIGURE 6.7 Voter assessments of party ideology, Sweden 2014 and the United States 2012

liberal, and a very large density of Americans perceives the Republican Party to be extremely conservative. However, the overall mean assessments are moderate because a countervailing, nontrivial group of Americans views the Democrats as conservative, and the Republicans as liberal. In contrast to the relatively tight distributions seen in Sweden, the American parties are different things to different people. Even though the overall means are close to each other, as we have seen, many American voters view the two parties as far from the center, far from each other, and far from themselves. The same phenomenon can be seen in other majoritarian democracies. While the means of voter assessments of party platforms are closer together than in proportional democracies, the standard deviations are substantially larger.

Thus, the small difference in party means estimated in the United States is misleading. For the United States, the difference between the mean assessment of the Democrats' ideology and that of the Republicans in the 2012 survey is only 0.59. However, if we calculate the absolute value of the difference in assessed ideology between the two parties for each individual, we see something radically different. The modal respondent perceives a 10-point difference between the Democrats and Republicans. If we take the average of those differences across all respondents, the perceived difference is actually 5.4. This is almost as high as the 6-point average perceived difference between the far-right Sweden Democrats and the far-left Vänsterpartiet.

Let us take this logic to the larger group of OECD countries. For each individual in each wave of the CSES, we can take the absolute difference between the perceived ideological location of the largest party and the perceived ideological location of every other party and then take a weighted average of these differences, where the weights are the parties' legislative vote shares. This tells us how spread out each individual perceives the party system to be. Figure 6.8 plots country means of this index against the effective number of political parties, with majoritarian democracies indicated by the diamond shape.

Figure 6.8 suggests that if anything, voters in countries with fewer political parties perceive the parties' platforms to be more spread out; in contrast to the Dalton Index, Americans are among the respondents who perceive their parties to be the furthest apart. Part of the reason for the disjuncture between the inferences we might draw from examining differences in party means and individual-level absolute differences between party placements is that respondents are not providing unbiased assessments of the parties' platforms. In addition to assessments of the parties,

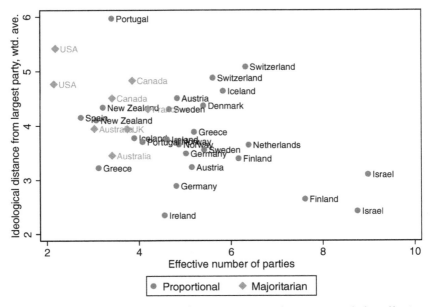

FIGURE 6.8 Voter assessments of party system polarization and the effective number of parties, CSES Modules 3 and 4

the CSES also asks voters to place *themselves* on the same unidimensional 11-point scale. In the United States, there is a U-shaped relationship between one's self-assessment and one's perception of difference between the parties. Americans who rate themselves as very conservative or very liberal perceive a large difference between the parties, while those who see themselves as in the ideological middle perceive a smaller (but still substantial) difference.

It is useful to calculate for each respondent, as in the ANES analysis, the distance between their self-placement and their assessment of each party's location. We can then calculate the average perceived ideological distance, within each country, to the most proximate party. Next, we can calculate the average perceived distance of each individual to all of the non-proximate parties, weighting these distances by party vote shares. The first indicator gives us a sense of the extent to which voters believe a party comes close to offering their preferred ideological position. We might think of this as the representativeness of the party system. The second indicator tells us how far away respondents believe the *other* parties to be. Thus, it provides an intuitive alternative measure of party system polarization: the further the ideological distance of the average voter from their non-proximate parties, the more polarized is the party system. We can conclude that a party system is polarized if a large number of voters view relatively large, non-proximate political parties as ideologically far away. A system is less polarized if voters perceive the non-proximate parties to be closer. Even if an objective measure of party platforms, like the text analysis of the Comparative Manifesto Project, suggests that parties' platforms are close together, voters might perceive the non-proximate party as very far away from themselves.

This approach has a methodological advantage over the Dalton Index in that it is unaffected by possible voter misunderstandings of the 11-point scale. A surprisingly large number of Americans who rated themselves as "very conservative" also rated the Democrats as very conservative and the Republicans as very liberal. It is plausible that they either switched the parties or, more likely, believed a higher number on all the scales corresponds to a more leftist position. Such mistakes would not affect a measure based on absolute differences between the self-assessment and the perceived party platform, or between perceived platforms, as long as respondents understand the direction of the scale to be the same for both the respondent and all of the parties.

This conceptualization of polarization also leads to very different cross-country characterizations than the Dalton Index. The average American respondent in 2012 perceived the most proximate party to be around 1.3 ideological units (on the 11-point scale) away from themselves, and they perceived the non-proximate party to be 4.4 units away. In Sweden, the average voter perceived their most proximate party to be only 0.3 units away, while the weighted average distance of the non-proximate parties was 2.97. Swedish respondents feel not only closer than American respondents to the party they identify as closest, but they also feel closer to their non-preferred parties. In other words, when it comes to perceived ideological distance, the Swedish party system is *less* polarized than the American system.

For the larger group of OECD countries in the CSES, the first panel in Figure 6.9 plots the average ideological distance of each respondent to the most proximate party against the effective number of political parties. Relative to other countries, American and British respondents view themselves as remarkably far from their most proximate party. And there is a rather strong relationship between the number of political parties and the ideological proximity of the closest party. Not surprisingly, in multiparty

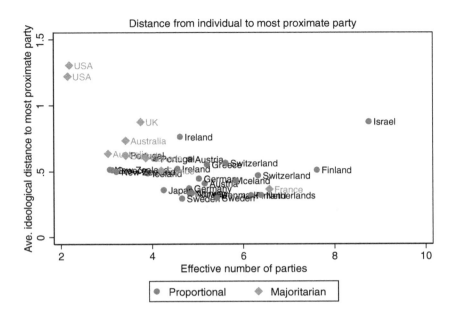

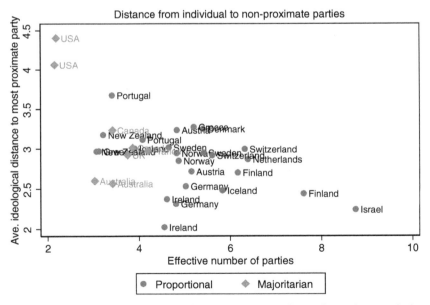

FIGURE 6.9 Voter assessments of party distances from themselves and the effective number of parties, CSES Modules 3 and 4

systems, voters are much more likely to identify a party with a platform that they perceive to be identical to their own.

The second panel in Figure 6.9 suggests that the United States is remarkably polarized relative to other countries, in that voters perceive the non-proximate party to be quite far away. Australia, with its system of compulsory voting and ranked-choice ballot procedure, is an outlier relative to other majoritarian democracies. But in contrast to the classic unidimensional political economy literature, if anything, voters perceive the parties to be further not only from one another but also from themselves in countries with majoritarian electoral institutions, higher levels of disproportionality, and fewer political parties.

PERCEIVED IDEOLOGICAL DISTANCE, GEOGRAPHY, AND SOCIAL POLARIZATION

As new issue dimensions have been added, it appears that American voters have come to see their partisan outgroup as moving further and further away. Lilliana Mason (2014) argues that as individuals with the same issue preferences sort into the same political party, they experience an increasing sense of the party as a social identity. This, in turn, can provoke the type of anger, mistrust, and "affective polarization" reported by Iyengar et al. (2019). As pointed out earlier, many of the issue dimensions that have been added over time are correlated with urban versus rural residence. Accordingly, Kathy Cramer (2016) reports a related sense of rural identity. She argues that recent support for conservative candidates in rural Wisconsin has been motivated in part by resentment toward urban elites that has rather little in the way of explicit policy content. A similar resentment of educated downtown Toronto elites seems to be part of the electoral appeal of Rob Ford in exurban and rural Ontario.

In short, polarization in majoritarian democracies has congealed as parties – pushed by activists – have bundled together a set of issues on which preferences are quite correlated with urbanization. As parties of the left have become champions of cities and parties of the right have become champions of exurbs and rural areas, these parties have also come to be more closely linked with distinct social and geographic identities. Legislative elections have come to feel like high-stakes battles between distinctive urban and rural policy agendas and different identities and ways of life, with the winner determined by a handful of pivotal districts in the middle-ring suburbs.

For the most part, this pattern of polarized geographic political competition appears not to have emerged in the proportional democracies of Northern Europe. As described earlier, when new issue dimensions arise in multiparty proportional democracies without small winner-take-all districts, new parties enter and old parties adapt. There is no logic pushing a single mainstream party of the left to bundle all urban issue positions and identities into one package. Likewise, there is no logic pushing a single party of the right to bundle together the interests of high-income fiscal conservatives and those of rural traditionalists. High-income, educated, cosmopolitan professionals in the knowledge economy cities of North America and Australia vote overwhelmingly for parties of the left, but their counterparts in European cities can choose from a far more diverse menu of choices. Some choose green parties that coalesce with the left, and many choose liberal or center-right parties with progressive social platforms.

As a result, European governments of the right typically contain substantial representation from the urban core of the major cities. Parliamentary elections are much less likely to take shape as winner-take-all geographic battles pitting the urban core against the countryside. In contrast, the legislative coalitions supporting conservative governments in the United Kingdom and Canada contain virtually no urban MPs. The same is true of Republican US House majorities in the United States.

European voters have a wider range of options than American voters; as suggested in the earlier analysis, for most voters, there is more than one ideologically proximate party, and one's preferred party often cannot govern without forming coalitions with some less-preferred parties. Moreover, unlike many Americans who live in politically homogeneous Democratic urban neighborhoods or Republican rural areas, Europeans in all geographic settings are much more likely to live in neighborhoods where others in their immediate social network vote for, and identify with, a different party. It is possible that the type of geographic partisan segregation that has emerged in the United States, Canada, and Britain exacerbates social polarization (Enos 2018).

Perhaps the ideological proximity of out-parties and lower levels of geographic partisan segregation in proportional democracies make it less likely that voters will come to view a specific party as a form of social identity, and less likely to form strong hostilities toward partisan outgroups. On the other hand, insofar as the parties of the left and right typically coalesce with the same partners, perhaps American-style social polarization merely reproduces across the broad left-right groupings.

Cross-national research on affective polarization, or "party-ism," outside the United States is in its infancy. A recent study by Heeremans (2018) finds evidence of party-based out-group hostility in the Netherlands, but it appears to be substantially less pronounced than that in the United States. Those who identify with the Liberal party, the VVD, for instance, have surprisingly warm feelings toward partisan outgroups. This makes sense, since the VVD has coalesced with parties of both the right and left in recent years, but Christian Democrats also report surprisingly warm feelings toward partisan out-groups. More generally, the average "feeling thermometer" (0 to 100) score given by voters of parties of the right toward parties of the left is actually more than 50, and the average score given by voters of left parties toward parties of the right is 39. In another study, Huddy, Bankert, and Davies (2018) find that the overall strength of partisanship as a social identity is lower in Sweden and the Netherland than in the United States.

An innovative study by Westwood et al. (2018) uses behavioral games in several countries to examine the extent to which partisans treat members of their in-group and out-group differently. Democrats and Republicans in the United States, and supporters of Labour and Conservatives in Britain, show a striking willingness to discriminate against each other. However, Liberal Democrats did not discriminate against Labour, and supporters of both of the major parties are much less likely to discriminate against Liberal Democrats than against each other. It is also interesting to note that American and British respondents only punished members of the opposite major party – they did not *reward* members of their in-group.

In the same study, the results were different in Belgium, with its multi-party system. Belgian voters showed a striking favoritism toward members of their partisan in-group. This is, perhaps, consistent with the notion that voters in multiparty systems feel closer to their most proximate parties than do voters in majoritarian democracies. And on the whole, discrimination against partisan outgroups was less pronounced than in the majoritarian democracies. Voters for the Flemish right discriminate against neither the Flemish Liberals nor the Flemish Socialists. The Francophone Socialists and Liberals – who were recently in a coalition together – do not discriminate against each other.

One of the interesting threads in each of these studies is the relative lack of evidence for social polarization involving *liberal* parties, whose platforms are typically to the right on economic issues but to the left on social issues. And more broadly, these initial comparative studies of social polarization seem consistent with the notion that proportional democracies – where voters perceive their out-parties as closer on average – are also less prone to social polarization. However, much work remains to be done to explore this possibility. And even if the perceived ideological and social distances between supporters of the various parties is indeed lower in Northern Europe than in Britain and its former colonies, it is plausible that this is driven not by electoral rules, but by a deeper cultural norm of cooperation and collaboration that took root in Northern Europe even before the adoption of proportional representation (Martin and Swank 2011). It is also plausible that the rise of far-right and populist parties, like the AfD in Germany, and the emergence of a cleavage between the winners and losers of globalization, is generating American-style social polarization between the traditional parties on the one hand and the new populist parties on the other (Helbling and Jungkunz 2018).

CONCLUSION

In Chapter 10 (this volume), Salas, Rosenbluth, and Shapiro focus primarily on the economic dimension of conflict and point out some dangers of proportional representation in the era of the postindustrial knowledge economy – above all, partisan fragmentation and the rise of extremist parties. The present chapter focuses on multiple issue dimensions and suggests that in spite of a tendency toward fragmentation, proportional representation might have a countervailing advantage: it helps inoculate against partisan and social polarization by preventing the two-party urban-rural bundling of issue platforms and social identities that have gradually fueled the rise of partisan hostility in majoritarian democracies. The United States, which has the purest two-party system in the world, is rather striking in the extent to which its voters view the parties as ideologically distinctive and far from themselves. In the postindustrial era, as self-described socialists vie for control of the Democratic Party, and rural nativists consolidate their control of the Republican Party, the centripetal logic of majoritarian democracy – so clear in simple one-dimensional theory – is difficult to see in practice.

Each of the industrialized majoritarian democracies has experienced some version of the same pattern of polarization, but each also has some mitigating features. Canada has largely avoided American-style nationalization of provincial politics and maintains distinct party systems in each province. Federalism may also provide a valuable antidote to polarization in the United States, where Republican governors in extremely liberal northeastern states and Democratic governors of conservative states are able to gain popularity by offering locally crafted solutions to local problems. Perhaps ranked-choice voting changes the dynamic in Australia, as does the multi-round process in France.

The United States is, in many ways, an outlier. Most majoritarian democracies do not have strict two-party systems. There is often a persistent divide on the left in majoritarian democracies, such as that between the NDP and Liberals (and increasingly the Greens) in Canada, or between Labour and the Liberal Democrats in the United Kingdom, not to mention the Scottish and Welsh parties. One might view these multiparty systems as a good thing, in that they provide voters with a greater range of choices, including some – like the Liberals in Canada and the Liberal Democrats in the United Kingdom – that might be described as "centrist." On the other hand, voters must engage in careful strategic voting in these systems; as long as parties can hope to exploit coordination failures among their enemies, extremist parties with broadly unpopular platforms can hope to form outright parliamentary majorities with as little as 35 percent of the vote. Such a party would have to expand its support base to win in a pure two-party system or find moderate coalition partners in a proportional system; however, in a multiparty majoritarian system, extremist parties can govern alone as long as their opponents fail to coordinate against them.

In the era of backlash to globalization, wage stagnation, and interregional and interpersonal inequality, proportional democracies are also being put to the test. The rise of rural and postindustrial xenophobic and nativist parties, for instance, has led to considerable anxiety throughout Europe. Yet these parties, while sometimes extreme in their rhetoric, will likely be forced to moderate to make themselves into palatable coalition partners. Moreover, in spite of its centripetal reputation, proportional representation brings a powerful advantage: it can allow the political system to absorb the rise of new issue dimensions, from environmentalism to women's rights to nativism, without the issue bundling and partisan identity construction that facilitate all-encompassing American-style polarization.

At the heart of political polarization in the United States is a paradox. The parties appear to be moving further and further apart precisely because they are offering evermore heterogeneous and incoherent bundles of platforms over time in response to their geographic bases as new issues arise. At the same moment that they appear to be implacable tribes on the cusp of civil war, they also appear to be obstreperous coalitions on the verge of collapse. While many Americans feel strong antipathy toward the more distant of the two parties, in comparison with citizens of other countries, they do not feel especially close to the most proximate party either.

A key claim in the comparative politics literature is that the number of parties in a country is a function of the number of cross-cutting cleavages – in other words, the number of distinct, salient issue dimensions in the mass public – and the extent to which the electoral system lowers barriers to entry for new parties (Amorim Neto and Cox 1997). This chapter suggests that the partisan and social polarization experienced by the United States in recent years might be a function of having a growing number of cleavages but, due to its political institutions, a fixed number of political parties.

REFERENCES

Abramowitz, Alan and Steven Webster. 2018. "Negative Partisanship: Why Americans Dislike Parties but Behave Like Rabid Partisans." *Political Psychology* 39, 1: 119–135.

Adams, James F., Samuel Merrill III, and Bernard Grofman. 2005. *A Unified Theory of Party Competition*. Cambridge: Cambridge University Press.

Ahler, Douglas and David Broockman. 2018. "The Delegate Paradox: Why Polarized Politicians Can Represent Citizens Best," *The Journal of Politics* 80, 4: 1117–1133.

Amorim Neto, Octavio and Gary Cox. 1997. "Electoral Institutions, Cleavage Structures and the Number of Parties," *American Journal of Political Science* 41: 149–174.

Baldassarri, Delia and Amir Goldberg. 2014. "Neither Ideologues nor Agnostics: Alternative Voters' Belief System in an Age of Partisan Politics," *American Journal of Sociology* 120, 1: 45–95.

Calvo, Ernesto and Timothy Hellwig. 2011. "Centripetal and Centrifugal Incentives under Different Electoral Systems," *American Journal of Political Science* 55, 1: 27–41.

Chua, Amy. 2018. *Political Tribes: Group Instinct and the Fate of Nations*. New York: Penguin.

Cox, Gary. 1990. "Centripetal and Centrifugal Incentives in Electoral Systems," *American Journal of Political Science* 34, 4: 903–935.

Cramer, Katherine. 2016. *The Politics of Resentment: Rural Consciousness in Wisconsin and the Rise of Scott Walker*. Chicago: University of Chicago Press.

Dalton, Russell. 1996. *Citizen Politics: Public Opinion and Political Parties in Advanced Industrial Democracies*. Washington, DC: CQ Press.
  2008. "The Quantity and the Quality of Party Systems: Party System Polarization, Its Measurement, and Its Consequences," *Comparative Political Studies* 41, 7: 899–920.

Downs, Anthony. 1957. "An Economic Theory of Political Action in a Democracy." *Journal of Political Economy* 65, 2: 135–165.
Enos, Ryan. 2018. *The Space Between Us: Social Geography and Politics*. Cambridge: Cambridge University Press.
Feldman, Stanley and Christopher Johnston. 2014. "Understanding the Determinants of Political Ideology: Implications of Structural Complexity," *Political Psychology* 35, 3: 337–358.
Fiorina, Morris. 2017. *Unstable Majorities: Polarization, Party Sorting, Rand Political Stalemate*. Palo Alto, CA: Hoover Institution Press.
Heeremans, Lauren. 2018. "Affective Polarization in the Netherlands," Masters Thesis, University of Amsterdam.
Helbling, Marc and Sebastian Jungkunz. 2020. "Social Divides in the Age of Globalization," *West European Politics* 43, 6: 1187–1210.
Hotelling, Harold. 1929. "Stability in Competition," *The Economic Journal* 39, 15: 41–57.
Huddy, Leonie, Alexa Bankert, and Caitlin Davies. 2018. "Expressive versus Instrumental Partisanship in Multi-Party European Systems." Unpublished paper, Stony Brook University.
Iaryczower, Matias and Andrea Mattozzi. 2013. "On the Nature of Competition in Alternative Electoral Systems," *The Journal of Politics* 75, 3: 743–756.
Inglehart, Ronald. 1990. *Culture Shift in Advanced Industrial Society*. Princeton: Princeton University Press.
Iyengar, Shanto, Yphtach Lelkes, Matthew Levendusky, Neil Malhotra, and Sean Westwood. 2019. "The Origins and Consequences of Affective Polarization in the United States." *Annual Review of Political Science*, 22, 129–146.
Laver, Michael and Norman Schofield. 1990. *Multiparty Government: The Politics of Coalition in Europe*. Oxford: Oxford University Press.
Layman, Geoffrey and Thomas Carsey. 2002. "Party Polarization and 'Conflict Extension' in the American Electorate," *American Journal of Political Science* 46, 4: 786–802.
Levendusky, Matthew. 2009. *The Partisan Sort: How Liberals Became Democrats and Conservatives Became Republicans*. Chicago: University of Chicago Press.
Lijphart, Arend. 2012. *Patterns of Democracy: Government Forms and Performance in 36 Countries*. New Haven: Yale University Press.
Martin, Cathie Jo and Duane Swank. 2011. "Gonna Party Like It's 1899: Party Systems and the Origins of Varieties of Coordination." *World Politics* 63, 1: 78–114.
Mason, Lilliana. 2014. "I Disrespectfully Agree: The Differential Effects of Partisan Sorting on Social and Issue Polarization," *American Journal of Political Science* 59, 1: 128–145.
Matakos, Konstantinos, Orestis Troumpounis, and Dimitrios Xefteris. 2016. "Electoral Rule Disproportionality and Platform Polarization." *American Journal of Political Science* 60, 4: 1026–1043.
McCarty, Nolan, Keith T. Poole, and Howard Rosenthal. 2008. *Polarized America: The Dance of Ideology and Unequal Riches*. Cambridge, MA: MIT Press.

Miller, Gary and Norman Schofield. 2003. "Activists and Partisan Realignment in the United States," *American Political Science Review* 97, 2: 245–260.
  2008. "The Transformation of the Republican and Democratic Party Coalitions in the U.S.," *Perspectives on Politics*, 6, 3: 433–450.
Pew Research Center. 2016. "Partisanship and Political Animosity in 2016," available at www.people-press.org/2016/06/22/partisanship-and-political-animosity-in-2016/
Rodden, Jonathan. 2015. "Geography and Gridlock in the United States," in Nathaniel Persily, ed., *Solutions to Political Polarization in America*. Cambridge: Cambridge University Press.
  2019. *Why Cities Lose: The Deep Roots of the Urban-Rural Political Divide*. New York: Basic Books.
Schickler, Eric. 2016. *Racial Realignment: The Transformation of American Liberalism*. Princeton: Princeton University Press.
Treier, Shawn and Sunshine Hillygus. 2009. "The Nature of Political Ideology in the Contemporary Electorate," *Public Opinion Quarterly* 73, 4: 679–703.
Westwood, Sean, Shanto Iyengar, Stefaan Walgrave, Refael Leonisio, Luis Miller, and Oliver Strijbis. 2018. "The Tie that Divides: Cross-National Evidence on the Primacy of Partyism." *European Journal of Political Research* 57, 333–354.

7

America's Unequal Metropolitan Geography

Segregation and the Spatial Concentration of Affluence and Poverty

Douglas S. Massey and Jacob S. Rugh

During the 1970s, income inequality and class segregation began to rise throughout the United States. At about the same time, black residential segregation began to fall, though the declines proved to be quite uneven and black hyper-segregation persists in many metropolitan areas. Levels of Asian and Hispanic segregation show no signs of declining, however, and if anything are edging upward, contributing to a sharp increase in spatial isolation as the Asian and Hispanic populations have grown. These spatial trends have had profound effects on the ecological structure of US metropolitan areas, since racial-ethnic segregation, when combined with rising class segregation and surging inequalities of wealth and income, constitutes a proven formula for spatial polarization along the lines of race and class (Massey and Fischer 2000; Quillian 2012; Massey and Tannen 2016).

Here we assess trends and patterns in the spatial concentration of affluence and poverty across US metropolitan areas. After describing our data and methods, we highlight trends in class distribution, class segregation, and spatial isolation among the affluent and the poor in four major racial-ethnic groups from 1970 to 2010. We then present maps showing the geographic distribution of concentrated affluence and poverty in metropolitan areas throughout the nation and go on to estimate multivariate models that link selected variables to the spatial isolation of poor and affluent metropolitan residents.

Our analyses reveal a stark ecology of inequality within metropolitan America in which whites and Asians benefit disproportionately from the increasing spatial concentration of affluence but largely escape the predations of concentrated poverty. In contrast, Hispanics and African

Americans enjoy only a tenuous hold in areas of concentrated affluence but are routinely exposed to high concentrations of poverty. This socioeconomic polarization across metropolitan areas is grounded in America's entrenched ecology of racial and class segregation, whose effects have been heightened by globalization to produce intense concentration of affluence on the coasts and high concentrations of poverty throughout the US interior.

DATA AND METHODS

We measure segregation and spatial isolation by race and class using data from the 1970–2000 Decennial Censuses and the combined 2008–2012 rounds of the American Community Survey (ACS), which provide tract-level estimates centered on 2010. By linking census tracts to their corresponding counties and merging them with metropolitan statistical areas (MSAs) and metropolitan divisions (MDIVs), we created a set of 287 consistently defined metropolitan areas for the period 1970–2010. Using census data on race and Hispanic origin, we define four broad racial-ethnic groups: non-Hispanic whites, non-Hispanic blacks, non-Hispanic Asians, and Hispanics, henceforth simply labeled whites, blacks, Asians, and Hispanics and abbreviated as "races."

Using data on household income, we define three income classes consisting of poor, middle class, and affluent individuals. Following Smith (1988) and others (Massey and Eggers 1990; Massey and Fischer 2003), we set the boundary between the poor and middle class at the annual poverty threshold for a family of four (\$22,314 in 2010), using the closest approximation available from census income categories (\$25,000 in 2010). For the middle-class–affluent boundary, we use the closest categorical approximation (\$100,000 in 2010) to four times the poverty threshold (\$89,256 in 2010). When combined, our three classes and four racial categories yield 12 distinct race-class groupings.

We then go on to measure residential segregation using the well-known index of dissimilarity (D), which for any two groups X and Y represents the relative share of X-members who would have to exchange tracts with Y-members to achieve an even residential distribution. We measure spatial isolation using within-tract $_xP_x^*$ isolation indices, which for any group X represent the share of X-members residing in the tract of the average X-member. The D index varies from 0 (when the proportion of X-members and Y-members within tracts equals their share in the metropolitan area) to 100 (when X-members and Y-members share no tract in common), whereas the $_xP_x^*$ index varies from the percentage of X-members in the metropolitan population (when they are evenly distributed across tracts) to 100 (when every X-member inhabits a tract made up only by other X-members).

Our multivariate analysis focuses on 2010 and regresses measures of class segregation and spatial isolation on metropolitan indicators of racial composition, demographic structure, housing circumstances, economic organization, and physical security. As shown in Table 7.1, measures of racial composition include the metropolitan percentage of Hispanics, blacks, and Asians, while indicators of demographic structure include metropolitan population size (logged), the percentage of people living in urbanized portions of metropolitan counties, the percentage of persons residing in owned homes, the percentage aged 65 or older, and the percentage foreign born. We also created an indicator of the prevalence of undocumented migrants, using the online tool provided by the Center for Migration Studies (2016) to obtain estimates of the number of undocumented migrants in each metropolitan area (which unfortunately is no longer available online). We then divided this number by the total number of foreign-born Hispanics (given that the vast majority of undocumented migrants are from Latin America).

To capture housing market circumstances, we used data from the US Department of Housing and Urban Development (2016) to derive the number of voucher-based and project-based subsidized housing units in each area and divided these numbers by the total number of housing units. The effect of local zoning regimes was assessed using an index of the permissiveness of density zoning in the suburbs developed by Rugh and Massey (2014) based on earlier work by Pendall, Puentes, and Martin (2006) and Rothwell and Massey (2009) but recoding it to indicate the *restrictiveness* rather than permissiveness of suburban density zoning. The age of the housing stock was measured using the median year of home construction.

Finally, we considered the effect of a metropolitan area's economic structure by computing the percentage of workers employed in manufacturing, education, and the FIRE sector (finance, insurance, and real estate). Since prior work by Farley and Frey (1994) found that areas with larger military populations are less segregated than others, we used census data to compute the log of the number of people living in military quarters per 100,000 persons. Likewise, since metropolitan areas dominated by "creative class" industries tend to be more diverse (Florida 2002), we included the rate of patent production using data from the US Patent

TABLE 7.1 *Metropolitan-level variables used in analysis of the concentration of affluence and poverty in 2010*

	Mean	SD	Min	Max
Group Economic Status				
Percentage Affluent	27.4	7.7	14.6	55.0
Percentage in Poverty	18.6	4.3	7.6	32.5
Residential Segregation				
Black-White Dissimilarity	48.2	12.6	15.1	79.6
Hispanic-White Dissimilarity	38.2	11.0	11.9	68.7
Asian-White Dissimilarity	34.9	8.3	14.7	57.1
Racial Composition				
Percentage Black	12.4	11.1	0.2	52.6
Percentage Hispanic	13.3	16.2	0.7	95.7
Percentage Asian	3.9	5.6	0.6	69.1
Demographic Structure				
Log of Metropolitan Population	13.0	1.1	11.3	16.3
Percentage Urban	80.7	11.9	42.3	99.9
Percentage Homeowner	66.1	5.6	38.4	79.9
Percentage Aged 65+	13.0	2.7	6.5	27.2
Percentage Foreign Born	8.9	7.8	0.8	51.2
Percentage Hispanics Undocumented	28.1	17.8	0.0	100.0
Housing Circumstances				
Percentage Project Housing	2.0	1.0	0.1	6.2
Percentage Voucher Housing	1.8	0.8	0.1	5.7
Density Restrictiveness in Suburbs	2.6	0.7	0.0	3.8
Median Year of Housing	1974	9.5	1950	1994
Economic Organization				
Percentage Manufacturing	11.4	5.0	2.2	34.3
Percentage in FIRE Sector	6.2	2.1	3.0	21.1
Percentage in Education	9.9	3.1	5.9	25.6
Log of Military Population	1.4	2.4	0.0	8.4
Patents per Capita	30.5	47.2	0.4	548.4
Safety and Security				
Violent Crime Rate per 100,000	443.6	206.9	76.0	1207.1

and Trademark Office (2012). Because affluent whites associate minority and the poor neighborhoods with higher crime rates and avoid them based on this perception (Emerson et al. 2001), we also include a control for the rate of violent crime per 100,000 persons using data from the US Federal Bureau of Investigation (2012).

TRENDS IN CLASS STRATIFICATION AND SEGREGATION

Figure 1 shows trends in class distribution by race across US metropolitan areas from 1970 through 2010. The top panel reveals that the percentage affluent has risen for all racial groups but that irrespective of the date considered, the share has always been greatest for Asians and whites and lowest for blacks and Hispanics. As of 2010, 46 percent of Asians were classified as affluent, up from 39 percent in 1980. The latter is a level that whites only achieved in 2010. In contrast, from 1970 to 2010 the share affluent among Hispanics rose only from 12 percent to 22 percent, whereas that for blacks increased from just 9 percent to 20 percent, leaving both groups well below the affluence levels exhibited by whites and Asians in 2010.

As shown in the bottom panel of Figure 7.1, the share of each group living in poverty displayed no clear trend. The poverty rate increased for all groups from 1970 to 1980, stabilized from 1980 through 2000, and then fell from 2000 to 2010, yielding little net change over the decades. As of 2010, the black poverty rate stood at 29 percent, compared to 22 percent for Hispanics, and 14 percent for both Asians and whites. As can be seen, the share occupying the middle of the income distribution steadily declined for all groups over the period. Whereas the percentage middle class ranged narrowly from 63 percent to 68 percent in 1970, by 2010 intergroup differentials had widened, with the figure falling to 56 percent for Hispanics, 51 percent for blacks, 48 percent for whites, and 40 percent for Asians. In general, then, over the four decades from 1970 to 2010, the percentage affluent mostly rose at the expense of the share in the middle class. The reasons for this increase in class inequality are well described by Thelen and Wiedemann (Chapter 12, this volume) and Ananat, Gassman-Pines, and Truskinovsky (Chapter 13, this volume).

Figure 7.2 shows trends in class segregation over the same period by displaying average indices of class dissimilarity computed separately within each race-class category. The indices measure the extent of segregation between racial group members of a particular income class from members of other class categories *whatever their race*. The top left quadrant, for example, shows trends in residential dissimilarity between affluent whites, blacks, Hispanics, and Asians and the poor of any race. These averages are weighted by the number of people in the first-named class

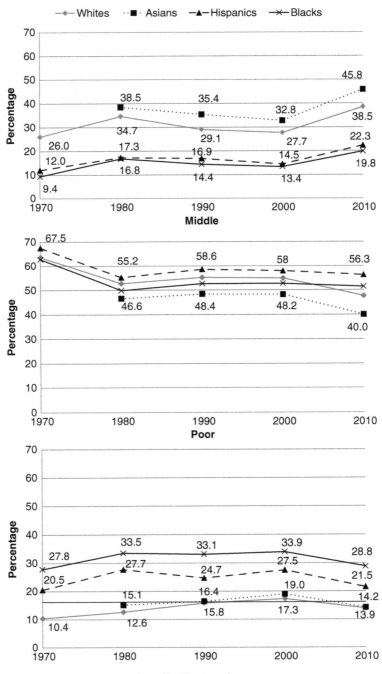

FIGURE 7.1 Class distributions by race 1970–2010

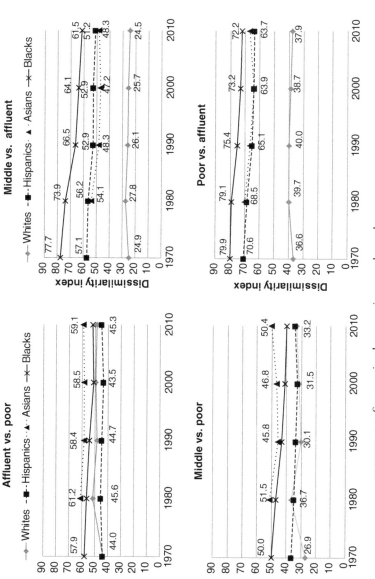

FIGURE 7.2 Segregation between income classes by race 1970–2000

category in each pairing. Thus the average affluent-poor dissimilarity index for whites is weighted by the number of affluent white people in each metropolitan area, thereby indicating the degree to which the average affluent white resident of the 287 metropolitan areas was segregated from poor people of any race.

A dissimilarity index of 60 is generally taken to indicate the threshold between a high and a moderate level of segregation, with 30 seen as the border between a moderate and low level of segregation. As shown in the upper left quadrant of the figure, according to these criteria the degree of segregation between affluent members of each racial group and the poor has consistently been in the upper reaches of the moderate range. As of 2010, affluent-poor dissimilarity stood at 59 for Asians, 52 for blacks, 49 for whites, and 45 for Hispanics. In contrast, the bottom left quadrant reveals that middle-poor dissimilarity has generally remained in the lower reaches of the moderate range, with the spread between races declining over time. As of 2010, the middle-poor dissimilarity index ranged from 33 for whites and Hispanics to 50 for Asians, with blacks falling in between at 40.

The upper right quadrant of Figure 7.2 reveals that the degree of middle-affluent dissimilarity has declined for all groups except whites, with the index dropping from 78 to 62 for blacks, from 57 to 51 for Hispanics, and from 54 to 48 for Asians. In contrast, middle-affluent dissimilarity varied narrowly from 25 to 28 with no particular trend. As of 2010, the middle-affluent dissimilarity index stood at just 25 for whites compared to respective values of 48, 51, and 62 for Asians, Hispanics, and blacks. Middle-class whites are also less segregated from the poor. In 2010, the middle-poor dissimilarity index for whites was just 33 (the same for Hispanics), compared with values of 40 and 50 for blacks and Asians, respectively. In general, then, class segregation has consistently been less intense among whites than other groups, at least on average, suggesting the salience of racial as opposed to class solidarity.

TRENDS IN THE SPATIAL CONCENTRATION OF AFFLUENCE AND POVERTY

Given increasing rates of affluence and relatively high levels of affluent-poor segregation, we would generally expect to observe a rising concentration of affluence within neighborhoods over time, especially for whites and Asians who display the highest rates of affluence and the highest indices of affluent-poor segregation. This scenario is exactly what we observe in the top panel of Figure 7.3, which presents trends in average class isolation by race. Once again, the averages are weighted such that the isolation index for affluent whites reflects the experience of the average affluent white metropolitan resident. Over time, the class isolation index rose from 36 to 45 for affluent whites and from 46 to 51 for affluent Asians. Although levels of class isolation also rose for affluent blacks and affluent Hispanics, the degree of spatially concentrated affluence remained well below the levels displayed by whites and Asians, coming in at 35 for blacks and 36 for Hispanics in 2010. Thus *affluent whites and Asians inhabit much more advantaged neighborhoods than do their black and Hispanic counterparts.*

As shown in the middle panel of Figure 7.3, the extent of middle-class spatial isolation is quite similar across racial groups and has consistently moved downward over time, dropping from an isolation index of around 66 for all groups in 1970 to 48 for Asians, 51 for whites, and 54 for blacks and Hispanics in 2010. In other words, *over time middle-class members of all groups have grown less likely to share neighborhoods with other middle-class people.* Over time, therefore, affluent households have come to enjoy ever more advantaged neighborhoods, while the spatial advantage once enjoyed by middle-class neighborhoods has steadily deteriorated, indicating the ecological correlates of what Ansel and Gingrich (Chapter 3, this volume) call "the end of human capital solidarity."

In contrast to the clear time trends in class isolation displayed at the top and middle of the class distribution, the isolation of the poor has followed an irregular pattern over time. Across all groups, the spatial concentration of poverty generally fell from 1970 to 1980, rose from 1980 to 1990, changed little between 1990 and 2000, and then fell once again from 2000 to 2010. At the latter date, the spatial concentration of poverty was greatest for blacks (33) and lowest for whites (21), with Hispanics and Asians falling in-between (at 28 and 24, respectively).

THE GEOGRAPHY OF CONCENTRATED AFFLUENCE AND POVERTY

Figure 7.4 maps the degree of concentrated affluence experienced by whites and Asians across metropolitan areas, which have been shaded to indicate three categories of class isolation: low (values less than 20), moderate (values from 20 to 40), and high (values more than 40). For both groups, the highest concentrations of affluence occur in five basic regions: the

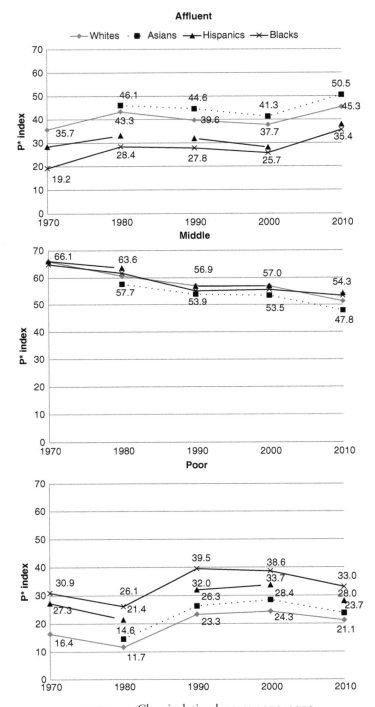

FIGURE 7.3 Class isolation by race 1970–2010

America's Unequal Metropolitan Geography

Percent Affluent in Neighborhood of Average Affluent White Resident

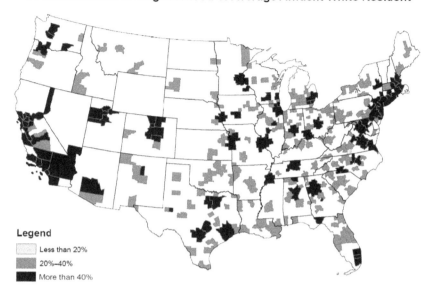

Percent Affluent in Neighborhood of Average Affluent Asian Resident

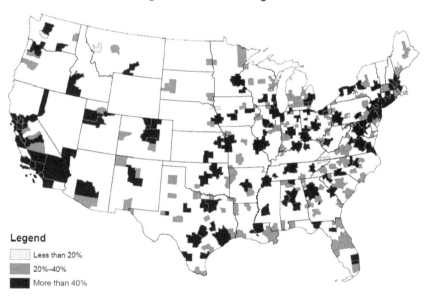

FIGURE 7.4 Spatial concentration of affluence for whites and Asians in US Metropolitan Areas 2010

Atlantic seaboard (the Boston-to-Washington megalopolis, along with Raleigh-Durham, Charlotte, Atlanta, and Miami–Fort Lauderdale–Palm Beach); the Pacific Coast (Seattle, Portland, the San Francisco Bay Area, Southern California, and Las Vegas); the Great Lakes (Cleveland, Detroit, Chicago, Milwaukee); the Mississippi River Basin (Minneapolis, St. Louis, Memphis, Nashville); and certain areas in the country's midsection (Lincoln, Kansas City, Dallas–Fort Worth, Houston, Austin, San Antonio, Denver-Boulder, Santa Fe, Phoenix, and Salt Lake).

Figure 7.5 shows the spatial concentration of affluence for blacks and Hispanics; it is immediately apparent that there are far fewer such areas for these groups than for whites and Asians. As with their white and Asian counterparts, locations of concentrated advantage for affluent blacks include metropolitan areas in the northeast (the outlying areas of Boston, Coastal Connecticut, New York–New Jersey, Baltimore, and Washington) as well as areas along the Pacific Coast (Seattle, the San Francisco Bay Area, and Southern California); apart from these regions, areas of concentrated black affluence are few and far between. Mostly they occur in smaller metropolitan areas containing small black populations.

Upper-class Hispanics similarly live under conditions of concentrated affluence along the Northeast Coast (around Boston, coastal Connecticut, New York–New Jersey, Albany and Almira in New York State, Baltimore, and Washington), the Southeast Coast (Wilmington, Delaware; Richmond; Raleigh-Durham; and Fort Lauderdale), and the West Coast (Seattle, the Bay Area, Oxnard, Santa Ana, and San Diego). Unlike their black counterparts, however, affluent Hispanics also enjoy areas of concentrated affluence in the Mississippi Basin (Minneapolis and Rochester, Minnesota; St. Louis; and Baton Rouge) as well as other metropolitan areas scattered around the country (Detroit; Cincinnati; Tallahassee; Gainesville; and Jackson, Tennessee). Nonetheless, *neither affluent African Americans nor well-to-do Hispanics enjoy the same neighborhoods of concentrated affluence as similarly well-off whites and Asians.*

Figure 7.6 shifts from the top to the bottom of the class distribution by showing the location of areas of concentrated poverty for whites and Asians, with metropolitan areas again shaded to indicate three categories: a low concentration of poverty (isolation indices less than 20), a high concentration of poverty (isolation indices 20–40), and an extreme concentration of poverty (isolation indices more than 40). A quick glance at the upper panel reveals that whites *never* experience an extreme concentration of poverty in any metropolitan area. That is, on average *in no metropolitan area do poor whites inhabit neighborhoods where more*

America's Unequal Metropolitan Geography

Percent Affluent in Neighborhood of Average Affluent Black Resident

Percent Affluent in Neighborhood of Average Affluent Hispanic Resident

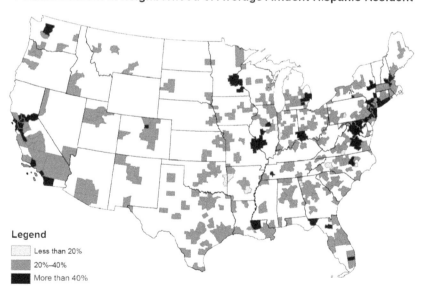

FIGURE 7.5 Spatial concentration of affluence for blacks and Hispanics in US metropolitan areas 2010

Percent Affluent in Neighborhood of Average Affluent Black Resident

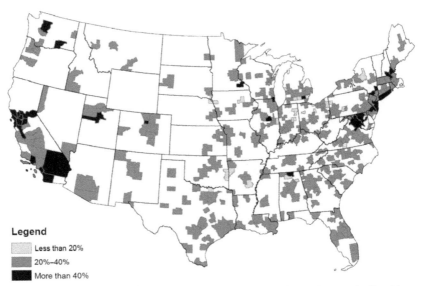

Percent Affluent in Neighborhood of Average Affluent Hispanic Resident

FIGURE 7.6 Spatial concentration of white and Asian poverty in US metropolitan areas 2010

than 40 percent of the residents are also poor. Areas characterized by merely high levels of concentrated poverty for whites (isolation indices in the 20–40 range) are generally located away from areas of concentrated affluence on the coasts and instead cluster in Appalachia, states of the former Confederacy, older industrial areas of the Northeast and Midwest, and the Great Plains. In contrast to whites, however, poor Asians quite often experience extreme concentrations of poverty, mainly in older industrial areas of the Northeast, Midwest, and South. Given their high level of affluence, this finding may seem puzzling. One possible explanation is that some Asians serve as middleman minorities and tend to reside in storefront locations in poor and minority neighborhoods, such as Korean grocers in black neighborhoods (Light and Gold 2000).

Figure 7.7 shows the distribution of concentrated poverty experienced by poor blacks and Hispanics throughout the United States. As seen in the top panel, black poverty concentration is high or extreme in most metropolitan areas, with the highest levels again being observed in the states of the former Confederacy and older industrial areas of the Northeast and Midwest. Many fewer metropolitan areas are characterized by extreme or even high concentrations of Hispanic poverty, with the highest concentrations being confined to the Northeast and portions of Texas, especially the Rio Grande Valley. High concentrations of poverty for Hispanics are also observed in and around Detroit, Chicago, and other older industrial centers.

In Table 7.2, we turn to an analysis of which factors predict the degree of spatially concentrated affluence experienced by affluent whites, Asians, blacks, and Hispanics in 2010, revealing a number of consistent effects across all four models. It is immediately apparent, for example, that in all models the concentration of affluence is significantly and positively predicted by both the percentage affluent and the degree of affluent-poor segregation. In other words, *as the relative number of affluent people increases and the degree of segregation between the affluent and the poor rises, then quite logically the spatial concentration of affluence rises and affluent people increasingly come to inhabit more advantaged neighborhoods in which they are surrounded by other affluent people, with little exposure to the poor.* In most of the equations, the spatial concentration of affluence is also positively predicted by the share of workers employed in the FIRE sector, patents per capita, and the home ownership rate, but negatively predicted by the percentage of elderly and the share of workers in manufacturing. Thus *affluence tends to concentrate spatially in highly urbanized, postindustrial, creative-class,*

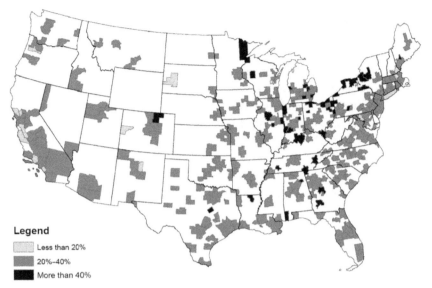

FIGURE 7.7 The production of concentrated affluence and poverty

TABLE 7.2 *Equations predicting concentration of affluence for whites, Asians, blacks, and Hispanics in 2010*

	Whites		Asians		Blacks		Hispanics	
Predictors	B	SE	B	SE	B	SE	B	SE
Group Economic Status								
Affluence Rate	0.935***	0.024	0.273***	0.038	0.478***	0.053	0.469***	0.059
Poverty Rate	0.090	0.048	-0.023	0.048	0.070	0.049	-0.031	0.050
Residential Segregation								
Affluent-Poor	0.238***	0.014	0.207***	0.062	0.048*^	0.027	0.085***	0.026
Black-White	-0.001	0.010	0.057	0.043	-0.098***	0.035	0.021	0.032
Hispanic-White	0.000	0.008	0.031	0.036	0.016	0.030	0.026	0.035
Asian-White	0.015	0.011	0.078	0.050	0.021	0.040	0.017	0.038
Racial Composition								
Percentage Black	-0.150***	0.011	-0.025	0.047	-0.051	0.042	-0.044	0.035
Percentage Hispanic	-0.102***	0.011	-0.130*	0.050	-0.018	0.038	-0.081*	0.038
Percentage Asian	-0.057***	0.017	0.095	0.077	0.178**	0.062	0.096	0.060
Demographic Composition								
Log of Metro Population	0.222*	0.108	0.716	0.481	0.415	0.396	0.024	0.380
Percentage Urban	0.034***	0.010	0.149***	0.044	0.088**	0.033	0.119***	0.032
Percentage Homeowner	-0.001	0.019	0.153*^	0.086	0.135*	0.067	0.133*	0.067
Percentage Aged 65+	0.067	0.039	-0.845**	0.151	-0.585***	0.121	-0.570**	0.116

(continued)

TABLE 7.2 (continued)

Predictors	Whites		Asians		Blacks		Hispanics	
	B	SE	B	SE	B	SE	B	SE
Percentage Foreign Born	0.002	0.023	0.065	0.093	0.089	0.078	0.149*	0.073
Percentage Undocumented	0.000	0.004	0.048*	0.019	0.026	0.015	0.001	0.015
Housing Characteristics								
Percentage Project Housing	-0.167	0.091	-1.192**	0.405	0.029	0.325	-0.307	0.314
Percentage Voucher Housing	-0.040	0.098	-0.286	0.444	-0.129	0.355	-0.081	0.340
Density Restrictiveness	0.436	0.248	0.836	1.143	2.041*	0.921	1.268	0.858
Median Year of Housing	0.040**	0.014	-0.078	0.060	0.083	0.050	0.067	0.048
Political Economy								
Percentage Manufacturing	-0.011	0.020	-0.359**	0.086	-0.250***	0.069	-0.302**	0.067
Percentage in FIRE Sector	0.113**	0.041	0.100	0.182	0.446**	0.144	0.398**	0.137
Percentage in Education	-0.040	0.029	0.070	0.131	-0.141	0.098	-0.050	0.096
Log of Military Population	0.115***	0.032	0.319*	0.140	0.296*	0.119	0.101	0.112
Patents per Capita	0.005**	0.002	0.033***	0.008	0.033***	0.006	0.032***	0.001
Safety and Security								
Violent Crime Rate	0.001	0.000	0.000	0.002	0.000	0.002	0.000	0.002
Constant	-89.845***	27.618	148.399	121.045	-164.268	100.600	-128.35	96.241
R-Squared	0.986		0.754		0.789		0.760	
N	287		287		287		287	

*p<0.05; **p<0.01; ***p<0.001; ^One-tailed test

metropolitan areas with younger populations and a high rate of home ownership.

Although the coincidence of a high rate of affluence with a high degree of affluent-poor segregation yields concentrated affluence for all groups, the combination is especially powerful for whites. Indeed, whites are able to translate their affluence into concentrated advantage at almost a one-to-one rate. Each point increase in affluence yields a 0.935 increase in the spatial concentration of white affluence, a conversion rate that is roughly twice that observed for blacks and Hispanics and more than three times that of Asians. Likewise, each point increase in affluent-poor segregation increases the concentration of white affluence by 0.238 points, a rate that is five times that observed for blacks and three times that observed for Hispanics (though admittedly only 15 percent greater than that observed for Asians). Mainly as a result of these differences, the variables in the model explain 99 percent of the variance in concentrated affluence for whites, compared to just 75 percent–80 percent of the variance for the other three groups.

In the black model, the positive coefficient for affluent-poor segregation is well below that observed in the other three models and barely significant statistically. Instead, what looms large in the black model is the very significant *negative* coefficient associated with black-white segregation. By way of contrast, Asian-white segregation and Hispanic-white segregation have no significant effect on the concentration of Asian or Hispanic affluence. Each point increase in the black-white dissimilarity index reduces the concentration of black affluence by almost 0.1 points. Simply put, *racial segregation undermines the ability of affluent blacks to isolate themselves in affluent neighborhoods and thereby achieve the same level of spatial advantage as whites and Asians.*

Although an increase of 0.1 per point of racial segregation may seem small, what makes it important is that half of all black metropolitan residents live in areas characterized by a high level of segregation (D>60), and in a third of all metropolitan areas African Americans experience a truly extreme pattern of racial isolation known as hyper-segregation (Massey and Tannen 2015). The ability of affluent African Americans to isolate themselves spatially is also constrained by the fact that the rate of black affluence is half that of whites and the degree of segregation from the poor achieved by affluent African Americans is 22 percent less than that achieved by affluent whites.

Turning to the determinants of concentrated poverty, as shown in Table 7.3, we again see a commonality of effects across the various models. Just as with the concentration of affluence, the concentration of poverty is analogously produced by the coincidence of a high rate of poverty with a high degree of poor-affluent segregation. *As the relative number of poor people rises and the segregation between them and the affluent increases, so does the spatial concentration of poverty.* In addition, across metropolitan areas the spatial isolation of the poor also tends to be associated with a higher percentage of workers in education and a relatively large share of project-based housing units (especially for African Americans) but is negatively associated with a high rate of home ownership. *Poverty thus tends to concentrate spatially in metropolitan areas with a larger stock of public housing, a large educational workforce, and a low rate of home ownership.*

As before, the white model explains far more of the variance in concentrated poverty (94 percent) than do the models estimated for the other groups (which range from 61 percent to 73 percent). Moreover, once again in an analogous manner, the white poverty rate translates into concentrated white poverty on almost a one-to-one basis. Other things equal, each point increase in the white poverty rate yields a 0.936 increase the spatial concentration of white poverty, compared to figures of just 0.371 for Hispanics, 0.346 for Asians, and 0.215 for blacks. Of course, other things are not equal. Although the rates of Asian and white poverty are similar, the average rate of black poverty is twice as high and the average rate of Hispanic poverty is 56 percent greater (see Table 7.1). In addition, poor-affluent segregation is more predictive of poverty concentration for African Americans and Hispanics (with respective coefficients of 0.301 and 0.292 compared to 0.215 for whites). Moreover, to make matters worse, their indices of poor-affluent dissimilarity are much higher (60.8 for blacks and 69.6 for Hispanics compared to 36.4 for whites).

Finally, the models in Table 7.3 show that the concentration of poverty is significantly exacerbated by residential segregation, especially for African Americans. For them, the regression coefficient associated with black-white dissimilarity is 0.116 and as already noted the index is greater than 60 in half of all metropolitan areas. Among Latinos, the coefficient associated with Hispanic-white segregation is lower at 0.084 and the average dissimilarity from whites is much lower at just 38.2 (see mean value in Table 7.1). In short, compared to whites and Asians, and to a lesser extent compared to Hispanics, residential segregation on the basis of race simultaneously reduces the likelihood that affluent blacks benefit from the advantages of concentrated affluence while increasing the odds that poor blacks suffer disadvantages of concentrated poverty.

TABLE 7.3 *Equations predicting the concentration of poverty for whites, Asians, blacks, and Hispanics in 2010*

Predictors	Whites B	Whites SE	Asians B	Asians SE	Blacks B	Blacks SE	Hispanics B	Hispanics SE
Group Economic Status								
Affluence Rate	-0.013	0.027	-0.088*	0.041	-0.095*^	0.056	-0.107*	0.052
Poverty Rate	0.936**	0.054	0.346***	0.054	0.215***	0.051	0.371***	0.045
Residential Segregation								
Poor-Affluent	0.215**	0.015	0.399***	0.060	0.301***	0.038	0.292***	0.030
Black-White	-0.001	0.010	-0.021	0.045	0.116*	0.037	0.084**	0.029
Hispanic-White	0.007	0.009	0.009	0.039	-0.058	0.031	0.020	0.028
Asian-White	-0.005	0.012	0.169**	0.054	-0.029	0.042	-0.016	0.034
Racial Composition								
Percentage Black	0.053***	0.011	-0.068	0.049	0.178***	0.042	0.043	0.031
Percentage Hispanic	0.030*	0.012	-0.030	0.053	0.185***	0.040	0.160***	0.034
Percentage Asian	-0.022	0.019	0.129	0.089	0.042	0.065	0.028	0.054
Demographic Composition								
Log of Metro Population	-0.119	0.121	1.057*	0.533	1.145**	0.407	-0.683*	0.343
Percentage Urban	-0.011	0.011	0.045	0.046	-0.093**	0.035	0.047	0.029
Percentage Homeowner	0.079***	0.022	-0.277**	0.096	-0.170*	0.070	-0.113*^	0.060
Percentage Aged 65+	0.030	0.044	0.206	0.159	0.624***	0.125	0.269**	0.104

(continued)

TABLE 7.3 (continued)

	Whites		Asians		Blacks		Hispanics	
Predictors	B	SE	B	SE	B	SE	B	SE
Percentage Foreign Born	-0.078**	0.025	-0.108	0.104	-0.255**	0.082	-0.142*	0.067
Percentage Undocumented	-0.003	0.005	0.015	0.021	-0.005	0.016	0.001	0.014
Housing Characteristics								
Percentage Project Housing	0.322***	0.100	0.904*	0.446	1.158***	0.339	-0.121	0.283
Percentage Voucher Housing	-0.045	0.110	-0.222	0.487	0.089	0.372	-0.161	0.306
Density Restrictiveness in Suburbs	-0.419	0.275	-2.327*^	1.260	2.898**	0.946	-1.344*	0.776
Median Year of Housing	0.008	0.015	0.052	0.066	0.148**	0.052	-0.065	0.044
Political Economy								
Percentage Manufacturing	0.040	0.023	0.076	0.094	0.085	0.071	0.142*	0.061
Percentage in FIRE Sector	-0.002	0.046	-0.134	0.196	-0.197	0.150	0.022	0.125
Percentage in Education	0.257***	0.032	0.712***	0.139	0.481***	0.101	0.604***	0.086
Log of Military Population	-0.079*	0.036	-0.363*	0.158	-0.127	0.124	-0.085	0.101
Patents per Capita	0.004*	0.002	0.004	0.009	-0.004	0.006	-0.007	0.005
Safety and Security								
Violent Crime Rate	0.001	0.000	0.005*	0.002	0.005**	0.002	0.004**	0.001
Constant	-11.805	30.695	-122.30	133.110	314.011**	105.027	126.714	87.449
R-Squared	0.935		0.612		0.696		0.730	
N	287		287		287		287	

*p<0.05; **p<0.01; ***p<0.001; ^One-tailed test

CONCLUSION

In his seminal book *The Truly Disadvantaged*, William Julius Wilson in 1987 called attention to the growing concentration of poverty in black neighborhoods and the high degree of spatial isolation experienced by poor African Americans. Indeed, as we have shown, the spatial concentration of black poverty did rise sharply during the 1980s; however, it leveled off thereafter and trended downward, though a sizeable gap in the spatial isolation of poor blacks and poor whites remains. Paradoxically, it wasn't poverty that became much more concentrated over the past four decades, but affluence, especially for whites and Asians. As of 2010, the average affluent Asian in metropolitan America occupied a neighborhood that was 50.5 percent affluent, and for affluent whites the figure was 45.3 percent, figures that are much greater than the concentration of poverty experienced by poor blacks and Hispanics in that year, when the average poor African American occupied a neighborhood that was 33 percent poor and the average Hispanic one that was 28 percent poor.

Across the United States, concentrations of affluence tend to arise in highly urbanized, postindustrial metropolitan areas with a high rate of home ownership and containing an innovative, creative elite and a concentration of workers in finance and insurance. In contrast, concentrations of poverty tend to arise in metropolitan areas dominated by employment in education with limited home ownership and relatively large stocks of project-based public housing. Maps indicate that the concentrations of affluence are greatest in US metropolitan areas well connected to global networks of trade, governance, and immigration that are on the nation's three coasts (Atlantic, Pacific, and the Great Lakes). In contrast, concentrations of poverty are greatest in places bypassed by globalization, located in the industrial heartland, the South, and the Great Plains.

In some of these locations, the isolation of the poor is often extreme. In Youngstown, Ohio, for example, the average poor African American inhabits a neighborhood that is 45 percent poor and the average poor Hispanic occupies one that is 44 percent poor. In Waco, Texas, the average poor white person lives in a neighborhood that is 33 percent poor and the average Asian occupies one that is 47 percent poor. As others have shown, the concentration of poverty is, in turn, associated with high rates of violent crime, disorder, and social isolation (see Peterson and Krivo 2010; Sampson 2012; Sharkey 2013). For African Americans, of course, the extremes of class isolation brought about by broader structural sifts in American society are magnified by racial segregation, which undermines the ability of affluent blacks to achieve co-residence with other affluent people while confining poor blacks to the nation's most disadvantaged neighborhoods (Massey and Denton 1993).

In sum, over the past four decades, the United States has come to be characterized by a geography of extreme inequality in which the poor inhabit neighborhoods with other poor people and the rich, especially, enjoy unprecedented concentrations of advantage. Moreover, these oases of privilege and islands of deprivation are located far from one another in different regions of the country. Across metropolitan areas, concentrations of poverty and affluence are produced by affluent and poor people living under conditions of relatively high class segregation, which inevitably produces spatial agglomerations of privilege and deprivation, with profound political implications for the nation. Salas, Rosenbluth, and Shapiro (Chapter 10, this volume) identify a "new politics of insecurity" in the United States, and Weir and King (Chapter 8, this volume) speak of a "politics of spatial inequality." Rodden (Chapter 6, this volume) sees a stark "partisan polarization" and attributes it to the nation's peculiar two-party electoral system, while Hacker and Pierson (Chapter 11, this volume) point out that it also stems from the country's "fragmented, veto-ridden structure of national authority and the degree to which it empowers those seeking to stop, rather than enable, government activity."

It is perhaps no coincidence that we observe the very highest concentration of affluence in Washington, DC, where affluent whites and Asians typically inhabit neighborhoods in which two-thirds of the residents are also affluent, with few middle-class and virtually no poor neighbors. The growing chasm in political attitudes and behavior between affluent elites and other Americans has been well documented. Compared to the average US resident, the affluent are more likely to worry about deficits than the economy and to prefer private over public solutions to social problems (Sides 2014). They are vastly more engaged politically. Whereas 99 percent of the wealthy voted in the 2012 presidential election and 60 percent gave money to a political candidate, the corresponding figures were just 78 percent and 18 percent for Americans in general (Cook, Page, and Moskowitz 2014). As a result, the affluent are far more likely than other Americans to have their political preferences reflected in public policies (Gilens 2012; Bartels 2016).

To a significant degree, the schism between self-satisfied elites and angry populists is grounded in spatial segregation by income and social class. Like all people, the affluent form their perceptions about society by extrapolating from their immediate circumstances. Unfortunately, over time the neighborhoods of the affluent have grown increasingly unrepresentative of broader conditions in the nation as a whole, most notably in the nation's capital. Under conditions of concentrated affluence, Thal (2016:1) finds that the affluent take on perceptions of social conditions that are significantly more positive than the perceptions of everyone else in society, which he asserts lead them "to develop the false sense that others' lives are as problem-free as their own, and in so doing, imperil the prospects for improving social conditions in the United States." Under these circumstances, the populist backlash that carried Donald Trump into the White House should hardly have been unexpected.

REFERENCES

Bartels, Larry M. 2016. *Unequal Democracy: The Political Economy of the New Gilded Age* Second Edition. Princeton, NJ: Princeton University Press.

Center for Migration Studies. 2016. *Data Tool: US Unauthorized and Eligible-to-Naturalize Population by PUMA*. Accessed January 15, 2016. No longer publicly available.

Cook, Fay L., Benjamin I. Page, and Rachel L. Moskowitz. 2014 "Political Engagement by Wealthy Americans." *Political Science Quarterly* 129 (3):381–398.

Emerson, Michael O., Karen J. Chai, and George Yancey. 2001. "Does Race Matter in Residential Segregation? Exploring the Preferences of White Americans." *American Sociological Review* 66(6):922–935.

Farley, Reynolds, and William H. Frey. 1994. "Changes in the Segregation of Whites from Blacks during the 1980s: Small Steps toward a More Integrated Society." *American Sociological Review* 59(1):23–45.

Florida, Richard. (2002). *The Rise of the Creative Class: And How It's Transforming Work, Leisure, Community and Everyday Life*. New York: Basic Books.

Gilens, Martin. 2012. *Affluence and Influence: Economic Inequality and Political Power in America*. Princeton, NJ: Princeton University Press.

Light, Ivan H., and Steven J. Gold. 2000. *Ethnic Economies*. Bingley, UK: Emerald Group Publishing.

Massey, Douglas S., and Jacob S. Rugh. 2018. Zoning, Affordable Housing, and Segregation in US Metropolitan Areas." In Gregory Squires, ed., *The Fight for Fair Housing: Causes, Consequences and Future Implications of the 1968 Federal Fair Housing Act*, pp. 245–265. New York: Taylor and Francis.

Massey, Douglas S., and Jonathan Tannen. 2015. "A Research Note on Trends in Black Hypersegregation." *Demography* 52:1025–1034.
2016. "Segregation, Race, and the Social Worlds of Rich and Poor. "In Henry Braun and Irwin Kirsch, eds., *The Dynamics of Opportunity in America: Evidence and Perspectives*, pp. 13–33. New York: Springer.
Massey, Douglas S., and Mary J. Fischer. 2000. "How Segregation Concentrates Poverty." *Ethnic and Racial Studies* 23:670–691.
2003. Introduction. In William G. Gale and Janet Rothenberg Pack, eds., *Brookings-Wharton Papers on Urban Affairs 2003: The Geography of Inequality in the United States 1950–2000*, pp. 1–40. Washington, DC: Brookings Institution.
Massey, Douglas S., and Mitchell E. Eggers. 1990. "The Ecology of Inequality: Minorities and the Concentration of Poverty 1970–1980." *American Journal of Sociology* 95:1153–1188.
Massey, Douglas S., and Nancy A. Denton. 1993. *American Apartheid: Segregation and the Making of the Underclass*. Cambridge, MA: Harvard University Press.
Moskos, Charles, and John S. Butler. 1996. *All That We Can Be: Black Leadership and Racial Integration the Army Way*. New York: Basic Books.
Pendall, Rolf, Robert Puentes, and Jonathan Martin. 2006. *From Traditional to Reformed: A Review of Land Use Regulations in the Nation's 50 Largest Metropolitan Areas*. Washington, DC: Brookings Institution Research Brief.
Peterson, Ruth D., and Lauren J. Krivo. 2010. *Divergent Social Worlds: Neighborhood Crime and the Racial-Spatial Divide*. New York: Russell Sage Foundation.
Quillian. Lincoln. 2012. "Segregation and Poverty Concentration: The Role of Three Segregations." *American Sociological Review* 77(3):354–379.
Rothwell, Jonathan, and Douglas S. Massey. 2009. "The Effect of Density Zoning on Racial Segregation in US Urban Areas." *Urban Affairs Review* 44:799–806.
Rugh, Jacob S., and Douglas S. Massey. 2014. "Segregation in Post-Civil Rights America: Stalled Integration or End of the Segregated Century?" *The DuBois Review: Social Science Research on Race* 11(2):202–232.
Sampson, Robert J. 2012. *Great American City: Chicago and the Enduring Neighborhood Effect*. Chicago, IL: University of Chicago Press.
Sharkey, Patrick. 2013. *Stuck in Place: Urban Neighborhoods and the End of Progress toward Racial Equality*. Chicago, IL: University of Chicago Press.
Sides, John. 2014. "The Politics of the Top 1 Percent." The Five Thirty-Eight Blog. Accessed on January 7, 2017 at https://fivethirtyeight.blogs.nytimes.com/20 11/12/14/the-politics-of-the-1-percent/?_r=1
Smith, James P. 1988. "Poverty and the Family." In Gary D. Sandefur and Marta Tienda, eds., *Divided Opportunities: Minorities, Poverty, and Social Policy*, pp. 141–172. New York: Plenum Press.
Thal, Adams. 2016. "Class Isolation and Affluent Americans' Perception of Social Conditions." *Political Behavior*. Published online September 2 at DOI:10.1007/s11109-016-9361-9

US Department of Housing and Urban Development. 2016. HUD Data Website. Accessed on January 16, 2017 at https://data.hud.gov/data_sets.html
US Federal Bureau of Investigation. 2012. *Uniform Crime Reporting Statistics*. Washington, DC: US Department of Justice. Accessed May 28, 2013 at www.ucrdatatool.gov/
US Patent and Trademark Office. 2012. Website of the US Patent and Trademark Office. Washington, DC: US Department of Commerce. Accessed May 28, 2013 at www.uspto.gov/about/stats/index.jsp

8

Redistribution and the Politics of Spatial Inequality in America

Margaret Weir and Desmond King

In the United States, the politics of inequality and poverty has long been linked to the political geography of the metropolis. Fueled by waves of immigration, American cities developed a distinctive spatial politics defined by class, ethnicity, and race. Postwar suburban development added a new dimension of separation that sharpened spatial inequality by establishing racial walls between cities and suburbs. The division of the metropolis along racial lines forged the white middle class even as it denied economic opportunities to black Americans. Separated by political boundaries, cities and suburbs effectively formed "two Americas, one black, one white," as the Kerner Commission memorably declared (United States 1968).

Over the past half century, however, the old lines between cities and suburbs have lost the significance they once had. Growing numbers of African Americans have moved to suburbs even as new cohorts of immigrants have transformed the populations of cities and suburbs. Moreover, the economic divisions of the past no longer define the geography of the metropolis: many cities have experienced economic booms and an influx of affluent residents, while poverty in the suburbs has risen. Intertwined with these spatial shifts is growing economic inequality that has richly rewarded those at the top of the income spectrum and left the middle class increasingly stressed.

Making sense of the new metropolis is critical for understanding opportunity and inequality in the United States. Place of residence

---

We would like to thank William Gomberg for research assistance and members of the SSRC Working Group on Distribution for helpful comments.

presents a uniquely formidable risk in the United States, amplifying the constellation of risks discussed by Thelen and Wiedemann (Chapter 12, this volume). Legally sanctioned racial segregation created a template for a particularly vicious form of inequality that has endured long after formal residential segregation was outlawed (King 2007; Rothstein 2017 Taylor 2019). Since the 1980s, spatial inequalities have been exacerbated by the federal government's turn away from place-based assistance. Growing economic inequality has magnified spatial differences, turning place of residence into a coveted prize – or deep disadvantage. As a result, the United States has become "a collection of societies, some of which are 'lands of opportunity' with high rates of mobility across generations, and others in which few children escape poverty" as Raj Chetty and his coauthors put it in an influential study (Chetty et al. 2014, 1). The profound effect of place means that understanding inequality and opportunity in America requires assessing the economic and political forces that exacerbate spatial inequalities and those that temper them.

This chapter argues that metropolitan America is now defined by two divergent political trends with very different implications for inequality, redistribution, and economic opportunity. On the one hand, most metropolitan areas exhibit a pattern of segmented localism that partitions the public sector by income and race. We show that metropolitan America is fragmenting across political jurisdictions, allowing affluent residents to cluster into separate municipalities shielded from fiscal responsibility for low-income residents. Lower-income people, by contrast, increasingly reside in political jurisdictions with weak public capacities. This form of urbanism, we argue, creates a skewed distribution of public resources allowing richer jurisdictions to enjoy better services and lower taxes, while jurisdictions with high numbers of low-income residents struggle to provide basic services. Political fragmentation leaves little room for redistribution across boundaries.

By contrast, a very different approach to poverty and inequality is germinating in affluent cities. Once left for dead, many big cities are now thriving as they benefit from the agglomeration effects of the knowledge economy and connections to the global economy. These cities have the economic means and the political inclination to champion a bundle of polices that aim to reduce inequality and promote opportunity. Ranging from minimum wage to universal prekindergarten, these initiatives chart a very different approach to using local public resources and public power to reduce inequality.

We begin with an analysis of the rules for creating separate local jurisdictions, showing how these rules create incentives for exit from and avoidance of economically and racially heterogeneous jurisdictions. The very limited role of higher levels of government in mitigating differences across place exacerbates those differences. We then examine the development of segmented localism, showing that jurisdictions within metropolitan areas have pulled apart economically in recent decades. We analyze the attitudes about taxes and redistribution that underlie the impulse to separate economically. The third section explores the rise of progressive urbanism, outlining the political possibilities presented by economic agglomeration and discussing the political limits of urban-based redistributive initiatives.

THE SIGNIFICANCE OF THE AMERICAN LOCAL PUBLIC SECTOR

In assessing the significance of place as a component of inequality, Freemark, Steil, and Thelen (2020) highlight the interaction of two distinct dimensions. The first encompasses the rules for placemaking and preserving the autonomy of local jurisdictions. The second includes policies that promote spatial equalization by expanding the supply of regional public goods or redistributing from richer to poorer areas. On both dimensions, American policies create strong incentives for the emergence and preservation of sharp economic and racial differences among localities.

Table 8.1 draws from their analysis to show how unique the United States is in facilitating inequality across place and how little it does to

TABLE 8.1 *Public policies and spatial inequalities*

Country	Governmental Fragmentation	Federal/State/Provincial Education Funding	Fiscal Equalization
United States	High	Low-Medium	Low
Canada	Low	High	High
France	High	High	High
Sweden	Low	High	High
Switzerland	High	High	High

Sources: Blöchliger, Charbit, 2008; Blom-Hansen, Kora, Serritzlew, Treisman 2016; Freemark, Steil, and Thelen 2000; Sellers, 2017

remedy the resulting place inequalities. The table displays variation among three policy domains that amplify or mitigate place inequality: governmental fragmentation, educational financial arrangements, and policies for fiscal equalization. Greater degrees of local governmental fragmentation promote inequality by allowing more affluent residents to choose the level of services and taxes they wish to pay for, while less affluent residents may remain trapped in jurisdictions with weak tax bases and poor services (Sellers 2017).

Arrangements for educational finance can mitigate or enhance spatial inequality: when higher levels of government foot the bill for education, place differences matter less, reducing incentives to move to obtain good schooling. Finally, higher levels of government can mitigate spatial inequalities through programs that promote fiscal equalization across place, either taking from richer places to assist poorer places or offering supplements for poorer places. As Table 8.1 indicates, American policies promote spatial inequality by the combination of high local governmental fragmentation and weak action from federal and state governments to mitigate those inequalities.

Beginning in the 1950s, many rich democracies aggressively amalgamated their local governments to suit broader economic and social goals (Blom-Hansen et al. 2016). Many national governments merged localities so that they would have the scale needed to implement the social programs delegated to them. For example, in the immediate postwar decades, Scandinavian countries undertook amalgamations that greatly reduced the numbers of localities. Canadian provinces created large metropolitan governments that had authority over the city as well as its suburbs. However, France and Switzerland, like the United States, did not undertake comparable municipal reorganization.

The fragmentation score is low if the country reduced the number of localities by more than 50 percent over the past fifty years. Education spending on the part of higher levels of government is scored as low if local government's share is more than 40 percent. Fiscal equalization is low if there is no federal or state-mandated plan to reduce fiscal inequalities among local governments.

The United States could have followed a path similar to that of Canada, if the states, which retain authority over land use, had taken action. But by the early decades of the twentieth century, most states had established rules that made it easy to create local governments, and they had granted those governments considerable autonomy. Once established, localities used their near exclusive control over land use to restrict the type of housing that could be built. In most states, local governments had the power to ban multifamily housing and to reject public housing. They could also enact "large lot" zoning requirements to ensure that only residents with higher incomes could afford to live there (Briffault 1990; Rothstein 2017). State legislatures, increasingly filled with representatives from suburban political districts, had no interest in challenging these powers (Weir 2005). In contrast to Canada and Europe, the racial politics of place in the United States made the political costs of metropolitan amalgamation prohibitive. A large literature has documented how central racial exclusion was to postwar suburban development, as real estate interests took the lead in incorporating new local governments and enacting racially restrictive covenants designed to preserve housing values (Burns 1994; Connolly 2014; Self 2005). Legal challenges to these powers – even when they result in racial exclusion – stood little chance of success. After 1973, the Supreme Court issued decisions affirming the inviolable status of local boundaries. The result, as legal scholar Michelle Anderson put it, was that "where state autonomy had long issued a license to shape local borders, local autonomy now constituted a defense of existing local borders, even those drawn using segregation's pen" (Anderson 2010, 971).

Local political fragmentation created a bias for exit and for the segmentation of public resources, well documented by a variety of studies. For example, in a study examining the number and size of local jurisdictions, Alesina, Baquir, and Hoxby (2004) show that more racially and economically heterogeneous counties create more local jurisdictions and that whites will exit to new jurisdictions as their own becomes more economically and racially diverse. Trounstine (2018) offers a more political explanation, finding that when city politics and spending favor nonwhites and the poor, whites and affluent residents will exit for a different locality.

Yet, incentives for exit and resource hoarding at the local level can be mitigated by a variety of federal and state policies that reduce spatial inequalities (Freemark, Steil, and Thelen 2020). Educational financing systems that make local governments shoulder a large part of the cost can dramatically exacerbate spatial inequalities. As Table 8.1 indicates, most rich democracies limit this source of inequality by making educational finance a national responsibility or by devising systems that redistribute from richer to poorer school districts or that greatly supplement the finances of less affluent school districts. France and Switzerland, like the United States, have many local governments, but they reduce spatial inequality through educational financing systems that limit local responsibility. The United States stands out as the only advanced democracy that does not have a robust system designed to equalize school finance. Because the federal government provides little financial support for elementary and high school education, efforts to equalize depend on state action. Despite decades of litigation to promote more equal funding for schools – and some successes – local governments continue to bear nearly half the cost of education (National Center for Education Statistics 2016).

Finally, most rich democracies have policies of territorial equalization that help buffer differences in resources and needs across localities (Sellers 2017). These take many forms, including grants from the national government and revenue-sharing schemes across local governments (Blöchliger and Charbit 2008; Kübler and Rochat 2018; Sellers 2017). The United States, by contrast, has no formal policies to promote equalization across the states or municipalities. During the 1960s, a variety of federal programs directed at cities sought to directly assist the poor and to promote economic development (Mollenkopf 1983). Even after this version of "forceful federalism" was abandoned, a series of block grants, including general revenue sharing, was put into place (King 2017). Although broadly spread across municipalities, federal revenue sharing operated on a mildly redistributive formula that disproportionately benefited less affluent jurisdictions. But even these modest forms of equalization were slashed in the 1980s. Deep cuts to place-based federal policies and the outright elimination of revenue sharing left municipalities increasingly reliant on own-source revenue, further driving a wedge between the haves and the have-nots (Caraley 1992). States did not step in to promote regional redistribution when federal support declined. Only one metropolitan area – Minneapolis–St. Paul – mandates a formal tax base sharing program, and efforts to build broad support for regional redistribution schemes have met with little success (Orfield 1997).

The United States stands as an outlier among rich democracies. It allows local governments with greatly different needs and capacities to proliferate, and it does very little to buffer those inequalities through educational financing and spatial equalization programs. When combined with the very high rates of economic inequality in the United States, these policies have set the stage for a fractured local public sector that shields the affluent and leaves low-income residents with only fragile handholds for economic security and mobility.

THE POLITICS OF SEGMENTED LOCALISM

In metropolitan areas across the United States, growing economic inequality is reflected in an increasingly stark political geography of inequality. The uneven distribution of local public goods exposes residents of some places to a severe form of the risk contagion discussed by Thelen and Wiedemann (Chapter 12, this volume), while residents of affluent places are buffered against risk. The disadvantages and rewards associated with place have often generated bitter conflict between those seeking to mitigate spatial differences and those working to reinforce existing boundaries or to introduce new ones. While these political battles are fought out in debates about local autonomy, democracy, and fairness, efforts to enforce racial exclusion are never far beneath the surface of conflict.

The Politics of Separation

The pattern of separation across political jurisdictions emerges from choices that individuals make about where to live; however, these choices are framed by the active use of public powers. Restrictive land-use policies limit the location of affordable housing much as decisions about how to draw new boundaries determine who lives in which political jurisdiction. Throughout metropolitan America, efforts to enact policies that mitigate or further entrench spatial inequalities provoke rancorous conflict. These battles reveal how deeply entrenched ideas about the desirability of economic separation have become and how closely connected they are to the preferences of white residents for racial segregation.

The most important strategy to combat concentrations of rich and poor involves spreading affordable housing throughout the metropolitan area. Yet, even people who support redistributive policies express opposition when confronted with the prospect of affordable housing being built near their own homes. In a survey of American metropolitan areas, Marble and Nall (2020) found that liberal and conservative homeowners differed on whether federal policy should promote affordable housing, with liberals far more supportive of such efforts. However, when asked about whether dense affordable housing complexes should be located in their communities, the views of liberal homeowners became much more negative.

Even small initiatives to promote affordable housing regularly meet with fervent opposition. The opponents' arguments reveal deeply held assumptions about the need for spatial separation by income and indirectly by race. Chicago, which faces a significant spatial mismatch between housing and jobs, provides an example. Affordable housing is scarce in the largely white north and northwestern suburbs where job growth has been concentrated. But opponents have been able to block most affordable housing initiatives in these suburbs. Opponents express fears about the negative impact on existing home values, a reduction in the quality of life, and the likelihood of higher taxes due to greater density. In addition, references to the city of Chicago's high-rise public housing – occupied mainly by African Americans – infuse debates about affordable housing (Hertz 2012). Many opponents invoke the specter of Cabrini-Green – one of Chicago's notoriously problematic high-rise housing projects – as a reason to oppose affordable housing. Residents and officials in affluent jurisdictions often regard the current characteristics of their municipalities as immutable. Although political boundaries and land-use regulations are the product of political decisions, public officials resist affordable housing initiatives on the ground that they are not "natural." In the words of one suburban official, "We've prided ourselves as a high-end, low-density community.... It's not natural for [affordable housing] to be here" (Yednak and Flynn, 2005, 2C).

Battles over political boundaries also provoke arguments about the best mix of incomes in a municipality. These conflicts emerge primarily in Sunbelt areas, which in contrast to the Northeast and Midwest, had laws facilitating annexation and restricting municipal incorporation. This framework for local governance left large swaths of developed territory unincorporated. Communities in these areas rely on county government for public services, supplemented for many residents by private homeowners' associations (McKenzie 1994). But when county governments expand redistribution, growing dissatisfaction with taxes and services frequently set off movements to escape county governance by establishing separate municipalities. These controversies have broad implications for redistribution because such governance changes replace a single overarching tax system with a set of separate and unequal tax bases. The debates that arise in campaigns to secede from county rule reflect beliefs that taxes and services should align in ways that leave very little room for redistribution.

In a study of clusters of new metropolitan incorporation, Waldner and Smith (2015, 187) analyzed the forces behind these governance changes. Relying on Proquest and local news sources, they examined the Atlanta, Miami, Sacramento, and Seattle areas, all metros where counties had experienced at least two incorporations in a single county between 1990 and 2009. They found that dissatisfaction with counties was the most consistent theme running through the decision to incorporate, calling it a "mass revolt against the county government" (Waldner and Smith 2015, 187). Three types of complaints stood out: dissatisfaction with services, revenue, and land use, especially the siting of apartment buildings. In each metropolitan area, it was the most affluent communities that led the push to secede from county government.

A closer look at the statements of public officials and residents in these metros reveals the contrasting ideas about fairness and redistribution that underlie these conflicts. Proponents of breaking away from county government often think of communities in terms of "donors" and "receivers," and they express acute awareness that they pay more into the county than they are getting from it. In the Atlanta suburbs, proponents of the proposed city of Brookhaven found it unfair that their community had "14 percent of unincorporated DeKalb's [County] tax base but less than 9 percent of the population" (Torpy 2012, B1). Similarly, a supporter of the effort to create the new city of Arden Arcade in Sacramento County noted that his area served as "the revenue generator of the county.... Sixty percent of the tax revenue earned in Arden Arcade goes out"(Garvin 2010). Eve Galambos, the leader of the move to incorporate affluent Sandy Springs in Georgia and later mayor of the new city, reflected on the impetus for incorporation: "We were a cash cow. We were tired of subsidizing everybody else's police department, and we had no policemen" (Pomerance, 2008, D1).

By contrast, opponents of municipal incorporation praise the benefits of a broader tax base. In the Atlanta area, a leader of a local civic association argued that the cityhood movement could be seen as "cynical": "You peel away affluent areas, get enough commercial and the heck with people left behind. Before, we kind of spread the load" (Torpy 2012, B1). African American public officials pointed to the way redistribution and taxes intertwined with race. Reacting to the 2005 incorporation of the affluent Sandy Springs in Atlanta's Fulton County, State Senator Vincent Fort rued, "You're going to have this different tax distribution that is going to have an impact.... That's nothing but apartheid" (Barry 2005). Indeed, the municipal carving up of Fulton County, which had a majority Black government, can be seen as a way to prevent minorities "from making claims on the property of affluent whites through the political system" (Connor 2015, 40). In that sense, the municipal incorporation movement echoes Trounstine's (2018) finding that whites exit political systems when Blacks gain power and increase public spending.

Conflicts over affordable housing and local government reflect broader public attitudes about taxes, redistribution, and community in the United States. Williamson's study of attitudes about taxation argues that Americans express a willingness to pay taxes when they feel a "sense of *fellowship*" (Williamson 2017, 8). In a national survey and in-depth interviews, she finds that "Americans like when their taxes clearly go to the people with whom they feel a strong sense of shared interest" (2017, 80). In addition, they prefer public spending that is "visible and proximate" (2017, 80; see also Mettler 2011). In metropolitan America, local governments with homogenous populations help create that sense of commonality. Indeed, Williamson, in line with other researchers, finds that local public investments are among the most popular forms of government spending (2017, 80). Not surprisingly, when big county governments increase redistributive spending and perceptions arise that public spending benefits some areas more than others, pressures to redefine local government emerge. Likewise, initiatives to build affordable housing in affluent communities confront resident concerns about possible impacts on local taxes. When combined with deeply embedded attitudes that define community in racial terms, these views support exclusion and exit.

The desire of affluent suburbs to secede also reflects the nostalgia analyzed by Andra Gillespie (Chapter 2, this volume). In the mid-1990s, Newt Gingrich, who represented the Atlanta suburbs in Congress, praised Atlanta's white suburbs in explicitly nostalgic terms, describing them as "a sort of Norman Rockwell world" where "the values ... of the mid-50's are the values of most of these people now" (Applebome, 1994, 1A). Although they are now embedded in racially diverse metropolitan areas and serve as major employment centers, seceding municipalities have sought to retain a small-town ambiance. Demolishing existing multifamily housing and preventing new apartments from being built have been very high on the agenda of new municipalities in the Atlanta region. The price of nostalgia is one borne by lower-income residents – especially people of color – who cannot find affordable housing close to employment centers or who cannot find affordable housing at all.

The Growth of Spatial Inequality

These attitudes have contributed to growing spatial inequality in metropolitan America. Examining census tract data from 1990 to 2010, Bischoff and Reardon (2014) demonstrate that income segregation in metropolitan areas grew rapidly from 2000 to 2009 and that, over time, middle-income neighborhoods shrunk while poorer and richer neighborhoods grew. Their work shows that most of the increase in income segregation results from the segregation of affluence rather than the segregation of poverty. Florida and Mellander (2015) provide a complementary analysis, charting the rise in economic segregation by using income, education, and occupation as indicators. Massey and Rugh (Chapter 7, this volume) highlight the growth of neighborhood-level economic segregation over time and show how it is reinforced by segregation of Blacks and Latinos.

Segregation by neighborhood is not the only way to understand spatial inequality. As racially exclusive suburbanization grew in the 1950s, political boundaries between city and suburb – not simply neighborhood – became even more significant. With suburbanization, Trounstine shows, a greater share of metropolitan racial segregation occurs across cities rather than within them (2018, 167). These patterns affect the public resources that residents can access. Research has shown that cities with the strongest fiscal capacity spend the most on redistributive purposes (e.g., Hajnal and Trounstine 2010, 1144, 1150). Jurisdictions with lower incomes have weaker tax bases and less capacity to redistribute. Even though most local governments do not directly spend significant sums on redistributive programs, their fiscal capacity nonetheless matters for low-income residents. Local expenditures on a wide range of public goods – including police, fire, roads, transportation, public libraries, parks, and recreation programs – all affect the well-being and future prospects of low-income residents.

The growing population of suburbs makes it important to assess economic divisions not only between the historic central city and its suburbs but also across suburban municipalities. In many parts of the country, the central city accounts for a relatively small fraction of the metropolitan area population. Moreover, since 1990, poverty in suburbs has grown. By the mid-2000s, a majority of poor residents in major metropolitan areas lived outside the historical central city (Kneebone and Berube 2012). Recognizing the importance of political jurisdictions, researchers have begun to track inequality across all political jurisdictions in a metropolitan area to understand emerging patterns of economic and political segregation. In a study of fifty metropolitan areas from 1980 to 2000, Swanstrom and his coauthors found that the suburban population was increasingly sorted into affluent and poor jurisdictions, with the proportion of middle-income municipalities declining (Swanstrom, Casey, Flack, and Dreier 2004, 7). In 1980, 75 percent of suburban residents lived in middle-income suburbs but only 60 percent did so in 2000.[1] At the same time, they found that the gap between the richest and poorest suburbs had grown.

The expanding economic gap across political jurisdictions has produced significant fiscal segregation. Examining the fifty largest metropolitan areas, Orfield and Luce (2013, 403) found that predominantly nonwhite suburbs had a per capita tax base that was 66 percent of the regional average, while the per capita tax base of predominantly white suburbs was 108 percent.

Separate and Unequal

Attitudes and laws that promote racial and income separation have sorted much of metropolitan America into places that protect higher income people from the costs of redistribution while other jurisdictions have little to offer their residents, even at high tax rates. The political geography of inequality varies in regions of the country. In the Northeast and Midwest, greater governmental fragmentation and the anti-density zoning that accompanies it have enhanced segregation by income and race (Rothwell and Massey 2009). As we have seen, some Sunbelt metros have embraced political fragmentation in recent decades. Sunbelt metros also achieve separation when municipalities pursue annexation strategies that bypass low-income communities.

In the Northeast and Midwest, high levels of fragmentation have resulted in a growing number of small high-poverty jurisdictions: by 2014, more than a third of the poor outside the historic central city lived in small high-poverty jurisdictions in these regions (Mattiuzzi and Weir 2019). In all regions of the country, Blacks and Latinos were overrepresented in such small high-poverty cities. Small high-poverty jurisdictions face special challenges. With high needs and restricted resources, they are vulnerable to "death spirals" of reduced services, higher taxes, and population loss (Mallach 2018, 164–165).

Harvey, Illinois, a majority Black town of 24,908 in Chicago's south suburbs, provides a stark example. Struggling with pension payments, a budget shortfall, and a 38 percent poverty rate, the town laid off a quarter of its police force and 40 percent of its firefighters in 2018

---

[1] These authors define middle-income jurisdictions as those falling between 75 percent and 125 percent of the regional per capita income.

(Koeske 2018; Slowik 2018). Yet, the town had a high tax rate. A 2019 study comparing the tax rates of selected municipalities in the Chicago area showed that the poorest municipalities had the highest tax rates. The tax rate in Harvey was three times as high as that in affluent largely white municipalities (Civic Federation 2019, 6). High tax rates stand in the way of commercial development and depress housing values. In contrast with more affluent communities, where homeowners can expect their property to appreciate, homeowners in these distressed municipalities experience declining property values (Mallach 2018, 164–165). Moreover, these communities suffered the highest rate of foreclosures during the 2008 recession. Housing, which for a majority of white Americans serves as the central vehicle for building wealth, instead drains resources from such poor, largely minority communities.

The experience of affluent jurisdictions differs markedly. Wealthier places can offer ample public services at a low tax rate. The well-off suburb of Naperville featured one of the lowest tax rates of the municipalities in the Chicago suburbs (Civic Federation 2019, 6). In the Sunbelt, many affluent communities that incorporated to escape county governance benefited from lower taxes and better services. For example, Key Biscayne, Florida, whose decision to incorporate in 1991 set off a wave of municipal incorporations in Miami-Dade County, was able to reduce taxes by 20 percent at the same time that it dramatically raised the quality of services (Waldner and Smith 2015, 188).

Many cities in Sunbelt metros restrict redistribution through their annexation strategies. The highest and fastest growing proportion of the metropolitan poor in unincorporated areas is found in southern metros (Mattiuzzi and Weir 2019). With generally more lenient annexation powers, Sunbelt cities routinely annex affluent areas that will add to their tax base while skipping over poorer areas that require more services (Anderson 2007). This process of *underbounding* leaves poorer, often minority communities reliant on county governments. Many such communities lack even the most basic services, including water and sewers. Swanstrom and his coauthors found that 40 percent of the poorest suburbs were unincorporated communities, the vast majority in Sunbelt metros (Swanstrom et al. 2004, 16–17). Throughout the Sunbelt, a lopsided distribution of local resources is achieved not only by a patchwork of unequal municipalities but also by deliberate decisions to leave some places out of municipalities.

BIG CITIES AND THE POLITICS OF REDISTRIBUTION

Even as metropolitan America divides into fiscally separate worlds, the big cities at the heart of the metropolis have become more economically and demographically diverse. Through a combination of immigration and gentrification, many big cities have disrupted the downward demographic spiral that once seemed inevitable. At the same time, the rise of the knowledge economy has brought extraordinary prosperity to some cities. Animated by liberal cosmopolitan ideas, these thriving cities combine the economic and political elements needed to promote local redistribution. Over the past decade, a cluster of new municipal ordinances and spending plans points to a significant local role in redistribution. Yet, questions remain about how far these initiatives can spread and whether they can be sustained.

Theories of fiscal federalism posit that competition among local governments prevents them from engaging in redistribution (Peterson 1981). Because they are responsible for raising their own revenue, the theory argues, American cities necessarily seek taxpaying residents and industries. They avoid redistribution for fear of attracting residents who consume costly services. But considerable research has shown that cities do, in fact, redistribute. Many cities spend their own source revenue on housing, health care, and other social services directed at lower-income residents (Craw 2015). Researchers have shown that larger cities and those with greater fiscal capacity are more likely to redistribute (e.g., Craw 2010; Hajnal and Trounstine 2010, 1144, 1150). As this suggests, the competitive position of cities varies across place and over time as they benefit or suffer from economic and governmental changes (Craw 2015).

Over the past three decades, the possibilities for urban redistribution have been amplified by the move away from manufacturing toward the innovation-based knowledge economy. A growing body of research has documented the emergence of economic agglomerations as industries colocate to innovation hubs (Moretti 2012; Storper 2013). Cities that become innovation hubs benefit from concentrations of skilled workers, specialized service providers, and knowledge spillovers (Moretti 2012, 124). Once established, the competitive advantage of these cities escalates. Firms that require access to agglomerations risk failure if they locate elsewhere. But it is not only firms in the knowledge economy that face constraints about where they locate. Hotels, for example, require some downtown locations. These constraints on business raise the cost of exit, giving cities more room to redistribute than the fiscal federalism model posits (Schragger 2016).

The demographic and political characteristics of big cities also predispose them toward redistribution. Researchers have shown that more racial and ethnic diversity leads cities to engage in more redistributive spending (e.g., Craw 2010; Trounstine 2018, 153).[2] Urban residents are also more likely than those in rural areas to hold economically liberal views. In an examination of data from the General Social Survey from 1970 to 2010, Rodden (2019) shows that residents of the urban core of big cities are far more likely to express support for government intervention in the economy than are their counterparts in suburbs, smaller cities, or rural areas (Rodden 2019, 87–88). Even as cities have attracted more affluent residents over the past two decades, the economic liberalism of big cities has not declined.

Cities are also home to a constellation of organizations that influence public attitudes, strengthen politicians' resolve, and uncover sources of leverage to promote redistribution. Advocacy groups, community-based organizations, philanthropies, and labor unions separately and in coalition have put redistributive polices on urban agendas. Since the early 1990s, community-labor coalitions have become active in cities across the country. The translocal organization of labor and of some community-based organizations, such as the now defunct social justice organization ACORN, has facilitated the spread of policies across different cities. While there is considerable criticism of philanthropy's limited engagement with advocacy, philanthropic dollars have been essential to the operation of the campaigns for redistribution. Through lobbying, mobilizing, protesting, these groups have forged new models for urban redistribution.

The earliest policy victories rested on the contracting and regulatory functions of the city. The "living wage movement" launched by ACORN and organized labor in the 1990s required city contractors to pay a wage substantially higher than the federal minimum wage and, in some cases, to provide benefits (Martin 2001). By 2016, 140 cities had adopted some form of the living wage (Bernhardt and Osterman 2017). Organized labor turned to the regulatory power of cities as it launched the "Fight for Fifteen," passing city ordinances requiring employers to raise the minimum wage to fifteen dollars an hour. In the face of federal inaction, these efforts to raise the minimum wage in cities and counties across the country

---

[2] Trounstine (2018, 156), however, shows that racial segregation decreases redistributive spending in diverse cities.

have achieved significant success. By 2019, 44 cities and counties had enacted new minimum wage laws (University of California, Berkeley Labor Center 2019). Reflecting the leverage provided by the combination of agglomeration economies and activist mobilization, half of these were in the San Francisco Bay Area. Others included Chicago and Cook County; Seattle and surrounding suburbs; cities in the Los Angeles area; Minnesota's Twin Cities; and the Washington, DC, area. Most of these cities and counties have high education levels, as would be expected from the agglomeration literature.[3] Unions have also deployed strategies to intervene in economic development projects to wrest benefits for local communities. Community-benefit agreements use the city's land-use authority and unions' contracting relationships to require that developers provide affordable housing, jobs, and parks and other amenities (Schragger 2016, 149–161).

Urban success in enacting policies to assist low-income residents has dramatically raised the profile of concerns about inequality and low-wage work. But urban redistribution remains inherently limited. Researchers have confirmed that urban public spending varies in accordance with local ideology (Einstein and Kogan 2016; Tausanovich and Warshaw 2014). While these findings challenge the emphasis on constraints that drive theories of fiscal federalism, they also underscore the fact that redistributive efforts involving spending will vary across municipalities. More conservative municipalities will aim to keep taxes and spending low. Likewise, the use of urban regulatory power to impose new demands on employers will vary. Struggling cities that are the losers in the new knowledge economy have less leverage for using their regulatory authority to promote redistribution. Even when they adopt living wage policies, for example, economically distressed cities impose significant restrictions on the scope of the policies. Regulations and city ordinances that promote redistribution have also been limited by state preemption of local authority (Briffault 2018). "Blue cities" in "red states" have been especially subject to state laws that revoke local authority to enact such policies. By 2018, 60 percent of Americans lived in states that prohibited localities from raising the minimum wage (Hertel-Fernandez 2019, 240–241).

The impact of such polices is also limited by rising property values, which especially affect low-income residents in cities with the most

---

[3] Three-quarters of the local governments that raised the local minimum wage were in metropolitan areas where education levels (measured by percentage with BA and above) were in the top 25 percent out of 389 metros (SSTI 2017).

leverage over employers. Rising housing costs have made life in the most prosperous cities much less advantageous for low-wage workers, effectively erasing any wage benefits that these locations offer (Florida 2017).[4] Such costs may also lead poorer residents to leave prosperous cities altogether. While there is little agreement among scholars about the displacement effects of gentrification, rising suburban poverty is undoubtedly linked to rising home prices in some metropolitan areas (Freeman 2004; Schafran 2018).

These limits suggest that the remarkable movement for urban redistribution may only directly assist a relatively small percentage of low-wage workers. But in animating a movement and creating new policy models, these urban innovations pave the way for state and federal initiatives that may ultimately make place a less significant factor in the risks and rewards that confront Americans.

CONCLUSION

The bias for localism in American law and policy laid the foundation for a patchwork metropolis of separate political jurisdictions divided by income and by race. Once the federal government began to shrink place-based investment in the 1980s, prospects for mitigating economic differences across place dimmed. Instead, the risk of living in resource-poor places was pushed onto the shoulders of individuals, a version of the "risk shift" identified by Jacob Hacker (Hacker 2019). Disadvantaged jurisdictions expose their residents to an extreme form of risk amplification. Because place is linked to so many resources essential for well-being – school quality, housing values, vulnerability to foreclosures, public resources for children, social services, and access to transit – residents of resource-poor places face risks on multiple fronts.

The United States shows little sign of moving toward the municipal amalgamation strategies so common in European nations. Indeed, if anything, the laws governing placemaking are moving to support more fragmentation and difference in most states. But initiatives are underway in metropolitan areas across the country that provide starting points for a less divided metropolis.

Three types of initiatives stand out. The first involves supporting public investments in boundary-crossing transit systems. With the growth of

---

[4] In fact, David Autor's recent work (2019) suggests that there may be no benefits in terms of wages for service sector workers.

poverty in suburbs, the need for transportation to work and services has become acute. The greater racial diversity of suburbs may make suburban places long opposed to transit more supportive, as the recent extension of public transportation into Atlanta's suburbs suggests (Karner 2018). A second strategy is the continuing effort to locate affordable housing throughout the metropolitan area. Efforts to institute region-wide housing vouchers provide one avenue for change. A 2015 Supreme Court ruling opened new possibilities by upholding challenges to the common practice of building publicly supported affordable housing in distressed, racially segregated communities. Fundamental to all housing strategies is the enforcement of federal fair housing laws (Orfield and Luce 2013). A third initiative for diminishing the significance of place entails building translocal networks that can help address the collective action problems that block cooperation across local political boundaries. Such networks can begin to knit together systems of support for low-income residents of different municipalities. They can also provide political support for advocates confronting local resistance in their efforts to win political influence or change local policy.

Similar to the minimum wage regulations being pioneered in progressive cities, efforts to reduce the risks associated with place currently have relied primarily on local initiatives. Significant progress on both agendas will be difficult to achieve without the support of states and the federal government. For most of its history, the laws and policies of the United States supported the separation of people by race; now divisions fall increasingly along income lines as well. Federal interventions that press against these divisions are essential for creating equal opportunity regardless of place.

REFERENCES

Alesina, Alberto, Reza Baqir, and Caroline Hoxby. 2004. "Political Jurisdictions in Heterogeneous Communities." *Journal of Political Economy* 112, no. 2: 348–396.

Anderson, Michelle Wilde. 2008. "Cities Inside Out: Race, Poverty, and Exclusion at the Urban Fringe." *UCLA Law Review* 55, no. 5: 1095–1160.

2010. "Mapped Out of Local Democracy." *Stanford Law Review* 62, no. 4: 931–1003.

Applebome, Peter, 1994. "A Suburban Eden Where the Right Rules." *New York Times*, p. 1A. www.nytimes.com/1994/08/01/us/a-suburban-eden-where-the-right-rules.html

Autor, David. 2019. "Work of the Past, Work of the Future." NBER Working Paper No. 25588, Feb. www.nber.org/papers/w25588

Barry, Ellen. 2005. "Nascent City Trying to Keep Its Money Close to Home." *Los Angeles Times*, www.latimes.com/archives/la-xpm-2005-aug-29-na-sandy29-story.html

Bernhardt, Annette, and Paul Osterman. 2017. "Organizing for Good Jobs: Recent Developments and New Challenges." *Work and Occupations* 44, no. 1: 89–112.

Bischoff, Kendra, and Sean F. Reardon. 2014. Residential Segregation by Income, 1970–2009. Pp. 208–233 in John R. Logan (ed.), *Diversity and Disparities: America Enters a New Century*. New York: Russell Sage Foundation.

Blöchliger, Hansjörg, and Claire Charbit. 2008. "Fiscal Equalisation." *OECD Journal: Economic Studies*, no. 1: 1–22.

Blom-Hansen, Jens, Kurt Houlberg, Søren Serritzlew, and Daniel Treisman. 2016. "Jurisdiction Size and Local Government Policy Expenditure: Assessing the Effect of Municipal Amalgamation." *American Political Science Review* 110, no. 4: 812–831.

Bridges, Amy. *Morning Glories: Municipal Reform in the Southwest*. Princeton, NJ: Princeton University Press, 1997.

Briffault, Richard. 1990. "Our Localism: Part I–The Structure of Local Government Law." *Columbia Law Review* 90, no. 1: 1–115.

2018. "The Challenge of the New Preemption." *Stanford Law Review* 70, no. 6: 1995–2027.

Burns, Nancy. 1994. *The Formation of American Local Governments: Private Values in Public Institutions*. New York: Oxford University Press.

Caraley, Demetrious. 1992. "Washington Abandons the Cities." *Political Science Quarterly* 107, no. 1: 1–30.

Chetty, Raj, Nathaniel Hendren, Patrick Kline, and Emmanuel Saez. 2014. "Where Is the Land of Opportunity? The Geography of Intergenerational Mobility in the United States." *The Quarterly Journal of Economics* 129, no. 4: 1553–1623.

The Civic Federation. 2019. *Estimated Effective Property Tax Rates, 2007–2016*. Chicago January 9. www.civicfed.org/sites/default/files/civic_federation_effective_tax_rates_report_2007–2016.pdf

Connolly, N. D. B. 2014. *A World More Concrete: Real Estate and the Remaking of Jim Crow South Florida*. Chicago: University of Chicago Press.

Connor, Michan Andrew. 2015. "Metropolitan Secession and the Space of Color-Blind Racism in Atlanta." *Journal of Urban Affairs* 37, no. 4: 436–461.

Craw, Michael. 2010. "Deciding to Provide: Local Decisions on Providing Social Welfare." *American Journal of Political Science* 54, no. 4: 906–920.

2015. "Caught at the Bottom? Redistribution and Local Government in an Era of Devolution." *State and Local Government Review* 47, no. 1: 68–77.

Einstein, Katherine Levine, and Vladimir Kogan. 2016. "Pushing the City Limits: Policy Responsiveness in Municipal Government." *Urban Affairs Review* 52, no. 1: 3–32.

Ertas, Nevbahar, Jungbu Kim, John Matthews, and Laura Wheeler. 2009. *A Comparison of County Services Provided by the Counties of Cobb, DeKalb, Fulton and Gwinnett*. Report 6 of *Creating a New Milton County*. Fiscal Research Center Andrew Young School of Policy Studies Georgia State

University, February 2009. https://cslf.gsu.edu/files/2014/06/Report_6_Service_Comparison_3-3-09.pdf

Florida, Richard. 2017. *The New Urban Crisis*. New York: Basic Books.

Florida, Richard, and Charlotta Mellander. 2015. *Segregated City: The Geography of Economic Segregation in America's Metros*. Toronto: Martin Prosperity Institute, University of Toronto.

Freeman, Lance, and Frank Braconi. 2004. "Gentrification and Displacement: New York City in the 1990s." *Journal of the American Planning Association* 70, no. 1: 39–52.

Garvin, Cosmo, 2010. "Is Sacramento Cracking Up?" newsreview.com www.newsreview.com/sacramento/is-sacramento-cracking-up/content?oid=1447274

Gourevitch, Ruth, Solomon Greene, and Rolf Pendall. 2018. *Place and Opportunity*. Washington DC: Urban Institute.

Frasure-Yokley, Lorrie. 2015. *Racial and Ethnic Politics in American Suburbs*. New York: Cambridge University Press.

Freemark, Yonah, Justin Steil, and Kathleen Thelen. 2020. "Varieties of Urbanism: A Comparative View of Inequality and the Dual Dimensions of Metropolitan Fragmentation." *Politics and Society* 48, no. 2: 235-274.

Hacker, Jacob S. 2019. *The Great Risk Shift: The New Economic Insecurity and the Decline of the American Dream*, 2nd edn. New York: Oxford University Press.

Hajnal, Zoltan L., and Jessica Trounstine. 2010. "Who or What Governs?: The Effects of Economics, Politics, Institutions, and Needs on Local Spending." *American Politics Research* 38(6): 1130–1163.

Hertel-Fernandez, Alexander, 2019. *State Capture: How Conservative Activists, Bug Businesses, and Wealthy Donors Reshaped the American States-and the Nation*. New York: Oxford University Press.

Hertz, Daniel. 2012. "Exiling the Poor." *In These Times*. Sept. 2. https://inthesetimes.com/article/exiling-the-poor

Karner, Alex, and Richard Duckworth. 2018. "Pray 'for Transit': Seeking Transportation Justice in Metropolitan America." *Urban Studies*, 56, no. 9: 1882–1900.

King, Desmond. 2007. *Separate and Unequal: African Americans and the US Federal Government*. New York: Oxford University Press.

2017. "Forceful Federalism against Racial Inequality." *Government and Opposition*, 52: 256–282.

Kneebone, Elizabeth, and Alan Berube. 2012. *Confronting Suburban Poverty in America*. Washington DC: Brookings Institution Press.

Koeske, Zak. 2018. "Harvey Lays Off 40 Police and Fire Employees, Union Officials Say." *Daily Southtown*, April 10. www.chicagotribune.com/suburbs/daily-southtown/ct-sta-harvey-layoffs-st-0411-story.html

Kübler, Daniel, and Philippe E. Rochat. 2018. "Fragmented Governance and Spatial Equity in Metropolitan Areas: The Role of Intergovernmental Cooperation and Revenue-Sharing." *Urban Affairs Review*, 55, no. 5: 1247-1279.

Mallach, Alan. 2018. *The Divided City: Poverty and Prosperity in Urban America*. Washington, DC: Island Press.

Marble, William, and Clayton Nall. 2020. "Where Interests Trump Ideology: Liberal Homeowners and Local Opposition to Housing Development," forthcoming *Journal of Politics*. williammarble.co/docs/MarbleNallJOP.pdf

Martin, Isaac. 2001. "Dawn of the Living Wage: The Diffusion of a Redistributive Municipal Policy." *Urban Affairs Review* 36, no. 4: 470–496.

Mattiuzzi, Elizabeth, and Margaret Weir. 2020. "Governing the New Geography of Poverty in Metropolitan America," *Urban Affairs Review*, 56, no. 4:1086–1131.

McKenzie, Evan. 1994. *Privatopia: Homeowner Associations and the Rise of Residential Private Government*. New Haven: Yale University Press.

Mettler, Suzanne. 2011. *The Submerged State: How Invisible Government Policies Undermine American Democracy*. Chicago: University of Chicago Press.

Miller, Gary J. 1981. *Cities by Contract: The Politics of Municipal Incorporation*. Cambridge, MA: MIT Press.

Mollenkopf, John H. 1983. *The Contested City*. Princeton: Princeton University Press.

Moretti, Enrico. 2012. *The New Geography of Jobs*. New York: Houghton Mifflin Harcourt.

National Center for Education Statistics. 2016. Table 235.10 Revenues for public elementary and secondary schools, by source of funds: Selected years, 1919–20 through 2013–14. https://nces.ed.gov/programs/digest/d16/tables/dt16_235.10.asp

Orfield, Myron. *Metropolitics: A Regional Agenda for Community and Stability*. Washington DC: Brookings Institution Press, 1997.

Orfield, Myron, and Thomas F. Luce. 2013. "America's Racially Diverse Suburbs: Opportunities and Challenges." *Housing Policy Debate* 23, no. 2: 395–430.

Peterson, Paul. 1981. *City Limits*. Chicago: University of Chicago Press.

Pomerance, Rachel. 2008. "The New City Next Door? – Dunwoody Has a Lot in Common with Neighboring Sandy Springs." *Atlanta Journal Constitution*. May 22. https://infoweb-newsbankcom.revproxy.brown.edu/apps/news/document-view?p=WORLDNEWS&docref=news/120D4B2A798868A8

Reich, Robert B. 1992. *The Work of Nations: Preparing Ourselves for 21st-Century Capitalism*. New York: Vintage.

Rodden, Jonathan A. 2019. *Why Cities Lose: The Deep Roots of the Urban-Rural Political Divide*. New York: Basic Books.

Rothstein, Richard. 2017. *The Color of Law*. New York: Liveright.

Rothwell, Jonathan, and Douglas S. Massey. 2009. "The Effect of Density Zoning on Racial Segregation in US Urban Areas." *Urban Affairs Review* 44, no. 6: 779–806.

Rusk, David. 2013. *Cities Without Suburbs: A Census 2010 Perspective*. Washington DC: Woodrow Wilson Center Press.

Schafran, Alex. 2018. *The Road to Resegregation: Northern California and the Failure of Politics*. Oakland: University of California Press.

Schragger, Richard. 2016. *City Power: Urban Governance in a Global Age*. New York: Oxford University Press.

Self, Robert O. 2005. *American Babylon: Race and the Struggle for Postwar Oakland*. Princeton: Princeton University Press.

Sellers, Jefferey M. 2017. "Metropolitan Inequality and Governance: A Framework for Global Comparison." Pp. 1–23 in Jefferey M. Sellers, Marta Arretche, Daniel Kübler, and Eran Razin (eds.), *Inequality and Governance in the Metropolis: Place Equality Regimes and Fiscal Choices in Eleven Countries*. London: Palgrave Macmillan.

Slowik, Ted. 2018. "South Suburban Group Joins Lawsuit Claiming Berrios 'Systematically and Illegally' Discriminated Against Black, Latino Homeowners." Daily Southtown, March 20. www.chicagotribune.com/suburbs/daily-so

SSTI, Educational Attainment by Metropolitan Area. 2017. https://ssti.org/blog/useful-stats-educational-attainment-metropolitan-area–2007–2017

Storper, Michael. 2013. *Keys to the City: How Economics, Institutions, Social Interaction, and Politics Shape Development*. Princeton: Princeton University Press.

Swanstrom, Todd, Colleen Casey, Robert Flack, and Peter Dreier. 2004. *Pulling Apart: Economic Segregation among Suburbs and Central Cities in Major Metropolitan Areas*. Metropolitan Policy Program. Washington, DC: Brookings Institution.

Tausanovitch, Chris, and Christopher Warshaw. 2014. "Representation in Municipal Government." *American Political Science Review* 108, no. 3: 605–641.

Taylor, Keeanga-Yamahtta. 2019. *Race for Profit*. Chapel Hill: N.C.: University of North Carolina Press.

Torpy, Bill. 2012, "New Cities Movement – Incorporation Gripping DeKalb – Revenue Concerns Drive Debate." *Atlanta Journal-Constitution*. September 23.

Trounstine, Jessica. 2018. *Segregation by Design: Local Politics and Inequality in American Cities*. New York: Cambridge University Press.

United States. National Advisory Commission on Civil Disorders. 1968. *Report of the National Advisory Commission on Civil Disorders*. Washington, DC: Government Printing Office.

University of California, Berkeley Labor Center. 2019. "Inventory of US City and County Minimum Wage Ordinances." http://laborcenter.berkeley.edu/minimum-wage-living-wage-resources/inventory-of-us-city-and-county-minimum-wage-ordinances/

Waldner, Leora, and Russell M. Smith. 2015. "The Great Defection: How New City Clusters Form to Escape County Governance." *Public Administration Quarterly* 39, no. 2: 170–219.

Weir, Margaret. 2005. "States, Race, and the Decline of New Deal Liberalism," *Studies in American Political Development* 19, no. 2: 157–172.

Williamson, Vanessa S. 2017. *Read My Lips: Why Americans Are Proud to Pay Taxes*. Princeton: Princeton University Press.

Weiher, Gregory. 1991. *The Fractured Metropolis: Political Fragmentation and Metropolitan Segregation*. Albany: State Universtiy of New York Press.

Yednak, Crystal, and Courtney Flynn. 2005. "Affordable Housing Law Deadline Looms," *Chicago Tribune*, April 1, p. 2C. https://search-proquest-com.libproxy.berkeley.edu/hnpchicagotribune/docview/2351488788/fulltextPDF/8ECCE79FA7834964PQ/3?accountid=14496

PART III

POLITICS

9

Electoral Realignments in the Atlantic World

Carles Boix

In 1958, while putting together all his essays at Palo Alto's Center for the Advanced Study of Behavioral Sciences into what would become *The End of Ideology*, Daniel Bell wrote a strong epilogue concluding that "the old ideologies have lost their 'truth' and the power to persuade." Instead, he wrote, "in the Western world, there is today a rough consensus among intellectuals on political issues: the acceptance of the Welfare State; the desirability of decentralized power; a system of mixed economy and of political pluralism."[1] Indeed, as the Cold War period unfolded, democratic rule stabilized across Western Europe under the rule of broad mass parties that, leaving behind the tragic conflicts that had erupted on that continent during the interwar period, now saw democracy, capitalism, and welfare states as inextricably intertwined.

Sixty years later, however, the politics of advanced democracies are in a state of turmoil. Trust in national politicians is at an all-time low. Electoral participation, which averaged 80 percent in Europe during the Cold War, has declined to about 65 percent – with abstention mostly clustered among low-income strata and young cohorts. The old traditional alignment that pitted moderate social democratic parties against a reformist right has been challenged by new politicians who promise, mostly through a combination of protectionist trade measures and strict

---

This chapter was initially prepared for the Anxieties of Democracy meeting that took place at Yale University on November 30, 2018. I am grateful for the comments of its participants and the suggestions of Frances McCall Rosenbluth and Margaret Weir and two anonymous referees.

[1] Reproduced in Bell (1988).

barriers to migration, to restore the declining fortunes of America's and Europe's old industrial working class. Right after wrapping up the presidential nomination in the last wave of primaries in May 2016, Trump stated, in an interview with *Bloomberg Businessweek*, that the Republican party would be "five, 10 years from now – a different party. You're going to have a worker's party. A party of people that haven't had a real wage increase in 18 years, that are angry." Across the Atlantic, and already twenty year earlier, the leader of the National Front, Jean-Marie Le Pen, referred to his party as "the party of the working class" in the presidential campaign of 1995. Several electoral campaigns later, her daughter, Marine Le Pen, would ask Florian Philippot, a former supporter of Pierre Chevènement, a left-wing member of the French Socialist Party, to write a new economic program for the National Front. In declarations to a French newspaper, Phillipot claimed, "Jean-Pierre Chevènement's project is carried forward by Marine Le Pen."[2] In fact, populist and nationalist alliances now govern a handful of European countries. And, in a context of increasing polarization, almost half of American voters elected Trump and, with him, a policy agenda allegedly intent on challenging the liberal system of global cooperation and open economies designed by the United States after 1945.

In this chapter, I consider three topics. First, I explore the economic foundations of this remarkable political turnaround. Second, I describe the historical sequence through which populist movements took advantage of those changes. Finally, I discuss, necessarily in a succinct manner, what may be the responses to the new economic and political challenges faced by advanced economies.

TECHNOLOGICAL CHANGE AND ITS EMPLOYMENT AND WAGE EFFECTS

Following a sweeping wave of technical innovations, which ranged from the systematic use of electricity and electric motors to the invention of the assembly line and the use of mass production techniques, Western economies experienced large productivity gains and an unprecedented period of economic growth throughout most of the twentieth century. Between 1900 and 1975, the economy expanded on average at an annual rate of about 2.5 percent in the United States and almost 3 percent in Western Europe – a pace two times faster than in the previous century. Per capita

---

[2] Both quotes are taken from Judis (2016), pages 103 and 145.

income doubled in the forty years preceding World War II. It then doubled again during the Cold War. More fundamentally, economic growth was spread quite uniformly across all social strata. Unskilled workers, in high demand during the first Industrial Revolution, were replaced by semiskilled individuals capable of reading the operating instructions of machines as well as installing, repairing, and improving them. Moreover, a systematic fall in communication and transportation costs led to the rise of global markets, the formation of large firms, and with them the growth of new layers of white-collar jobs needed to manage those corporations. With semiskilled and skilled jobs in higher demand, wages grew across the board, particularly among middle social strata.

Figure 9.1 shows the evolution of US average real earnings from 1913 to 1936, median real earnings from 1937 to 2016, and labor productivity (output per hour worked) of commerce and industry workers in the United States for the whole period (1913–2016) – after normalizing all of them to their value (expressed as 100) in 1937. Output per hour worked, growing at an average annual rate of 2.5 percent, rose by almost 80 percent between 1913 and 1937 and by 250 percent from 1937 to 1975. Average earnings of commerce and industry workers essentially tracked productivity throughout the whole period – growing by 69 percent between 1913 and 1937 and by 215 percent from 1937 to 1975. Median

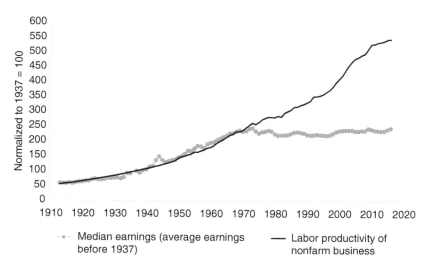

FIGURE 9.1 Evolution of labor productivity and median earnings in the United States, 1913–2016

earnings, that is, the earnings of a worker located in the middle of the whole earnings distribution, grew slightly faster than average earnings, pointing to a process of wage equalization.

After 1975, that parallel growth trend in labor productivity and median earnings broke down. On average, US labor productivity continued to grow at a similar rate during the postwar period, doubling between 1975 and 2016. By contrast, median earnings remained flat throughout the whole period after the oil shocks of the 1970s. That abrupt transformation coincided with the invention of the personal computer and, later on, the creation of the Internet, email, and mobile phones – a set of information and communication technologies that eroded the previously dominant position of skilled blue-collar workers and white-collar employees in the production process. The intensification of automation in manufacturing – due to the availability of extraordinarily fast microprocessors – made a substantial fraction of qualified blue-collar workers redundant. The number of US factory workers shrunk from nearly 19.5 million in 1979 to about 12 million in 2014. By contrast, total manufacturing output roughly doubled in the same period of time.[3] In Europe, manufacturing jobs represented more than one-fifth of all employment in 1970 but less than one-tenth in the middle of the 2010s. Automation reached non-manual jobs as well. The generation of complex software programs able to reproduce a growing set of routine administrative tasks transformed employment conditions in a wide range of traditional white-collar jobs, from accounting and banking to travel agencies. In the meantime, the number of professional and managerial jobs, which are low in routinized tasks and highly reliant on abstract, relatively creative thought processes, rose steadily.

Table 9.1 displays the change in the share of employment of different occupational groups in the United States in the periods 1910–1950, 1950–1980, and 1980–2010. The different groups are displayed according to their average level of skills: from those with a low-qualification content (industrial laborers) to those generally linked to high educational requirements (professionals). While unskilled jobs fell as a share of total employment over the whole century, the share of blue-collar jobs grew until 1950. Both middle-skill jobs (clerical and sales) and high-skill occupations (managers and professionals) rose – by 10 and 16 percentage

---

[3] Data on manufacturing employment comes from the Bureau of Labor Statistics: https://fred.stlouisfed.org/series/MANEMP. Data on industrial output is taken from the Bureau of Economic Analysis: https://bea.gov/industry/index.htm

TABLE 9.1 *Change in employment share of each category in the United States*

	Percentage Points		
	1910–1950	1950–1980	1980–2010
Operative, Laborers	−2.4	−4.7	−3.8
Skilled Blue Collar	+2.2	−2.0	−3.9
Clerical, Sales	+3.6	+6.3	−2.8
Professional, Managers	+5.6	+10.0	+11.5

Source: Katz and Margo (2014)

points, respectively – until 1980. Afterward, the fall in the share of blue-collar workers intensified and the share of moderately skilled occupations started to shrink. Clerical and sales jobs declined by almost 3 percentage points in the following three decades. By contrast, managerial and professional occupations rose as a share of total employment.

European economies experienced similar employment shifts in the past decades. Between 1993 and 2006, their employment share in high-wage occupations rose by an average of 4 percentage points. Demand for low-skilled jobs, with a high manual component and arguably less affected by the computer revolution, grew as well. By contrast, the process of substitution by computers struck mid-skilled occupations, mainly concentrated in manufacturing production, administrative positions, and sales and technical staff. As a result, the structure of employment gradually polarized – with a shrinking center and growing tails – across the advanced industrial world.

In combination with a sharp drop in transportation costs, the ongoing information and communication revolution also globalized trade after the late 1970s, intensifying, as a result, the direct employment effects triggered by the invention of the personal computer. The Cold War's international system of production, characterized by a clear split between an industrial North, tightly interconnected through intra-industry trade, and a broad South specialized in exporting raw material, was put to rest by the emergence of newly industrialized countries, such as the East Asian Tigers, and the rise of job offshoring. An increasing number of American, European, and Japanese companies, from toy and other consumer-goods makers in the 1970s to electronics in the 2000s, unbundled their production operations across the world, moving low-wage jobs to developing countries; the job status and wages of blue-collar industrial workers and the administrative middle class in advanced industrial economies declined accordingly.

A falling demand for routine manual and clerical positions and a growing need for jobs with high-skills content translated into a wider wage structure and a more unequal distribution of incomes. Still, the breadth and depth of that change differed across countries. In the United States as well as those economies that had regulatory structures closer to the American model of flexible labor markets, wages of low and semiskilled workers adjusted downward while employment in privately owned firms grew in net terms. Since the middle of the 1970s, wages for those in the bottom quintile of the earnings distribution dropped in real terms in the United States. Median male earnings, that is, the income received by men at the 50th percentile of the earnings distribution, remained stagnant in real terms in the United States. In the meantime, earnings doubled for individuals with postgraduate education and grew by almost 50 percent for those with bachelor degrees. In exchange, the United States added 35 million jobs in net terms between 1980 and 2006. Less dramatic but similar wage dynamics took place in a majority of advanced industrial economies. By 2010, the earnings of an individual in the 90th percentile of the wage distribution were three to five times higher than the earnings of an individual at the 10th percentile of the same distribution. By contrast, those European countries where low wages rose and where earning inequality remained unchanged, experienced negligible employment growth, such as Belgium or France, or even a fall in jobs in the private sector in net terms, such as Finland or Italy.

ELECTORAL REALIGNMENT

As the technologies of mass production invented at the turn of the twentieth century spread out, raising productivity and wages and equalizing incomes, partisan politics moderated first in the United States and then, particularly after the growth miracle of the 1950s and 1960s, in Europe. In the United States, Democrats and Republicans converged toward the ideological center throughout the first quarters of the twentieth century. According to calculations by McCarty et al. (2006) based on congressional roll-call votes, both parties were far apart at the turn of the twentieth century – at −0.41 and 0.46 in the conservative-liberal spectrum. By 1977, the difference between both parties had declined to 0.49 or half of what it had been 100 years earlier. Throughout the

1950s, extreme right-wing parties disappeared in northwestern Europe. In Germany, Christian democracy absorbed the support for fringe conservative and authoritarian parties. In Italy and France, reactionary movements such as the Ouomo Qualunque and Puojadisme collapsed quickly. The Italian Fascist Party, MSI, remained marginal. French Gaullism and moderate Christian democratic parties now occupied most of the conservative electoral space. The left experienced similar changes. In Britain, Labour's leadership launched a campaign to drop Clause Four, which called for the nationalization of industry, from the party's platform. German Social Democrats discarded from their party program any reference to orthodox Marxism as an instrument of analysis and guide to action, rejected their label as a "[working-]class party," and reasserted their commitment to democracy and peaceful reform in 1959. Socialist parties in Austria, Belgium, the Netherlands, and Scandinavia also wholeheartedly embraced the market economy, embedded in an extensive welfare state. In the 1970s, the once combative French and Italian Communist parties eventually adopted the doctrine of "Eurocommunism," ditching Lenin's doctrine in favor of the proletarian revolution and a one-party dictatorship and promising instead socialist policies adopted through exclusively democratic means.

Relying on the data on party positions from the "Party Manifesto Project," Figure 9.2 shows the degree of ideological dispersion (in economic policy) across the party system for each country and election year from 1945 onward.[4] The level of dispersion is calculated as the standard deviation of the policy positions of all parties contesting each election (weighted by their electoral strength). In the figure, each dot represents one electoral contest. Higher numbers imply higher levels of policy dispersion or polarization among the parties running in each specific election. For clarification purposes, Figure 9.2 highlights two cases: the elections of 1961 in Sweden and of 1969 in West Germany. In the former, a polarized electoral arena results in the

---

[4] Party positions are derived from the data collected in the "Party Manifesto Project" (Volkens et al. 2012) as follows. The position of party i in the left-right scale is calculated as the logs odd-ratio θi = (log Ri + 0.5) − (log Li + 0.5) where R is the sum of references to right-wing themes in party i's manifesto (categories 104, 201, 203, 305, 401, 402, 407, 414, 505, 601, 603, 605, and 606 in the Party Manifesto Project), and L is the sum of references to left-wing themes in party i's manifesto (categories 103, 105, 106, 107, 202, 403, 404, 406, 412, 413, 506, and 701). For a description of the log odds-ratio scaling method, see Lowe et al. (2011). The countries included are all Western European countries with continuous democratic elections since 1948 plus Australia, Canada, Japan, New Zealand, and the United States.

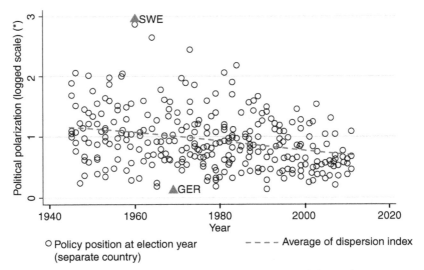

FIGURE 9.2 Polarization in economic policy positions in Europe

highest index of dispersion of the whole sample (3.12). In Germany, where the three main parties (FDP, CDU/CSU, and SPD) hardly differed from each other (with policy positions of −1.12, −1.67, and −2.21, respectively), the dispersion index is a very low 0.40. A casual inspection of the data reveals that the dispersion index declined over time. This pattern is confirmed once we estimate the average of the dispersion index across all cases and over time (represented by the Left-right dashed line). The line shows a gradual but significant drop in the level of political polarization starting in the aftermath of World War II – from about 1.5 to 0.9 or about one standard deviation of the entire sample.

Policy Stability

The policy moderation of the postwar period persisted for a long while in the wake of the economic and social transformations triggered by the computerization of jobs and hyper-globalization. Figure 9.3 displays the average position of the main center-right and social democratic parties in the left-right scale in those advanced countries that had been democratic since the end of World War II. Both mainstream political families

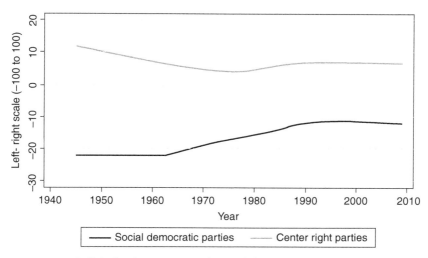

FIGURE 9.3 Political polarization in advanced democracies, 1945–2010
Source: Manifesto Project Dataset – Volkens et al. (2012)

maintained close and very stable policy commitments since the early 1990s well through the end of the Great Recession.

Social democracy's political moderation was rooted in the explicit decision taken by socialist politicians to court middle-class voters even to the point of sacrificing their historical reliance on blue-collar workers. A secular decline of the manufacturing sector, which fell from comprising a third or more of all employment until the 1970s to about one-tenth of all jobs in 2010, made it impossible to remain a viable governmental party by appealing only to blue-collar workers. To attract service sector employees, who represented more than two-thirds of total employment in most countries by the early twenty-first century, socialist parties adopted a liberal stance in social policies and offered a pro-globalization economic platform. Economic openness may have hurt their old electoral core. But broad swaths of middle-class voters benefited from the importation of cheap manufactures and from the employment of foreign workers in low-paid jobs ranging from restoration to domestic services (Scheve and Slaughter 2001, 2006).[5]

Silja Häusermann (2017) has estimated that social democrats mobilized about twice as many working-class voters than middle-class

---

[5] In fact, many European social democratic parties ended up reinforcing some of the macroeconomic policies (most fundamentally, the adoption of the euro with its quasi gold-standard quality) that "narrowed" their room of maneuver in monetary and regulatory policies.

individuals in 1980. Forty years later, that proportion is roughly the opposite.[6] A great deal of that compositional shift within the center-left electorate was a direct result of the growth of non-manufacturing jobs and the decision of center-left parties to court their holders. But following such a "supraclass" strategy (as opposed to relying on the strict mobilization of working-class individuals) led to the electoral alienation of part of the historical electoral supporters of socialist parties. The proportion of workers voting for left-wing candidates fell from about two-thirds in 1980 to less than one-half in 2010.[7] By contrast, the share of middle-class voters voting for left parties rose from 40 percent to 50 percent on average (with considerable variation across countries) over the same period of time (Gringich and Häusermann 2015).

The Dog That Didn't Bark (Immediately)

In response to the programmatic stability of mainstream parties, a growing section of the electorate first responded by voting less. Figure 9.4 plots the proportion of nonvoters in legislative elections conducted in Western Europe from 1918 until 2016. Abstention in Western Europe stayed at around 20 percent until the 1980s but then started to grow consistently in the early 1980s (Franklin et al. 2004; Hooghe and Kern 2017). By 2016, almost one out of every three European adults refrained from voting. Figure 9.4 also displays the nonvoting share of the electorate in American presidential elections since 1932 for the sake of comparison. It excludes participation in Southern states, where blatant discriminatory rules suppressed black turnout until the introduction of the Civil Rights Act.[8] Abstention rates were not particularly different in the American non-South and in Western Europe in the late 1930s. Right after World War II, however, the nonvoting gap between the two continents grew to 10 percentage points, perhaps driven the presence of strong socialist and Christian democratic mass parties in Europe, unmatched by American parties in

---

[6] For additional research on the electoral transformation of social democratic parties, see Cronin et al. (2011), McCrone (2013), Kitschelt and Rehm (2015), Rennwald and Evans (2014).
[7] The incapacity of social democratic parties to retain blue-collar workers was arguably due to the gradual decline of unions and to a growing divergence of policy preferences between the old working class and the new middle class.
[8] Alex Kerchner, at Princeton University, has generously shared the data. In the US South, turnout fluctuated around 25 percent in the 1930s and 1940s.

Electoral Realignments in the Atlantic World 223

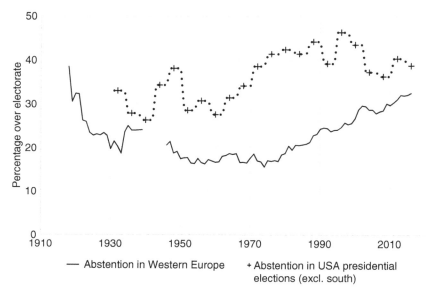

FIGURE 9.4 Abstention, 1918–2016

organizational terms. Coinciding with a generalized decline in trust toward politicians and political institutions, abstention began to drift upward in the American non-South in the mid-1960s. A decade later, it did as well in Europe. By the end of the Great Recession, and following a modest upturn in participation in the United States, the difference between both continents was only 6 percentage points.

Until the 1970s, socioeconomic status had been unrelated to the likelihood to vote in Britain, where Crewe, Fox, and Alt (1977) noted that class and education "fail to have any bearings on propensity to vote regularly" (p. 54), Germany (Kleinhenz 1998), France (Abrial et al. 2003), Italy (Tuorto 2010), and Scandinavia (Andersen and Hoff 2001; Martikainen et al. 2005). By contrast, today's abstention is higher among those social sectors that had become most vulnerable to recent economic transformations – low-income citizens and younger cohorts entering an inhospitable labor market.

Table 9.2 reports the share of nonvoters in three selected countries (Finland, France, and the United Kingdom) that have witnessed a substantial fall in turnout. For each country, it reports nonvoting shares within the top, middle, and bottom quintiles of the income distribution and, within each quintile, three age groups: younger than 35, between 35

TABLE 9.2 *Rate of Abstention in Finland, France, and the United Kingdom*

	Finland			France			United Kingdom		
	Young	Middle	Senior	Young	Middle	Senior	Young	Middle	Senior
Top Quintile	32	19	10	50	19	7	29	23	11
Middle Quintile	41	30	18	65	40	12	48	32	10
Bottom Quintile	53	48	33	68	64	29	73	50	20

and 54 years of age, 55 or older.[9] Across all countries and age groups, participation levels are much lower among low-income voters. Individuals in the bottom quintile are two to three times more likely to abstain than those in the richest quintile.

Age has its own independent effect on turnout. In Finland; within each income quintile, electors whose age is 55 or older are twice more likely to vote than those younger than 35. Age plays an even larger role in France. About two-thirds of all young electors in the three lowest quintiles abstained in the legislative elections of 2013. But even among people younger than 35 years in the top quintile of the income distribution, the nonvoting share was, at 50 percent, very high. The United Kingdom displays an extreme version of the French case. With the exception of young individuals in the top quintile, whose abstention is close to the national average, young individuals' non-participation rate is uniformly high, peaking at a dismal 73.4 percent among 34-years-old or younger in the bottom income quintile.

A cohort or generational effect – as opposed to a life cycle effect – has driven the decrease in turnout correlated with age. Using Finnish data,

---

[9] The Finnish data, taken from Martikainen et al. (2005), refers to the parliamentary elections of 1999 and consists of actual individual-level observations of turnout linked, through Finland's national population register, to the demographic, social, and economic characteristics of each elector. The data analyzed cover all Finnish electors between 25 and 69 years of age – a total of 2,941,834 persons – and avoid sample bias and over-reporting. The data for France and the United Kingdom comes from the latest wave of the European Social Survey in 2014, a multi-country survey with a vast array of political, economic, demographic, and attitudinal questions administered in more than 30 countries. I select them because the deviation between the official turnout data in their latest legislative elections and the aggregate turnout rate uncovered through the survey is relatively small: 2.3 percent in the United Kingdom and 6.0 percent in France. By contrast, the deviation between survey and official data is much higher in the majority of the remaining countries, reaching 11 percentage points in Germany and 19 percentage points in Switzerland, for example.

Wass (2007) has shown that whereas 70.4 percent of those born in 1960 voted when they were age 19 (in the 1979 election), only 57.7 percent and 49.6 percent of those who were 19 in 1987 and 1999 did so, respectively. The probability of voting remained stable within each generation – in fact, falling slightly with age. For example, among those born in 1960, the average turnout in 1979 fell 1.7 percentage points to 68.7 percent in both 1987 and 1999. Blais et al. (2004) find similar generational effects in Canada, where turnout among the generation born in the 1970s has been 25 points lower than among pre–baby boomers.

The Anti-Globalization Turn

Because political discontent first took the form of growing abstention, mainstream parties hardly lost their capacity to govern for a long while. Figure 9.5 displays the electoral performance of European mainstream and extreme parties from 1918 to 2016 – both as a proportion of the whole electorate (dashed line) and of all voters (solid line). Mainstream parties are those political organizations that embrace the economic and institutional architecture of the golden age of democratic capitalism: social democrats, Christian democrats, liberals, and conservatives. Vote

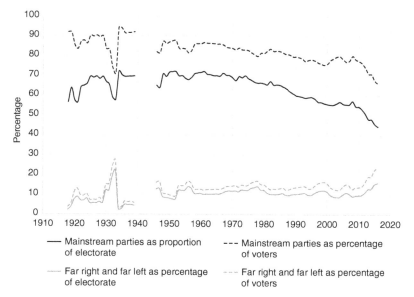

FIGURE 9.5 European parties – as proportion of voters and electors, 1918–2016

for extreme parties comprise both far left organizations (mainly, communist parties but also, and more recently, parties such as Syriza and Podemos) and far-right organizations (such as the Nazi party in Germany or radical anti-immigration parties today).[10]

Throughout the interwar period, mainstream parties experienced a steady increase in electoral support – from about 56 percent of the whole electorate in 1918 to 69 percent right before the crash of 1929 – due to the gradual electoral mobilization of low-income citizens who had been recently enfranchised and whose participation benefited center-left and left parties. The rise of the Nazi party in Germany temporarily brought the overall support of mainstream parties down to its 1918 levels. After World War II, about 70 percent of the whole electorate voted systematically for parties that favored some variant of the political and economic architecture of "embedded liberalism." In the aftermath of two oil shocks and in what at first looked like a standard response to a disappointing economy, support for mainstream parties as a fraction of the electorate declined gently in the late 1970s and early 1980s. However, even after the economic cycle swung back up, traditional political forces kept bleeding votes. Their total vote equaled 60 percent of the electorate in 1990 and 55 percent in 2007. After the end of the Great Recession, they only received the support of 45 percent of all those entitled to vote. However, and crucially for their parliamentary representation and their chances to form a government, their share over actual votes barely changed until 2008. Mainstream parties still received 80 percent of all ballots cast in both the late 1970s and, recovering from a brief decline in the later 1990s, the late 2000s. As a result, even though they had lost overall support, they commanded stable majorities in terms of votes and, therefore, in parliamentary seats. All in all, their incentives to switch policy positions were low.

Except for a short-lived uptick in the vote for communist parties in the mid- and late 1970s, the total share of far-left and far-right parties remained unchanged at 10 percent of the electorate and 15 percent of voters for several decades. The Great Recession, however, changed their fortunes. An array of populist candidates was able to frame the

---

[10] The countries included are Austria, Belgium, Cyprus, Denmark, Finland, France, Germany, Greece, Ireland, Italy, Luxembourg, Netherlands, Norway, Portugal, Spain, Sweden, Switzerland, and the United Kingdom. Each year's data corresponds to the result from the previous year's election or (for a very small number of years) as the closest election (resulting in a t2-year lag). Simon Hix at the London School of Economics has generously shared the data.

governmental bailout of the financial sector as a blatant example of a political establishment working for the benefit of the economic elite. Several migration crises of the 2010s then exacerbated the sense of loss and overall discontent across part of the Western electorate.

According to the emerging populist narrative, globalization and the overall policies of aloof mainstream parties were to blame for the economic (and cultural) transformations of the past decades. Low tariffs, production offshoring, and loose immigration policies had multiplied the supply of labor, forcing national workers to compete with foreigners and, in the process, freezing or even reducing domestic wages. They also threatened the generous welfare state in place since the middle of the twentieth century. Protectionism and the strengthening of national borders were the proper responses to decades of economic backsliding – a way to restore living standards without necessarily engaging in more social spending and higher levels of taxation. That anti-globalization program could glue together a new electoral coalition encompassing the "old" working class, outsiders in the labor market such as the younger cohorts just beginning to enter the labor market, and a fraction of middle-class voters.[11]

Using the European Social Survey of 2014, Table 9.3 reports the percentage of voters supporting "populist" parties in six European countries: two Nordic countries, Denmark and Finland; two continental cases with high support for non-mainstream parties, France and the Netherlands; Germany; and the United Kingdom. For each country, Table 9.3 reports the "populist" vote share in the top-, middle-, and low-income quintiles.[12]

---

[11] For an alternative, mostly cultural-ideational interpretation of the new electoral politics of today, see Häusermann and Kriesi (2015), who claim that far-right parties benefit from a cultural chasm between enlightened, mobile professionals and a traditional, "authoritarian" working class and from the latter's lack of tolerance toward migrants. In America, the Republican vote of low-income voters has been explained as a function of religiosity and, more recently, of emotions, such as resentment (Cramer 2016), and of underlying ideas of justice and deservingness (Cramer 2016; Hochschild 2016). Although sparser, material accounts seem more promising. Dancygier (2010) emphasizes material conflicts of natives and newcomers over the allocation of local goods. Gest (2016) traces the change in electoral behavior of blue-collar workers to declining material and status conditions. See also Mayer (2009) and Ford and Goodwin (2014) for France and Britain, respectively. Jonathan Rodden, in both Rodden (2019) and Chapter 6, this volume, has suggested that we should examine current politics as a two-dimensional space defined by economic and social or moral issues.

[12] Inclusion in the income quintile is based on household's total net income (question F41 in ESS 2014). Past experience of unemployment is taken from question F36. Working on a tradable sector is derived from recoding question F31. Italy was not included in the of

TABLE 9.3 *Reported vote for "populist" parties in selected countries, mid-2000s*

	Denmark	Finland	France	Netherlands	Germany	United Kingdom
QUINTILE						
Top	13	13	7	9	8	4
Middle	22	20	16	24	13	5
Bottom	25	25	20	30	18	9

Source: European Social Survey (2014)

Total support for non-mainstream parties is low in Germany and the United Kingdom and high otherwise.[13] Those differences in electoral performance derive from two factors: the structure of the economy and the electoral system. Low-value sectors, which are arguably more sensitive to automation and globalization, are (or were) located in the European periphery but much less so in Mitteleuropa. Hence, non-mainstream parties' poor performance in (the western part of) Germany seems to be a direct outcome of that country's reliance on high-value-added industries that are still highly competitive in the world economy. As for the United Kingdom, demand for nonstandard policies is strong in its Northern regions, which score lower in terms of education, income, and unemployment – as attested by the outcome of the Brexit referendum (Becker et al. 2017). However, United Kingdom Independence Party (UKIP)'s poor electoral performance in national elections is the result of Britain's first-past-the-post electoral system.

Independently of the average level of support, "populist" parties are stronger among low-income voters. Whereas one out of four Danish voters in the bottom quintile supported the People's Party, only one out of eight voters in the top quintile cast a ballot for any populist party. That electoral ratio (or a factor of two poor voters to one rich voter) is similar in

---

2014. Belgium is not reported here because the regional divide makes classifying parties complex. The classification between left and right parties is based, following Simon Hix's work, on their membership in the European Parliament. Left parties are those included in the European United Left-Nordic Green Left (GUE-NGL) Parliamentary Group. Right parties are part of two European Parliamentary Groups: Europe of Nations and Freedom and Europe of Freedom and Direct Democracy. The True Finns and the Danish People's Party, which were founding members of the Europe of Freedom and Democracy, are also counted as right-wing parties.

[13] In Sweden, which is not shown here, support is moderate to high.

Finland (25 percent to 13 percent), Germany (18 percent to 8 percent), and Britain (9 percent to 4 percent). It rises to a factor of three to one in France (20 percent to 7 percent) and the Netherlands (30 percent to 9 percent).

A DIFFERENT POLITICAL RESPONSE?

Although the fight against globalization has become the main plank of populist campaigns, it is highly unlikely that a protectionist agenda would be able to curb the structural transformations that we have witnessed during the past few decades. Recent economic estimations attribute just about one-third of all employment losses in the past decades to trade and the relocation of production abroad (cf. Los, Timmer and De Vries, 2014). The rest is the result, instead, of a process of automation that has reduced the demand for "routinizable" jobs and depressed the earnings associated with them.

Addressing the polarization of employment opportunities and the stagnation of wages as the result of ongoing technological innovation requires two types of responses: some of them, strictly economic and others, mostly political.[14] Before examining them, however, we need to acknowledge first that there is little consensus about the future pace and depth of automation. In one of the first and most publicized studies on the effects of automation, Oxford researchers Carl Frey and Michael Osborne assign to each job (and, by aggregation, to economic sectors), a given risk of computerization, from low to high, as a function of the kinds of knowledge, abilities, and skills needed to perform each occupation successfully. According to those calculations, 47 percent of total US employment falls under "the high-risk category," mainly "transportation and logistic occupations, together with the bulk of office and administrative support workers, and labour in production occupations" (Frey and Osborne 2017: 265). In turn, 33 percent of jobs have a low computerization risk, corresponding to "generalist occupations requiring knowledge of human heuristics, and specialist occupations involving the development of novel ideas and artifacts" (p. 266). By contrast, Arntz, Gregory, and Zierahn (2016) estimate that only 9 percent of jobs in OECD countries are highly automatable. In any case, notice that despite their differences, all these studies share one common trait: they contain no detailed calendar of the future automation process. As Frey and Osborne (2017: 265) write, their analysis simply implies that "[high-risk] occupations are potentially

---

[14] For a full discussion of these options, see Boix (2019), chap. 6.

automatable over an *unspecified* number of years, *perhaps* a decade or two" (my emphasis added here). Therefore, any policy response to automation can only proceed in a piecemeal (rather than a comprehensive) fashion.

On the economic front, responses to automation fall into three categories, ordered as follows according to their increasing controversial nature among policy experts and the public in general: educational investment, a universal basic income, and the socialization of capital. There is wide agreement that policy makers should facilitate the adjustment to the new economy by spending heavily on human capital formation. As happened throughout most of the twentieth century, the benefits of technological change are expected to spread out to everyone provided the supply of the right type of workers matches the labor needs of firms. However, this strategy would only work if, first, all individuals can acquire the kind of high skills demanded by ICTs, and, second, the creation of new jobs makes up for those tasks that have become automatized. If educational investments cannot overcome initial deficiencies in natural talents or if automation replaces most jobs (including new ones), policy makers may have to consider more direct methods of compensation and redistribution toward the losers of today's capitalism – such as a universal basic income.

A universal basic income, that is, a regular income paid by public authorities to all individuals regardless of their income or need and independently of whether or not they work, has two important advantages. First, it should free individuals from routine, repetitive tasks, allowing them to engage in more creative and inventive professional paths. Second, it could reduce poverty and equalize conditions. The extent to which it could equalize the income distribution will be a function, among other things, of its volume. In a country with a per capita income of about $50,000 (a rich European country today) and public spending (excluding police and defense) equivalent to about 40 percent of GDP, transforming all that spending into a universal basic income would amount to an annual direct transfer of about $20,000 per person. A family of four would receive an annual income of $80,000 – not far from the median household income (in any of those countries). Such a proposal would lead to a very sharp compression of the income distribution. But any direct transfer significantly below that amount would reproduce or even exacerbate current levels of inequality.

The introduction of a universal basic income comes with important costs. First, results from pretrials of the universal basic income in Canada and the United States show that it distorts the incentives people have to work (Sage and Diamond 2017). Second, it may sustain preexisting inequalities and subsidize the wages paid by firms, which, knowing that some basic needs are met by a publicly paid income, can offer lower wages. Third, it may reduce individuals' incentives to school themselves and to go through the normal processes of character formation and development of internal discipline that result from preparing for and having a job. Fourth, although voters support the existence of mechanisms such as unemployment benefits or universal health services to protect the unemployed and the sick in the short and medium run, they also value having jobs and a full employment economy over receiving a permanent stream of subsidies from politicians. A fixed universal income may not meet the true preferences of an electorate about how to organize the economy and the welfare state. At the end of the day, the political success of the universal basic income will be a function of the extent of automation. It is only in a situation of complete or very widespread automation, where jobs had become scarce and individual effort would be not enough to earn one's living for the vast majority of the population, that the universal basic income should gather strong public support.

A more radical solution than a universal basic income would consist of socializing the ownership of capital and dividing it among all citizens – especially if and when both labor disappeared as a production input and capital became highly concentrated in the hands of a few owners. Dividing the ownership of machines and robots would curb the political power of a capitalist oligarchy (if the latter indeed emerged). It would also be preferable to transferring all property to a central planner controlling, soviet-style, all the wealth and then managing its distribution among the population. The socialization of capital faces two important problems, however. First, innovation would suffer under that system, especially if the returns generated by new patents and industries were to be allocated equally. Second, it is unclear whether, even in the absence of differential technological change and productivity growth across sectors and firms, redistributing property in equal lots at some point in time would result in maintaining an equal society in the long run. In former socialist economies that privatized (parts of) their business sector and distributed it equally among their citizens, such as the Czech Republic and Poland, the property of capital became again concentrated rather quickly (Grosfeld and Hashi 2007).

A program of economic interventions to take advantage or, at least, to mitigate the potential downsides of widespread automation would remain insufficient without a strategy to deal with the potentially adverse political consequences of robotization. Although the effects of future technological innovation are not clear-cut, it is likely that, were inequality to intensify, the main winners of that change could employ their dominant position to capture the state, through campaign contributions, political lobbies, and personal connections, to regulate the economy, block the entry of any potential rivals, and lock in their initial economic advantage. The open market economies of the past would give way to some form of oligarchical capitalism and, with that, weak democratic institutions and a declining interest in helping those most affected by technological change.

Both the reduction in market competition and growing concentration of wealth that have taken place in the past few decades do not bode well in that regard for the immediate future. In the past two decades, more than three-fourth of all US industries have become more concentrated. Since the 1980s, corporate profits of large firms have grown considerably – relative to those of small firms, concentrating in a declining number of firms. Some sectors such as communications services, health care, and information technology show evidence of monopoly-like profits (Jarsulic et al. 2019). The US labor share of national income fell from about 64 percent throughout the postwar period to 58 percent from the mid-1980s onward (Elsby et al. 2013). Karabarbounis and Neiman (2014) report a fall of 5 percentage points in the labor share of income in a sample of 59 countries in the period from 1975 to 2013. By economic sectors, the labor share of income decreased rapidly in US sectors with high research and development (R&D) intensity – from 80 percent in the mid-1970s to 60 percent in 2011 – while remaining flat over the same period of time in less R&D-intense sectors over the same period (Guellec and Paunov 2017). Overall income inequality has also grown. The top 1 percent of the US income distribution earned 8 percent of the national income in the early 1980s but 17.5 percent in 2010. In a correlated manner, campaign contributions in US federal elections have gradually become concentrated among the super-wealthy. The top 0.01 percent of households (in the income distribution) donated between 10 percent and 15 percent of all campaign contributions until the early 1990s. In 2012, they gave 40 percent. Besides direct contributions, large corporations and industry associations have ramped up lobbying efforts and spending (Bonica et al. 2013). At least in the United States, money appears to be shaping policy makers' preferences and votes. According to Larry Bartels, the views of members of Congress are closer to those of their wealthy constituents than to low-income voters (Bartels 2008).

To tame inequality and its potential political effects, a few things seem advisable: capping campaign donations by corporations; democratizing the distribution of electoral funds along the lines of the reform proposed by Bruce Ackerman and Ian Ayres and approved in places such as Seattle;[15] disclosing the (ownership and marketing) relations between media and large firms; and, arguably, taxing robots to reduce the political consequences of excessive economic inequality. It is very likely, however, that checking the crony tendencies of the capitalism of the future would only be possible under three circumstances: a higher level of electoral participation, which would reinforce the position of the common voter; a much stronger set of civil society associations to make politicians accountable; and systems of institutional representation (such as the one that characterize most small Western European countries) that, in sustaining a tight connection between electorates and their representatives, ensure that policy makers resist crony capitalists and defend the idea of free markets and open economies while devising policies to help the most disadvantaged by economic change.

REFERENCES

Abrial, Stephanie, Bruno Cautres, and Nadine Mandran. 2003. "Turnout and Abstention at Multilevel Elections in France." Fifth Framework Research Programme (1998–2002): Democratic Participation and Political Communication in Systems of Multi-level Governance. Working paper, Centre d'Informatisation des Donnes Socio-Politiques, Centre National de la Recherche Scientifique, Grenoble.

Ackerman, Bruce, and Ian Ayres. 2008. *Voting with Dollars: A New Paradigm for Campaign Finance*. New Haven, CT: Yale University Press.

Adserà, Alícia, and Carles Boix. 2002. Trade, democracy, and the size of the public sector: The political underpinnings of openness. *International Organization*, 56 (2): 229–262.

Andersen, Jorgen G., and Jens Hoff. 2001. "Electoral Participation." In *Democracy and Citizenship in Scandinavia*, edited by Jorgen G. Andersen and Jens Hoff, 31–46. London: Palgrave.

Arntz, Melanie, Terry Gregory, and Ulrich Zierahn. 2016. "The Risk of Automation for Jobs in OECD Countries: A Comparative Analysis." OECD Social, Employment and Migration Working Papers, no. 189. Paris: OECD.

---

[15] See Ackerman and Ayres (2008). The Ackerman and Ayres' system consists in giving to each citizen a fixed number of dollars to be spent in the electoral campaign in the way (that is, on the candidate) each voter prefers. That proposal is complemented with the decision to establish a blind trust in which all private donations are put – to be transferred to the candidate or parties chosen by each donor. As with the secret ballot, the secrecy of donations should reduce the lobbying by well-identified donors.

Bartels, Larry M. 2008. *Unequal Democracy: The Political Economy of the New Gilded Age*. Princeton, NJ: Princeton University Press.

Becker, Sascha O., Thiemo Fetzer, and Dennis Novy. 2017. "Who Voted for Brexit?: A Comprehensive District-Level Analysis." *Economic Policy* 32 (92): 601–650.

Bell, Daniel. 1988. *The End of Ideology (with a new afterword)*. Cambridge, Mass.: Harvard University Press.

Blais, Andre, Elisabeth Gidengil, and Neil Nevitte. 2004. "Where Does Turnout Decline Come From?" *European Journal of Political Research* 43 (3): 221–236.

Bonica, Adam, Nolan McCarty, Keith T. Poole, and Howard Rosenthal. 2013. "Why Hasn't Democracy Slowed Rising Inequality?" *Journal of Economic Perspectives* 27 (3): 103–123.

Boix, Carles. 2019. *Democratic Capitalism at the Crossroads*. Princeton, NJ: Princeton University Press.

Cramer, Katherine J. 2016. *The Politics of Resentment: Rural Consciousness in Wisconsin and the Rise of Scott Walker*. Chicago: University of Chicago Press.

Crewe, Ivor, Anthony Fox, and James Alt. 1977. "Non-voting in British General Elections 1966–October 1974." In *British Political Sociology Yearbook*, vol. 3, edited by Colin Crouch, 38–109. London: Croom Helm.

Cronin, James E., George W. Ross, and James Shoch, eds. 2011. *What's Left of the Left: Democrats and Social Democrats in Challenging Times*. Durham, NC: Duke University Press.

Dancygier, Rafaela M. 2010. *Immigration and Conflict in Europe*. New York: Cambridge University Press.

   2017. *Dilemmas of Inclusion: The Political Representation of Muslims in Europe*. Princeton, NJ: Princeton University Press.

Elsby, Michael W. L., Bart Hobijn, and Ayşegül Şahin. 2013. "The Decline of the US Labor Share." *Brookings Papers on Economic Activity* (2): 1–63.

European Social Survey (ESS). 2014. European Social Survey Round 7 Data. Data file edition 2.1. NSD (Norwegian Centre for Research Data) Data Archive and distributor of ESS data for ESS ERIC.

Ford, Robert, and Matthew J. Goodwin. 2014. *Revolt on the Right: Explaining Support for the Radical Right in Britain (Extremism and Democracy)*. London: Routledge.

Franklin, Mark N., Patrick Lyons, and Michael Marsh. 2004. "Generational Basis of Turnout Decline in Established Democracies." *Acta Politica* 39 (2): 115–151.

Frey, Carl Benedikt, and Michael A. Osborne. 2017. "The Future of Employment: How Susceptible Are Jobs to Computerisation?" *Technological Forecasting and Social Change* 114: 254–280.

Gest, Justin. 2016. *The New Minority*. New York: Oxford University Press.

Gingrich, Jane, and Silja Hausermann. 2015. "The Decline of the Working Class Vote, the Reconfiguration of the Welfare Support Coalition and Consequences for the Welfare State." *Journal of European Social Policy* 25 (1): 50–75.

Grosfeld, Irena, and Iraj Hashi. 2007. "Changes in Ownership Concentration in Mass Privatised Firms: Evidence from Poland and the Czech Republic." *Corporate Governance: An International Review* 15 (4): 520–534.

Guellec, Dominique, and Carolina Paunov. 2017. "Digital Innovation and the Distribution of Income." NBER Working Paper no. 23987.
Hausermann, Silja. 2017. "Electoral Realignment and Social Policy Positions of Social Democratic Parties." Working paper, University of Zurich.
Häusermann, Silja, and Hanspeter Kriesi (2015). "What Do Voters Want?" In *The Politics of Advanced Capitalism*, edited by Pablo Beramendi, Silja Häusermann, Herbert Kitschelt, and Hanspeter Kriesi, 202–230. New York: Cambridge University Press.
Hooghe, Marc, and Anna Kern. 2017. "The Tipping Point between Stability and Decline: Trends in Voter Turnout, 1950–1980–2012." *European Political Science* 16: 535–552.
Hoschschild, Arlie R. 2016. *Strangers in Their Own Land*. New York: New Press.
Jarsulic, Marc, Ethan Gurwitz, and Andrew Schwartz. 2019. "Toward a Robust Competition Policy." Center for American Progress. www.americanprogress.org/issues/economy/reports/2019/04/03/467613/toward-robust-competition-policy/
Judis, John B. 2016. *The Populist Explosion: How the Great Recession Transformed American and European Politics*. New York: Columbia Global Reports.
Karabarbounis, Loukas, and Brent Neiman. 2014. "The Global Decline of the Labor Share." *Quarterly Journal of Economics* 129 (1): 61–103.
Katz, Lawrence F., and Robert A. Margo. 2014. "Technical Change and the Relative Demand for Skilled Labor: The United States in Historical Perspective." In *Human Capital in History: The American Record*, edited by Leah Platt Boustan, Carola Frydman, and Robert A. Margo, 15–57. Chicago: University of Chicago Press.
Keating, Michael, and David McCrone, eds. 2013. *The Crisis of European Social Democracy*. Edinburgh: Edinburgh University Press.
Kitschelt, Herbert, and Philipp Rehm. 2015. "Party Alignments: Change and Continuity." In *The Politics of Advanced Capitalism*, edited by Pablo Beramendi, Silja Hausermann, Herbert Kitschelt, and Hanspeter Kriesi, 179–201. New York: Cambridge University Press.
Kleinhenz, Thomas. 1998. "A New Type of Nonvoter? Turnout Decline in German Elections, 1980–94." In *Stability and Change in German Elections: How Electorates Merge, Converge, or Collide*, edited by Christopher J. Anderson and Carsten Zelle, 173–198. Westport, CT: Praeger.
Los, Bart, Marcel Timmer, and Gaaitzen deVries. 2014. "The Demand for Skills 1995–2008: A Global Supply Chain Perspective." *OECD Economics Department Working Papers*, No. 1141. Paris: OECD Publishing. http://dx.doi.org/10.1787/5jz123g0f5lp-en
Lowe, Will, Kenneth Benoit, Slava Mikhaylov, and Michael Laver. 2011. "Scaling Policy Preferences from Coded Political Texts." *Legislative Studies Quarterly* 36 (1): 123–155.
Martikainen, Pekka, Tuomo Martikainen, and Hanna Wass. 2005. "The Effect of Socioeconomic Factors on Voter Turnout in Finland: A Register-Based Study of 2.9 Million Voters." *European Journal of Political Research* 44 (5): 645–669.

Mayer, Nonna. 2009. "What Remains of Class Voting?", In *Politics in France and Europe*, edited by Pascal Perrineau and Luc Rouban, pp. 167–181. New York: Palgrave.

McCarty, Nolan, Keith T. Poole, and Howard Rosenthal. 2006. *Polarized America: The Dance of Ideology and Unequal Riches*. Cambridge, MA: MIT Press.

Rennwald, Line, and Geoffrey Evans. 2014. "When Supply Creates Demand: Social Democratic Party Strategies and the Evolution of Class Voting." *West European Politics* 37 (5): 1108–1135.

Rodden, Jonathan. 2019. *Why Cities Lose: The Deep Roots of the Urban-Rural Political Divide*. New York: Basic Books.

Sage, Daniel, and Patrick Diamond. 2017. "Europe's New Social Reality: The Case against Universal Basic Income." Policy Network paper. February.

Scheve, Kenneth F., and Matthew J. Slaughter. 2001. "Labor Market Competition and Individual Preferences over Immigration Policy." *Review of Economics and Statistics* 83 (1): 133–145.

  2006. "Public Opinion, International Economic Integration, and the Welfare State." In *Globalization and Self- Determination: Is the Nation-State under Siege?* edited by David R. Cameron, Gustav Ranis, and Annalisa Zinn, 51–94. London: Routledge.

Tuorto, Dario. 2010. "La partecipazione al voto." In *Votare in Italia, 1968–2008: Dall'appartenenza alla scelta*, edited by Paolo Bellucci and Paolo Segatti, 53–79. Bologna: Il Mulino.

Volkens, Andrea, Pola Lehmann, Sven Regel, Henrike Schultze, and Annika Werner, with Onawa Promise Lacewell. 2012. *The Manifesto Data Collection. Manifesto Project (MRG/CMP/MARPOR)*. Version 2012a. Berlin: Wissenschaftszentrum Berlin fur Sozialforschung.

Wass, Hanna. 2007. "The Effects of Age, Generation and Period on Turnout in Finland 1975– 2003." *Electoral Studies* 26 (3): 648–659.

10

Political Parties in the New Politics of Insecurity

Christian Salas, Frances McCall Rosenbluth, and Ian Shapiro

INTRODUCTION

Citizen trust in American political parties has hit lows unmatched since the 1850s, dramatically underscored in 2016 by Donald Trump's stampede to the US presidency. In Britain in the same year, widespread voter disenchantment produced the Brexit vote against the majorities of both parliamentary parties. The world watched with bewildered anxiety as these leading countries of the postwar order appeared to give in to xenophobic populism at the cost of global political stability and collective prosperity. The world had not reckoned that whole groups of American and British citizens, left behind in the postindustrial economy, would be willing to second-guess their traditional political institutions and sacrifice global economic integration for better deals at home. The apparent collapse of traditional politics in America and Britain, which had long been counted on to promote global security and free trade, put allies on edge.

The sources of economic insecurity are well understood. Rich democracies have shed manufacturing jobs to labor-saving machines and to countries with lower wages. In the United States, workers with steady, stable manufacturing jobs dropped from 35 percent of the workforce in 1975 to less than 10 percent by 2010. The rise of the service sector has created unimaginable wealth among small numbers of managers and entrepreneurs; but for many other citizens, jobs are part time, temporary, and without reliable retirement benefits or health insurance. Large numbers of insecurely employed workers are potent voices for economic protectionism, undermining the postwar commitment to free trade and immigration.

It is a paradox of democratic politics that economic suffering seems to make voters vulnerable to symbolic politics rather than fight for economic policies that would help them. The Tea Party's successful assault on Republican incumbents in legislative and presidential primaries has capitalized on many voters' willingness to give up social insurance such as health care, unemployment insurance, and other welfare benefits (all of which require robust taxation) for extremist social positions on abortion, gun rights, and religious and racial intolerance (Hochschild 2016; Williamson, Skocpol, and Coggin 2011). The low-tax coalition in American politics includes bafflingly large numbers of voters who would be economically better off with a higher-tax, higher-spending configuration of policies. They like low taxes because they assume "their" benefits – social security and Medicare – are safe. Meanwhile, they overestimate the costs and disapprove of the benefits for everyone else (Williamson et al. 2011).

In seeking antidotes for the Anglo-American populist lurch to the right, one appealing model is northern Europe, where proportional representation electoral rules underpinned a decades-long cross-class alliance capable of balancing economic competitiveness with employment stability. As Thelen and Wiedemann (Chapter 12, this volume) show, Europe's social welfare schemes have been far more successful in alleviating economic insecurity than those in Britain and especially in the United States. The more effectively government can protect workers from dire straits, the fewer voices for political and economic extremism. Security, it would seem, produces political moderation.

Unassailable though the evidence may be for the efficacy of social insurance, even in Europe the political coalitions supporting it are threatened by the unprecedented (at least since Weimar) rise of anti-establishment parties and candidates. At a quickening pace, Europeans have rejected government recommendations in referendums and plebiscites, and they have elected anti-establishment figures who would not have been taken seriously half a generation ago. In stalwart Germany, for example, it took then–Prime Minister Angela Merkel more than six months to form a government after the September 2017 elections because of the increased strength of the anti-immigrant AfD (Alternative for Germany) and libertarian Free Democrats to her right and the Greens to her left, and the decentralized control of the opposition Social Democrats that made negotiations all but impossible and allowed the Social Democrats to extract massive concessions from Merkel's electorally more successful CDU (Christian Democratic Union of Germany).

Merkel was forced to give the Social Democrats six ministries in her new government including the crucial Finance Ministry, and three ministries to her Christian Socialist Union (CSU) partners, leaving her own Christian Democrats with only five ministerial portfolios. The problem for the German people is not only that forming a government took so long; a fragmented government is hard to manage and raises ongoing challenges for electoral accountability: it is unclear to voters whose campaign promises will be honored, and what deals will be implemented after closed-door negotiations. One result is that the large, traditional parties took major hits from the AfD and the Greens in the regional elections in Bavaria and Hesse in October 2018, forcing Merkel to step down as head of the CDU/CSU by 2021.

This chapter presents the case that plurality (single-member district) countries such as the United States and the United Kingdom are not alone in being vulnerable to populist politics. Proportional representation countries, as wise and steady as they seemed to be in the postwar period, may be *particularly* vulnerable. Because proportional representation in these countries permits smaller parties to proliferate more easily than in the United States and the United Kingdom, it is important to pay close attention to the trend toward political fragmentation. It is possible, as some evidence suggests, that the splintering of parties on the left reduces governments' inclination and ability to implement the blend of economic openness and employment stability that marked Europe's golden postwar years. First, we turn to the variety of electoral rules to understand how they mediate the decline of industrial jobs.

THE BASELINE: ELECTORAL RULES AND ECONOMIC POLICIES

Rich democracies enjoyed unprecedented prosperity and stability in the decades after World War II, as global free trade rewarded their economic competitiveness with rising profits and, most importantly for democratic stability, rising incomes for the large numbers of workers who were employed in industrial firms. In the heyday of manufacturing, stable, well-paying jobs turned factory workers into the bulwark of political moderation. Their lives were visibly improving, and they had reason to expect that the system would continue working for them into the foreseeable future. Ed Leamer (2007) suggested the image of a forklift, which both equalizes and amplifies the productivity of an otherwise heterogeneous population of workers. Moreover, as political scientists have pointed out, the resulting relative income equality translates into political stability if the rich have less reason to fear taxation and redistribution at their expense (Boix 2003, 2019; Ahlquist and Ansell 2017; Ansell, Broz, and Flaherty 2018). The demand for moderation was high.

On the institutional supply side, there are theoretical reasons to believe that electoral systems matter for policy making, but all boats rise in high tide, making the prosperous decades after World War II a poor basis from which to consider the policy effects of electoral systems. The policy consequences of electoral incentives on parties and politicians are more likely to show up when the underlying distribution of economic interests becomes discordant. As Warren Buffet has said, you only find out who's been swimming naked when the tide goes out.[1] Recent decades of growing insecurity among large numbers of voters put the spotlight on how well institutions respond to conflicts among voters. Our overall aim in this chapter is to understand how different institutional setups compare in their ability to provide their citizens with public as opposed to private goods – or at least, as a looser measure, how well they supply policies that are good for most voters over the long haul.

In this section, we explore the complex and sometimes countervailing incentives that electoral institutions confer on politicians and by which, by extension, they shape policy outcomes. Proportional representation (PR) systems potentially have several features that lend themselves to the provision of national public goods. If they are based in large rather than small geographic districts, they can aggregate interests at or close to the national level, considering the costs and benefits of a given policy on the entire population. Second, if they have closed lists, PR parties are disciplined and capable of enforcing policies deemed best for the entire constituency they seek to represent. Third, if they are large, encompassing parties, as Germany's Social Democratic Party (SPD) and CDU/CSU deliberately sought for decades to be, they aim at the broad interests of voters in the political middle, eschewing policies desired by narrow groups that would be costly to many others. This configuration would appear nearly ideal for the production of public goods and predictive of inclusive and long-term prosperity. Germany did, in fact, perform so admirably over the postwar decades that many countries in the second and third waves of democratization emulated Germany's mixed member electoral system, which was anchored in PR but had an element of single member districts (SMDs) to foster large parties that would aim at the middle.

---

[1] "Swimming naked when the tide goes out," Money. April 2, 2009. http://money.com/money/2792510/swimming-naked-when-the-tide-goes-out/

Plurality political systems, we suggest, have some countervailing advantages to PR systems. First, forcing two large parties to compete for the political middle reduces the hold that smaller, niche parties might have on final coalition building in legislative politics.[2] When only two parties compete for votes, political competition is more likely to be based on economic interests aimed at the broad interests of the nation. By contrast, if parties in a PR system join a government coalition and then logroll the intense preferences of their respective constituencies, the population at large pays for the costs of those logrolls in the form of higher prices for protected industries, higher taxes for privileged recipients of redistribution, and possibly lower long-term growth (Bawn and Rosenbluth 2006; Persson, Roland, and Tabellini 2007). It is an empirical question, still much debated, whether and under what conditions separately elected parties in PR systems can and will subordinate the interests of their respective constituencies to those of the coalition government (Powell 2002; Hallerberg and von Jurgen 2009; Martin and Vanberg 2011). Second, plurality systems create strong, unified opposition parties that can hold governments to account between elections.

In either PR or plurality systems, however, the strength of party discipline is likely to be more important than the number of parties. With Britain's traditional Westminster system, in which one political party at a time controls the government, voters can count on strong party discipline to deliver on promised policies – at least they could until leaders began relying on referendums to avoid internal party conflicts and decentralizing leadership selection procedures and adopting such innovations as the Fixed Term Parliaments Act of 2011 (Rosenbluth and Shapiro 2018: 248). Contrast this with the many veto players who, by design, check one another even within parties in the American federal, presidential, and bicameral system. In addition, primaries in predominantly red or blue congressional districts pit against one another candidates from the same party, putting a premium on costly campaigns that highlight personal legislative positions and achievements. Money in politics is nefarious,

---

[2] Warwick and Druckman (2001) argue that small parties are less likely to be pivotal in government formation – and therefore distorting of legislative politics – when the existence of a large number of small parties reduces the value of their bids to join the government coalition. On the other hand, small religious parties in Israel seem to maintain outsized influence in coalition politics on the dimension of religion and territorial aggrandizement to the extent they all agree on those points.

and it is important to see from where the demand for it comes. The need to establish a personal brand name is not only costly in itself, but it also opens candidates to attacks from better-funded candidates in their same party. It is no wonder that legislative elections in the United States cost several multiples of what they cost in Britain, giving moneyed interests greater leverage over policy measures in the absence of disciplined and unified parties.

Parties tend to be stronger in parliamentary systems; however, open lists in proportional representation systems, which give voters the option of boosting individual candidates' positions on the party's list, undercut the ability of party leaders to reward candidate loyalty and, by extension, weaken a party's ability to whip votes in line to deliver promised policies. Money plays a smaller role in Germany's closed-list proportional representation than in PR systems with open lists, common in Latin America and Eastern Europe, which pit individual candidates against one another for a winning berth. Carey and Shugart (1995) show why this is so: intraparty competition in either PR or plurality systems breaks the connection between voters and expected policy outcomes that only disciplined parties can deliver. Without party discipline, individual politicians cannot credibly commit to policies that voters might care about.

Note that polarization and party discipline are not the same thing. Empirically, contemporary American politics is polarized because the Republican and Democratic Parties occupy policy positions at opposite ends of the ideological spectrum. But much of the extreme position taking is the result of primaries between co-partisans in safe (for the party) seats. Because American districts to a significant extent have become overwhelmingly red or in urban areas overwhelmingly blue, fewer "purple" districts remain to force the parties to adopt policies that are *broadly* popular. A candidate more worried about their primary challenger than about the candidate of the other party will reasonably ignore the party's guidance on policy, especially if I can secure financial backing from PACs on their own.

Conceptually, polarization and party strength are not only different; they are opposite concepts. Parties are a mirror of their elected members in that they are stronger when their representatives are more alike and weaker when their representatives have less in common. When a party's representatives span the distance between the political middle and the extreme, a party's leadership is powerless to whip them to support policies that put many of them at electoral risk.

In the table below, we array party systems along two dimensions: Whether there are many parties, as in Proportional Representation systems (PR) or two parties, as in plurality systems; and whether the parties are disciplined or undisciplined.

	PR: Many Parties	Plurality: Two Parties
Disciplined parties	Closed list: e.g., Sweden or Germany	Westminster
Undisciplined parties	Open list: e.g., Brazil or Poland	veto players, e.g., United States

Postwar prosperity generated political moderation that masked institutional differences only now beginning to reveal themselves. Large and well-organized groups such as unionized workers, able to support a strong party of the left, would moderate their demands for higher wages if organized labor were such a large proportion of the total population to encompass their interests as consumers and exporters as well as workers (Calmfors and Driffill 1988; Iversen and Soskice 2006 and 2019). Plurality electoral systems force parties to aim at broader coalitions than industrial workers alone, but the governments and policies produced by plurality and PR systems would be much the same if industrial workers encompass the median voter. If organized labor shrinks as a percentage of the population, its interests could diverge from those of voters in the middle, pulling labor parties to the political left. Because PR systems make it easy for parties to fragment and gain election as small parties, parties on the left have begun to fragment as economies deindustrialize.

The challenges facing plurality systems are somewhat different. Winner-take-all electoral rules weaken strategic incentives for extremists to break off into splinter parties. But if the parties are weak, as in the United States, extremist groups like the Tea Party can exert enormous influence within a mainstream party. Even Britain is not immune. Its parliamentary system gives party leaders far greater power to select or deselect who stands for election than they have in the United States, contributing to greater party discipline. But as in the United States, deindustrialization is eating away at British institutions. The economic fortunes of British citizens have varied so starkly by geography over the past few decades, with London growing while the North shrinks, that the parties are no longer internally homogeneous. Pro- and anti-Brexit forces rive both of the two main parties.

THE DECLINE OF INDUSTRIAL JOBS

In this chapter, we explore empirically the effects of declining industrial jobs on party fragmentation, focusing on the thirty-four OECD countries from 1966 to 2015. Over this period, industrial jobs have declined in rich democracies everywhere. Voters have responded by abandoning traditional parties in favor of new splinter groups further to the left. Voters appear to blame traditional left parties for their inability to protect industrial jobs against automation or foreign competition.

As Table 10.1 below shows, a 10 percent decrease in the share of industrial jobs (Ind Jobs) is associated with a 9 percent increase in the vote share of new splinter parties (nontraditional) on the left. These numbers understate the collapse of the traditional left, since our data pool the entire postwar period, which includes times of prosperity with the less prosperous times. This splintering does not occur in plurality or single-member-district (SMD) electoral systems, presumably because voters are reluctant to throw away their votes.

One consequence of a shift in votes to new splinter parties on the left is an increase in the total number of parties. Table 10.2 shows that a

TABLE 10.1 *Industrial jobs and voter support*

	Left		Right	
	Traditional (1)	Nontraditional (2)	Traditional (3)	Nontraditional (4)
Ind Jobs	0.41	−0.89**	0.54	−0.24
	(0.57)	(0.43)	(0.32)	(0.18)
SMD	0.12	−0.02	−0.11*	0.05
	(0.10)	(0.07)	(0.05)	(0.05)
Open list	−0.03	0.05	0.06**	0.01
	(0.05)	(0.03)	(0.02)	(0.03)
Presidential	−0.02	0.03	0.02	−0.09***
	(0.03)	(0.02)	(0.02)	(0.02)
GDP per cap	0.05	0.03	−0.01	0.04
	(0.08)	(0.06)	(0.04)	(0.05)
R2	0.907	0.646	0.927	0.822
N	222	222	222	222
Mean of Dep Var	0.272	0.060	0.298	0.047

Statistical significance: *0.10, **0.05, ***0.01. The relatively high R2 suggests that these variables capture much of the variation. The means of the dependent variable indicate that votes for traditional parties are still considerably greater than for splinter parties, over all.

TABLE 10.2 *Industrial jobs and fragmentation on left parties*

	Left	
	By Vote (5)	By Seats (6)
Ind Jobs	-4.73*	-5.73**
	(2.59)	(2.50)
SMD	0.47	0.03
	(0.72)	(0.64)
Open list	0.68**	0.55**
	(0.27)	(0.25)
Presidential	0.25	0.25
	(0.36)	(0.40)
GDP per cap	0.60	0.52
	(0.75)	(0.60)
R2	0.792	0.795
N	221	222
Mean of Dep Var	1.821	1.697

Statistical significance: *0.10, **0.05, ***0.01

10 percent drop in the share of industrial jobs corresponds with an increase in the number of effective parties by about a half a party, on average, across all of these country-years. Although it is harder to see this from these data, parties on the right may also fragment in strategic response to the collapse of traditional left parties. We notice in Germany, for example, that the Social Democrats (SPD) have lost votes to their left, to Die Linke and the Greens, forcing the SPD in turn to move leftward or at least to spread out ideologically. The CDU under Merkel took tactical advantage of their move by staking a larger claim to the political middle, which in turn may have spawned AfD activism on her right as she did so. Fragmentation on the left, in response to fewer industrial jobs, motivated parties to spread out their appeals across the political spectrum.

Column (1) in Table 10.3 shows that fragmentation occurs in non-SMD systems, as we would expect. Plurality systems, even if beset with the same loss of industrial jobs, do not reward a political strategy of starting a smaller party to capture the disaffected.

Column (2) in Table 10.3 shows the same substantive results if, for robustness, we measure the effects of plurality systems by the minimum

TABLE 10.3 *Industrial jobs and left party fragmentation*

	Effective Number of Left Parties			
	(1)	(2)	(3)	(4)
Ind Jobs	−5.21**	−7.19***	−5.87**	−5.46**
	(2.39)	(2.57)	(2.55)	(2.50)
Ind Jobs × SMD	8.91**			
	(4.01)			
Ind Jobs × Min %		25.51**		
		(11.51)		
Ind Jobs × Open list			1.76	
			(3.50)	
Presidential				11.40**
				(3.91)
R2	0.799	0.803	0.795	0.800
N	222	212	222	222
Mean of Dep Var	1.697	1.685	1.697	1.697
+ p-value	0.445	0.505	0.032	0.232

Statistical significance: *0.10, **0.05, ***0.01

share of votes within a district necessary for a party to secure one seat (rather than SMD per se). At very high levels of proportionality, a 10 percent loss of industrial jobs increases the number of parties by more than one-half on average (0.71). With every 10 percent increase in the minimum share of votes needed to win a seat, approaching plurality, the number of parties decreases by about a quarter of a party on average. Column (3) shows that in PR systems with open or closed lists – that is, irrespective of internal party discipline – the decline in industrial jobs is significantly associated with left party fragmentation. For reasons we do not explore in this chapter but may reflect clientelistic spending in the presidential systems of Latin America, column (4) shows that the connection between the loss of industrial jobs and left party fragmentation only exists in parliamentary systems.

PARTY FRAGMENTATION AND ECONOMIC POLICIES

We have surmised, as does much of the relevant literature (e.g., Boix 2018; Iversen and Soskice 2019), that prosperity underpinned political moderation by giving the mass of voters a stake in the status quo. It

TABLE 10.4 *Fragmentation on left parties and policy choice and outcome*

	Gov. Spending on Community (1)	Agricultural Producer Support (2)	Gov. Spending on Redistribution (3)	Unemployment Rate (4)
Left Frag	−0.03	0.25***	−0.42**	0.01
	(0.04)	(0.06)	(0.19)	(0.20)
Left Frag × Left Gov	−0.15**	0.06	1.01**	1.02***
	(0.07)	(0.08)	(0.39)	(0.37)
Left Gov	0.18***	−0.32**	−0.06	0.30
	(0.05)	(0.13)	(0.22)	(0.27)
R2	0.544	0.913	0.948	0.746
N	478	302	478	639
Mean of Dep Var	0.759	1.430	15.370	7.165
+ p-value	0.008	0.000	0.107	0.030

Statistical significance: *0.10, **0.05, ***0.01

follows from this logic that if parties on the left splinter in response to voter dissatisfaction, these parties will be less inclined to support moderate policies that benefit the political middle or, more broadly, the long-term interests of most voters. A decrease in left vote cohesiveness away from the median voter is likely to amplify the influence of smaller and more dispersed groups of voters.

Table 10.4 offers some suggestive evidence that when the left is in government but is fragmented, spending on community services declines. By contrast, agricultural producers' support, which is a classic example of spending on a narrow group, increases with left party fragmentation. As in the past, spending on redistribution continues to increase when the left is in government and decreases when the right is in power, but the degree to which redistribution is aimed broadly at the middle or becomes more narrowly targeted is more important. The association of the redistribution with higher rather than lower unemployment is worrisome. One additional left party causes a 1 percent increase in the share of workers who are unemployed. Perhaps the fall in industrial jobs forces the left to continue serving well-organized workers with employment benefits and protection at the expense of workers who have lost their jobs and who find it hard to get a new job given the high costs of employment.

CONCLUSIONS AND POSSIBLE SOLUTIONS

Industrial jobs have disappeared in rich democracies, undercutting the motivations and means for political moderation. This has occurred everywhere but nowhere more dramatically than in the proportional representation countries of Europe where small, extremist parties have grown with astonishing speed and effectiveness. In the United Kingdom, despite a rise in xenophobia, neither the racist British National Party nor the anti-European UKIP has made significant parliamentary inroads. With a 12.6 percent of the vote in the 2015 election, UKPI would have netted 86 seats in the House of Commons instead of the solitary seat it won.[3] As in the 1920s and 1930s, when extremist parties exploited economic stagnation to make major inroads in Europe, the splinter group of the day, Oswald Mosley's fascists, got nowhere in British electoral politics.

The chapters in this volume describe many deplorable trends in American politics, including the rise of polarization and racism in response to economic insecurity. Boix (Chapter 9) and Kessler-Harris (Chapter 5), each in their own way, describe the unraveling of moderate politics. As Rodden (Chapter 6) shows, demographic sorting of Democrats into cities leaves large numbers of Americans unrepresented and economically vulnerable. Weir and King (Chapter 8) recount the strategies of rich suburbanites to wall themselves off from the needs of the less well off. Hacker and Pierson (Chapter 11) describe how the Republican Party has lurched to extreme positions as floods of money support right-wing causes. Politics in America is a tale of bad decisions and sad outcomes.

It would be wrong, however, to think wishfully about greener grass without appreciating the source of water, so to speak. The proportional representation countries of Europe have, without question, modeled a superior set of policy outcomes: prosperity without sacrificing equality. As Thelen and Wiedemann (Chapter 12) show, support for these policies remains strong. However, deindustrialization strains the capacity of these countries as well, and voter frustration has motivated reforms in many proportional representation countries of the wrong kind: opening list systems to let voters select individual representatives on party lists and using primaries to draw up lists. These measures produce intraparty competition that rewards small groups with intense preferences and

---

[3] "Election 2015: What difference would proportional representation have made?" *BBC News*, May 9, 2015. www.bbc.com/news/election-2015-32601281

undermine healthy competition over national programs. It would be far better to increase thresholds, forcing small parties to combine, retain closed lists to strengthen party leaderships, and use counting rules that tilt in favor of the largest parties.

Internally disciplined and hierarchical parties have an undemocratic ring and are vulnerable to attack in hard times. When voters do not know whom to blame, parties are easy targets. But weakening parties also weakens their ability to formulate and implement policies with an eye to the long run. Far better is for party leaders' authority to be conditional on parliamentary backbenchers' preference for strategic moderation. If party members know they are better able to get and stay elected when they offer coherent policies, they can choose new leaders who can – as the swift departures of Margaret Thatcher in 1990 and David Cameron in 2016 underscore. Parties that are broad-gauged, encompassing an electoral majority, and are disciplined enough to enforce majority-enhancing deals give voters clear signals of what the party stands for, and what it will implement in the event that it wins the election and becomes the government.

Populism in the United States and the United Kingdom has corroded the major parties, to be sure. But first-past-the-post electoral rules in these countries force groups like the Tea Party to fight for prominence within the established parties rather than establish separate political parties. Electoral competition in single member districts has blunted the force of extremist groups, though decentralizing reforms have rendered them more vulnerable to hostile takeovers – as Jeremy Corbyn's reelection by the membership in September 2016 following an overwhelming no-confidence vote from the Parliamentary Labour Party and Donald Trump's takeover of the Republicans underscore (Rosenbluth and Shapiro 2018: 62–127). The more electoral districts remain competitive between the two major parties, the more electoral competition benefits the average citizen. Parties forced to compete for the political middle must be strategically moderate or fail.

PATHWAYS FOR REFORM

Democratic accountability rests on political competition between strong parties that can craft and deliver good policies. Improving democracy is not about returning "more power to the people" in a literal sense, but in improving electoral institutions so that voters have a meaningful choice. In proportional representation systems, raising the electoral threshold for legislative representation would reduce the toehold of small extremist parties and would force party leaders to bundle policies at the level of aggregation that benefits most voters over the long term. Eliminating open lists and primaries would give party leaders the levers of control with which to enforce this kind of strategic moderation. Scrapping run-off elections would also promote moderation by robbing narrow interest groups of a source of power – their ability to swing elections in the second round of voting in exchange for special favors. Proportional representation countries, which have an advantage over district-based systems in controlling backbenchers to offer nationally competitive platforms, forfeit that advantage when they succumb to the false promises of decentralizing forms of "party democratization."

District-based systems such as the United States and Britain need radical restructuring in the direction of national competition. Ideally, every electoral district would be diverse in ways that mirror the nation's diversity across the range of issues that voters care about. Given the wealth and prosperity differentials between New York and London and many other parts of their respective countries, an ideal system would include a sliver of cities, suburbs, and rural areas in every constituency. The median voter in each constituency would then better resemble the national median voter, and their elected representatives would find it comparatively easy to agree on policy priorities. Backbenchers in the legislature would be willing to delegate authority to their party leaders to get legislative work done and protect the party's brand into the future. In Britain, this would also mean substantially increasing the size of constituencies and correspondingly reducing the number of MPs. Average British constituencies are a third the size of Germany's single member districts and a tenth of the size of the typical US congressional district.

American geographic diversity is locked into constitutionally mandated powers of the Senate that pose even bigger challenges. This could be mitigated somewhat by admitting Puerto Rico and the District of Columbia to statehood and breaking up states like California and Texas. A perhaps more realistic reform in the short run would be redistricting in favor of competitive congressional elections. State legislatures have relentlessly redistricted with exactly the opposite purpose: to create the maximum number of districts for their own party while wasting as many votes for the opposite party as possible with super-safe districts. In most districts, this means that the primary election is the only contest of any consequence, fostering Tea Party takeovers and other kinds of extremism.

Majority-minority districts have, in a cruel twist, reduced partisan competition and thereby failed to serve the interests of the minority voters that they are intended to benefit. Alternative ways to achieve diversity in legislatures include the reservation of 7 out of New Zealand's 120 parliamentary seats for Māoris, or the comparable provision in India dating back to the Poona Pact of 1934, which reserves 84 out of the parliament's 543 seats for Untouchables and other scheduled castes. Requiring parties to nominate a diverse field of candidates could also enhance gender and other forms of diversity without diluting democracy's competitive lifeblood. Making every district accountable to the preferences of voters in the political middle would moderate the stances of American legislative parties by strengthening their leaders at the expense of the shrinking number of outliers. There may be some vulnerable minorities that will not be adequately protected by any electoral arrangements, particularly when ethnic and racial inequalities consistently map onto inequalities of income.

Even in that case, vulnerable minorities would be better served when politicians are given incentives to campaign on political platforms defined by economic interests rather than ethnicity and race. Identity politics tends to breed more identity politics, as the scramble to benefit from set-asides and other benefits for scheduled castes in India and the recent rise of white identity politics in the United States underscore. African Americans in the United States would be better served if both major parties had incentives to compete for their votes, rather than the current status quo in which Democrats can take them for granted and Republicans' main incentive is to find ways to suppress minority turnout (Rosenbluth and Shapiro 2018: 42–61).

American checks and balances, hailed as antidotes to tyranny, have often fallen prey to powerful groups rather than working to protect weak ones. Most advances that vulnerable minorities have achieved in the United States have come through legislatures, not the courts – protestations by lawyers to the contrary notwithstanding (Rosenberg 2008). Comparative evidence suggests that separation-of-powers systems with independent courts do no better than parliamentary democracy at protecting vulnerable minorities. Indeed, courts have undermined democratic competition in the United States since 1976 by declaring money to be speech protected by the First Amendment to the Constitution, disproportionately empowering the well-heeled to work their will in the American political process (Shapiro 2016: 93–102).

Plebiscites and referendums undermine rather than enhance democratic accountability. Britain had never had a referendum before Harold

Wilson called one in 1975 over remaining in the European Union. In those pre-Thatcherite days, it was Labour that was divided over Europe, which was seen less hospitable than Britain to workers' legal protections under UK law. Rather than do the hard work of fighting it out within his party, Wilson put it to a referendum in which "Remain" beat "Leave" by 67.2 percent to 32.8 percent. Pleased with himself, Wilson (1979: 109) opined in his autobiography: "It was a matter of some satisfaction that an issue which threatened several times over thirteen years to tear the Labour movement apart had been resolved fairly and finally ... all that had divided us in that great controversy was put behind us." Five years later, in 1980, a referendum split the Labour Party nevertheless. When Michael Foot, having retracted his earlier acceptance of the referendum result and declaring that Britain should leave Europe without another referendum, won the leadership contest in 1980, the Gang of Four – Roy Jenkins, David Owen, Shirley Williams, and Bill Rodgers – stormed out to form the Social Democratic Party. Had Dennis Healey not defeated Tony Benn for the deputy leadership, the exodus would have been a lot larger. Thirty-five years later David Cameron made a comparable blunder as the path of least resistance to avoid confronting the Tory rifts over Brexit.

It is the job of political parties to bundle issues, so that voters discount some things they want against other things they also want. American voters support unilateral tax cuts when asked about them in referendums such as Proposition 13 in California in 1978, limiting property taxes to 1 percent of assessed value. The downstream effect was to decimate California's public schools and local governments. Polls show that voters will support any tax cut when asked about them in isolation, but not if they are told that a particular cut will be accompanied by losing a popular program such as free medical prescriptions (Birney, Shapiro, and Graetz 2008). Then they are forced to discount their preference for lower taxes by their preference for free medical prescriptions.

Parties are in a better position than individual voters to consider the costs and benefits of alternatives when they bundle policies into programs. They must discount everything they propose by everything else they propose in ways that they hope will appeal to as large a swath of the population as possible. The fewer the parties, the more voters they must consider. This is why both Labour and the Tory parliamentary parties strongly favored remaining in Europe. When they discounted the costs of leaving against everything else they knew most voters wanted, Remain made better sense. Considering one issue at a time in a referendum creates an artificial choice for voters, as in the case of the Brexit vote.

Weakening parties in favor of increasing local and diverse voices has a democratic ring. This has been the dominant response to rising insecurity. Unfortunately, decentralized control also undermines the ability of parties to work out the trade-offs among policies in a complex world. As E. E. Schattschneider (1942, p. 1) said three-quarters of a century ago, "the condition of the parties is the best possible evidence of the nature of any regime." Whatever the system, political parties play a vital role in identifying, competing over, and defending the broad interests of the voting public. Strengthening rather than weakening political parties is democracy's best hope.

Appendix

DATA

We collect data on electoral rules, electoral results of legislative elections, and economic performance of the thirty-five OECD countries for 1945 to 2017. For every election held democratically in this sample, we record the rules regarding parliamentary or presidential system, district system (majoritarian, proportional, or mixed), district magnitude, PR formula (Danish, Hare, Sainte-Lague, LR-Droop, D'Hont, LR-Imperiali, Imperiali highest averages), list system (Open or preferential, Closed), PR legal threshold (minimum percentage of votes required for a party to be admitted into parliament), number of districts, and number of seats available or filled.

For every election, we record whether the election was scheduled beforehand or called early, the number of rounds, and the turnout for each round. Only France has two rounds; we record the second round whenever a choice needs to be made. In the case of countries that use two votes with different electoral systems, such as Germany and Mexico, we code the PR one. We record the vote share and seat share obtained by every party elected to parliament, recording which parties were "traditional" and which "nontraditional," and which parties were right leaning and which left. Finally, we record the vote share for parties not elected to parliament if categorized as nontraditional (e.g., far right, far left).

In general, we follow standard coding rules such as Carey-Hix's (2011). We use several sources, including previous publications containing such information (e.g., Carey-Hix (2011) and DPI (2015)), official records (in print and online), and unofficial online sites (e.g., Google,

Wikipedia). Economic indicators such as the share of employment accounted for the industrial sector, GDP, and unemployment and inflation were obtained from the OECD, the ILO, and the World Banks public databases. All variables containing monetary amounts are measured in real terms, and with purchasing power parity when available; when used in estimation, these variables are logged.

Data availability varies with variable. The estimations shown in the text use the maximum number of years and countries for which data are available for our main variables, namely party fragmentation and the share of employment accounted for the industrial sector. Since some potentially relevant controls are available only for a subset of years and/or countries, in the text we present estimates using only those controls available for the maximum sample.

RESEARCH DESIGN

To examine the effect of the fall of industrial jobs on the support for different political factions and party fragmentation we estimate

$$y_{it} = \alpha_i + \lambda_t + \beta \, IndJobs_{it-1} + X_{it-1} \Pi + \varepsilon_{it} \tag{1}$$

where i indexes countries where, and t indexes years when, an election was held. Given the data limitations and the year of elections, we are able to consider all 35 OECD but 2, South Korea and Latvia, and all years from 1966 until 2015. With the exception of 8 years when no election was held, in every year elections are held in a median of 4.5 countries, with as few as 1 (1995) and as many as 13 (2011).

Our dependent variable y_{it} will measure an electoral outcome, of which we will consider two sets: (i) share of votes obtained by a political faction (traditional left, traditional right, nontraditional left, nontraditional right) and (ii) the resultant party fragmentation in parliament, as measured by the number of parties and by the classic *effective number of parties* measure, which basically weights each party by its share of seats.[4] Our preferred measure for fragmentation is *effective number of parties*, because it better accounts for actual fragmentation of forces in parliament.[5] Our main

---

[4] Formally, effective number of parties is equal to one over the sum of the shares of each party squared, where shares are measured in decimals (or percentage).
[5] We wish to use a measure that captures the fact that a parliament consisting of four parties with equal share of seats is a far more "fragmented" than one consisting of four parties with shares 45 percent, 45 percent, 5 percent, and 5 percent. Number of parties would

coefficient of interest is β, which accompanies $IndJobs_{it\text{-}1}$ the share of employment that corresponds to the industrial and manufacturing sector. Since some elections are held in the middle of the year and to avoid reverse causality issues, we measure $IndJobs_{it\text{-}1}$ the year previous to the election. All standard errors are clustered at the year level to correct for non-independence of observations across countries within a year, for example, due to global political or economic trends.[6]

The specification includes country fixed effects α_i and year fixed effects γ_t. The country fixed effects capture any time-invariant differences across countries, such as persistent differences in ideological stigma or in corruption. Year fixed effects control for global trends that affect all countries similarly.

To account for the fact that the timing of election may be endogenous, we restrict the sample to exclude elections that were called ahead of the next scheduled election, about 13 percent of all elections in our sample. To control for country-specific time-varying unobservables, the specification includes a vector of covariates $X_{it\text{-}1}$, including GDP per capita of the year previous to the election to avoid reverse causality issues, and a collection of controls for the political system valid the year of the election. Political controls include indicator variables for parliamentary, vis-à-vis presidential, systems, for closed list systems and for electoral systems with single-member districts (SMDs). We also include a variable we call *Min %* that calculates for each election the minimum percentage of votes within a district that a party requires to secure at least one seat. This variable intends to measure, in top of the SMD dummy, the degree of proportionality of an electoral system, and it is constructed using three pieces of information: the median district magnitude; the formula used to allocate seats to parties in a proportional system (e.g., D'Hont); and the PR legal threshold, if one exists.

Finally, in addition to equation (1), for our main variable of interest – fragmentation on the left – we estimate (1) including an interaction of industrial jobs with SMD and Min % to test whether the result differs across degrees of proportionality.

---

indicate that both parliaments have 4 parties, while *effective number of parties* would indicate that the first has 4 parties while the second 2.44, exactly what intuition calls for.
[6] Findings are similar when clustering by country. We use year clusters as the preferred method since the number of countries (33) is low (lower than 42 years), and we worry that our standard error estimates may be biased with the small number of clusters.

To examine the effect of fragmentation of the left on labor policy choice and outcomes, we estimate

$$y_{it+1} = \alpha_i + \lambda_t + \beta\, LeftFrag_{it} + \gamma\, LeftGov_{it} \times LeftFrag_{it} + X_{it}\,\Pi + \varepsilon_{it} \quad (2)$$

where i indexes countries and t years. Given the data limitations and the year of elections, we are able to consider all thirty-five OECD countries but South Korea, and all years from 1966 until 2015. Fragmentation changes only at elections, and elections are held in different years for different countries. This staggered nature of elections allows us to employ a differences-in-differences design to test how left fragmentation $LeftFrag_{it}$ has affected policy choice and outcome, when the left was in government ($LeftGov_{it}$) as opposed to when it was not.

Depending on the country, elections are held in various times of the year, and some countries hold elections every two or three years. Thus, to focus on the effect of the recent fragmentation change without contaminating the results with future political phenomena, we measure all outcomes in the year posterior to the election, which inevitably limits our analysis to short-run policies.

As part of the differences-in-differences design, equation (2) includes country fixed effects α_i and year fixed effects γ_t. The main identifying assumption in this design is the parallel trends assumption, which requires that the trajectory of our dependent variable in a country where an election was held would, if it had not been held, have been similar to that of a country where no election occurred. Here again we exclude from the sample elections that were called ahead of the next scheduled election, about 13 percent of all elections in our sample. To account for omitted country-specific time-varying factors, the specification also includes a vector of covariates X_{it}, containing the same covariates as the first research design, together with an indicator variable of whether the governing party or coalition is from the left and a variable that measures the fragmentation of the right parties, which allows us to isolate the effect of left fragmentation alone, as opposed to general parliament fragmentation, on the policy outcome. Results are robust when using the full sample and, for the restricted and full sample, including linear time trends for each country, a parametric way of relaxing the parallel trends assumption allowing each country to have a unique trend over time.

REFERENCES

Ahlquist, John S., and Ben Ansell. 2017. "Taking Credit: Redistribution and Borrowing in an Age of Economic Polarization." *World Politics* 69(4): 640–675.

Ansell, Ben J. Lawrence Broz, and Thomas Flaherty. 2018. "Global Capital Markets, Housing Prices, and Partisan Fiscal Policies." *Economics & Politics* 30(3): 307–339.
Bawn, Kathleen, and Frances McCall Rosenbluth. 2006. "Short versus Long Coalitions: Electoral Accountability and the Size of the Public Sector." *American Journal of Political Science* 50(2): 251–265.
Birney, Mayling, Ian Shapiro, and Michael Graetz. 2008. "The elite uses of public opinion: Lessons from the estate tax repeal," in Ian Shapiro, Peter Swenson, and Daniela Donno, eds, *Divide and Deal: The Politics of Distribution in Democracies*. New York: New York University Press. 298-340.
Boix, Carles. 2003. *Democracy and Redistribution*. Cambridge: Cambridge University Press.
  2019. *Democratic Capitalism at the Crossroads: Technological Change and the Future of Politics*. Princeton: Princeton University Press.
Calmfors, Lars, and John Driffill. 1988. "Bargaining Structure, Corporatism and Macroeconomic Performance." *Economic Policy* 3(6): 13–61.
Carey, John, and Matthew S. Shugart. 1995. "Incentives to Cultivate a Personal Vote: A Rank Ordering of Electoral Formulas," *Electoral Studies* 14(4): 417–439.
Hallerberg, Mark, Rolf Rainer Strauch, and Jurgen von Hagen. 2009. "The Design of Fiscal Rules and Forms of Governance in European Union Countries," *European Journal of Political Economy* 23(2).
Hochschild, Arlie Russell. 2016. *Strangers in Their Own Land: Anger and Mourning on the American Right*. New York: The New Press.
Iversen, Torben, and David Soskice. 2006. "Electoral Institutions and the Politics of Coalitions: Why Some Democracies Redistribute More than Others," *The American Political Science Review* 100(2): 165–181.
  2019. *Democracy and Prosperity: Reinventing Capitalism through a Turbulent Century*. Princeton: Princeton University Press.
Leamer, Edward. 2007. "A Flat World, a Level Playing Field, a Small World After All, or None of the Above? A Review of Thomas L. Friedman's *The World Is Flat*," *Journal of Economic Literature*. 45: 83–126.
Martin, Lanny W., and Georg Vanberg. 2011. *Parliaments and Coalitions*. Oxford: Oxford University Press.
Persson, Torsten, Gerard Roland, and Guido Tabellini. 2007. "Electoral Rules and Government Spending in Parliamentary Democracies." *Quarterly Journal of Political Science* 20: 1–34.
Powell, Bingham G. 2002. "PR, the Median Voter, and Economic Policy: An Exploration," Paper presented at the annual meeting of the American Political Science Association.
Rosenberg, Gerald N. 2008. *The Hollow Hope: Can Courts Bring About Social Change*. 2nd ed. Chicago: University of Chicago Press.
Rosenbluth, Frances, and Ian Shapiro. 2018. *Responsible Parties: Saving Democracy from Itself*. New Haven: Yale University Press.
Shapiro, Ian. 2016. *Politics against Domination*. Cambridge, MA: Harvard University Press.
Shattschneider, E. E. 1942. *Party Government*. New Brunswick, NJ:Transaction.

Warwick, Paul, and James N. Druckman. 2001. "Portfolio Salience and the Proportionality of Payoffs in Coalition Governments," *British Journal of Political Science* 31(4): 627–649.

Williamson, Vanessa, Theda Skocpol, and John Coggin. 2011. "The Tea Party and the Remaking of Republican Conservatism." *Perspectives on Politics* 9(1): 25–43.

Wilson, Harold. 1979. *The Final Term: The Labour Government 1974–76*. London: Weidenfeld & Nicholson.

11

The Peculiar Politics of American Insecurity

Jacob S. Hacker and Paul Pierson

The last generation has witnessed a dramatic rise in the economic insecurity of American workers and their families. Although recent concern has centered on the prospect of widespread job losses due to automation and artificial intelligence, these tides have yet to be fully felt. Instead, the main story of the past three decades is what one of us has called the "Great Risk Shift" (Hacker 2008, 2019) – the shift of risk from the broad shoulders of government and corporations onto the fragile backs of workers and their families.

This change has not brought mass joblessness, though some segments of the workforce (particularly white male workers without a college degree) have experienced declining employment prospects. But it has brought mass insecurity, with risks once faced mainly by the working poor steadily creeping up the income ladder to reach all but the best-off Americans. Amid the COVID-19 pandemic, the shift of risk onto American households has rapidly accelerated, with tens of millions of workers losing their jobs – and often their employment-based health benefits as well. Meanwhile, those who work in face-to-face settings have confronted an intensified set of health and safety risks – risks that many state workers' compensations programs do not cover and that conservative political leaders have insisted should not be borne by employers.

The growing insecurity of American households is often seen as an exogenous economic change beyond political control – a result of deep shifts in technology, finance, and the global economy. In this chapter, we argue that as important as these exogenous changes have been, the Great Risk Shift is to a very large extent a result of endogenous political and policy developments. Moreover, we suggest that many, though certainly not all, of these developments are specific to the United States – which is why both the politics and the experience of American insecurity stand out in cross-national perspective.

In particular, we focus on three fundamental developments: (1) the erosion of America's distinctive framework of social provision, which is uniquely reliant on private risk pooling by employers – risk pooling that has become less and less attractive to American business in a financialized, globalized economy with weak labor power; (2) the weakness of social solidarity and resonance of racial (rather than class) appeals in our increasingly geographically, racially, and politically polarized society; and (3) the growing extremism of the Republican Party, enabled and propelled by its capacity to maintain (at least until now) an uneasy "plutocratic-populist" coalition of upscale economic conservatives and downscale social conservatives. Understanding these three developments – the retrenchment of private provision, the resurgent impact of racial resentment, and the radicalization of the GOP – is essential to grasping not just how America insecurity arose but also whether it might yet be addressed.

THE GREAT RISK SHIFT

To understand the Great Risk Shift, we must first understand America's distinctive framework of social protection. As Thelen and Wiedemann (Chapter 12, this volume) show, the United States stands out for the high levels of risk uncushioned by social policy. Unique among rich democracies, the United States fostered a social contract based on stable long-term employment and widespread provision of private workplace benefits. As Figure 11.1 shows, our government framework of social protection is indeed smaller than those found in other rich countries. Yet, when we factor in tax levels and include private health and retirement benefits – mostly voluntary, but highly subsidized through the tax code – the United States has an overall system that is similar in size to that of other rich countries. The difference is that America's hybrid system is distinctively private (Hacker 2002; Howard 2007).

This framework, however, is coming undone. The unions that once negotiated and defended private benefits have lost tremendous ground. Meanwhile, the pressures on corporations from global competition, technological change, and impatient financial markets have greatly intensified. Partly for these reasons, employers face strong incentives to reduce the burdens they took on during more stable economic times. At the same

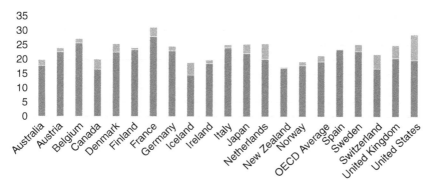

■ After-tax public spending   ■ After-tax private spending

FIGURE 11.1 Public and private social protection spending by country
Source: Jacob S. Hacker, "The Great Risk Shift That Helped Deliver Donald Trump," Talking Points Memo, 24, October 2018, https://talkingpointsmemo.com/feature/the-great-risk-shift-that-helped-deliver-donald-trump. Data: Organisation for Economic Co-operation and Development. Graphic: Christine Frapech/TPM.

time, they no longer place as much value on the long-term relationships with workers that these arrangements reflected and fostered.

To be sure, not all firms have faced intensified competition. Many sectors – from health care to retail trade to technology – have instead seen concentration and consolidation. Indeed, economists have found strong tendencies toward both monopsony (one buyer, many sellers) and monopoly (one seller, many buyers) in a wide range of labor and product markets (CEA 2016; Grullon 2019). And yet these trends, too, have mostly pushed toward greater insecurity. Alongside declining unions, the increase in the monopsony power of employers appears to be an important reason for the persistent wage stagnation of recent decades (Naidu and Posner 2018). In other sectors, monopoly power has increased prices or dependence on particular sellers. In the tech industry, for example, the biggest players – Apple, Google, Facebook, Amazon – can leverage their huge networks of locked-in users and the near-zero cost of expanding those networks to destroy or acquire potential competitors (Kahn 2016).

Perhaps because of the prominence of these companies, recent commentary about the changing labor market has focused on the digital revolution – and, in particular, on online employment platforms, such as the transportation application Uber and piecework sites like Task Rabbit and Amazon's Mechanical Turk. Yet online employment represents a miniscule share of the total employment picture: about 0.5 percent of all workers, according to a 2015 survey (Katz and Krueger 2016). The significance of these new platforms does not lie in their prevalence, or at least not yet. Rather, it reflects the extent to which they exemplify a long-term move away from traditional career patterns and job structures toward a more unstable set of arrangements in which workers change jobs frequently, pay and benefits vary greatly from worker to worker and firm to firm, and reciprocal loyalty between employers and employees is limited.

The essence of this new set of arrangements is not the particular form that work takes, or how exactly it is managed, but rather the locus of risk in the employment relationship. Put simply, American employers have ceased to pool risks as consistently or durably as they once did. Median job tenure is down, particularly for younger workers. The prevalence of employer-employee arrangements that imply little in the way of reciprocal obligations – and, with them, individualized assessment and "incentive" pay – are up. To use a domestic analogy, workers and employers used to be more or less stably married. Now, they are cohabitating for comparatively brief periods of time, and sometimes not even that.

The shift has been most pronounced for industrial workers with limited formal education: once fairly well protected from the economy's vagaries, they now find their options limited, fueling the decline of small towns and resentment of blue-collar workers that have contributed to America's peculiar variant of right-wing populism. Yet even those who are better poised to profit in today's postindustrial economy face heightened insecurities. Workers and their families need to invest more and more in education to earn a middle-class living. Even so, in an economy marked by huge differentials in pay and benefits between high-end professional work and low-end service employment, these costly investments are no guarantee of a high, stable, or upward-sloping path (Hacker 2019).

Moreover, the workplace is not the only site of heightened insecurity. Americans are also at greater risk because of changes in the role and character of families. Although median wages have essentially remained flat over the past generation, median-income families have seen stronger income growth (Boushey and Vaghul 2016). The whole of this rise is because women are working many more hours outside the home than they once did. Indeed, without the increased work hours and pay of women, median family incomes would have *fallen* over the past generation. As a result, families with two earners now rely on continuous work by both partners to maintain a middle-class standard of living. This heightens the potential for disruption when they need to take time off to care for children, parents, or themselves; when they face unexpected expenses; or when their partnerships end in divorce or separation. Of course, many of these risks are even greater for the substantial minority of parents who are raising children on their own (Iversen and Rosenbluth 2011).

In all these ways, the new world of work and family has undermined key pillars of the more secure economy of the mid-twentieth century. The decline of more stable forms of employment and changes in the family have directly increased the risks facing American households. At the same time, they have gravely undermined America's unique employment-based system of social benefits, which places primary responsibility for health insurance and family policies like childcare and paid leave, as well as secondary responsibility for retirement savings, in the hands of employers.

At the lower end of the labor market, generous benefits have all but disappeared. In firms where they have not, they have shifted more risk onto workers (as in defined-contribution pension plans). And even in sectors where private benefits remain strong, they can be legally denied to workers classified as temporary or contingent or employed through subcontracting arrangements. Frequently, such workers are also ineligible for key public protections tied to work, such as unemployment insurance, because legal definitions of workers – so crucial to the ability to get both public and private benefits – remain tied to a traditional employment model that is less and less common (Hacker 2019).

Of course, policy makers could have responded to these changes by shoring up existing programs of economic security. However, at the same time that the corporate world turned away from an older model of employment, the political world turned away from a long-standing approach to insecurity known as "social insurance." The premise of social insurance is that widespread economic risks can be dealt with effectively only through institutions that spread their costs across differing income, age, and risk classes. The idea is most associated with Franklin Roosevelt, but from the 1930s well into the 1970s private insurance companies and unionized corporations promoted it, too. During this era of rising economic security, both public and private policy makers assumed that a dynamic capitalist economy required a basic foundation of protection against economic risks.

That changed during the economic and political turmoil of the late 1970s. With the economy becoming markedly more unequal and conservatives gaining political ground, many policy elites began to emphasize a different credo, one premised on the belief that social insurance was too costly and inefficient and that individuals should be given "more skin in the game" so they could manage and minimize risks on their own. Instead of a guaranteed benefit from Social Security, for example, workers should have individualized retirement accounts regulated by the government. Instead of providing public insurance, Medicaid and Medicare should be less generous and rely on individual private plans. Instead of pooling risks, in short, government should privatize them.

To be sure, actual retrenchment of public social protections has proved limited (Pierson 1994; Hacker and Pierson 2018). Indeed, there have been important expansions of government insurance, as occurred in 2010 with the passage of the Affordable Care Act. As important as these policy departures have been, however, they have not halted the shift of risk. In most domains, policies have not kept pace with changing circumstances, leaving workers and their families to deal with heightened risks on their own. This policy "drift," in turn, has reflected vigorous efforts by employers and conservatives to push back against the updating of these laws in the face of rising insecurity as well as to undermine existing protections (Hacker et al. 2015). To explain why these efforts have been successful, we must first understand why there has been such limited voter pressure on elected officials to repair America's tattered safety net.

"SECOND-DIMENSION" POLITICS

The failure of public officials to respond to rising insecurity poses two intertwined puzzles. The first is why changes as consequential as those just discussed have not led to larger shifts in effective voter *demand* for policy updating. The second is why there has been so little elite effort to *supply* such updating.

Among students of American politics, these two questions are often seen as synonymous – no demand, no supply. Yet a growing body of research suggests that the actions and agendas of elected representatives often depart greatly from the preferences and priorities of their constituents (Gilens 2012; Gilens and Page 2014; Bartels 2016). To make assessments of representation even more complex, elite communications and organized structures of participation – such as interest groups and party organizations – can profoundly shape how citizens come to understand issues, as well as how, whether, and when their views come to shape policy development.

Still, it is worth thinking separately about issues of demand and supply – without assuming the former drive the latter or treating public preferences as independent of political contestation. The relative quiescence of Americans in the face of rising economic insecurity does pose a puzzle, one that is cast in sharp light by the growing body of research on how citizens react to major economic shocks. A consistent finding of this work is that those who experience such shocks become more supportive of public policies designed to address them (Hacker et al. 2013; Margalit 2013). Nor are these effects small; in some studies, a life-altering economic loss has effects that are comparable to the difference in attitudes between Republicans and Democrats (Hacker et al. 2013). Since the likelihood of these shocks has increased, it would be natural to assume that public support for new policies providing economic security has too.

Natural, but wrong: public preferences have not shifted markedly over the past generation. While support for most existing social policies remains high, public views about *new* policies show little consistent trend. Instead, public opinion exhibits two main features: heightened partisan polarization and highly conditional support. That is, Republicans and Democrats disagree more about contested social policies than in the past, and both Republicans and Democrats appear less trusting of the capacity of government to successfully carry out large-scale policies (Pew 2012; Kuziemko et al. 2015). Although polarization may not influence average levels of support, it implies much more intense opposition to the expansion of public social protections. Meanwhile, widespread distrust of government makes *all* citizens less willing to believe that even clearly recognized problems will be effectively dealt with by new policy measures.

These barriers are compounded by differences in political engagement and participation. For example, behavioral research suggests that those experiencing economic insecurity withdraw politically relative to their more secure fellow citizens (e.g., Marx 2016), in part, as Adam Seth Levine (2015) has argued, because appeals that emphasize insecurity are "self-undermining" – reminding people of their time and resource constraints. What's more, while all Americans have faced heightened insecurity, the effects have been most pronounced among less affluent Americans, who are both less likely to participate in politics and less likely to see their preferences reflected in policy.

In addition – and this is what we focus on in the remainder of this section – an enormous amount of evidence indicates that voters' perceptions of public protections are highly racialized (e.g., Tesler 2012; Gilens 1999). Although long-standing, this racialization has become more consequential because of the heightened need for an affirmative government response to rising insecurity and because of changes in the position and character of the two parties. In this section, we focus mostly on the electoral dimensions of this change; in the next section, we turn to the dynamics of "asymmetric" elite polarization that we believe provide the primary explanation both for these electoral dimensions and for the policy drift that has left Americans so insecure.

Race enters into the politics of social policy through at least two channels, what Woojin Lee and John Roemer (2006) call the "solidarity" and "policy bundling" effects. The solidarity effect is the simplest: people are less likely to trust and less willing to share risks with those whom they see as "the other" – in the case of white Americans, racial and ethnic minorities, including recent immigrant groups. There is an active debate about whether economic dislocations or racial animus are the fundamental explanation for voters' support for ethnonationalist positions (see, e.g., Mutz 2018; Iversen and Soskice 2019). But this framing of the debate is far too stark: in the United States at least, racial animus and a sense of economic decline appear clearly linked through long-term processes of opinion formation. Perhaps more important, they have been linked by conservative political elites who have strong incentives to respond to economic grievances with racialized appeals (Tavits and Potter 2015).

We come, then, to the second process highlighted by Lee and Roemer, policy bundling. Policy bundling arises in the context of a competitive party system in which political elites can appeal to voters on the basis of their group identities rather than their material interests. In the American context, this might be called the "George Wallace" effect, after the racist populism Wallace successfully deployed in the 1968 election, winning five southern states and the allegiance of nearly 10 million (mostly less educated and affluent) voters despite the well-known barriers to third-party candidates in the United States (Kozak 2014). Though Wallace's hard-edged racism was too hard for most GOP candidates, the themes he emphasized – particularly "law and order" and "states' rights" – became a staple of GOP campaigns in the South, which gradually shifted from a one-party Democratic region into a Republican stronghold.

Of course, President Donald Trump doubled down on Wallace-style rhetoric in his successful 2016 campaign for the GOP nomination and then the US presidency. But he did not invent the strategy of attracting less affluent voters with such "second-dimension" appeals (as opposed to the "first dimension" of economic and size-of-government issues). Since the realignment of the parties around race in the 1960s and 1970s and around social conservatism in the 1970s and 1980s, emphasizing noneconomic wedge issues has always been an attractive approach for a party that includes business groups and affluent donors, on the one hand and less affluent white voters, on the other.

Despite the ongoing moderation of Americans' views on race, the incentives to deploy this strategy have increased over time. For one, rising inequality has sharpened the economic conflict between the upscale and downscale parts of the GOP coalition, making it harder to please "intense policy demanders" (Bawn et al. 2012) at the top without turning to the second dimension to appeal to GOP voters below the top. For another, as discussed in the next section, Republican political elites – who in theory could have moderated on economic issues in response to rising inequality – have forged a strong alliance with these intense policy demanders, especially highly organized elements of the business community and superrich donors (Hacker and Pierson 2016). This alliance is most apparent in the GOP's hard-right positions on taxation and regulation, which are generally unpopular even among Republican voters (Kuo and McCarty 2015). Thus, the rising economic standing and political power of GOP-allied corporate organizations and big donors have increased the party's incentives to emphasize the second dimension in the policy bundle offered to less affluent white voters.

Finally, and fatefully, the growing diversity of the electorate has made Republicans more reliant on precisely those less affluent voters. To counter the growing nonwhite share of the electorate – voters who lean strongly Democratic – Republicans have come to depend on outsized winning margins among white voters without a college degree (the so-called white working class). Among Republican-favorable segments of the electorate, these downscale white voters are at once the least supportive of conservative economic policies and the most prone to racial resentment, making second-dimension appeals with strong racial elements an effective strategy for increasing their allegiance to the GOP and their likelihood of turning out to vote.

Electoral geography is a key contributor to and enabler of this strategy. Over the past two decades, as Rodden (Chapter 6, this volume) notes, rural areas have grown more Republican and urban areas more Democratic. This has gone hand in hand with the growing concentration of prosperity and diversity in urban and coastal areas. The most affluent regions of the country are increasingly Democratic and racially and ethnically pluralistic; the most depressed are increasingly Republican and hostile to the changing face of the nation. While these areas are still overwhelmingly white, there is evidence that some have experienced unusually large *increases* in low-skilled, nonwhite immigrants, albeit from a low base (Adamy and Overberg 2016; Mayda et al. 2018). Salient *changes* appear to be far more important than absolute levels in explaining backlash against demographic shifts (Hopkins 2010).

Of course, these trends are happening in many affluent democracies (Rodden 2019). America's electoral system, however, makes them both more attractive and more effective: the same geographic sorting that is creating a more isolated and disaffected GOP voting base is also giving Republicans a significant bonus in national electoral contests (Stephanopoulus and McGhee 2015). The unique American electoral system combines a Senate highly biased toward less populous states (a bias that partially carries over to the Electoral College, which decides the presidency) with single-member, winner-take-all districts. This system naturally rewards parties that are broadly distributed across large swaths of sparsely populated territory. It also makes it much easier for such parties to gerrymander districts to maximize their ability to translate votes into seats, especially because they are likely to control state governments (and hence redistricting) in less populous states. Increasingly, the party that fits this description is the GOP.

This Republican electoral edge has, ironically, heightened the party's audacity in pursuing upwardly redistributive policies that will be devastating in many of the areas of the country where Republican voting strength is greatest. Electoral insulation means that Republicans can adopt more extreme stances with less fear of backlash from moderate voters. Meanwhile, it increases their fear of primary challengers from their right flank as opposed to general-election opponents.

The conservative media bubble – another highly distinctive feature of the American context – has added to this insulation, fostering a GOP electorate that is motivated primarily by "negative" or "affective" partisanship (that is, hatred of the other side). This is a key reason why Trump won the support of the substantial share of Republicans who thought he was unqualified for the presidency; they could not bring themselves to vote for the Democratic Party. Many of the core Trump voters come from places prosperity has left behind. But he could not have won without the support of many suburban and upscale Republicans who were mainly motivated by negative partisanship.

Thus, geographic and media isolation have worked in tandem to intensify the opposition of the GOP base to government, the Democratic Party, and new social policies that can be portrayed as giveaways to racial and ethnic minorities. Recent scholarship on conservative media sources has shown they are both highly influential and highly distinctive from both mainstream and liberal outlets (e.g., DellaVigna and Kaplan 2007; Arcenaux et al. 2016; Martin and Yurukoglu 2017; Roberts et al. 2018). Conservative media sources mostly rely on other conservative sources for amplification and verification; even the most liberal news outlets, by contrast, operate in an environment where their claims must relatively quickly confront the routines of fact-checking and commitment to nonpartisanship (not always observed, of course) of major media institutions.

Right-wing media is also driven by a distinctive business model that rests heavily on discrediting alternative sources of expertise and emphasizing conspiratorial and oppositional thinking – often with strong themes of racial and cultural backlash, as evidenced, for example, by Fox News's fixation on an "invasion" of immigrants across the Southern border in the run-up to the 2018 midterms. These characteristics have further facilitated the emphasis on the second dimension by GOP candidates and officeholders.

The key to this strategy is a continual ratcheting up of racialized antigovernment appeals. These appeals, however, carry long-term risks. They not only threaten Republicans' electoral support beyond their base; they also mobilize growing opposition to the GOP governing approach. It is this approach – and its consequences for economic insecurity – that are the focus of the next section.

ASYMMETRIC POLARIZATION

The dramatic polarization of political elites over the past generation has not been symmetrical (Hacker and Pierson 2015, 2016). Republicans have moved much further right than Democrats have moved left. This asymmetry can be seen not just in congressional voting patterns but also in the relative positions of presidential and vice-presidential nominees, as well as in the relative positions of each party's judicial nominees. It can also be seen, to a lesser extent, in the polarization of state-level elected officials and when comparing the policy conservatism or liberalism of Republican "trifectas" (control of both houses of the state legislature as well as the governor's office) and Democratic trifectas (Grumbach 2018).

Moreover, this asymmetry is apparent even when the focus is on the *absolute* rather than *relative* positions of elected officials. Most measures of polarization are effectively blind to shifts in the central tendencies of ideological conflict. If, for example, all politicians become more supportive of free trade but still equally polarized regarding it, measures of polarization will miss this consistent shift. And, indeed, there have been such consistent shifts over the past generation, as discussed earlier: the 1970s and 1980s saw both parties moving to the right on issues of social insurance, with an increased emphasis on personal responsibility and individualized approaches to risk management.

But it is also possible to say that Republicans have moved *much* more to the right on these and related policy disputes – not just relative to Democrats but also in absolute terms (Hacker and Pierson 2016). Consider just two examples: health care and taxation. In the debate over President Bill Clinton's health plan in 1993 and 1994, more than half of Senate Republicans backed a competing, market-oriented approach advocated by the Heritage Foundation. The Heritage blueprint later became the guiding vision for a health plan passed in Massachusetts with the support of GOP Governor Mitt Romney. Yet when these same principles became the template for President Obama's health plan in 2009, every national Republican, including Romney, denounced it in the most apocalyptic terms. In 2017, Republicans came within a few votes of repealing core elements of the Affordable Care Act and dramatically scaling back Medicaid – a package that, had it passed, would have been the most substantial and regressive retrenchment in the history of U.S. social policy, far exceeding the 1996 welfare reform legislation in scope or impact (Hacker and Pierson 2018).

Similarly, the Republican Party once worked closely with Democrats to restrain the growth of federal health spending by using Medicare's bargaining leverage to hold down provider charges. (In fact, Presidents Reagan and George H. W. Bush each spearheaded new payment controls, with substantial GOP support in Congress.) Beginning in the 1990s under House Speaker Newt Gingrich, Republicans renounced these once-bipartisan efforts to control costs within the health care industry. Instead, GOP leaders focused their proposals on cuts in benefits, even ones that would in practice have little impact on overall costs. They advocated turning Medicaid into a limited "block grant" to the states and proposed raising the eligibility age for Medicare and transforming it into a voucher-style system in which the federal government made a fixed contribution to the cost of private plans, shifting the risks of health spending from the federal government onto beneficiaries.

The Republicans have also turned right on issues related to taxes. Ronald Reagan agreed to raise taxes on numerous occasions, maintaining the established bipartisan formula for handling budget deficits: modestly cut spending and moderately raise taxes. After 1990, however, Republicans refused to support *any* tax increases in budget packages. Indeed, they went further. On numerous occasions, they insisted that "deficit reduction" include (deficit-raising) tax cuts. At the same time, Republicans increasingly focused on tax cuts for the highest income groups: cuts in the estate, dividends, corporate, and capital gains taxes, as well as the top marginal income tax rate. Republicans' focus on tax cuts for the affluent reached its apotheosis (to date at least) in the "Trump tax cuts" of 2017, which delivered more than 80 percent of their long-term benefits to the richest 1 percent of Americans (Tax Policy Center 2017). This distributional skew is all the more striking because opinion polls consistently indicate that voters' biggest complaint about the tax system is that the rich did not pay their fair share (Pew Research Center 2015).

The Republican Party has moved toward the far right not just when you compare its current stances with its own past positions but also when you compare its current stances to the current stances of conservative parties in other rich democracies. Analyses based on systematic coding of the campaign platforms of leading parties (the "Manifestos Project") show that the Republican Party is an outlier relative not just to center-right parties in other nations but in some cases to right-wing parties that place themselves well to the right of mainstream conservatives, too (Chinoy 2019).

These shifts in positions have made it exceedingly difficult to construct new social policies that attract bipartisan support. (In fact, the ACA passed without a single GOP vote in either house of Congress.) But ideological shifts have not been the only barrier to an effective response to heightened insecurity. In addition to moving right, Republicans have become much more confrontational – willing to use hardball tactics that while technically legal in most cases, had previously been shunned as uncivil or anti-democratic. Among the major examples of such "constitutional hardball" (Tushnet 2004; Fishkin and Pozen 2018), Republicans have led the way and deserve exclusive or primary responsibility for

- Routinized use of the filibuster to block virtually all initiatives of the majority party.
- Repeated government shutdowns.
- Resort to mid-decade reapportionments (which are traditionally done following the census counts that occur once every ten years) in order to gerrymander House seats.
- Systematic efforts to disenfranchise younger, lower-income, and non-white voters viewed as unlikely to support the GOP.

- Using the periodic raising of the authorized ceiling on federal debt (to finance spending *already appropriated* by Congress) to extract concessions from Democrats – in effect, taking the full faith and credit of the federal government hostage so as to ransom it for favored GOP policies.

The list is neither short nor are the items trivial. Together, they are what led veteran Congress watchers Thomas Mann and Norman Ornstein to call the GOP "an insurgent outlier in American politics" (Mann and Ornstein 2012, xiv).

The GOP is not just a conservative party, in other words. It increasingly displays characteristics of what comparative scholars call an "anti-system party" (Zulianello 2018) – one oriented not toward governing but toward making governing nearly impossible. Even when out of power in Congress or the White House, Republicans have been able to block most major initiatives to address economic insecurity since the mid-1990s, breaking norm after norm along the way. The revealing exception is the passage of the Affordable Care Act (ACA) in 2010 – which Republicans have successfully sought to undermine ever since, even though they have proved unable to repeal it outright.

Again, the effects of this confrontational strategy are limited where strong social policies are in place and protected against erosion by automatic updates (such as indexation to price levels). But it has proved much more consequential where policies require regular updating and especially where existing policies increasingly fall short because of changes in the world of work and family and the erosion of private benefits. In these highly important areas – ranging from wage and labor laws to health care, pension, and family leave policies – the Great Risk Shift has continued apace.

Finally, the GOP's anti-system strategy is a key contributor to the unfavorable electoral and opinion dynamics discussed in the previous section. Given the lack of effective progress in addressing economic insecurity, GOP appeals to disaffected voters have emphasized racial resentment; the pathologies of government; and, above all, the tribal need for those living in the "real America" to band together to defeat the other side. Even before Trump's rise, moreover, it was increasingly clear this strategy relied on continually escalating negative partisanship among an outraged voting base that Republicans elites had cultivated but, in many ways, could not fully control. In 2016, these party elites lost command altogether, and Donald Trump won the GOP nomination.

Once in office, however, Trump has largely gone along with Republicans' preexisting approach to domestic social policy. During his campaign, Trump defended core programs of the American welfare state and said he would restore economic security to regions devastated by deindustrialization and the rise of the knowledge economy, with its fundamentally urban orientation. In practice, however, his presidency has been even more focused on cutting taxes on the affluent and deregulating key sectors of the economy than the presidency of George W. Bush (2000–2008). The clearest example is the aforementioned 2017 tax cuts, but Trump has also pursued cutbacks in Medicaid and the ACA (through executive means after the failure of the GOP health care push in Congress) and called for radical retrenchment of almost all labor protections and safety-net policies, while conspicuously failing to follow up on repeated promises to fund job-creating infrastructure investments, lower health care costs, and provide support for family leave. Virtually all the policies that Trump and the GOP Congress have pursued are highly unpopular – even, in many cases, among strong GOP voters (Kuo and McCarty 2015; Clement et al. 2017; Hacker and Pierson 2018).

This gap between rhetoric and reality is not simply a reflection of Trump's erratic personality or the ambiguity of his core policy commitments. Instead, it is mostly a product of America's distinctive party dynamics and political system – the same factors, we have argued, that have militated against an effective response to rising insecurity. After all, Trump did not build his own party; instead, he took over a going concern. Nor, for the most part, is Trump able to achieve durable policy shifts on his own. Instead, America's separation of powers gives Congress a pivotal role in domestic lawmaking.

In other words, America's unusual political structure is a double-edged sword. It makes it easier (when combined with negative partisanship) for a right-wing populist to grab the presidency. But it does not give the president full authority to make policy. To achieve big changes, presidents must work with Congress.

For congressional Republicans in 2017, this meant embracing Trump, and all he represented, to advance long-sought legislative goals. For Trump, it meant deep-sixing the more economically populist aspects of his 2016 campaign, not that there was any sign he was eager to pursue them. Americans were greeted with the spectacle of Speaker of the House Paul Ryan – the architect of a string of extreme fiscal plans known as the "Ryan budget" – embracing a man he had once denounced as a racist (Alberta 2018).

Indeed, if another Republican had captured the presidency in 2016, the GOP agenda in Congress would probably not have looked radically different. Back in 2012, conservative activist Grover Norquist, head of the virulently anti-tax Americans for Tax Reform, described the key qualities a future GOP president needed to have:

> We are not auditioning for fearless leader. We don't need a president to tell us in what direction to go. We know what direction to go. We want the Ryan budget. ... We just need a president to sign this stuff. We don't need someone to think it up or design it. The leadership now for the modern conservative movement for the next 20 years will be coming out of the House and the Senate. Pick a Republican with enough working digits to handle a pen to become president of the United States. ... His job is to be captain of the team, to sign the legislation that has already been prepared. (Quoted in Frum 2012)

Given the role of the filibuster and the unpopularity of Republicans' core priorities, the "team" and its "captain" have struggled to pass elements of their inegalitarian agenda. Despite the abnormality of his behavior and rhetoric, however, Trump as president has largely stuck to the Norquist script. Although the Republicans' health bill failed, the president and congressional Republicans achieved two of their biggest goals: a string of conservative judicial appointments that are certain to constrain state and federal efforts to address economic insecurity going forward, and massive tax cuts that directly worsen inequality and threaten future spending cuts. It was these achievements that led Senate Majority Leader Mitch McConnell, first elected in 1984, to say in September 2018, "If you want America to be a right of center nation, this last year-and-a-half has been the best year-and-a-half in my time in the Senate" (Donachie 2018). Needless to say, it has been far less sunny for those who would like the federal government to address the Great Risk Shift.

PROSPECTS FOR THE FUTURE

What then are the prospects for a more vigorous response to rising insecurity? This is a question of political economy, and it hinges on three broad factors: individual voter response, political organization, and the structure of the political economy. Without providing anything like a full answer, we offer final reflections with regard to each.

If the past generation has taught us anything, it is that voters' responses to economic insecurity are highly mediated by the structure of partisan conflict and the electoral system. Vigorous clarifying and mobilizing efforts by groups are particularly crucial if voters are to recognize their economic interests and act on behalf of them. Here, however, the sharp decline of unions in the United States stands out as a major barrier to government responsiveness. Meanwhile, employers appear to have become *more* effective at mobilizing their workers in support of their aims, and they appear most effective when workers feel insecure (thus worrying that their job is vulnerable if they do not support the company line) (Hertel Fernandez 2018). More broadly, the imbalance between business groups, on the one hand, and labor and public interest groups, on the other, has become increasingly acute. Without serious efforts to rebuild groups representing workers and other diffuse constituencies, efforts to respond to rising insecurity are likely to be anemic, episodic, and vulnerable to backsliding.

Another barrier that must be confronted is the fragmented, veto-ridden structure of national authority and the degree to which it empowers those seeking to stop, rather than enable, government activity. As we have emphasized, the status quo bias of American political institutions – coupled with the asymmetric polarization of the parties – has made comprehensive national efforts to address insecurity all but impossible. We would add to this observation that because of this gridlock as well as the success of Republicans in confirming conservative judges, battles in the federal courts will be fundamental to future prospects. The failure to update the legal status of unions and workers, even as these laws have been interpreted in more and more constricted ways, has greatly compounded insecurity. Yet, bringing about such changes is very hard for political actors who lack durable organizations and high levels of expertise – attributes that business groups in particular have developed. Here again, advocates of policy updating will need to support laws and investments that facilitate the development and mobilization of organizations that can serve as a counterweight to narrow interests that are already well organized.

Finally, American federalism provides its own distinctive constraints – and some potential opportunities. Though federal law matters enormously, state policies have a large impact on economic security, too. Even so, state policy making advantages mobile employers, who can threaten exit if their interests are threatened. Moreover, employers have become adept at lobbying states. Witness the substantial influence of the American Legislative Exchange Council (ALEC), a pro-business lobby that has had considerable success at the state level (Hertel-Fernandez 2014) or Uber's impressive lobbying in key states.

In short, if durable reforms are challenging at the federal level because of polarization and gridlock, they are also challenging at the state level because of the structural power of mobile employers and the increased lobbying prowess of employer organizations. The state fiscal crisis caused by the pandemic added another powerful barrier, since states lack the borrowing capacity of the federal government and virtually all have balanced-budget requirements. Still, states are likely to continue to diverge in their response to the Great Risk Shift, as the number of Republican trifectas declines from its mid-2000s peak (again, trifectas are where both houses of the statehouse and the governor's office are in a single party's hands) and the number of Democratic trifectas increases. The result may well be a growing divergence *within* the political economy between "red" and "blue" states, with workers in blue America enjoying a modicum of security, while those in red America continue to bear the brunt of the Great Risk Shift.

As we write in August 2020, President Trump looks more vulnerable than any incumbent president since at least Jimmy Carter in 1980. His average approval rating has been lower than any first-term president in the history of modern polling, and the president's disastrous handling of the COVID-19 pandemic has only added to the headwinds he faces. Moreover, the Democratic Party is moving left on economic issues, driven by a combination of the anti-Trump wave, the enthusiasm of younger voters, and the growing diversity of the party's voters and elected officials. In the 2018 midterm elections, Democrats took the House in part because of their vigorous defense of the ACA and Medicaid, especially the ACA's protections for patients with preexisting health conditions. Democratic candidates also hammered their opponents for votes on key pieces of GOP legislation, bills that garnered the lowest public support of any seriously considered in the past quarter century (Hacker and Pierson 2018).

These signs raise the prospect that state and national policy making may shift toward a more robust response to rising insecurity in the future. As we have argued, the main barriers to such an agenda are not economic or fiscal; they are political and institutional. To succeed over the long term, those who seek greater security for American workers and their families will have to tackle directly the negative political dynamics showcased in this chapter.

WORKS CITED

Adamy, Janet, and Paul Overberg. 2016. "Places Most Unsettled by Rapid Demographic Change Are Drawn to Donald Trump," *Wall Street Journal*, November 1. https://www.wsj.com/articles/places-most-unsettled-by-rapid-demographic-change-go-for-donald-trump-1478010940

Alberta, Tim. 2018. "The Tragedy of Paul Ryan," *Politico*, April 12 https://www.politico.com/magazine/story/2018/04/12/how-donald-trump-upended-paul-ryans-plans-217989

Arceneaux, Kevin, Martin Johnson, René Lindstädt, Ryan J. Vander Wielen. 2016. "The Influence of News Media on Political Elites: Investigating Strategic Responsiveness in Congress." *American Journal of Political Science* 60(1): 5–29.

Bartels, Larry. 2016. *Unequal Democracy: The Political Economy of the New Gilded Age*, 2nd ed. Princeton, NJ: Princeton University Press.

Bawn, Kathleen, Marty Cohen, David Karol, Seth Masket, Hans Noel, and John Zaller. 2012. "A Theory of Political Parties: Groups, Policy Demands, and Nominations in American Politics." *Perspectives on Politics* 10(3): 571–597.

Boushey, Heather, and Kavya Vahgul. 2016. "Women Have Made the Difference for Family Economic Security." Washington Center for Equitable Growth Issue Brief. April. Available online at http://cdn.equitablegrowth.org/wp-content/uploads/2016/04/04153438/Women-have-made-the-difference-for-family-economic-security-pdf.pdf

Chinoy, Sahil. 2019. "What Happened to America's Political Center of Gravity?" *New York Times*. June 26. https://www.nytimes.com/interactive/2019/06/26/opinion/sunday/republican-platform-far-right.html

Clement, Scott, Emily Guskin, and Shelly Tan. 2017. "America's Chaotic, Crazy, Challenging, Great, Tumultuous, Horrible, Disappointing Year: A Look Back at the Ups and Downs of Public Opinion in 2017." *Washington Post*, Dec. 15.

Council of Economic Advisers (CEA). 2016. *Labor Market Monopsony: Trends, Consequences, and Policy Responses*. October. Available online at https://obamawhitehouse.archives.gov/sites/default/files/page/files/20161025_monopsony_labor_mrkt_cea.pdf

DellaVigna, Stefano, and Ethan Kaplan. 2007. "The Fox News Effect: Media Bias and Voting." *The Quarterly Journal of Economics* 122(3): 1187–1234.

Donachie, Robert. 2018. "McConnell: Last 18 Months under Trump Have Been My 'Best' Time in the Senate." *Washington Examiner*. September 21. https://www.washingtonexaminer.com/news/white-house/mcconnell-last-18-months-under-trump-have-been-my-best-time-in-the-senate

Fishkin, Joseph, and David E. Pozen. 2018. "Asymmetric Constitutional Hardball." *Columbia Law Review* 118(3): 915–982.

Frum, David. 2012. "Norquist: Romney Will Do as Told." *Daily Beast*. February 13. https://www.thedailybeast.com/norquist-romney-will-do-as-told-david-frum

Gilens, Martin. 1999. *Why Americans Hate Welfare: Race, Media, and the Politics of Antipoverty Policy*. Chicago: University of Chicago Press.

  2012. *Affluence and Influence: Economic Inequality and Political Power in America*. Princeton, NJ: Princeton University Press.

Gilens, Martin, and Benjamin I. Page. 2014. "Testing Theories of American Politics: Elites, Interest Groups, and Average Citizens." *Perspectives on Politics* 12(3): 564–581.

Grullon, Gustavo, Yelena Larkin, and Roni Michaely. 2019. "Are U.S. Industries Becoming More Concentrated?" *Review of Finance* 23(4): 697–743.

Grumbach, Jacob M. 2018. "From Backwaters to Major Policymakers: Policy Polarization in the States, 1970–2014." *Perspectives on Politics* 16 (2): 416–435.

Hacker, Jacob S. 2002. *The Divided Welfare State: The Battle over Public and Private Benefits in the United States*. New York: Cambridge University Press.

　2008. *The Great Risk Shift: The New Economic Insecurity and the Decline of the American Dream*, rev. and exp. paperback ed. New York: Oxford University Press.

　2019. *The Great Risk Shift: The New Economic Insecurity and the Decline of the American Dream*, 2nd ed. New York: Oxford University Press.

Hacker, Jacob S., and Paul Pierson. 2015. "Confronting Asymmetric Polarization." In *Solutions to Polarization*, ed. Nathaniel Persily. New York: Cambridge University Press.

　2016. *American Amnesia: How the War on Government Led Us to Forget What Made America Prosper*. New York: Simon & Schuster.

　2018. "The Dog That Almost Barked: What the ACA Repeal Fight Says about the Resilience of the American Welfare State." *Journal of Health Politics, Policy, and Law* 43(4): 551–577.

Hacker, Jacob S., Paul Pierson, and Kathleen Thelen. 2015. "Drift and Conversion: Hidden Faces of Institutional Change." In *Comparative Historical Analysis in the Social Sciences*, ed. Kathleen Thelen and James Mahoney. New York: Cambridge University Press.

Hacker, Jacob S., Philipp Rehm, and Mark Schlesinger. 2013. "The Insecure American: Economic Experiences, Financial Worries, and Policy Attitudes." *Perspectives on Politics* 11(1): 23–49.

Hertel-Fernandez, Alexander. 2014. "Who Passes Business's 'Model Bills'? Policy Capacity and Corporate Influence in U.S. State Politics." *Perspectives on Politics* 12(3): 582–602.

　2018. *Politics at Work: How Companies Turn Their Workers into Lobbyists*. New York: Oxford University Press.

Hopkins, Daniel J. 2010. "Politicized Places: Explaining Where and When Immigrants Provoke Local Opposition." *American Political Science Review* 104(1): 40–60.

Howard, Christopher. 2007. *The Welfare State Nobody Knows: Debunking Myths about U.S. Social Policy*. Princeton, NJ: Princeton University Press.

Iversen, Torben, and David Soskice. 2019. *Democracy and Prosperity: Reinventing Capitalism through a Turbulent Century*. Princeton, NJ: Princeton University Press.

Iversen, Torben, and Frances McCall Rosenbluth. 2011. *Women, Work, and Politics: The Political Economy of Gender Inequality*. New Haven, CT: Yale University Press.

Katz, Lawrence F., and Alan B. Krueger. 2016. "The Rise and Nature of Alternative Work Arrangements in the United States, 1995–2015." National Bureau of Economic Research Working Paper No. w22667.

Khan, Lina M. 2016. "Amazon's Antitrust Paradox." *Yale Law Journal* 126(3): 710–805.

Kozak, Warren. 2014. "George Wallace 1968 Presidential Campaign," *History on the Net*. Available online at www.historyonthenet.com/george-wallace-1968-presidential-campaign

Kuo, Didi, and Nolan McCarty. 2015. "Democracy in America." *Global Policy* 6(S1): 49–55.

Kuziemko, Ilyana, Michael I. Norton, Emmanuel Saez, and Stefanie Stantcheva. 2015. "How Elastic Are Preferences for Redistribution? Evidence from Randomized Survey Experiments." *American Economic Review* 105(4): 1478–1508.

Lee, Woojin, and John E. Roemer. 2006. "Racism and Redistribution in the United States: A Solution to the Problem of American Exceptionalism." *Journal of Public Economics* 90(6–7): 1027–1052.

Levine, Adam Seth. 2015. *American Insecurity: Why Our Economic Fears Lead to Political Inaction*. Princeton, NJ: Princeton University Press.

Mann, Thomas E., and Norman J. Ornstein. 2012. *It's Even Worse Than It Looks: How the American Constitutional System Collided with the New Politics of Extremism*. New York: Basic Books.

Margalit, Yotam M. 2013. "Explaining Social Policy Preferences: Evidence from the Great Recession." *American Political Science Review* 107(1): 80–103.

Martin, Gregory J., and Ali Yurukoglu. 2017. "Bias in Cable News: Persuasion and Polarization." *American Economic Review* 107(9): 2565–2599.

Marx, Paul, and Christoph Nguyen. 2016. "Are the Unemployed Less Politically Involved? A Comparative Study of Internal Political Efficacy." *European Sociological Review* 32(5): 634–648.

Mayda, Anna Maria, Giovanni Peri, and Walter Steingress. 2018. "The Political Impact of Immigration: Evidence from the United States." National Bureau of Economic Research Working Paper No. w24510.

Mutz, Diana C. 2018. "Status Threat, Not Economic Hardship, Explains the 2016 Presidential Vote." *Proceedings of the National Academy of Sciences* 115(19): E4330–E4339.

Naidu, Suresh, and Eric A. Posner, 2018. "Labor Monopsony and the Limits of the Law." Working Paper. Columbia University. Available online at https://irs.princeton.edu/sites/irs/files/naidu%20posner%20limits%20of%20law%20conference%20draft.pdf

Pew Research Center. 2012. "Partisan Polarization Surges in Bush, Obama Year – Trends in American Values: 1987–2012." Available online at www.people-press.org/2012/06/04/partisan-polarization-surges-in-bush-obama-years/

2015. "Federal Tax System Seen in Need of Overhaul – Top Complaints: Wealthy, Corporations 'Don't Pay Fair Share.'" Available online at www.people-press.org/2015/03/19/federal-tax-system-seen-in-need-of-overhaul/

Pierson, Paul. 1994. *Dismantling the Welfare State? Reagan, Thatcher and the Politics of Retrenchment*. New York: Cambridge University Press.

Roberts, Hal, Robert Faris, and Yochai Benkler, 2018. *Network Propaganda: Manipulation, Disinformation, and Radicalization in American Politics*. New York: Oxford University Press.

Rodden, Jonathan A. 2019. *Why Cities Lose: The Deep Roots of the Urban-Rural Political Divide*. New York: Basic Books.

Stephanopoulos, Nicholas, and Eric McGhee. 2015. "Partisan Gerrymandering and the Efficiency Gap." *University of Chicago Law Review* 82: 831–900.

Tavits, Margit, and Joshua D. Potter. 2015. "The Effect of Inequality and Social Identity on Party Strategies." *American Journal of Political Science* 59 (3): 744–758.

Tax Policy Center. 2017. *Distributional Analysis of the Conference Agreement for the Tax Cuts and Jobs Act*. Washington, DC: Tax Policy Center, December 18.

Tesler, Michael. 2012. "The Spillover of Racialization into Health Care: How President Obama Polarized Public Opinion by Racial Attitudes and Race." *American Journal of Political Science* 56(3): 690–704.

Tushnet, Mark. 2004. "Constitutional Hardball." *John Marshall Law Review* 37: 523–553.

Zulianello, Mattia. 2018. "Anti-System Parties Revisited: Concept Formation and Guidelines for Empirical Research." *Government and Opposition* 53(4): 653–681.

12

The Anxiety of Precarity

The United States in Comparative Perspective

Kathleen Thelen and Andreas Wiedemann

INTRODUCTION

The COVID-19 crisis has underscored the critical importance of policy in protecting lives and livelihoods in the face of life's unexpected risks. Viewed from a comparative frame, it has also shone a singularly unflattering light on the ability of the American social policy regime to shield the country's citizens from the health and economic impact of a deadly virus. While the current challenges are in some ways new and unprecedented, the COVID crisis also brings into sharp relief what are in fact long-standing weaknesses in the American social safety net by exacerbating trends that have been much longer in the making.

For decades now, and across the advanced industrial world, a growing number of people have been experiencing heightened risk relating to trends in labor markets, social policy regimes, and in some cases personal finance. One important labor market development, for example, concerns the growth of various forms of "atypical employment." As David Weil has pointed out, firms have become increasingly "fissured" (Weil, 2014), as companies construct extensive networks of outsourcing, subcontracting, and franchising that allow them to streamline operations and cut costs, particularly labor costs. Such practices are well known in manufacturing (e.g., Palier & Thelen, 2012) but have become even more

---

We would like to thank Bruno Palier for numerous conversations about this chapter, which have deeply influenced and strengthened our thinking about these issues. Thanks also to the other members of our SSRC working group, especially Frances McCall Rosenbluth and Margaret Weir.

pronounced with the rise of the service economy, where employment at all skill levels is characterized by more atypical, nonstandard, or discontinuous work (Häusermann, Kurer, & Schwander, 2015: 238; Oesch, 2006). Digital platforms such as Uber and Deliveroo have elevated such strategies to new levels by forgoing normal employment contracts altogether and using "independent contractors" instead. The upshot of all of these strategies is that firms are increasingly abdicating the responsibilities (and above all the benefits) once attached to the standard employment relationship (see especially Davis, 2015).

Meanwhile, contemporary trends in social policy regimes heighten the precarity associated with these labor market developments. A broad trend, shared across many of the rich democracies, has been in the direction of outright retrenchment (Pierson, 1996). Moreover, even the most resilient welfare regimes are increasingly turning away from policies of passive support to policies organized around labor market activation. Less visible but often equally consequential is the growing inadequacy of welfare programs to cover new social risks associated with evolving gender and family dynamics (Bonoli, 2005; see also Ananat, Gassman-Pines, and Truskinovsky, Chapter 13, this volume). Policy makers in many countries have failed to adapt policies to changing conditions, resulting in widespread policy drift (Hacker, 2004; Hacker and Pierson, Chapter 11, this volume). Together, these social policy and labor market trends have produced a growing disconnect between new forms of work and the policies that were designed in a period of manufacturing dominance and organized around assumptions, particularly male breadwinners with a stable long-term attachment to a specific company or sector, that no longer hold.

Finally, in the United Kingdom and the United States especially, the turn away from Keynesianism has famously ushered in neoliberal macroeconomic growth regimes that reflect a turn to what Colin Crouch has called "privatized Keynesianism" (Crouch, 2009). The classic Keynesianism that informed government policy for much of the postwar period kept unemployment at bay by smoothing market fluctuations and promoting growth through demand management (Crouch, 2009: 386). With the ascendance of neoliberalism since the 1970s and 1980s, however, governments have abandoned countercyclical spending and relied instead on an alternative form of "privatized Keynesianism." Thus, rather than the government taking on debt to stimulate the economy, policy makers expanded opportunities for individuals themselves to take on debt through bank loans and credit cards (Crouch 2009: 390).

All of these developments have contributed to what Jacob Hacker (2006) has called the "Great Risk Shift" in which the risks and uncertainties previously covered by firm-based benefits or government policies are increasingly shifted onto citizens themselves.[1] While the impact is most keenly felt among low-skill, low-income individuals, even high-skill employees face new risks associated with heightened income volatility, the need for self-provisioning in the absence of employment-related benefits, and ongoing skill obsolescence in a period of rapid technological change.

This chapter explores the dynamics of precarity, situating the United States in a comparative perspective. We argue that precarity, as we define it, involves exposure to financial and social insecurity stemming from a *combination* of high levels of individual labor market vulnerability and low levels of collective coverage against such risks.[2] The scope and intensity of *labor market risk* varies as a function of a country's regulatory and institutional environment. Variation in *risk coverage*, by contrast, captures how the consequences of such risks are addressed, either collectively through the welfare state or individually by individuals themselves. We show that while some countries share with the United States high levels of risk on one or the other dimension, the United States stands out in comparative perspective for the way it combines these two. Moreover, citizens in the United States are much more vulnerable than their counterparts in other rich democracies to what we call *risk contagion*: the phenomenon that misfortune in one domain can cascade to increase risk in other dimensions. Much as a secondary infection is both a new problem and a complication arising from an existing problem, risks in one arena (e.g., unexpected job loss) in the United States are more likely to trigger knock-on risks in other arenas (e.g., arrears on home mortgage payments) in ways that can cause individuals to spiral into precarity and poverty.

The chapter proceeds as follows. We begin by exploring some of the ways in which other scholars have approached the problem of assessing precarity and point out the ways in which the existing literature either provides only a slice of the problem or lacks a comparative perspective, before introducing our alternative framework. We then provide a

---

[1] See also Hacker and Pierson, Chapter 11, this volume.
[2] Although we focus on the risk side, this distinction shares many similarities with those drawn by other scholars focusing on the policy side, e.g., Nathan Kelly's (2008) distinction between "explicit redistribution" and "market conditioning" mechanisms for reducing inequality and Jacob Hacker's (2011, 2013) distinction between redistribution and "predistribution."

comparative empirical assessment of how the United States compares to other rich democracies in the prevalence of important sources of risk, as well as their potential mediators. We then discuss two prominent pathways through which risk spreads in the American context. A final section summarizes the argument.

RISK AND PRECARITY AS MULTIDIMENSIONAL PHENOMENA

The trends in labor markets, social policy, and finance mentioned at the outset have all contributed to new economic insecurities and new forms of social and economic precarity (Castel, 1995; also Standing, 2011). The literature in this area is vast and space does not allow for a full consideration of all the important contributions. However, in general, we observe a disconnect between two distinct literatures – one focusing on precarity in the American context, and the other on more comparative, treatments of the problem. The Americanist literature has provided insightful analyses of low-wage work (see, especially, Newman, 2006 and Kalleberg, 2013), inadequate social policy coverage (Hacker, 2006), and financial insecurity (Morduch and Schneider, 2017). Focusing as they do on the US case, however, they do not tell us whether precarity is worse in the United States than in other rich democracies – or if it is, why exactly that is the case. For this we need to situate the American case in a broader comparative context.

Comparativists, for their part, have also produced important studies of the growth of precarity across the full range of rich democracies (see, e.g., Häusermann et al. 2015; Chauvel, 2016; Rovny & Rovny, 2017, among many others). Several of the most prominent of these, however, focus on indicators of precarity that make sense in a European context but do not provide much leverage on the American case. For example, a common measure of growing precarity via heightened labor market risk in the comparative literature is the share of workers on various forms of "atypical" employment contracts (e.g., Chauvel, 2016; Häusermann et al. 2015). The rise of atypical employment is a useful and meaningful measure in the European context, where employers have increasingly turned to the use of atypical employment contracts, among other reasons, to avoid strong employment protections attached to standard employment contracts. By this measure, the United States would not be seen as having a precarity problem, since the share of atypical work is among the lowest in the Organization for Economic Cooperation and Development

(OECD).³ However, the measure itself is misleading for the case of the United States, where employment protections are weak for *all workers*, irrespective of the type of employment contract. Thus, we clearly need to adopt a different approach to assessing precarity, one that is more sensitive to such differences.

In this chapter, we provide a framework that attempts to capture precarity as a multidimensional phenomenon, and one that manifests differently in diverse national contexts. Simplifying greatly, we can distinguish two separate analytic issues. The first captures the extent to which individuals are exposed to socioeconomic risks that result in sudden and significant loss of income (e.g., unemployment) or a steep and unexpected rise in expenses (e.g., major medical costs). Exposure to such risks can be either high or low across individuals within a country – depending, for example, on a person's education level. But it also varies at the macro level – being either broadly or narrowly distributed – depending, for example, on employment protection and other labor market regulations. Increasing risk on this dimension is most often a result of *employers' strategies* to reduce labor costs.

A second, separate issue, however, relates to the consequences of misfortune and, in particular, whether the costs of protection are borne by the collective (society) or by the individual. Variation on this dimension, by its nature, is primarily a function of macro institutions, both legal and social policy frameworks. It varies cross-nationally due, for example, to differences in the level and scope of unemployment insurance or health care coverage – although other features such as union density and collective bargaining coverage also play a role. Growing risk on this dimension is thus often a function of deliberate policy choices. The most visible are welfare state reforms such as social policy retrenchment that are frequently undertaken in the interest of fiscal austerity, but we include as well the less visible but equally important forms of government inaction, that is, "policy drift" (Hacker, 2004).

A Macro-Level Typology

Breaking out risk into these two dimensions – one that captures the extent and scope of labor market risks, the other describing the degree to which such risks are mitigated collectively or individually – allows us to draw important distinctions both across different policies and across countries.

---

³ See, for example, OECD Employment Outlook 2002.

		Type of social policy coverage	
		Risk borne collectively	Risks borne individually
Labor market risk	High probability of risk	Denmark, Netherlands, Labor market outsiders in Germany or France	US, "Freeters" in Japan
	Low probability of risk	Sweden, Labor market insiders in Germany or France	Labor market insiders in Japan

FIGURE 12.1 Illustrative typology of risk amplification for labor market risk.

Figure 12.1 provides a stylized typology that sorts countries broadly using the example of risks associated with job loss.[4] Thus, for example, the United States shares with Denmark (and to an extent also the Netherlands) a flexible labor market with weak employment protection that can result in severe earnings volatility, that is, high labor market risk on this measure. But in Denmark and the Netherlands, high unemployment insurance coverage and generous benefits, as well as universal social guarantees to health care, to training, or to minimum social assistance mean that these risks are more heavily borne collectively by the welfare state.

Other combinations are also possible. Protected core workers with lifetime employment guarantees in Japan experience low risk of unemployment, but if a person does become unemployed, the weakness of the social net means that the risks are borne by the individual. Similarly, strong employment protection in Germany reduces the labor market risk faced by most full-time employees, but recent welfare reforms that cut unemployment insurance coverage, especially for those on atypical employment contracts, mean that the consequences are increasingly borne by

---

[4] Of course, the countries might sort differently for other policy areas, such as pensions, and empirical metrics for various policies are discussed in detail later. Moreover, although in this chapter we are focused primarily on cross-national differences, this same template could also be applied to study risk differentiation at the subnational level. For example, US states have different rules about eligibility for unemployment benefits and different coverage rates that create risk fragmentation and differential exposure to financial insecurity across states (see especially Michener 2018).

individuals. Sweden might be a case of (relatively) low risk exposure and (relatively) high collective risk coverage. Japanese "freeters," a very precarious category of workers in "nonregular," employment (especially prominent in low-wage, low-skill service jobs), and most American workers would be in the opposite quadrant for most categories of labor market risk.

MAPPING THE COMPARATIVE LANDSCAPE OF RISK

There are many sources of labor market vulnerability and social insecurity. We have identified six main ones that contribute to precarity: job loss, income loss, insufficient pay, loss of social protection, lack of skills, and household indebtedness.[5] Without claiming to have exhausted all the relevant measures (and for many measures there are simply no comparative statistics), we can situate the United States comparatively on these six general sources of risk. To simplify and streamline the analysis, we compare the United States to five other rich democracies that are commonly associated with distinct varieties of capitalism (Hall and Soskice 2001) and different welfare regimes (Esping-Andersen 1990), namely Denmark, France, Germany, Japan, and the Netherlands.

1. **Risk of job loss.** Among working-age individuals, for all but the very wealthy, the main source of income is their job. The possibility of losing one's job therefore is a first obvious source of risk. Such risk is unevenly distributed across individuals, depending, for example, on the extent to which they possess skills that make them indispensable to their employer (or at least difficult to replace). In terms of broader institutional factors, however, prevailing legal and collective bargaining frameworks heavily condition the risk of job loss. In some countries, employers are tightly constrained by rules that make it difficult or costly to lay workers off, while in others, the barriers to layoffs are very low. In much of Europe, different rules apply to workers employed on different types of contracts; for example, workers on regular contracts often enjoy stronger job protections than those hired on various atypical employment contracts. Figure 12.2 shows that employment protection for regular workers across different types of political economies is far stronger than that in the United States. It also shows that labor market liberalization since the 1990s in Europe has increased the risk of job loss among atypical workers, while leaving permanent workers less affected.

---

[5] The risks we elaborate here parallel those identified by Standing (2011: 12).

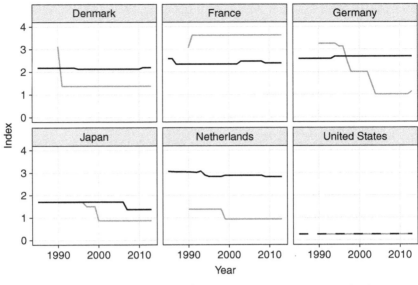

FIGURE 12.2 Strictness of employment protection *Note*: The index measures the procedures and costs involved in dismissing individuals or groups of workers and the procedures involved in hiring workers on fixed-term or temporary work agency contracts. Higher values indicate stronger employment protection. *Source*: OECD (2017), Employment Database.

What is striking about the United States in this context is the overall low level of employment protection and the lack of any distinction in levels of job protection between the "permanent" and "temporary" employees. As noted earlier, the number of American workers on atypical contracts is very low by international standards. However, far from signaling a lack of precarity, the risk of job loss in the United States is in fact greater – for all workers. Unlike their European counterparts, American employers need not resort to atypical work contracts when it is just as easy to fire permanent workers.

2. **Risk of income loss.** Job loss inevitably brings income loss, but the depth of the net income shock is again something that varies both across individuals and cross-nationally. Differences in unemployment policies – their scope, generosity, and eligibility criteria – figure most prominently here. The overall generosity of unemployment insurance (UI) benefits has always varied across countries, but the rise of precarious types of jobs and

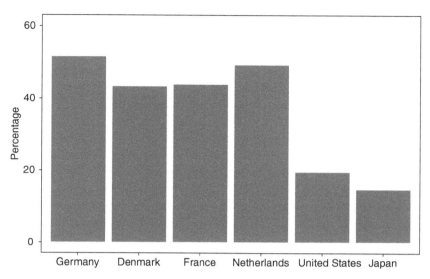

FIGURE 12.3 Unemployment insurance replacement rate, weighted by share of unemployed receiving regular unemployment benefits, average in the 2000s *Note*: Average UI replacement rates for single person, weighted by the average share of unemployed individuals who receive regular social security unemployment benefits. Sources: Replacement rates come from Scruggs, Lyle, Detlef Jahn, & Kati Kuitto, 2013. "Comparative Welfare Entitlements Data Set 2, Version 2017-09" Share of coverage of unemployed comes from ILOSTAT (2017). Germany: 2004–2012; Denmark: 2000–2013; France: 2000–2013; Netherlands: 2012; UK: 2007–2012; USA: 2000–2012.

more unstable employment trajectories make many workers ineligible for such benefits altogether. For example, in most countries UI depends on uninterrupted employment tenure for a certain period of time. Yet because of temporary work or frequent job switches, more workers now fall through the cracks of the UI system.

The problem of spottier UI coverage is thus by no means unique to the United States. In most OECD countries, fewer people are eligible for benefits because of changing work patterns as well as changing eligibility criteria. Figure 12.3 provides a summary measure, displaying the average unemployment insurance replacement rate weighted by the share of unemployed people who are actually receiving benefits. Averaging across the 2000s, the average weighted replacement rate in the United States stands at a mere 20 percent, as compared to weighted rates that are more than twice as high in most European countries.

3. **The risk of loss of key benefits.** The risks associated with job loss are amplified to the extent that receipt of other crucial benefits (e.g., pensions, health care) is itself tied to employment. In the United States, as in much of continental Europe, pensions are tied to employment history, while other countries (the Nordics but also the Netherlands) have a guaranteed pension to which all citizens are entitled regardless of their employment history.[6] These arrangements directly affect the risk of poverty in old age cross-nationally, depending on whether pensions are universal or contribution based. This difference can lead to significant variation across individuals, causing higher vulnerability especially among women, who often have less continuous career paths (Häusermann et al. 2015).

The COVID pandemic has drawn our attention to an even more striking example of risk via benefit loss, namely, the loss of health care. In the United States, medical expenses – if accompanied by a lack of health care coverage or underinsurance and combined with the high cost of care – play an enormous role in fueling insecurity (see Hacker, 2006 and Morduch & Schneider, 2017). The problem is not uniquely American: institutional differences in the design of health care systems across countries, in particular the cost structure and the importance of co-payment can translate into considerable health and financial costs. However, the United States is alone in the extent to which coverage depends on one's employment status and the scope and generosity of firm-sponsored benefits. The lack of universal health care thus exacerbates risk by exposing individuals to private decisions by firms based on economic rather than social considerations. According to data from the 2013 Commonwealth Fund International Health Policy Survey, close to a quarter of American households reported that they had serious problems paying medical bills or were even unable to pay them at all, compared to less than 7 percent and 4 percent of German and Swedish families, respectively. While out-of-pocket health spending has grown across many OECD countries, Figure 12.4 shows that even after the passage of the Affordable Care Act, the United States still stands out with an average of more than $1,000 in out-of-pocket health spending, more than twice as high as in other OECD countries.[7] In general,

---

[6] This is often supplemented by collectively bargained occupational pensions.

[7] The introduction of the Affordable Care Act (ACA) in 2010 reduced the number of uninsured Americans from around 46.5 percent to 27.4 percent in 2017 (Kaiser Family Foundation, 2019). What concerns us here, however, is the rather stable share of Americans with employer-based health insurance. That number stands rather stable at around 67 percent (US Census 2018), which means that two-thirds of Americans face potential risk of losing their employer-based health insurance when they face unemployment.

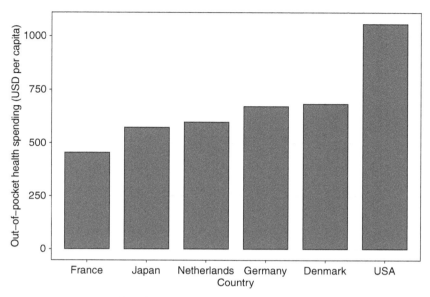

FIGURE 12.4 Out-of-pocket health spending, 2015 *Note*: Health spending measures the final consumption of health care goods and services. *Source*: OECD (2018a), Health Statistics.

the high financial costs of health care in the United States results in stratified access to medical services and levels of medical bankruptcy that are much less common or even unheard of in European countries (cf. Himmelstein et al. 2009).

4. Risk of insufficient income from employment. The three risk types already discussed can affect workers at any income level, but some of the deepest sources of persistent precarity are concentrated at the low end. One such source of precarity is insufficient income from employment – that is, the inability to climb out of poverty despite holding a job (or jobs). Here again there is significant cross-national variation, attributable among other causes to variation in union strength and collective bargaining coverage, as well as the existence and generosity of a minimum wage. Figure 12.5 provides an overview of the extent of in-work poverty across the OECD both before and after taxes and transfers. It shows that by this measure, precarity in the United States is rivaled only by Japan, a country notorious for extreme labor market dualization and meager social spending, and whose social programs clearly do even less to redress inequalities generated by the market (Estevez-Abe, 2008; Gordon, 2017).

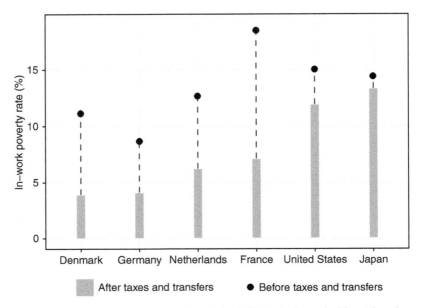

FIGURE 12.5 Poverty rates among individuals living in households with at least one worker, 2016 *Source*: OECD Income Distribution Database. 2018

A broader comparative view would show that the rates of in-work poverty in both Japan and the United States exceed even what are often considered Europe's weakest economies (e.g., Greece and Italy) (OECD, 2018b).

Beyond Labor Markets and Social Policy: Educational and Financial Institutions and Risk

Until now we have stressed the labor market and social institutions, but other arrangements in the political economy can either exacerbate or mitigate the risks that individuals face (micro level) or diffuse or contain the scope of such risks across the population as a whole (macro level). We single out arrangements in two arenas that interact closely with the labor market and social policy institutions just discussed, namely educational institutions and financial institutions.

5. **Educational institutions.** In today's "knowledge economy," not having the necessary skills to access (good) jobs heightens the risk of precarity, especially though not exclusively for young people.[8] Educational

---

[8] See also Ansell and Gingrich, Chapter 3, this volume.

institutions play an important role in shaping the risk of precarity. The literature on skill and skill formation systems has identified two dimensions that are especially important in this respect – inclusiveness and skill type.[9]

The first dimension is the level of inclusiveness of the higher education system, whether elitist (as in the United States, the United Kingdom, or France) or more encompassing (as in much of non-Anglo Europe). Americans tend to think of the United States as having a very inclusive system of higher education, and it is true that the United States was a pioneer and leader in tertiary education. However, the share of the US population with tertiary education has barely budged over the past generation, while many European countries in the meantime have matched or surpassed the US level (OECD, 2015). More importantly, like the other elite systems, the United States also allows relatively large numbers of youth to leave the school system with very low skills or even without skills.

More encompassing systems, by contrast, aim to provide skills to most of a cohort, either in a stratified way where students are tracked into vocational or academic paths early on (as in Germany) or on an egalitarian basis where secondary education is more uniform for all (as in most of the Nordic countries). In encompassing systems, government policies to enhance youth employment usually promote employability through additional skill acquisition and training. In the more selective systems, by contrast, government policies tend to promote employment among low-skill youth simply by lowering the cost of hiring them, for example, through exemptions from minimum wage or social contribution requirements (Chevalier, 2016: 8). These "workfare" or "work-first" policies often translate into a higher share of young people in precarious situations in the labor market.

These differences are reflected, among other indicators, in the share of young adults who are not in education, employment, or training (NEETs). Comparisons of the number of NEETs show how education systems based on high selectivity and general skills drive precarity among young people. Figure 12.6 shows that countries with encompassing educational systems and especially those with a strong vocational component are better able to avoid unemployment or inactivity among young adults.

6. **Financial institutions/risk of insolvency.** A final factor contributing to financial insecurity in some countries relates to trends in households' financial lives, particularly their debt burdens. Household debt, including

---

[9] See especially Chevalier (2016), on whom we draw, but also Ranci 2010.

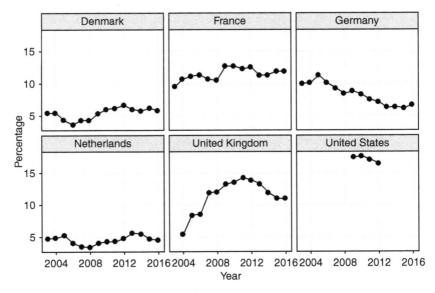

FIGURE 12.6 Share of youth not in employment, education or training *Note*: Youth are defined as persons between the ages of 15 and 24. *Source*: ILO (2017). ILOSTAT Statistical Database.

mortgages, personal and educational loans, and credit card debt, has grown to unprecedented levels in many countries over the past few decades. Indeed, in the five years leading up to the Great Recession, the share of total household debt relative to disposable income – a measure that captures the exposure of families to debt – has risen across rich democracies by an average of 39 percentage points to a level of 138 percent in 2007 (International Monetary Fund [IMF], 2012: 89). Yet as Figure 12.7 shows, countries vary considerably in the degree to which their respective households are indebted. American households on average carry consumer credit, mostly credit card debt, of around a quarter of their income, while in other European countries that number is much lower. Mortgage debt, however, is much larger in Denmark and the Netherlands compared to the United States.

These differences reflect in part differential demand for credit across households and in part different institutional underpinnings of countries' financial regimes. Broadly speaking, households take on debt for two main reasons. First, they may use credit to finance investments in assets – financial and personal. This would include the use of credit to buy a home or a car, but it would also include private investments in human

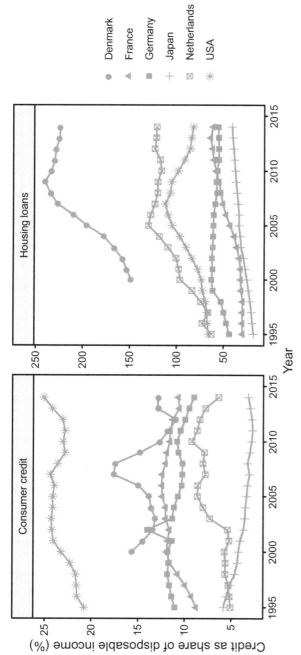

FIGURE 12.7 Consumer credit and housing loans as a share of disposable income *Note*: Consumer credit corresponds to the outstanding amounts (stocks) of loans at the end of the year granted by the resident monetary-financial institutions to resident households and non-financial corporations for consumption purposes. Consumer credit includes loans related to credit cards as well as overdrafts. *Source*: European Credit Research Institute (ECRI), 2015.

capital – for example, student loans to finance a college degree. Second, households may draw on credit to smooth consumption to fill temporary income losses or meet rising expenses. In many cases, households respond to welfare state retrenchment by going into debt and borrowing money to pay for basic social services, including income losses, education, or even childcare (see, esp. Wiedemann, 2021). Credit, in other words, has turned into a private alternative to publicly provided welfare states. One study in the United States found that in 2004, around one-third of families reported drawing on credit cards to cover basic living expenses during an average of four months per year (Draut, 2005: 11).

As households' burden of debt rises, so does the risk of financial failure. Monthly debt repayment requires a constant and stable stream of income. If households miss debt repayments because of irregular incomes or unemployment or are unable to repay their loans altogether, they face insolvency, bankruptcy, or even home foreclosure.[10]

The COVID pandemic rapidly turned households' exposure to debt into a new source of risk. When millions of people suddenly lost their jobs, the financial fragility of many highly leveraged households resurfaced. Although the US government tried to protect debtors from further hardship by allowing some to temporarily delay or adjust payments, existing debt needs to be repaid.

The risks documented here, ranging from volatile incomes to declining benefit coverage, can have severe downstream consequences for indebted families.

A Comparative View of Risk Exposure

At this point we can pause to pull together the various strands of the argument and compare how the different dimensions of risk vary cross-nationally and over time by providing an overview of eleven categories of risk that capture the changes in labor markets, social policies, and financial markets outlined earlier. The radar charts in Figure 12.8 visualize the degree to which different risks are borne by individuals in these countries in the early and mid-2000s in panel (a) and the mid-2010s in panel (b). Higher values farther out in the circles indicate higher exposure to risk. The first seven categories (R1 through R7) represent risks associated with the flexibility of labor markets and employment protection of workers

---

[10] Unfortunately, comparative statistics on personal bankruptcy in the OECD are not available.

The Anxiety of Precarity

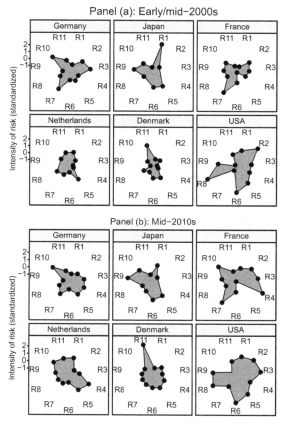

- R1: Share discouraged workers
- R2: Share youth NEET
- R3: Labor market insecurity for low skilled individuals
- R4: Unemployment rate among low-skilled individuals (25–64yo)
- R5: Weakness of temporary employment protection
- R6: Weakness of regular employment protection
- R7: Labor force non-participation rate
- R8: Share of individuals without health insurance coverage
- R9: Share of unemployed not receiving benefits
- R10: Unemployment duration more than 12 months
- R11: Total credit to households as share of disposable income

Risk Domain

FIGURE 12.8 The comparative view of intensity of different types of risks over time *Notes*: All scores are normalized to allow comparison across categories and over time. R1 through R7 are risks associated with labor market institutions; R8 through R11 are risks associated with welfare state institutions, education, and private debt levels. For more details on the year coverage and data sources see the Appendix.

before welfare states can mitigate parts of that risk. The last four categories (R8 through R11) capture risks associated with social policies, including unemployment, sickness and health insurance, the chances of finding new jobs or educational opportunities, as well as the burden of debt. The larger the area spanning between the different risk categories, the larger is the overall risk for individuals.

This overview allows us to visualize cross-national differences on different dimensions of risk, and how they have changed over time. On average, the sum of risks has increased for individuals in nearly all countries, as indicated by the growing surface area of the radar charts. But there is also considerable variation across countries in the types of risks that matter most for individuals in these countries and the degree to which these risks rest on the shoulders of individuals or society. In France and the Netherlands, for example, unemployment among low-skilled individuals (R4) increased and long-term unemployment (R10) became more prevalent. In Germany, temporary employment protection (R5) was weakened considerably while youth NEET (R2) and labor force nonparticipation rate (R7) declined, which suggests an overall stronger labor market outlook at the expense of more labor market segmentation and insecurity on the periphery. In Denmark, by contrast, unemployment among low-skilled individuals (R4) declined but because of labor market and social policy reforms, slightly more unemployed individuals do not receive benefits (R9). Private debt levels (R11) have grown in the Netherlands and Denmark. In the United States, labor market insecurity for low-skilled individuals (R3) and overall labor force nonparticipation (R7) increased while fewer unemployed individuals receive benefits (R9). However, the Affordable Care Act expanded medical insurance considerably and led to fewer individuals without health insurance coverage (R8).

The charts also highlight significant cross-national variation. For example, they reveal that the fluidity of the American labor market is a double-edged sword. Weak employment protection and the fact that benefits are contingent upon employment are a source of great risk. But this very flexibility also allows workers to find new jobs much faster than in other countries such as Germany, where structural long-term unemployment is a bigger problem (R10). The continental Bismarckian welfare systems thus produce their own kinds of risks, mostly because of more rigid labor markets (Palier 2010). Long-term unemployment is a particular problem in Germany, the Netherlands, and France, resulting in especially high-risk exposure for labor market "outsiders." In addition, segmented labor markets and declining benefits expose low-skilled employees to much greater labor market insecurity in Germany and France compared with the Netherlands.

Denmark, by contrast, mitigates the flexibility of its labor markets and the weak protection of employees with a generous social safety net (the "flexicurity" model) that collectivizes the costs of coping with these labor market risks. Private debt, which as we have seen, can be a source of financial instability and economic risk, is highest in Denmark, followed by the Netherlands, the United States, and the United Kingdom. Danish households have greater exposure to credit markets than American households, but the encompassing Danish welfare state and the comparatively higher quality of jobs in Denmark make indebtedness and default a much smaller risk than in the United States.

Finally, and unsurprisingly in light of the foregoing discussion, the United States stands out as the country with the largest exposure to risk, even in comparison with the United Kingdom, another liberal market economy. As noted earlier, employment-based benefits play a significant role in exacerbating risk, because benefit reduction is a matter of decentralized employer choice and thus not subject to the same public scrutiny and contestation as social policy reforms elsewhere. In sum, the interaction of high labor market risk, a weak welfare state, insufficient health insurance coverage, and growing debt burdens puts American families at much higher risk of precarity compared with families in other countries.

PRECARITY AND RISK CONTAGION: THE UNITED STATES IN A COMPARATIVE PERSPECTIVE

Each dimension of risk laid out in the previous section increases individuals' socioeconomic insecurity. What makes matters worse and strongly shapes the precarity of many individuals' daily lives occurs when risks amplify as they spill from one domain into another. Risk contagion captures the idea that risks stemming from one dimension are compounded when they trigger contingent risks in another dimension. While labor market risks (and resulting income losses) and the welfare states' risk-buffering functions are first-order effects, risk contagion involves second-order, indirect consequences – for example, as unemployment leads to loss of health care coverage, which in the event of significant medical expenses is then compounded by the risk of housing foreclosure or bankruptcy.

It is not only loose labor markets and weak social policy coverage that create uncommonly high levels of precarity; it is also educational institutions that confer few skills on low-income groups combined with financial institutions that provide easy access to credit to such groups to cover gaps in medical and social policy coverage and to smooth income. These interaction effects compound risk wherever a lack of backstops prevents the cascading of risk and misfortune in one realm from snowballing to affect others. Conceptually, risk contagion has general applicability; yet, empirically it is the United States that is particularly prone to its effects.

This section focuses on two of the most important "gateway" risks that can cascade to intensify risks in other domains, namely health care coverage and household debt.

Employment-Based Social Policies and Risk Contagion

Earlier we noted that workers on temporary contracts in Europe (and all workers in the United States) are exposed to a higher risk of job loss than permanently employed workers in most European countries. The impact of these differences in employment contracts is either amplified or mitigated by social policies. Häusermann et al.'s (2015) analysis of the difference in temporary employment status in Europe emphasizes these interaction effects. Their analysis reveals, for example, that the higher incidence of atypical employment among women not only exposes them to greater risk of job loss; they are also more likely to have spottier contribution-based entitlements, resulting in lower levels of, for example, pension coverage.

These observations about differences in benefits apply *a fortiori* in the United States, where a large share of part-time (even many full-time workers) are not entitled to benefits that are standard for all workers in Europe (e.g., paid sick leave, parental leave, vacation pay; Thelen, 2019). Moreover, and as the COVID crisis made painfully clear, employment-based health insurance puts the United States in a category by itself. With health insurance heavily tied to employment, Americans who lose their jobs are immediately exposed to a heightened risk of major uncovered medical expenses.[11] Moreover, and perhaps most strikingly in comparative perspective, receipt of government-provided minimum health benefits not only does not mitigate precarity; it also requires it. That is, receipt of Medicaid requires that individuals are *and remain* poor to qualify for benefits – that is, precarity is a prerequisite for receipt of the benefit (Campbell, 2014).

---

[11] In both Hacker (2006) and Morduch & Schneider (2017), medical expenses – lack of health care coverage or underinsurance, combined with the high cost of care – play an enormous role in fueling insecurity in the United States.

Household Debt and Risk Contagion

As noted earlier, high levels of household debt can further exacerbate the problem of income loss, and the rich democracies exhibit significant variation on this measure – highest in Denmark and lowest in Germany. However, the implications of these differences depend heavily on social policy. In the United States, income losses can easily spiral into financial insecurity for indebted families because there is a lack of social benefits to smooth income (e.g., in the case of job loss). This is why American families are at much higher risk of bankruptcy than Danish families, even though the latter carry more debt (see Porter, 2012 on the United States; Gerhardt, 2009).

Moreover, a weak social safety net can also be a driver of household debt if families borrow to compensate for income losses. American families have taken on more debt in response to welfare retrenchment, in particular through credit cards or payday loans (Montgomerie, 2013). In Denmark, by contrast, families are less likely to turn to credit to cover unplanned income shortfalls (such events being covered by social policies such as unemployment benefits) and more likely to do so more proactively (e.g., to invest in further education) in ways that reduce rather than amplify the risks they face. This explains the diverging trajectories of household debt in the two countries in the aftermath of the financial crisis. Denmark saw a strong decline in outstanding debt level, while consumer debt in the United States remained high and even rose somewhat after 2012.

Debt repayment, in most cases on a monthly basis, requires a constant and stable stream of income. If households miss debt repayments because of irregular incomes or unemployment or are unable to repay their loans altogether, they face insolvency, bankruptcy, or even home foreclosure. The risks documented earlier, ranging from volatile incomes to declining benefit coverage, can have severe downstream consequences for indebted American families. Although middle-income Americans have not been shielded from these developments, the burden is even greater for lower-income families because debt is typically more expensive for them, that is, they pay higher interest rates, and, relatedly, they devote a larger share of their income to debt repayments. Easy access to credit in the United States may operate as a risk *mediator* for high-income individuals (buffering against fluctuations in income over time) but often acts as a *source of risk contagion* for low-income groups, as resort to credit to cover income shocks in one arena can lead to great exposure to risk in other areas.

The COVID-19 pandemic not only sheds light on households' financial fragilities but also amplifies their precarious situations and further feeds into a downward spiral of risks. It shows the limited ability of the United States and its welfare state and labor market institutions to contain socioeconomic risks in the face of a large pandemic.

CONCLUSION

Economic insecurity and precarity are no longer limited to lower-income or low-skilled individuals and have become a pervasive problem and, in consequence, a growing concern for policy makers in the OECD countries. In this chapter, we adopt a comparative approach to precarity, focusing on two analytically distinct dimensions of risk that influence individuals' socioeconomic insecurity, shaped by countries' labor market and social policy regimes, respectively. While both dimensions have their own origins and can vary independently, the interaction of the two exacerbates individuals' socioeconomic precarity through a process we call risk contagion. By examining different types of risks and situating the United States in a comparative perspective, the sources and extent of American precarity come into especially sharp relief.

Space does not permit a full discussion of the policy implications that flow from this analysis, but two points stand out. The most obvious is that publicly provided universal benefits clearly mitigate the risks that individuals face, as the varying abilities of countries to contain the economic fallout of COVID-19 pandemic show. Such policies become even more important in the context of the trends cited at the outset – the fissurization of work and employers' heightened reliance on atypical employment contracts of various sorts. A second, perhaps less obvious, implication points to the importance of public investment in human capital development. The OECD has long advocated social investment policies that involve robust state funding to expand educational opportunities at all levels – from public day care and high-quality early childhood education, to strong systems for vocational education and training, to generous public funding for tertiary education, to abundant resources for adult retraining. We are aware that public investment in human capital – an inherently private good – does not address the many profound structural labor market and social challenges the rich democracies now face. However, by socializing the costs, such investment can underwrite efforts by individuals to mitigate a host of new risks associated with accelerated technological change and the transition to the new knowledge economy.

Appendix

Data sources and year coverage for radar charts

Risk type	Data source	Panel (a): Early/mid-2000s	Panel (b): Mid-2010s
R1: Share discouraged workers	ILO Labor Statistics	2000; Japan: 2002	2017
R2: Share youth NEET	ILO Labor Statistics	2003; Japan: 2003	2017
R3: Labor market insecurity for low-skilled individuals	OECD Job Quality Database	2007; Japan: NA	2015; Germany: 2013; Japan: NA
R4: Unemployment rate among low-skilled individuals (25–64yo)	OECD Education Statistics	2000; Japan: NA	2015; Japan: NA
R5: Weakness of temporary employment protection	OECD Employment Database	2000	2013
R6: Weakness of regular employment protection	OECD Employment Database	2000	2013
R7: Labor force nonparticipation rate	ILO Labor Statistics	2000; Japan: NA	2016
R8: Share of individuals without health insurance coverage	OECD Health Statistics	2000	2015
R9: Share of unemployed not receiving benefits	ILO Labor Statistics	2000; Japan: 2001; Netherlands: NA	2012; Japan: 2010
R10: Unemployment duration more than 12 months	ILO Labor Statistics	2002	2017
R11: Total credit to households as share of disposable income	ECRI Statistical Package	2000	2014

Note: The labor market insecurity index is the composition of unemployment risk and unemployment insurance's income support:

The unemployment risk component is measured as the monthly unemployment inflow probability times the expected average duration of unemployment spells (in months). Unemployment inflow probability: the ratio of unemployed persons who have been unemployed for less than one month over the number of employed persons one month before. Expected unemployment duration: the inverse of the unemployment outflow probability where the latter is defined as one minus the ratio of unemployed persons who have been unemployed for one month or more over the number of unemployed persons one month before.

The unemployment insurance component is defined as the coverage rate of unemployment insurance (UI) times its average net replacement rate among UI recipients plus the coverage rate of unemployment assistance (UA) times its net average replacement rate among UA recipients. The average replacement rates for recipients of UI and UA take account of family benefits, social assistance, and housing benefits.

REFERENCES

Bonoli, G. (2005). The politics of the new social policies: Providing coverage against new social risks in mature welfare states. *Policy & Politics*, 33(3), 431–449.

Castel, R. (1995). *Les metamorphoses de la question sociale*. Paris, France: Fayard. (Ed.). (2017). *From manual workers to wage laborers: Transformation of the social question* (R. Boyd, Trans. & Ed.). Oxford: Routledge [translated and edited by Richard Boyd; first published 2003 by Transaction Publishers].

Campbell, A. L. 2014. *Trapped in America's safety net: One family's struggle*. Chicago: University of Chicago Press.

Chauvel, L. (2016). The intensity and shape of inequality. *Review of Income and Wealth*, 62(1), 52–68.

Chevalier, T. (2016). Varieties of youth welfare citizenship: Towards a two-dimension typology. *Journal of European Social Policy*, 26(1), 3–19.

The Commonwealth Fund. 2013. International Health Policy Survey. www.commonwealthfund.org/series/international-health-policy-surveys

Crouch, C. 2009. "Privatised Keynesianism: An unacknowledged policy regime." *The British Journal of Politics & International Relations* 11(3), 382–399.

Davis, G. F. (2015). Corporate power in the twenty-first century. In S. Rangan (Ed.), *Performance and progress: Essays on capitalism, business, and society*, pp. 395–414. Oxford: Oxford University Press.

Draut, T. (2005). *The plastic safety net: The reality behind debt in America*. New York: Demos and the Center for Responsible Lending.

ECRI. 2015. *Statistical package*. Brussels: European Credit Research Institute.

Esping-Andersen, G. 1990. *The three worlds of welfare capitalism*. Cambridge: Polity Press.

Estevez-Abe, Margarita. 2008. *Welfare and capitalism in Postwar Japan*. New York: Cambridge University Press.

Gerhardt, Maria. 2009. Consumer Bankruptcy Regimes and Credit Default in the US and Europe: A Comparative Study. CEPS Working Document No. 318/July.

Gordon, Andrew. 2017. New and enduring dual structures of employment in Japan: The rise of non-regular labor, 1980s–2010s. *Social Science Japan Journal* 20(1), 9–36.

Hacker, J. S. (2004). Privatizing risk without privatizing the welfare state: The hidden politics of social policy retrenchment in the United States. *American Political Science Review*, 98, 243–260.

(2006). *The great risk shift: The assault on American jobs, families, health care, and retirement and how you can fight back*. Oxford: Oxford University Press.
(2011). The foundations of middle-class democracy. In *Priorities for a new political economy: Memos to the left*, pp. 33–38. London: Policy Network.
(2013). Pre-distribution: Rebuilding the organizational foundations of democratic capitalism. In O. Cramme (Ed.), *Progressive politics after the crash: Governing from the left*, pp. 117–130. London: Policy Network.
Hall, Peter A., and Soskice, D. W. 2001. *Varieties of Capitalism: The Institutional Foundations of Comparative Advantage*. Oxford: Oxford University Press.
Häusermann, S., Kurer, T., and Schwander, H. (2015). High-skilled outsiders? Labor market vulnerability, education and welfare state preferences." *Socio-Economic Review* 13(2): 235–258.
Himmelstein, D. U., Thorne, D., Warren, E., and Woolhandler, S. (2009). Medical bankruptcy in the United States, 2007: Results of a national study. *The American Journal of Medicine* 122, 741–746.
ILO. 2017. ILOSTAT Statistical Database. https://ilostat.ilo.org/data/
International Monetary Fund. (2012). *World economic outlook: Growth resuming, dangers remain*. Washington, DC: International Monetary Fund.
Kaiser Family Foundation. (2019). *The Uninsured and the ACA: A Primer*. San Francisco: The Kaiser Family Foundation.
Kalleberg, A. L. (2013). *Good jobs, bad jobs: The rise of polarized and precarious employment systems in the United States, 1970s to 2000s*. New York: Russell Sage Foundation.
Kelly, N. (2008). *The politics of income inequality in the United States*. New York: Cambridge University Press.
Michener, J. 2018. *Fragmented democracy: Medicaid, federalism, and unequal politics*. New York: Cambridge University Press.
Montgomerie, J. (2013). America's debt safety-net. *Public Administration* 91(4), 871–888.
Morduch, J., and Schneider, R. (2017). *The financial diaries: How American families cope in a world of uncertainty*. Princeton, NJ: Princeton University Press.
Newman, K. S. (2006). *Chutes and ladders: Navigating the low-wage labor market*. New York: Russell Sage Foundation; Cambridge, MA: Harvard University Press.
OECD. (2002). *Employment Outlook 2002*. Paris: OECD.
(2015). *Economic policy reforms 2015: Going for growth*. Paris. OECD.
(2017a). *Employment database*. Paris: OECD.
(2017b). *Job quality database*. Paris: OECD.
(2017c). *National accounts*. Paris: OECD.
(2018a). *Health statistics*. Paris: OECD.
(2018b). *Income distribution database*. Paris: OECD.
Oesch, D. (2006). Coming to grips with a changing class structure: An analysis of employment stratification in Britain, Germany, Sweden and Switzerland. *International Sociology* 21(2): 263–288.
Palier, B., (Ed.). (2010). *A long goodbye to Bismarck? The politics of welfare reform in continental Europe*. Amsterdam: Amsterdam University Press.
Palier, B., and Thelen, K. (2012). Dualization and institutional complementarities: Industrial relations, labor market and welfare state changes in France and

Germany. In P. Emmenegger, S. Häusermann, B. Palier, & M Seeleib-Kaiser (Eds.), *The age of dualization: The changing face of inequality in deindustrializing societies*, pp. 201–225. Oxford: Oxford University Press.

Pierson, P. (1996). The new politics of the welfare state. *World Politics*, 48(2), 143–179.

Porter, K. (Ed.). (2012). *Broke: How debt bankrupts the middle class*. Stanford, CA: Stanford University Press.

Ranci, C. (2010). *Social vulnerability in Europe: The new configuration of social risks*. Basingstoke, UK: Palgrave Macmillan.

Rovny, A. E., and Rovny, J. (2017). Outsiders at the ballot box: Operationalizations and political consequences of the insider–outsider dualism. *Socio-Economic Review*, 15(1), 161–185.

Standing, G. (2011). *The Precariat: The dangerous new class*. London: Bloomsbury.

Thelen, K. (2019). The American precariat: U.S. capitalism in comparative perspective. *Perspectives on Politics*, 17(1), 5–27.

US Census. (2018). *Health insurance coverage in the United States: 2017. Report Number P60-264*. www.census.gov/library/publications/2018/demo/p60-264.html#:~:text=The%20percentage%20of%20people%20with,million%2C%20up%20to%20294.6%20million

Warren, E., and Tyagi, A. W. (2003). *The two-income trap: Why middle-class mothers and fathers are going broke*. New York: Basic Books.

Weil, D. (2014). *The fissured workplace: Why work became so many and what can be done to improve it*. Cambridge, MA: Harvard University Press.

Wiedemann, A. (2021). *Indebted Societies: Credit and Welfare in Rich Democracies*. Cambridge: Cambridge University Press.

13

Increasing Instability and Uncertainty among American Workers

Implications for Inequality and Potential Policy Solutions

Elizabeth O. Ananat, Anna Gassman-Pines, and Yulya Truskinovsky

INTRODUCTION

The bulk of this chapter describes the rising instability and uncertainty facing American workers, particularly those at the lower end of the wage distribution, to establish a shared set of facts to inform the political discussions in the previous chapters. This chapter concludes by discussing the most promising policies emerging, particularly in state and local "laboratories of democracy," to address the problems facing workers to establish a set of potential policy goals to evaluate in the context of the political dynamics described in the rest of the volume.

Earnings and income volatility among US workers has increased at every socioeconomic level since the 1970s and continues to be highest among people with low levels of education and lower incomes (Gottschalk and Moffitt 2009; Dynan, Elmendorf, and Sichel 2012; Morduch and Schneider 2017). Several examples highlight these trends. For instance, across all working-age individuals in the United States, the share whose family income falls by more than half in at least one year has more than doubled, from 4 percent in the early 1970s to 10 percent in the mid-2000s (Jacobs and Hacker 2008). Comparing income volatility across income groups, more recent US Financial Diary data show that low-income households have more income variability over the course of a year than moderate-income households and that the majority of low-income households (with income between 100 percent and 200 percent of the poverty level) spent at least one month of the year in poverty (Morduch and Schneider 2017; Morduch and Siwicki 2017).

Even among low-income households, the most disadvantaged (with income less than 50 percent of the poverty level) have experienced the largest increases in household income instability in the past two decades (Bania and Leete 2009).

Further examination of trends in earning and income volatility by important demographic groups highlights the ways in which these patterns are unevenly distributed across the country. First, during this time period men have experienced more earnings volatility than women (Western et al. 2012), and women's earnings volatility may have actually declined (Moffitt and Zhang 2018). Most recently, male earnings volatility increased substantially during and after the Great Recession (Koo 2016; Moffitt and Zhang 2018). Although there are likely several reasons for the increase in earnings volatility among men, one key hypothesis is that the decline of labor unions during this period has particularly affected men's earnings (Western et al. 2012), while sectors that disproportionately employ women, such as hospitality and health care, have flourished.

Although women have not experienced the same increases in earnings volatility as men, it is important to underscore that women's experiences are not homogenous. In particular, single-parent, female-headed households experience much higher instability than married households (Hardy 2017). Among women, there are also substantial differences between Black and white women in income instability, with increased instability for Black women but not white women across the 2000s (Hardy 2012). (Kessler-Harris, Chapter 5, this volume, explores the uneven experiences among women, and the political implications thereof, in greater depth.)

Finally, considering difference by race and ethnicity, research has consistently shown that Black households both experience higher levels of instability and have seen larger increases in instability than white households. Income instability is much higher for Black households than white households, and the safety net has become less responsive to reducing income instability for Blacks (Hardy 2017). Income instability has increased over time for both white and Black individuals but has increased more among Blacks (Hill 2018). Much less research has focused on differences by ethnicity but emerging evidence suggests that among households with children, the lowest-income Hispanic households have slightly less income instability than non-Hispanic Black or white households (Gennetian et al. 2018). The relative earnings stability of Hispanic fathers may play a role in buffering the lowest-income Hispanic households from instability. Gillespie (Chapter 2, this volume) provides a more in-depth discussion of the racialized ways in which US citizens have interpreted and made sense of these patterns over time, often in ways that are at odds with the empirical evidence of who has been harmed the most by increasing instability.

CAUSES OF INCREASED VOLATILITY FOR LOW-SKILLED INDIVIDUALS

Shift toward Service-Sector Employment

Behind this increase in volatility for low-skilled workers is a set of phenomena – including changes in domestic production due to globalization and continuing automation due to technological innovation – that has contributed to a steady decrease in the employment share of manufacturing. The share of US workers employed in manufacturing has fallen from a peak of 32 percent in 1948 to less than 9 percent in 2017. Rather than tapering off, this trend accelerated in the new century, with more than a 30 percent decline in the number of manufacturing jobs since 2000 – much of which occurred even prior to the start of the Great Recession (Charles, Hurst, and Schwartz 2018).

Taking the place of manufacturing has been the service sector, including retail and food service and (increasingly) health care. These jobs are less routinized and require more "human touch" than manufacturing, making them less subject to either automation or off-shoring. Health care, in particular, has grown, due to both innovation and the aging of the population. It is currently the fastest-growing sector in the economy and is expected to add 2.3 million jobs between 2016 and 2026. The health care and social assistance sector is projected to be the single largest major sector in the economy by 2026 (Bureau of Labor Statistics 2018b).

While popular images of this sector include high-skilled jobs such as physician and medical technologist, most of these new jobs are predicted to be concentrated among low-skilled, direct care work (nursing assistants, home health aides, and personal care aides). Home health aides and personal care aides are at the top of the list of the ten fastest-growing occupations over the next two decades, projected to grow by more than 40 percent in the next twenty years (Bureau of Labor Statistics 2018c). Wages, hours, and benefits in direct care work are similar to those of retail and fast-food workers.

Instability and Uncertainty Effects of the Shift toward Service Employment

Manufacturing has historically played a key role in ensuring security and stability for less-skilled workers (Charles, Hurst, and Schwartz 2018). For workers without a college education, the manufacturing sector offers a significant wage and benefit premium: in 2013, total compensation in the manufacturing sector was 10.9 percent higher than in other occupations (Scott 2015). Moreover, manufacturing jobs have traditionally had high rates of union membership, and on an aggregate level, unions raise wages for less-skilled workers and significantly reduce income inequality (Farber et al. 2018). In addition, manufacturing has the highest tenure among major industries within the private sector, making manufacturing jobs more stable and secure than the jobs that have typically replaced them (Bureau of Labor Statistics 2016).

As employment has shifted away from manufacturing toward service work, the wage and job tenure conditions of workers have eroded. Work in retail, hospitality, and health care is characterized by low wages and benefits, low unionization, high turnover, and few prospects for career growth and promotion. Median pay in these sectors was just over $23,000/year or 11.25/hour in 2017, while median tenure in service occupations, including health care support, was less than 36 months in 2016 (Bureau of Labor Statistics 2018c). The combination of low pay and irregular hours or part-time status means that in many states, workers in these industries have earnings too low to qualify for Unemployment Insurance when they are laid off, amplifying the effects of employment and earnings instability.[1] Furthermore, less-skilled direct care health professions such as home health care have a large degree of informality and are often structured as contract or gig work, denying workers in these professions even the most basic benefits and protections.

Thus, the structural shift in the labor market has had major implications for less-educated workers (and, as Ansell and Gingrich, Chapter 3, this volume, note, potential implications for more-educated workers, as well). Underscoring the momentousness of this change, regional declines in traditional manufacturing employment have been linked to a range of negative outcomes in the communities that have long relied on these jobs,

---

[1] For example, a Michigan employee laid off from a job paying the state minimum hourly wage of $9.25 in 2018 would not qualify for Unemployment Insurance if they worked fewer than thirty hours per week, as is common in many service jobs.

including suicide, crime, falling marriage rates, declines in public goods provision, growing drug use, and others (Autor, Dorn, and Hanson 2017; Feler and Senses 2017; Charles, Hurst, and Schwartz 2018; Fort, Pierce, and Schott 2018). Many of these negative outcomes are, of course, themselves the result of policy choices to provide minimal levels of collective insurance (as discussed by Thelen and Wiedemann, Chapter 12, this volume), which leave workers and communities affected by structural shifts with no supports other than the service sector work they find for themselves.

Changing Conditions within Industries

At the same time that low-skilled employment has shifted toward the service sector, the nature of service work has also changed significantly. While it has long been the case that service employment was more volatile than manufacturing employment, today's service workers face additional forms of uncertainty even *within* employment.

In this sector, technology has so far not so much displaced labor as augmented it, in ways that lead workers to experience much more daily uncertainty in both pay and hours. As one important example, sophisticated scheduling software is now commonly used in service establishments; firms selling such software purport that it allows managers to "optimize" staffing. This software uses customer flow data to predict a range of staffing needs for a particular date and time and then recommends that managers schedule a minimum number of workers, while requiring additional workers to be "on call" (available for work but not paid if they are not needed). On-call schedules thereby allow employers to shift the costs of demand uncertainty from themselves to their employees, reducing the volatility of profits while increasing the volatility of hours and earnings.[2]

While questions remain about whether sophisticated scheduling is a cause rather than a symptom of schedule uncertainty, quite clear empirical evidence shows that schedule instability is today endemic among low-skilled workers. For example, in studying a national sample of young

---

[2] While this represents the widely promoted promise of scheduling software, in reality researchers have found that the managers transfer much more than 100 percent of their demand volatility to their workers via volatile scheduling (Henly and Lambert 2014) – that is, individual workers' schedules are much more volatile than customer demand can account for.

workers (26–32 years old), researchers found that 41 percent of workers received notice of their schedules only one week ahead of time or less (Lambert, Fugiel, and Henly 2014). Fluctuations in work hours are also substantial, with almost 75 percent of the young hourly workers reporting fluctuations in the number of hours they worked per week over the past month. Similarly, a survey of hourly workers in large retailers found that 60 percent of workers report variable hours and that 60 percent of workers have less than two weeks' notice of their work schedules (Schneider and Harknett 2016). While these numbers are quite striking in themselves, such global reports may actually understate the level of instability that workers face: a daily diary study of hourly retail and food service workers in one city found that 89 percent had experienced a schedule disruption in the past month, and that the probability of a last-minute schedule change was quite high even among workers who had described their job globally as having a stable schedule (Ananat and Gassman-Pines, 2020).

Moreover, instability in work hours is a leading cause of monthly variation in income (Morduch and Schneider 2017). Volatile income, in addition to its other obvious harms, poses particular problems for low-wage workers with families, as many means-tested assistance programs require re-certification when income changes. Re-certification itself can entail taking (unpaid) time off work for administrative appointments, leading to additional volatility. Failure to re-certify can lead to loss of benefits, compounding consumption volatility and, in the case of child care subsidies, impeding work.

Finally, the declining quality of service jobs has fed back into employment in manufacturing, where uncertainty and job instability have risen as well. Over the past several decades, employment even in this traditionally stable sector has shifted away from direct hire employees, who benefit from union-negotiated compensation packages and job protections, toward temporary workers contracted through staffing agencies. The total number of temporary help workers in core production jobs has more than doubled between 1989 and 2015. Specifically among low-skill manual workers, nearly one in five was employed by a temporary staffing agency in 2015 (Dey, Houseman, and Polivka 2012, 2017). Beyond lower wages and job tenure, domestically outsourced jobs tend to be characterized by higher incidence of workplace injuries and lower rates of employee control over job features such as tasks and hours (Bernhardt et al. 2016). Thus, the growing instability that characterizes service work, by worsening the outside options of manual workers, has degraded their work conditions as well.

Effects of Increasing Hours and Earnings Instability

The combination of these trends has led to increasing family instability for low-wage workers. Prior research has established that schedule instability, with its attendant earnings instability, is associated with worse worker and family well-being. Surveys of low-wage workers at a single point in time have shown that those with more unstable schedules report more psychological distress, worse sleep quality, and more parenting stress (Schneider and Harknett 2016). Unstable work schedules are also correlated with lower-quality parent-child interactions (Henly, Shaefer, and Waxman 2006). Further, new innovative research shows that on days when workers experience unexpected work schedule changes, they also report higher levels of negative mood and worse sleep quality (Ananat and Gassman-Pines, 2020), relative to that same family's baseline. Nighttime work hours also increase parental negative mood, harsh parenting behaviors, and negative child behavior (Gassman-Pines 2011). Overall, these findings are consistent with the notion that children are greatly influenced and constrained by their parents' lived experiences in the labor market (Ananat et al. 2013; Gassman-Pines, Gibson-Davis, and Ananat 2015).

If the schedule instability endemic to current low-wage service work harms children, then the increasing concentration of low-skilled workers in such jobs may portend poorly for the next generation's healthy development. This institutional practice of shifting the burden of decreased customer demand onto the worker by canceling shifts at the last minute may make it difficult for workers to advance economically. Further, an important way inequality may be perpetuated across generations is that heightened stress in poor families leads to negative parenting, which in turn causes poor children to have worse outcomes, such as poor mental health, in adulthood. Thus, one channel by which economic inequality may impact economic growth is that low-wage workers with little bargaining power face unpredictable schedules and earnings that increase the challenges of parenting and may harm the human capital development of the next generation.

THE GROWTH OF CAREGIVER-BREADWINNERS

The United States implicitly relies on the informal services of the working-age population as its main source of care for young children and a growing population of elderly and disabled individuals. The expense of formal care services, along with a cultural preference for home-based care, means that the responsibility for most care work falls within the family, typically to women. However, in most of the country the government does not provide, or require from employers, support such as paid sick and family leave for workers facing these often unpredictable caregiving demands at home (as discussed further in Thelen and Wiedemann, Chapter 12, this volume, and Kessler-Harris, Chapter 5, this volume).

While in the past many families had a stay-at-home adult, typically a woman, who could meet such demands, female labor force participation has increased dramatically, leaving policy far behind. The rising share of households led by single parents or dual-earner couples in the past four decades means that society's caregivers are now much more likely to be juggling caregiving with paid work obligations. A young child's or elderly family member's unexpected illness or injury can create a family financial crisis when no one is available to provide necessary care without sacrificing a paycheck.

Seventy percent of mothers with children younger than age 18 were in the labor force in 2015, compared to 47 percent in 1975, an increase of nearly 50 percent. For mothers with children younger than age 3, this growth is even more dramatic, with labor force participation increasing by 80 percent, to 61.4 percent in 2015 (Women's Bureau 2016). More than half of new mothers with a birth in the past twelve months are employed (Monte and Ellis 2014).

Not only are women more likely to be working – meaning that family income declines if they step into full-time caregiving – but women are increasingly the primary or sole family breadwinner, meaning family income can fall to zero when their care demands overtake paid work. Single mother–headed households make up a quarter of all households with children, and families headed singly by women are on the rise: more than one-third of children born in 2011 were in single mother–headed households, and 40 percent of households with children younger than age 18 have mothers as sole or primary breadwinners (Wang, Parker, and Taylor 2013). While this phenomenon results from a complex and disputed set of factors, one clear cause is, again, the rise in service sector employment, which disproportionately employs women, and the fall of manufacturing employment, which disproportionately employs men.

At the same time that families are less likely to have a full-time caregiver, the population continues to age rapidly, with the number of Americans age 65 and older expected to double by 2050. As the elderly are living longer and with more chronic conditions, the demand for long-term, non-acute elder care is expected to grow apace. Two-thirds of all Americans who reach age 65 will need regular assistance with basic functioning during their lifetimes, while 80 percent of those who develop dementia will need constant care (Hagen 2013). Coupled with lower fertility, higher divorce rates, and the growth in female labor force participation, these changing demographics mean that there will be greater numbers of those who need care at the same time that there are fewer family members who are available to take care of them without incurring serious financial instability.

Lack of Support for Low-Skilled Caregiver-Breadwinners

Low-skilled workers especially are finding themselves caring for multiple dependent generations with limited formal assistance or workplace protections. High-earning households can sometimes address caregiving needs without disrupting their labor force attachment by purchasing care on the market (a tactic that drives the demand for home health and personal care aides, as described earlier), or because their employers offer paid sick and family leave. However, low-skilled jobs rarely offer such benefits, and formal care is often prohibitively expensive for low- and middle-income families. Formal center-based childcare costs more than flagship college tuition in most states, and by some estimates exceeds 35 percent of single parent families' median income (Fraga et al. 2017). The average nursing home costs more than $85,000 annually, and that cost is expected to double in the next twenty years (Genworth 2018).

Some public policies and mechanisms do exist to help low-income families afford formal care. These include subsidies and tax benefits for childcare and Medicaid and long-term care insurance for the elderly. However, these programs fall short of meeting the needs of families in a variety of ways.

Only one in six families that are income-eligible for subsidies through the Child Care Development Fund – the primary source of funding for subsidized childcare for low-income families – actually receive them, because of insufficient funding and long waiting lists (Chien 2015; Glynn and Corley 2016). Churn within the subsidy program is very high, meaning that even families who manage to receive vouchers may not have a consistent source of childcare (Medeiros 2014). Additionally, in most states the income thresholds for subsidies are set so low that many low-income families are not eligible. At the same time, tax benefits for childcare go mainly to the top of the income distribution (Ananat et al.

2017). Head Start, the federally funded preschool program for low-income children, offers only part-day, part-year care, and only to a minority of those eligible. And 47 percent of single mothers work nonstandard schedules (often of the unpredictable variety previously described) (Knop 2017), which fits poorly with the 92 percent of child care centers that are open only during the traditional work hours of 8am to 6pm (National Survey of Early Care and Education Project Team 2015). Moreover, even families who manage to access formal care frequently find themselves having to find informal care to fill in gaps in formal coverage; for example, even healthy children typically get sick every year (Monto et al. 2014), which requires exclusion from formal care and the substitution of informal care.

Fewer than 10 percent of the elderly have any long-term care insurance, with most expecting to rely on their children for informal care in old age. Many also count on Medicaid, currently the only public source of funding for long-term care, if they need more intense care. But Medicaid is a means-tested program that requires recipients to spend down assets until reaching indigence to qualify for benefits, which can reduce families' economic security (Kaye, Harrington, and LaPlante 2010; Mommaerts 2015). And as with childcare, formal eldercare does not negate the need for informal care: 90 percent of elderly Americans who receive paid help also report receiving informal care from family members.

Effects of the Lack of Caregiving Support

The United States currently lacks both a comprehensive public approach to providing formal care to the young, the disabled, and the elderly and a formal set of universally available policies to support informal caregivers, the majority of whom also work for pay. A large body of evidence documents the myriad ways in which caregiving disrupts women's labor force participation, in particular, across their working lives, increasing women's income volatility and reducing economic security (Ettner 1995; Waldfogel 1998; Van Houtven, Coe, and Skira 2013; Weber-Raley and Smith 2015). Coordinating care, juggling multiple providers, and responding to health emergencies can lead to work and earnings disruptions. Breakdowns in formal childcare arrangements cause parents to miss work on average at least once in a six-month period (Glynn and Corley 2016), and adults who provide regular elder care report a 25 percent increase in workplace absences in the first six months after caregiving starts (Maestas and Truskinovsky 2018). Workers without job flexibility (a group that includes the majority of low-skill workers) may have a harder time remaining at work and meeting caregiving obligations, and those without workplace legal protections find themselves at increased risk of termination.

Elder caregivers respond to these challenges by reducing their labor supply on both the extensive margin, by dropping out of the labor force, and on the intensive margin, by reducing work hours (Van Houtven, Coe, and Skira 2013; Fahle and McGarry 2017). Even those who do not leave the labor force experience increases in workplace absences and significantly reduced hourly wages after two years (Maestas and Truskinovsky 2018), suggesting that caregiving imperils their long-term economic prospects. Significantly, eldercare obligations frequently arise when adult children are nearing their fifties, an age when women see their earnings trajectories starting to make up for delayed or intermittent labor force attachment due to child-rearing (Maestas 2018). Women for whom caregiving spans their entire working life are at an additional disadvantage in terms of both immediate and long-term economic security.

Informal caregiving and its associated work interruptions are not limited to mothers of young children or daughters of the elderly, however. Grandparents and other relatives provide a significant amount of childcare in the United States. Among children with employed mothers, nearly one-third were cared for by a grandparent, and an additional 10.4 percent by another non-parent relative (Laughlin 2013). The grandmothers of young children are frequently women nearing the end of their working lives, a time when interruptions can be especially damaging to both immediate and long-run economic security (Truskinovsky 2018). Similarly, spouses, grandchildren, siblings, and other relatives provide a significant amount of eldercare. It is not uncommon for a woman to spend all her working years caring for her own children, then her aging relatives, and then her grandchildren.

The demographic changes that place high levels of caregiving burden on the working-age population affect workers across income levels. However, the main way of reducing uncertainty and the consequences of unanticipated care needs – purchasing paid care and relying on employer-provided leave – are not equally accessible across all income levels. As discussed earlier, paid formal care is unaffordable for many median and low-earning families. In addition, access to employer-provided leave is highly unequal: 81 percent of middle-earning workers and 93 percent of top earners have access to paid sick days, compared with 31 percent of the lowest-paid workers (Bureau of Labor Statistics 2018a).

Even many employers that do offer paid leave only extend it to full-time workers, which often excludes the very workers with unstable hours who already face such high income and employment volatility.

The United States, unlike the overwhelming majority of its OECD partners, does not provide federal paid leave coverage for workers.[3] The Family and Medical Leave Act (FMLA), passed in 1993, guarantees twelve weeks of *unpaid* leave per year for employees who are new mothers, need to care for a family member with a serious illness, or have a serious illness themselves. Due to restrictions in eligibility (tenure, hours, firm size), however, approximately 40 percent of the workforce does not qualify for FMLA leave, and again most low-wage and variable-hours employees are among those excluded. Moreover, many workers, particularly the less skilled, report that they cannot afford to take leave that is unpaid (Horowitz et al. 2017).

Unpredictable caregiving emergencies arise for almost all working families across the income distribution eventually; in the US context, the resolution to such emergencies typically falls to the individual caregiver-breadwinner to sort out. Because low-earning families have fewer resources and less employer support, however, such emergencies are much more likely to derail their finances than the finances of high earners, further exacerbating existing income disparities.

POTENTIAL POLICY SOLUTIONS

This chapter has documented several trends in demographics and in the US labor market that are combining to increase instability and uncertainty among low-wage workers. First is the long-run move of low-skilled employment demand toward the service sector, which is lower paying and less stable than manufacturing. Second is the related rise of both dual-earner and single-headed households, which have dramatically reduced the share of households with a stay-at-home caregiver. Third is decreasing schedule and earnings stability within service employment, which increases income volatility and decreases family functioning for caregiver-breadwinners. Fourth is the growth of the elderly population in the

---

[3] Six states, including California, New Jersey, New York, Rhode Island, Massachusetts, and Washington, as well as the District of Columbia, have passed legislation mandating some form of statewide paid family leave coverage, often with coverage gaps similar to those in FMLA. This leaves at least three-quarters of Americans without legislated access to paid leave.

context of our societal dependence on informal caregiving for both children and the elderly, typically by family members who also work for pay. Together these changes have increased strain on low-skilled workers in the United States, particularly the growing group of such workers who combine caregiving and breadwinning.

Public policy is ill suited to address some of these trends, such as deindustrialization and the growing population share of the elderly. By contrast, public policy can ameliorate some of the uncertainty currently endemic in low-wage service sector employment and can better support low-wage workers who are balancing caregiving and employment responsibilities. Since high-wage workers both face less uncertainty at work and have access to many market-based (and tax-subsidized) tools to address uncertainty, continued policy neglect of these problems facing low-wage workers will only exacerbate our already unprecedented levels of inequality. Next we discuss policies that may help low-wage workers and reduce this inequality and describe some promising strategies for getting such policies enacted. Kris-Stella Trump (Chapter 4, this volume) explores in more depth voters' beliefs and behaviors related to policies aimed at reducing inequality.

New Labor Market Regulation of Hours and Schedules

Historical precedent exists for regulating labor markets with the aims of reducing inequality and improving child and family well-being. Indeed, much of the legislation that revolutionized work during the Progressive Era was motivated by exactly those goals, including minimum wages and workplace safety requirements. Moreover, legal standards also created the current US norms around scheduling, including the eight-hour workday and the weekend.

But in recent years, regulation of the labor market has focused little attention on hours and scheduling, despite the fact that the nature of work schedules has been shifting dramatically. In particular, while the earlier generation of scheduling regulation concentrated on preventing employers from extracting *too much labor* from workers, many of today's workers fear instead *too much variability* in work and pay. Labor advocates, raising concerns about employers shifting the risk of variable customer demand from themselves to their employees by giving workers neither hours nor pay when demand is unexpectedly low, have called for a new set of laws to reduce the unpredictability workers are facing.

So-called "schedule stability" legislation is a relatively new type of workplace policy that has been adopted by several localities, including San Francisco, Seattle, Emeryville in California, New York City, Philadelphia, and Chicago, as well as one state, Oregon. As of this writing, it is under consideration in other jurisdictions as well, including Los Angeles. These laws typically mandate that workers receive advanced notice of their schedules (around two weeks) and compensation for last-minute schedule changes, with the goal of reducing the unpredictability of their daily lives and incomes.

An evaluation of one such law, the 2017 Fair Workweek Act in Emeryville, California, found that the policy cut the share of workdays experiencing a short-notice schedule change, while a comparison group of similar workers unaffected by the law saw no changes (Ananat, Gassman-Pines, and Fitz-Henley 2019). Moreover, the policy caused a significant reduction in stress among affected workers, as proxied by sleep quality. Although it is too early to know how these schedule stability policies affect low-skilled workers and their families in the longer term, such approaches remain a potentially promising avenue for policy intervention.

These laws have many shortcomings, however, including that while they increase short-term predictability, they do not actually affect stability of work schedules, which can still vary radically from week to week as long as workers are informed two weeks ahead of time. Thus challenges remain for workers who must rearrange childcare from week to week, and for workers who are also in school 70 percent of undergraduates work, and one in five of these are also parents (Carnevale et al. 2015). These laws also do not guarantee total work hours per month, instead simply requiring employers to provide a "good faith estimate" of expected hours when hiring, and requiring that employers offer additional hours to existing employees before hiring new employees – thus, workers still have no assurances of their monthly earnings. In addition, these laws are typically written to include only retail (a shrinking sector in the economy) and hospitality workers (often only food service or even just fast-food workers), leaving out important sectors such as janitorial as well as health workers, the fastest-growing service sector. Further, these laws typically apply only to large employers, reducing the share of vulnerable workers affected even more.

Finally, it is as yet unknown whether or how regulating scheduling practices in the service sector will affect the size and health of the sector. However, a recent study found that the overwhelming majority of individual employees' schedule variability at a major retailer was unexplained by variation in demand, and that a randomized intervention to reduce employees' schedule instability both reduced turnover and increased sales (Williams et al. 2018). Besides lowering costs for businesses, reduced turnover in itself means greater job and earnings stability for workers.

Universal Care Supports

While more stable work will clearly promote family stability, it will certainly not negate the need for children and the elderly to be cared for while caregivers are at work. While federal policy recognizes that low-earning families cannot pay market prices for care, it falls far short of fully funding the care supports for which its own agencies make families eligible. Funding childcare subsidies, including after-school care and Head Start slots, for all eligible children can greatly enhance the ability of caregivers to earn enough to support their families. In addition, Medicare and Medicaid reforms to better support at-home care for the elderly and disabled can reduce nursing home expenditures while improving labor force attachment among family members responsible for their care. Several jurisdictions, ranging from New York City to the state of Oklahoma, have enacted universal prekindergarten. Moreover, several 2020 presidential primary candidates, including Joe Biden and Kamala Harris, offered detailed proposals to create universal childcare and to expand Medicare and Medicaid, including by reforming treatment of elder care.

Paid Family Leave Insurance

Nearly every worker will, at some point, experience an illness or other life event, either their own or a family member's, that will require time away from work. Although many (though not all) high-wage workers have access to paid leave for such events through their employer or can cover such leave through their assets, such resources are scarce for low-wage workers (Western et al. 2012) and for those who work for small employers (Kaiser Family Foundation 2017). Further, as Thelen and Wiedemann (Chapter 12, this volume) note, universal benefits are an important strategy for providing collective coverage that buffers all citizens from negative shocks, including health shocks.

Paid family leave insurance, which has been adopted in eight states and numerous localities, is a universal policy available to all workers that can smooth income for families. Such social insurance programs are typically funded through payroll taxes (although they can also be structured as a mandate for employers to purchase firm coverage) at a cost of a few dollars a week per worker and replace a percentage of weekly earnings when an employee is away from work due to a qualifying event (generally either the worker's or a family member's negative health shock, or bonding with a new child).

For caregivers with access to paid family leave insurance, research in California, which has had statewide paid leave insurance in effect since 2004, suggests that the benefits are numerous and span the dependent generations. Paid leave increases the likelihood that a new parent takes leave, as well as the duration of leave taken. California's policy doubled the overall use of maternity leave, increasing it from an average of three to six weeks for new mothers (Rossin-Slater, Ruhm, and Waldfogel 2013). Considerable evidence causally links new mothers' returns to work with the health and developmental outcomes of their children; most strikingly, paid family leave reduces infant mortality (Ruhm 2000). Mothers returning to work full time within twelve weeks of giving birth exhibit reductions in breastfeeding practices and important immunizations, while their children tend to display increases in externalizing behavior problems (Berger, Hill, and Waldfogel 2005). Paid leave insurance also supports workers caring for elderly family members: in California, nursing home usage decreased by 11 percent following the passage of paid leave (Arora and Wolf 2018).

Promising Strategies for Enacting Policies That Reduce Uncertainty

Although some of the policies described here have been considered at the federal level, the current makeup of the US Congress and the level of partisanship suggests that federal policy change is unlikely in the near future. Policy change at the state or local level, however, currently holds more promise, as progressives control many city councils and several state legislatures.

A clear pattern of advocacy and labor organizing has emerged in states and localities that have passed such policy change, providing insights into strategies that may be effective elsewhere. The initial community organizing in places that have ultimately passed laws to address uncertainty occurred around efforts to increase the minimum wage, in particular the "Fight for Fifteen." Organizing around minimum wage increases appears to be very effective for several reasons. First, the issue is highly visible and easy to understand – workers can see clearly how they will benefit from a minimum wage hike. Second, increasing the minimum wage has high levels of support across the population (Kull et al. 2017), which has meant a high rate of success in converting organizing into legislation. Once workers have succeeding in raising the minimum wage, they have both the groundwork and momentum to organize around other labor policy changes. Organized workers have turned to paid sick days, paid family leave, and schedule stability laws as complements to minimum wage hikes, because simply increasing wages does not address the uncertainty and unpredictability that workers experience in their daily lives.

This general pattern and strategy can be seen in the states and localities that have already adopted policies that reduce uncertainty and unpredictability. Following minimum wage increases, for example, Seattle, Philadelphia, and Emeryville passed schedule stability laws. The District of Columbia and New York State passed paid family leave policies after increasing the minimum wage.

Moreover, momentum at the local level has often expanded to the state level. For example, following Seattle's minimum wage increase and passage of schedule stability policy, Washington State passed a paid family and medical leave insurance policy. New York State raised the minimum wage and established paid family leave insurance after New York City raised the wage, passed schedule stability legislation, and created paid sick leave. Many other states and localities have recently passed or are actively considering minimum wage increases, while several that have already done so are now considering paid family leave and/or schedule stability laws. Given the long history of state-level changes reaching a critical mass at which they are adopted nationally (everything from widows' pensions to same-sex marriage), it is plausible that momentum at the city and state levels will eventually translate into federal policy. Indeed, this is the intended strategy of organizations with recent grassroots success such as the Center for Popular Democracy and Moms Rising, which have independent state-level organizations that work locally but share strategies and tactics with their partners across the country.

CONCLUSION

Our society places strong emphasis on the value of every family supporting itself through work. Yet over the past 40 years, the share of jobs that provide high enough, stable enough income to financially support both dependents and a designated family member who can act as full-time caregiver has drastically declined – particularly for the less skilled. To provide stability to families across the income distribution, then, will require both increasing the stability of jobs and increasing support for caregiving. In particular, we will need to accommodate the increasingly common social role of the caregiver-breadwinner, who serves both as primary earner and as primary caregiver. To do so, we will need to find ways to increase the stability and predictability of low-wage work in today's economy, support and improve the quality of non-family care arrangements for when caregivers need to work, and stabilize family income when caregivers inevitably need time away from work for caregiving duties. In the absence of such coordinated policy, high-wage workers will continue to address these challenges through paid help, insurance, and other forms of consumption smoothing. In the meantime, the increasing strain on low-wage workers will continue to generate additional, insidious forms of inequality.

References

Ananat, Elizabeth Oltmans, Dania V. Francis, Anna Gassman-Pines, and Christina M. Gibson-Davis. 2013. "Children left behind: The effects of statewide job loss on student achievement." *NBER Working Paper No. 17104*.

Ananat, Elizabeth Oltmans, and Anna Gassman-Pines. 2020. "Work schedule unpredictability: Daily occurrence and effects on working parents' well-being." *Journal of Marriage and Family*. https://doi.org/10.1111/jomf.12696

Ananat, Elizabeth Oltmans, Anna Gassman-Pines, Hayley Barton, Katie Becker, Tamara Frances, Rob Rappleye, Tim Rickert, and Maria Suhail. 2017. *Where does the money go? Federal spending on young American children*. Durham, NC: Duke Center for Child and Family Policy.

Ananat, Elizabeth O., Anna Gassman-Pines, and John Fitz-Henley II. 2019. "The effects of the Emeryville Fair Workweek Ordinance on the daily lives of low-wage workers and their families." Manuscript in preparation.

Arora, Kanika, and Douglas A. Wolf. 2018. "Does paid family leave reduce nursing home use? The California experience." *Journal of Policy Analysis and Management* 37 (1):38–62.

Autor, David, David Dorn, and Gordon Hanson. 2017. *When work disappears: Manufacturing decline and the falling marriage-market value of men*. Cambridge, MA: National Bureau of Economic Research.

Bania, Neil, and Laura Leete. 2009. "Monthly household income volatility in the US, 1991/92 vs. 2002/03." *Economics Bulletin* 29 (3):2100–2112.

Berger, Lawrence M., Jennifer Hill, and Jane Waldfogel. 2005. "Maternity leave, early maternal employment and child health and development in the US." *The Economic Journal* 115 (501):F29–F47.

Bernhardt, Annette, Rosemary Batt, Susan N. Houseman, and Eileen Appelbaum. 2016. "Domestic outsourcing in the United States: A research agenda to assess trends and effects on job quality." *Upjohn Institute Working Paper No. 16-253*. Kalamazoo, MI: W. E. Upjohn Institute for Employment Research.

Bureau of Labor Statistics. 2016. *Employee tenure in 2016*. Washington, DC: Bureau of Labor Statistics, US Department of Labor.

2018a. *Employee benefits in the United States – March 2018*. Washington, DC: Bureau of Labor Statistics, US Department of Labor.

2018b. Employment projections – 2016–26. Washington, DC: Bureau of Labor Statistics, U.S. Department of Labor.

2018c. *Occupational outlook handbook*.Washington, DC: Bureau of Labor Statistics, U. Department of Labor. www.bls.gov/ooh/home.htm

Carnevale, Anthony P., Nicole Smith, Michelle Melton, and Eric W. Price. 2015. *Learning while earning: The new normal*. Washington, DC: Georgetown University Center on Education and the Workforce.

Charles, Kerwin Kofi, Erik Hurst, and Mariel Schwartz. 2018. "The transformation of manufacturing and the decline in US employment." In *NBER Macroeconomics Annual 2018, vol. 33*. Chicago: University of Chicago Press.

Chien, Nina. 2015. "Estimates of child care eligibility and receipt for fiscal year 2012." *ASPE Issue Brief*., Washington, DC: Office of the Assistant Secretary for Planning and Evaluation and Office of Human Services Policy, US Department of Health and Human Services.

Dey, Matthew, Susan N. Houseman, and Anne E. Polivka. 2012. "Manufacturers' outsourcing to staffing services." *ILR Review* 65 (3):533–559.

2017. "Manufacturers' outsourcing to temporary help services: A research update." *US Bureau of Labor Statistics, Working Paper 493*.

Dynan, Karen, Douglas Elmendorf, and Daniel Sichel. 2012. "The evolution of household income volatility." *The BE Journal of Economic Analysis & Policy* 12 (2).

Ettner, Susan L. 1995. "The impact of 'parent care' on female labor supply decisions." *Demography* 32 (1):63–80.

Fahle, Sean, and Kathleen McGarry. 2017. "Women working longer: Labor market implications of providing family care." In *Women Working Longer: Increased Employment at Older Ages*, Claudia Goldin and Lawrence F. Katz, eds. Chicago: University of Chicago Press.

Farber, Henry S., Daniel Herbst, Ilyana Kuziemko, and Suresh Naidu. 2018. *Unions and inequality over the twentieth century: New evidence from survey data*. Cambridge, MA: National Bureau of Economic Research.

Feler, Leo, and Mine Z. Senses. 2017. "Trade shocks and the provision of local public goods." *American Economic Journal: Economic Policy* 9 (4):101–143.

Fort, Teresa C., Justin R. Pierce, and Peter K. Schott. 2018. "New perspectives on the decline of US manufacturing employment." *Journal of Economic Perspectives* 32 (2):47–72.

Fraga, Lynette M., Dionne R. Dobbins, Fitzgerald Draper, and Michelle McCready. 2017. *Parents and the high cost of child care: 2017 report*. Arlington, VA: Child Care Aware of America.

Gassman-Pines, Anna. 2011. "Low-income mothers' nighttime and weekend work: Daily associations with child behavior, mother-child interactions and mood." *Family Relations* 60:15-29. DOI:10.1111/j.1741-3729.2010.00630.x

Gassman-Pines, Anna, Christina M. Gibson-Davis, and Elizabeth Oltmans Ananat. 2015. "How economic downturns affect child development: An interdisciplinary perspective on pathways of influence." *Child Development Perspectives* 9:233-238.

Gennetian, Lisa A., Christopher Rodrigues, Heather D. Hill, and Pamela A. Morris. 2018. "Income level and volatility by children's race and Hispanic ethnicity." *Journal of Marriage and Family* 81 (1):204-229.

Genworth. 2018. "Cost of care survey 2018." www.genworth.com/aging-and-you/finances/cost-of-care.html

Glynn, Sarah Jane, and Danielle Corley. 2016. *The cost of work-family policy inaction*. Washington, DC: Center for American Progress.

Gottschalk, Peter, and Robert Moffitt. 2009. "The rising instability of US earnings." *Journal of Economic Perspectives* 23 (4):3-24.

Hagen, Stuart A. 2013. *Rising demand for long-term services and supports for elderly people*. Washington, DC: Congressional Budget Office.

Hardy, Bradley L. 2012. "Black female earnings and income volatility." *The Review of Black Political Economy* 39 (4):465-475.

——— 2017. "Income instability and the response of the safety net." *Contemporary Economic Policy* 35 (2):312-330.

Henly, Julia R., and Susan J. Lambert. 2014. "Unpredictable work timing in retail jobs: Implications for employee work-life conflict." *ILR Review* 67 (3):986-1016.

Henly, Julia R., H. L. Shaefer, and E. Waxman. 2006. "Nonstandard work schedules: Employer- and employee-driven flexibility in retail jobs." *Social Service Review* 80 (4):609-634.

Hill, Heather D. 2018. "Trends and divergences in childhood income dynamics, 1970-2010." In *Advances in child development and behavior*, Janette B. Benson, ed., 179-213. Cambridge, MA: Elsevier.

Horowitz, Julia M., Kim Parker, Nikki Graf, and Gretchen Livington. 2017. *Americans widely support paid family and medical leave, but differ over specific policies*. Washington, DC: Pew Research Center.

Jacobs, Elisabeth, and Jacob Hacker. 2008. *The rising instability of American family incomes, 1969-2004*. Washington, DC: Economic Policy Institute.

Kaiser Family Foundation. 2017. *Paid family leave and sick days in the U.S.: Findings from the 2017 Kaiser/HRET Employer Health Benefits Survey*. San Francisco, CA: Kaiser Family Foundation.

Kaye, H. Stephen, Charlene Harrington, and Mitchell P. LaPlante. 2010. "Long-term care: Who gets it, who provides it, who pays, and how much?" *Health Affairs* 29 (1):11-21.

Knop, Brian. 2017. "Parents working nonstandard schedules: Who's burning the midnight (and weekend) oil?" Poster presented at the Annual Meeting of the

National Council on Family Relations, Orlando, FL. www.census.gov/content/dam/Census/library/working-papers/2017/demo/ncfr-poster.pdf

Koo, Kyong Hyun. 2016. "The evolution of earnings volatility during and after the Great Recession." *Industrial Relations: A Journal of Economy and Society* 55 (4):705–732.

Kull, Steven, Clay Ramsay, Evan Lewis, and Antje Williams. 2017. *Americans on federal poverty programs*. College Park, MD: Program for Public Consultation, University of Maryland.

Lambert, Susan J., Peter J. Fugiel, and Julia R. Henly. 2014. "Precarious work schedules among early-career employees in the US: A national snapshot." *Research Brief*. Chicago: University of Chicago, Employment Instability, Family Well-Being, and Social Policy Network (EINet).

Laughlin, L. 2013. "Who's minding the kids? Child care arrangements: Spring 2011." *Current Population Reports*, P70-135. Washington, DC: US Census Bureau.

Maestas, Nicole. 2018. *The return to work and women's employment decisions*. Cambridge, MA: National Bureau of Economic Research.

Maestas, Nicole, Matt Messel, and Yulya Truskinovsky. 2020. "Caregiving and Labor force participation: New evidence from the Survey of Income and Program Participation." (No. WI20-12). Madison, WI: Center for Financial Security University of Wisconsin Madison Retirement and Disability Research Center.

Medeiros, Melissa. 2014. "Barriers to maintaining child care coverage: an analysis of states' child care subsidy policies." Masters project submitted in partial fulfillment of the degree of Master of Public Policy, Sanford School of Public Policy, Duke University, Durham, NC.

Moffitt, Robert A., and Sisi Zhang. 2018. *Income volatility and the PSID: Past research and new results*. Cambridge, MA: National Bureau of Economic Research.

Mommaerts, Corina. 2016. "Long-term care insurance and the family." *Unpublished, November*. University of Wisconsin-Madison, Madison, WI.

Monte, Lindsay M., and Renee R. Ellis. 2014. Fertility of women in the United States: 2012. In *Population Characteristics*. Washington, DC: Census Bureau, Economics and Statistics Administration, US Department of Commerce.

Monto, Arnold S., Ryan E. Malosh, Joshua G. Petrie, Mark G. Thompson, and Suzanne E. Ohmit. 2014. "Frequency of acute respiratory illnesses and circulation of respiratory viruses in households with children over 3 surveillance seasons." *The Journal of infectious diseases* 210 (11):1792–1799. DOI:10.1093/infdis/jiu327

Morduch, Jonathan, and Julie Siwicki. 2017. "In and out of poverty: Episodic poverty and income volatility in the US financial diaries." *Social Service Review* 91 (3):390–421.

Morduch, Jonathan, and Rachel Schneider. 2017. *The financial diaries: How American families cope in a world of uncertainty*. Princeton, NJ: Princeton University Press.

National Survey of Early Care and Education Project Team. 2015. *Fact sheet: Provision of early care and education during non-standard hours*. (OPRE

Report No. 2015–44). Washington, DC: Office of Planning Research and Evaluation, Administration for Children and Families, US Department of Health and Human Services.

Rossin-Slater, Maya, Christopher J. Ruhm, and Jane Waldfogel. 2013. "The effects of California's paid family leave program on mothers' leave-taking and subsequent labor market outcomes." *Journal of Policy Analysis and Management* 32 (2):224–245.

Ruhm, Christopher J. 2000. "Parental leave and child health." *Journal of Health Economics* 19 (6):931–960.

Schneider, Daniel, and Kristen Harknett. 2016. "Schedule instability and unpredictability and worker and family health and wellbeing." *Washington Center for Equitable Growth Working Paper Series*.

Scott, Robert E. 2015. "The manufacturing footprint and the importance of US manufacturing jobs." *Economic Policy Institute, Briefing Paper 338*.

Truskinovsky, Yulya. 2020. "The unintended consequences of child care subsidies on older women's retirement security." *Journal of Human Resources* (conditional acceptance).

Van Houtven, Courtney Harold, Norma B. Coe, and Meghan M. Skira. 2013. "The effect of informal care on work and wages." *Journal of Health Economics* 32 (1):240–252.

Waldfogel, Jane. 1998. "Understanding the 'family gap' in pay for women with children." *Journal of Economic Perspectives* 12 (1):137–156.

Wang, Wendy, Kim Parker, and Paul Taylor. 2013. *Breadwinner moms*. Washington, DC: Pew Research Center.

Weber-Raley, Lisa, and Erin Smith. 2015. *Caregiving in the U.S.* Washington, DC: National Alliance for Caregiving and the AARP Public Policy Institute.

Western, Bruce, Deirdre Bloome, Benjamin Sosnaud, and Laura Tach. 2012. "Economic insecurity and social stratification." *Annual Review of Sociology* 38 (1):341–359. DOI:10.1146/annurev-soc-071811-145434

Williams, Joan C., Susan J. Lambert, Saravanan Kesavan, Peter J. Fugiel, Lori Ann Ospina, Erin Devorah Rapoport, Meghan Jarpe, Dylan Bellisle, Pradeep Pandem, Lisa McCorkell, and Sarah Adler-Milstein. 2018. "Schedule stability increases productivity and sales." Berkeley: Work Life Law, University of California–Berkeley.

Women's Bureau. 2016. *Working mothers issue brief*. Washington, DC: Women's Bureau, US Department of Labor.

Index

Affordable Care Act, 264, 270, 272, 290, 298
Affordable Housing, 194–195
American Community Survey, 162
American Exceptionalism, 94–96
American Legislative Exchange Council, 275
American National Election Study, 136, 141
Anti-Establishment, 238, 272
Anti-tax Movement, 252, 271
Australia, 153
Automation, 214, 216, 259
   Impact on Employment, 229
   Responses to, 230

Block Grants, 193, 270
Brexit, 52, 59, 135, 237

Canada, 156, 191, 230
Chetty, Raj, 189
Chicago, 194
Childcare, 9, 16, 315, 321
   Child Care Development Fund, 315
   Effect on Labor Market, 316
   Head Start, 316
   Universal, 109, 110
Christianity
   In American Politics, 25, 46, 48
Citizen Trust, 237
Civil Rights Act, 34, 107, 114, 222
Civil Rights Movement, 27, 29, 30, 113, 115, 134

Class Segregation, 165
Cold War, 213, 217
Comparative Manifesto Project, 145, 151
Comparative Study of Electoral Systems, 145
Constitutional Hardball, 271
Cox, Gary, 145
Credit, Demand for, 294

Dalton Index, 146, 149, 151
Debt, Household, 293, 301
Denmark, 16

Economic Inequality
   Information Effects, 80, 81, 84–85, 86, 87–88
   Political Consequences, 274
   Satisfaction with Democracy, 56
   Sources, 237
   Trends, 79
   United States, 4, 5, 232
   Western Europe, 5
Education, Returns to, 54
Eldercare, 316, 317
Electoral Geography, 267
Employment Protection, 286, 288, 298
Employment Shifts, 216
Employment, Atypical, 284
   Job Security, 281
Equal Employment Opportunity Commission, 108

329

Equal Rights Amendment, 118, 122
European Social Survey, 69, 227

Fair Employment Practices Act, 113
Family and Medical Leave Act, 318
Finance, Educational, 191, 192, 230
FIRE Sector, 66, 163, 175
Firms, Market-dominant, 57, 58, 74, 75
Fixed Term Parliaments Act, 241

Gentrification. *See* Spatial Inequalities
Germany, 130, 226, 238, 240, 245
GI Bill, 112
Gig Economy, 4, 5
Gingrich, Newt, 197
Ginsburg, Ruth Bader, 108
Grand Coalitions, 14, 130
Great Recession, 1, 14, 79, 123, 221, 294
  Political Impact, 226
Great Risk Shift, 259, 272, 276, 283
Gun Culture, 28, 29

Healthcare, Universal, 117, 123, 290
Heritage Foundation, 270
Higher education, 293
  Electoral Politics, 63
  Heterogeneity, 52, 56, 67
  Political Impact, 52, 53–54, 58, 62, *See* Mismatched graduates
Human Capital Theory, 55

Identity Politics, 106, 115, 251
Income Instability. *See* Social Protection
  Causes, 310–312
  Demographic Differences, 307
  Effects, 313
  Policy Solutions, 319–321, 322
Industrialization, Nineteenth-Century, 103
Issue Bundling, 133, 153, 252, 266
Issue Politics, 132, 135, 136

Job Offshoring, 217, 227
JWJI 2016 Election Survey, 34

Kennedy, John Fitzgerald, 106
Keynesianism, Privatized Neoliberalism, 282
Knowledge Economy, 8, 11, 135, 189, 201, 292

Labor Force Participation, Female, 314
Labor Movement, 120
Laboratories of Democracy, 307
Le Pen, Marine, 8
Liberal Democracy, 2, 112
Living Wage Movement, 202
Localism, Segmented, 189

Make America Great Again, 1, 7, *See* Trump, Donald
Manifestos Project, 271
Manufacturing, Decline of, 4, 5, 16, 221, 309, 314
  Political Consequences, 244, 246
Marxism, 109, 219
McConnell, Mitch, 274
Media, Conservative, 268, 269
Median Earnings
  Trends, 216, 218, 262, 308, 314
Meritocracy, 90, 91, 95
Merkel, Angela, 238, 245
Millionaire's Tax, 83
Minimum Wage, 202, 322, 323
Mismatched Graduates, 53, 55, 57
  Generational Differences, 72
  Political Behavior of, 57, 71
  Satisfaction with Democracy, 54, 57, 69–74

National Front, 214
National Organization for Women, 107–108, 110
National Welfare Rights Organization, 110
Neoliberalism, 117, 120, 282
New Deal, 4, 9, 11, 119, 134
New Zealand, 146
Norquist, Grover, 274
Nostalgia, 197
  Definition, 26
  Impact on Social Policies, 29
  In the 2016 Election, 32–33, 39, 41–43, 47, 48
  Racial Attitudes, 28, 30, 31, 33, 39

Obama, Barack, 19, 36, 39, 43, 46
Occupy Wall Street, 28, 79, 123
Operationalization, 85, 88

Paleoconservatism, 32
Partisan Sorting, 129, 141
Partisanship, Political, 268

Party Discipline, 241, 242
Party Manifesto Project, 219
Pensions, 290
Peterson, Esther, 106
Plurality Political System, 250
Plurality Political Systems, 241, 243
Polarization, Political, 133, 140, 147, 153
Policy Bundling, 266
Political Competition, Multidimensional, 131–132, 144
Political Polarization
  Asymmetric, 269
Populism, 7, 52, 59, 62, 249, 262
  Support for, 228
Precarity, 36
Precarity, Growth of, 284–285
Progressive Era, 191, 319
Proportional Representation, 238, 248
  Features, 240, 242
  Political Advantages, 157
  Political Fragmentation, 239
  Political Reform, 249
Protectionism, 135, 227

Racial Resentment
  In the 2016 election, 39, 43, 48
  Measurement of, 37
Racial Stereotypes
  Deservingness, 9, 81, 93
Rational Choice Theory, 80
Redistribution, Support for, 64, 66, 80
  Determinants, 82, 83, 88–92, *See* Economic inequality
Redistribution, Urban, 189, 201, 202, 203
Redistricting, 250
Residential Segregation, 12, *See* Spatially Concentrated Affluence
  Measurement, 162
  United States, 189, 199–200, *See* Spatial Inequalities
Retrospective Voting, 48
Revolution, Digital. *See* Automation
Risk Contagion, 16, 194, 283, 299, 301
Risk Exposure, 296–299
Risk, Dimensions of, 287
Risk-pooling, 262
Roll-call Voting, 129, 218
Rural-urban divide, 10, 11, 134
Ryan Budget, 273

Schedule Instability. *See* Income Instability
Segregation, Occupational, 104
Segregation, Residential. *See* Spatially Concentrated Affluence
Service Economy, 1, 4, 16, 282
Single Member District Systems, 15, 19, 249
Skill-biased Technical Change, 53, 55, 63
Social Protection, 301
  Impact of Race, 265
  In the United States, 260–261, 263–264, 270
  Perceptions of, 265
Social Security, 264
Spatial Inequalities
  Historical Origins, 192
  Political Consequences, 192–193, 196–197, 200
  Predictors, 191
Spatial Politics, 188
Spatially Concentrated Affluence
  In Washington D.C., 184–185
  Isolation of the Poor, 169, 183–184
  Predictors, 175, 179, 183
  Racial Differences, 165, 168–175, 179, 183
Students for a Democratic Society, 114
Sweden, 131, 144, 219

Tea Party, 130, 238, 243, 249
Trade Unions, 113, 115, 121
Tribalism, 129, 130, 141
Trump, Donald, 1, 7, 214, 237
  Policies, 273
  Rhetoric, 266

Uber, 261, 275, 282
Underbounding, 200
Unemployment Insurance, 112, 263, 286, 288
Unions, Decline of, 260, 308
Universal Basic Income, 14, 230–231
  Alternatives to, 231

Voter Participation
  Trends, 222, 223, 226

Wallace, George, 7, 266
War on Poverty, 114
Welfare State, 112, 286, 298, 299
  Reforms, 282, 285

White Privilege, 28, 31
Winner-take-all System, 130, 243, 268
Women's movement, Twentieth-Century
    Dissent within, 117–122
    Origins, 106–107
Women's Equity Action League, 114
Workplace Protections. *See* Social Protection
World War II, 3, 9, 105, 111, 220, 239

Lightning Source UK Ltd.
Milton Keynes UK
UKHW010048210721
387505UK00001B/30